AF478842

KATALOG / CATALOGUE

Diese Publikation erscheint anlässlich der Ausstellung / This book is published on the occasion of the exhibition
Matts Leiderstam – Seen from Here.

Herausgeber / Editor
Kunsthalle Düsseldorf

Konzeption / Concept
Jari Ortwig, Christoph Benjamin Schulz

Redaktion / Editing
Jari Ortwig, Christoph Benjamin Schulz

Autoren / Authors
Bettina Baumgärtel
Ulrike Groos
Gregor Jansen
Maria Lind
Friedemann Malsch
Jari Ortwig
Dieter Roelstraete
Christoph Benjamin Schulz

Lektorat / Copy-editing
Katrin Sauerländer (Deutsch / German)
David Galloway (Englisch / English)

Übersetzungen / Translations
Timothy Connell (Deutsch-Englisch,
Kurztexte / German-English, short texts)
Barbara Hess (Englisch-Deutsch / English-
German, Essays von / by Dieter Roelstraete
und / and Maria Lind, Interview)

Elena Polzer (Deutsch-Englisch / German-
English, Essays von / by Bettina Baumgärtel und /
and Friedemann Malsch, Vorwort / Preface)
Jan Teeland (Schwedisch-Englisch / Swedish-
English, Essay von / by Maria Lind)

Gestaltung / Design
Christoph Steinegger / Interkool

Gesamtherstellung / Production
Druckerei zu Altenburg GmbH, Altenburg

2010 © Kunsthalle Düsseldorf, der Künstler,
die Autorinnen und Autoren, die Fotografinnen
und Fotografen und / the artist, the authors, the
photographers and Verlag für moderne Kunst,
Nürnberg

2010 © VG Bild-Kunst, Bonn, für die abgebil-
deten Werke von / for the reproduction of
works by Matts Leiderstam

Diese Publikation erscheint im / This book is
published by Verlag für moderne Kunst
Nürnberg

www.vfmk.de

ISBN 978-3-86984-029-1

Printed in Germany

Distributed in the United Kingdom
Cornerhouse Publications
70 Oxford Street, Manchester M1 5NH, UK
phone +44-161-2001503, fax +44-161-2001504

Distributed outside Europe
D.A.P. Distributed Art Publishers, Inc.
155 Sixth Avenue, 2nd Floor, New York,
NY 10013, USA
phone +1-212-6271999, fax +1-212-6279484

Bibliografische Information der Deutschen
Nationalbibliothek / Bibliographic information
published by the Deutsche Nationalbibliothek

Die Deutsche Nationalbibliothek verzeichnet
diese Publikation in der Deutschen Nationalbibliografie; detaillierte bibliografische Daten sind im
Internet über http://dnb.d-nb.de abrufbar / The
Deutsche Nationalbibliothek lists this publication
in the Deutsche Nationalbibliografie; detailed
bibliographic data are available in the internet
at http://dnb.d-nb.de.

AUSSTELLUNG / EXHIBITION
Matts Leiderstam – Seen from Here

Kunsthalle Düsseldorf
20.3. – 24.5.2010

Malmö Konstmuseum
13.6. – 22.8.2010

Turun Taidemuseo, Turku
1.10.2010 – 16.1.2011

Kuntsi Museum of Modern Art, Vaasa
4.2. – 3.4.2011

Ausstellung / Exhibition Kunsthalle Düsseldorf

Kurator / Curator
Christoph Benjamin Schulz

Kuratorische Assistenz / Curatorial assistance
Jari Ortwig

Technischer Leiter / Technical manager
Jörg Schlürscheid

Aufbauteam / Technical team
Christian Forsen
Vincent Gootzen
Bianca Grüger
Julio Ernesto Herrera Flores
Benjamin-Novalis Hofmann
Andreas Johnen
Jörn Kruse
Friederike Mainka
Jon Merz
Marc Helmut Ohliger
Max Schulze
Constantin Wallhäuser

Restauratorische Betreuung / Restoration service
Christina Nägler

Kunsthalle Düsseldorf

Künstlerischer Leiter / Artistic director
Gregor Jansen

Kuratorinnen / Curators
Elodie Evers, Magdalena Holzhey

Kuratorische Assistenz / Curatorial assistance
Jari Ortwig

Volontariat / Trainee
Inka Christmann

Projektassistenz / Project assistance
Constanze Murfitt

Presse- und Öffentlichkeitsarbeit / Press and PR
Dirk Schewe

Sekretariat / Office
Claudia Paulus

Verwaltung / Administration
Ariane Berger, Stephanie Müller

Technik / Technical Team
Jörg Schlürscheid, Siegfried Verheyden

Kunsthalle Düsseldorf
Grabbeplatz 4
D-40213 Düsseldorf
Tel. +49 (0)211 8996243
Fax +49 (0)211 8929168
mail@kunsthalle-duesseldorf.de
www.kunsthalle-duesseldorf.de

Dank / Credits
Ein spezielles Wort des Dankes gilt dem Künstler, den Leihgebern und all denen, die uns auf
vielfältige Weise bei der Vorbereitung der Ausstellung und der Herstellung der Publikation

unterstützt haben. / We should like to extend a
special word of thanks to the artist, the lenders and
all those who assisted us in so many ways in the
preparation of the exhibtion and the production of
the catalogue.

Andréhn-Schiptjenko, Stockholm
Aquazoo-Löbbecke Museum, Düsseldorf
Badischer Kunstverein, Karlsruhe
Bettina Baumgärtel
Ulrike Groos
Hetjens Museum, Düsseldorf
Kalksteinwerk Neandertal GmbH, Mettmann
Jens Komossa
Kunstmuseum Liechtenstein, Vaduz
Maria Lind
Magasin 3 Stockholm Konsthall
Malmö Konstmuseum
Friedemann Malsch
MoCAB – Museum of Contemporary Art, Belgrade
Moderna Museet, Stockholm
Christoph Münstermann
Dieter Roelstraete
Schwedisches Honorarkonsulat, Düsseldorf
Stadtmuseum Landeshauptstadt Düsseldorf
Stiftung museum kunst palast, Düsseldorf
Stiftung Neanderthal Museum, Mettmann
Wilfried Lentz Rotterdam

Matts Leiderstam bedankt sich für die Unterstützung
bei / would like to thank the following persons for
their support:

Ulf Arlinghaus, Bettina Baumgärtel, Hans und / and
Jenny Berge, Senay Berhe, Richard Bödeker, Hanna
Eggerath, Torsten Gunnarsson, Mia Haltia, Frode
Haverkamp, Christian Hoffmann, Mako Ishizuka,
Anders Kreuger, Franz Leinfelder, Anders Ljungman,
Christoph Müller, Isabella Nilsson, Annika Nylund,
Marika Reuterswärd, Helena Röjder, Gertrud
Sandqvist, Willi Schaefer, Sabine Schroyen, Jeff
Werner, Mikael Westerback

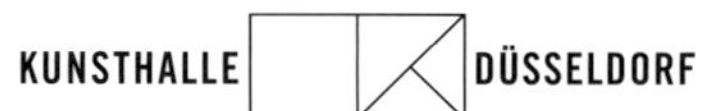

Verlag für moderne Kunst Nürnberg

Kunsthalle Düsseldorf wird gefördert durch / is supported by

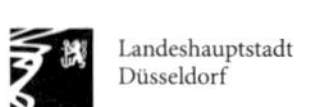
Landeshauptstadt
Düsseldorf

Ausstellung und Publikation wurden gefördert durch / Exhibition and catalogue were sponsored by

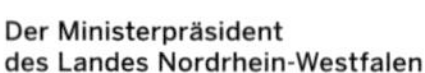
Der Ministerpräsident
des Landes Nordrhein-Westfalen

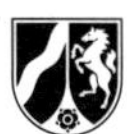

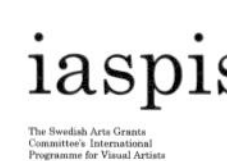
iaspis
The Swedish Arts Grants
Committee's International
Programme for Visual Artists

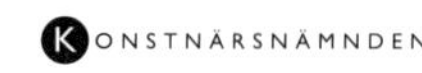
KONSTNÄRSNÄMNDEN

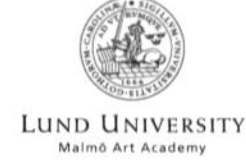
LUND UNIVERSITY
Malmö Art Academy

Stiftelsen Längmanska
Kulturfonden

*NO DIFFERENCE AT ALL, 1996
Temporäre Installation mit 2 Gemälden in /
Temporary installation with 2 paintings at
The Art Gallery of New South Wales, Sydney

Links / Left: John Constable, *Landscape with
Goatherd and Goats (after Claude Lorrain)*, 1823
Öl auf Leinwand / Oil on canvas, 50 x 43,5 cm
The Art Gallery of New South Wales, Sydney

Rechts / Right: Matts Leiderstam,
Landscape with Goatherd and Goats, 1996
(nach / after John Constable)
Öl auf Leinwand / Oil on canvas, 50 x 43,5 cm

S. / pp. 14–15, 10th Biennale of Sydney, 1996,
Photo: Jenni Carter

* * *

THE ERUPTION OF VESUVIUS, 2000
3 C-Prints
je / each 81 x 117, gerahmt / framed
Ed. 6 + 1 AP

Nach / After:
Pierre-Jacques-Antoine Volaire, *L'éruption du
Vésuve*, 1771
Öl auf Leinwand / Oil on canvas,
116,8 x 242,9 cm
The Art Institute of Chicago

S. / p. 16, The Art Institute of Chicago, 2000,
Photo: The Art Institute of Chicago
Ausklapper / Expander, Klemens Gasser & Tanja
Grunert, Inc., New York, 2001,
Photo: Mark Luttrell

* * *

THE ARTIST IS AT NIAGARA
FALLS, 2001
Installation mit Diaprojektion auf freistehender
Wand / Installation with slide projection on free
standing wall
Maße variabel / Dimensions variable

Nach / After:
O. A. / N. a., *View of Niagara*, 1807–1850
Öl auf Leinwand / Oil on canvas, 64 x 86 cm
Albright-Knox Art Gallery, Buffalo, New York

S. / pp. 20–23, Kunsthalle Düsseldorf, 2010,
Photos: Christoph Münstermann

* * *

PARIS, 15-03-1999 RETURNED,
PARC DES BUTTES-CHAUMONT
(MADE AFTER NICOLAS
POUSSIN'S SPRING OR THE
EARTHLY PARADISE, ROME
1660–1664), 2000–2001
Diaprojektion auf freistehender Wand, Bank /
Slide projection on free standing wall, bench
Maße variabel / Dimensions variable

Moderna Museet, Stockholm

S. / p. 25, Badischer Kunstverein, Karlsruhe,
2007, Photo: Thorsten Hallscheidt
S. / pp. 27–28, Centre Régional d'Art

Contemporain Languedoc-Roussillon, Sète,
2000, Photo: François Lagarde

* * *

FIRST SEEN, 2008
Historische Fotografie *Tropical Scenery,
Great Falls, Limon River*, 1871
(John Moran [1829–1902] zugeschrieben),
Wandregal, Buch mit einem eingeklebten Text
des Künstlers, Vergrößerungsglas / Vintage
album print *Tropical Scenery, Great Falls,
Limon River*, 1871 (attributed to John Moran
[1829–1902]), shelf, book with text by the
artist pasted in, magnifying glass

Photo: 28 x 20,3 cm
Wandregal / Shelf: 35,5 x 53 x 6,5 cm

Courtesy Wilfried Lentz Rotterdam

S. / p. 33, Wilfried Lentz Rotterdam, 2008,
Photo: John Bohnen

* * *

VIEW (WEST POINT), APRIL 30,
2003, 2004–2006
Installation mit Tisch, digitaler Projektion,
Leuchtkasten und historischen Claude-Gläsern /
Installation with table, digital projection,
lightbox and historical Claude glasses

Tisch / Table: 100 x 195 x 10 cm

Malmö Konstmuseum

S. / pp. 36–37, Lunds Konsthall, 2006,
Photo: Terje Östling

* * *

THE SUN (MADE AFTER
CLAUDE LORRAIN [1600–1682],
LANDSCAPE WITH REBEKAH
TAKING LEAVE OF HER FATHER,
1640/1641), 2003–2007
Installation mit 2 Tischen, 6 Büchern,
digitaler Projektion, Röntgenbild in
Leuchtkasten, 2 Gemälden, Öl auf Leinwand,
je 60,5 x 80 cm und 1 Gemälde, Öl auf
Holztafel, 22 x 27 cm, Vergrößerungsglas /
Installation with 2 tables, 6 books, digital
projection, X-ray in lightbox, magnifying glass,
2 paintings, oil on canvas, each 60.5 x 80 cm,
and 1 painting, oil on panel, 22 x 27 cm
Maße variabel / Dimensions variable

Malmö Konstmuseum

S. / pp. 38–39, Badischer Kunstverein, Karlsruhe,
2007, Photo: Thorsten Hallscheidt; S. / p. 40,
2010, Photo: Johanna Rylander; S. / p. 41,
Röntgenbild / X-ray, Photo: Erik Cornelius,
Nationalmuseum, Stockholm; S. / pp. 42–43,
Lunds Konsthall, 2006, Photo: Terje Östling

* * *

PROVENANCE, 2007
Digitale Doppelprojektion auf Eichenholztafel /
Digital double projection on oak panel

Tafel / Panel: 70 x 98 cm

Nach / After:
Jan van Goyen, 10 Ansichten von Dordrecht /
10 views of Dordrecht, Öl auf Leinwand und
Holztafel / Oil on canvas and wood panel
(alle zwischen / all between 1641–1655)
Jeronymus van Diest, *Ansicht von Dordrecht /
View of Dordrecht*, Öl auf Leinwand und
Holztafel / Oil on canvas and wood panel,
1660

Courtesy Andréhn-Schiptjenko, Stockholm

S. / pp. 44–45, Andréhn-Schiptjenko,
Stockholm, 2007, Photo: Peter Herrmann
S. / pp. 46–47, Fondation EDF, 2007,
Photo: Laurent Lecat
S. / pp. 48–49, Andréhn-Schiptjenko,
Stockholm, 2007, Photo: Peter Herrmann

* * *

MUSEUM (INSIDE/OUTSIDE), 2007
Digitale Projektion auf Skizzenblock, Staffelei,
Text des Künstlers / Digital projection on
sketchbook, easel, text by the artist
Maße variabel / Dimensions variable
Ed. 3 + 1 AP

Nach / After:
Miloš Gvozdenović, 11 Ansichten des / 11
views of the MoCAB – Museum of
Contemporary Art, Belgrade, c. 1985
Buntstift auf Papier / Colored pencil on paper
MoCAB – Museum of Contemporary Art,
Belgrade

Courtesy Andréhn-Schiptjenko, Stockholm

S. / p. 51, Salon MoCAB – Museum of
Contemporary Art, Belgrade, 2008,
Photo: Saša Relji

* * *

PROVENIENCE, 2008
Tisch, 2 Bücher mit eingeklebten Texten des
Künstlers, Vergrößerungsglas / Table, 2 books
with texts by the artist pasted in, magnifying
glass

Tisch / Table: 85 x 110 x 90 cm

Courtesy Wilfried Lentz Rotterdam

S. / pp. 54–55, Wilfried Lentz Rotterdam,
2008, Photo: John Bohnen

* * *

STORYLINE (SEEN FROM HERE),
2008
Bücher und Fotografien in einer vom Künstler
entworfenen Vitrine / Books and photographs
in a vitrine designed by the artist
63 x 570 x 80 cm

Courtesy Andréhn-Schiptjenko, Stockholm

S. / p. 65, Kunsthalle Düsseldorf, 2010,
Photo: Christoph Münstermann

NEANDERTHAL LANDSCAPE,
2008–2010
Installation mit 7 vom Künstler entworfenen
Tischen, Büchern (teils mit eingeklebten Texten
des Künstlers), Fotokopien, Texten und Zeichnungen, 2 digitalen Projektionen, Computeranimation, Staffeleien, Spektiven, Skiaskop,
historischen Gemälden und Grafiken / Installation with 7 tables designed by the artist, books
(partly with text by the artist pasted in),
photographs, texts and drawings, 2 digital
projections, computer animation, easels,
fieldscopes, skiascope, historical paintings
and sketches
Maße variabel / Dimensions variable

Gemäldewand / Wall with paintings:

Julius Rollmann, *Felshöhle mit Feueresse,* 1859
Öl auf Leinwand/Karton / Oil on canvas /
cardboard, 69,5 x 49 cm, gerahmt / framed

Julius Rollmann, *Landschaft bei Bad Aibling,*
1859
Öl auf Karton / Oil on cardboard,
45,3 x 60,5 cm, gerahmt / framed

Julius Rollmann, *Landschaft mit Blick auf
Brannenburg in das Inntal,* 1860
Öl auf Papier/Karton / Oil on paper/cardboard,
38 x 51,4 cm, gerahmt / framed

Julius Rollmann, *Wasserfall,* 1861
Öl auf Papier/Leinwand / Oil on paper/canvas,
39,3 x 55 cm, gerahmt / framed

museum kunst palast, Düsseldorf, Gemälde-
sammlung / painting collection, Sammlung
Kunstakademie / collection Art Academy
(NRW)

Andreas Achenbach, *Landschaft mit Charakter
des Hunsrück,* 1833–1839
Öl auf Leinwand / Oil on canvas, 45 x 57 cm,
gerahmt / framed

Oswald Achenbach, *Blick auf Bonn,* 1888
Öl auf Leinwand / Oil on canvas, 114 x 87 cm,
gerahmt / framed

Hans Frederik Gude, *Norwegische
Gebirgslandschaft,* 1860
Öl auf Holztafel / Oil on wood panel,
58 x 76 cm, gerahmt / framed

Anders Ascevold, *Bachbett,* 1856
Öl auf Papier/Leinwand / Oil on paper/canvas,
44 x 56 cm, gerahmt / framed

Caspar Scheuren, *Waldlandschaft,* 1845–1848
Öl auf Holz/Leinwand / Oil on wood/canvas,
62,5 x 56, gerahmt / framed

museum kunst palast, Düsseldorf,
Gemäldesammlung / painting collection

Adolf Hoeninghaus, *Landschaft – Felsenschlucht
mit Wildbach,* 1836
Öl auf Leinwand / Oil on canvas, 36,5 x 35 cm,
gerahmt / framed

museum kunst palast, Düsseldorf, Gemäldesammlung / painting collection, Dauerleihgabe
der Bundesrepublik Deutschland / permanent
loan by the Federal Republic of Germany

Gustav Rydberg, *Sjölandskap,* 1860
Öl auf Leinwand / Oil on canvas, 34 x 54 cm

Gustav Rydberg, *Landskap från Värmland,* 1859
Öl auf Leinwand / Oil on canvas,
68,5 x 101 cm

Axel Nordgren, *Motiv från Stördalen, Norge,*
1852
Öl auf Leinwand / Oil on canvas, 47 x 31,5 cm

Alfred Wahlberg, Motiv från Kolmården,
1860/1870
Öl auf Leinwand / Oil on canvas, 70 x 94 cm

Anders Kallenberg, *Skogslandskap,* 1868
Öl auf Leinwand / Oil on canvas, 100 x 134 cm

Malmö Konstmuseum

Peter Janssen, *Das alte Neandertal,* undatiert
(Düsseldorfer Malerschule, 19. Jh.) / undated
(Düsseldorf School of Painting, 19th century)
Öl auf Leinwand / Oil on canvas, 220 x 192 cm,
gerahmt / framed

Stiftung Neanderthal Museum, Mettmann

Andreas Achenbach, *Felspartie Neandertal,*
undatiert / undated
Öl auf Papier und Sperrholz / Oil on paper and
plywood, 30,3 x 22,8 cm
Inv.-Nr.: B 1332

P. K. Themistokles von Eckenbrecher,
Die Neanderhöhle im Gesteins, 1864
Öl auf Karton / Oil on cardboard, 47,5 x 30 cm
Inv.-Nr.: B 1107

Stadtmuseum Landeshauptstadt Düsseldorf

Freistehende Wand / Free standing wall:

Gustav Rydberg

Näckrosor (Wasserlilien / Waterlilies),
undatiert / undated
Ölskizze auf Leinwand / Oil sketch on canvas,
16,5 x 36,5 cm

Studie av trädstam (Studie eines Baumstumpfes /
Study of tree trunk), c. 1900
Ölskizze auf Leinwand / Oil sketch on canvas,
21 x 32,5 cm

Snösmältning (Schneeschmelze / Snowmelt),
1900/1930
Ölskizze auf Leinwand / Oil sketch on canvas,
25,8 x 34 cm

Höst (Herbst / Autumn), 1900/1930
Ölskizze auf Leinwand / Oil sketch on canvas,
25,9 x 34,2 cm

Sommarlandskap med höstackar, studie (Sommer-
landschaft mit Heuhaufen, Studie / Summer
landscape with haystacks, study), 1880/1930
Ölskizze auf Leinwand / Oil sketch on canvas,
27,3 x 39,6 cm

Landskap med gård (Landschaft mit Bauernhof /
Landscape with farm), c. 1900
Ölskizze auf Leinwand / Oil sketch on canvas,
12 x 38,8 cm

Studie av båtar (Studie mit Booten / Study
of boats), c. 1900
Ölskizze auf Leinwand / Oil sketch on canvas,
27 x 39,5 cm

Studie av hus i landskap (Studie mit Haus in
der Landschaft / Study of house in landscape),
c. 1900
Ölskizze auf Leinwand / Oil sketch on canvas,
38,3 x 62,4 cm

Landskap, studie (Landschaft, Studie /
Landscape, study), c. 1900
Ölskizze auf Leinwand / Oil sketch on canvas,
22,4 x 34,8 cm

Landskap, studie (Landschaft, Studie /
Landscape, study), c. 1900
Ölskizze auf Leinwand / Oil sketch on canvas,
32,3 x 47,8 cm

Molnstudie (Wolkenstudie / Cloud study), c. 1900
Ölskizze auf Leinwand / Oil sketch on canvas,
35,2 x 51 cm

Landskap, studie (Landschaft, Studie /
Landscape, study), undatiert / undated
Ölskizze auf Leinwand / Oil sketch on canvas,
35,2 x 48 cm

Landskap, studie (Landschaft, Studie /
Landscape, study), undatiert / undated
Ölskizze auf Leinwand / Oil sketch on canvas,
23,4 x 34,6 cm

Landskapstudie med ruin (Landschaftsstudie mit
Ruine / Landscape study with ruin), undatiert /
undated
Ölskizze auf Leinwand / Oil sketch on canvas,
38,2 x 60,5 cm

Landscapstudie med byggnader (Landschaftsstudie mit Häusern / Landscape study with
buildings), 1900/1930
Ölskizze auf Leinwand / Oil sketch on canvas,
38,4 x 56,1 cm

Landskap med äng (Landschaft mit Weide /
Landscape with meadow), c. 1900
Ölskizze auf Leinwand / Oil sketch on canvas,
37,6 x 61,7 cm

Motiv från Italien (Motive aus Italien / Motives
from Italy), 1901–1915
Ölskizze auf Leinwand / Oil sketch on canvas
38 x 64,8 cm

Malmö Konstmuseum

S. / pp. 82–87, Kunsthalle Düsseldorf, 2010,
Photos: Christoph Benjamin Schulz

S. / pp. 81, 88–99, Kunsthalle Düsseldorf,
2010, Photos: Christoph Münstermann
S. / pp. 109–112, Kunsthalle Düsseldorf, 2010,
Photos: Jens Komossa

* * *

DURCHBLICK, 2007
2 C-Prints in 1 Rahmen, Glasscheibe, Text des
Künstlers / 2 C-prints in 1 frame, glass panel,
text by the artist
70 x 100 cm
Ed. 6 + 2 AP

Courtesy Andréhn-Schiptjenko, Stockholm

Nach / After:
Johann Friedrich Overbeck, *Bildnis des Malers
Johann Carl Eggers / Portrait of the Painter
Johann Carl Eggers* 1816/20
Öl auf Leinwand / Oil on canvas, 26 x 19 cm
Staatliche Kunsthalle Karlsruhe

S. / pp. 126–127: Salon MoCAB – Museum of
Contemporary Art, Belgrade, 2008,
Photo: Saša Relji

* * *

BEFORE AND AFTER, 2000
2 C-Prints
70,5 x 62,5 cm, gerahmt / framed
Ed. 3 + 2 AP

Nach / After:
Bernardino Licinio da Pordenone, *Porträt
eines jungen Mannes / Portrait of a Young Man,*
1525
(vor und nach der Restaurierung / before and
after the restoration 1998)
Öl auf Leinwand / Oil on canvas,
45 x 37,5 cm
Kunstmuseum Liechtenstein, Vaduz

S. / p. 129, Salon MoCAB – Museum of
Contemporary Art, Belgrade, 2008
Photo: Saša Relji

* * *

SELBSTBILDNIS, 2002
2 C-Prints
je / each 48 x 38 cm, gerahmt / framed
Ed. 6 + 1 AP

Nach / After:
Franz von Lenbach, *Jugendliches Selbstbildnis /
Self-Portrait of a Young Man,* c. 1856
Öl auf Leinwand / Oil on canvas,
48 x 38 cm
Neue Pinakothek, München

Franz von Lenbach, *Bildnis eines jungen Mannes
(nach Andrea del Sarto) / Portrait of a Young Man
(after Andrea del Sarto),* 1865
Öl auf Leinwand / Oil on canvas,
60,3 x 45,7 cm
Schack-Galerie, München

S. / p. 130, Salon MoCAB – Museum of
Contemporary Art, Belgrade, 2008,
Photo: Saša Relji

*ADOLF LUDVIG STIERNELD, 2000
2 Cibachrome
je / each 131 x 106 cm, gerahmt / framed
Ed. 6 + 1 AP

Courtesy Andréhn-Schiptjenko, Stockholm

Nach / After:
Links / Left: Ulrika Pasch, *Adolf Ludvig
Stierneld,* 1780
Öl auf Leinwand / Oil on canvas, 78 x 64,5 cm
The Swedish National Portrait Collection,
Gripsholm

Rechts / Right: Kopie nach / Copy after Jacob
Björk, *Adolf Ludvig Stierneld,* 1782
Öl auf Leinwand / Oil on canvas,
58 x 47,5 cm
The Swedish National Portrait Collection,
Gripsholm

S. / pp. 134–135, Klemens Gasser & Tanja
Grunert, Inc., New York, 2001,
Photo: Mark Lutrell

* * *

HE AND SHE, 2001
2 Cibachrome
je / each 140 x 106 cm, gerahmt / framed
Ed. 6 + 1 AP

Nach / After:
Links / Left: Isak Wacklin, *Porträt des Vicars von
Laihela, Samuel Wacklin / Portrait of the Vicar of
Laihela, Samuel Wacklin,* 1755
Öl auf Leinwand / Oil on canvas,
72,5 x 58,5 cm
Ateneum – The Finnish National Gallery,
Helsinki

Rechts / Right: Isak Wacklin, *Elisabeth Wacklin,
Ehegattin des Vicars von Leihela, Samuel Wacklin /
Elisabeth Wacklin, Wife to the Vicar of Laihela,
Samuel Wacklin,* 1755
Öl auf Leinwand / Oil on canvas, 58,5 x 58,5 cm
The Finnish National Museum, Helsinki

Courtesy Andréhn-Schiptjenko, Stockholm

S. / pp. 134–135, Klemens Gasser & Tanja
Grunert, Inc., New York, 2001,
Photo: Mark Lutrell

* * *

*VIEWING POINTS (SHOWING
THREE RECOGNIZED, TWO
UNIDENTIFIED AND ONE
QUESTIONED – MADE BY TWO
RECOGNIZED, ONE ATTRIBUTED
AND THREE ANONYMOUS), 2002
Temporäre Installation mit 6 Porträts aus der
Sammlung des Malmö Konstmuseum /
Temporary installation with 6 portraits from
the collection of Malmö Konstmuseum

Gemälde von links nach rechts / Paintings
from left to right:

O. A. / N. a., *Porträt des Prinzen Hohenlohe,*
Österreichischer General / *Portrait of Prince*

Hohenlohe, Austrian General, undatiert /
undated
Öl auf Leinwand / Oil on canvas,
35,5 x 29 cm

O. A. / N. a., *Der Kaufmann Carl Petter Möller /
The merchant Carl Petter Möller,* 1823–1902
Öl auf Leinwand / Oil on canvas,
43 x 37 cm

Kilian Zoll, *Der Künstler N. J. O. Blommér (?) /
The artist N. J. O. Blommér (?),* 1840/1860
Öl auf Leinwand / Oil on canvas, 29,5 x 24 cm

O. A. / N. a., *Porträt eines unbekannten Mannes /
Portrait of an Unknown Man,* undatiert /
undated
Öl auf Leinwand / Oil on canvas, 45 x 38 cm

Alexander Roslin, *Porträt eines Mannes /
Portrait of a Man,* 1768
Öl auf Leinwand / Oil on canvas, 45 x 35 cm

Olof Johan Södermark, *Porträt von Frau Rosa
Michaelsen / Portrait of Mrs Rosa Michaelsen,*
1831
Öl auf Leinwand / Oil on canvas,
73 x 61 cm

S. / pp. 138–139, Rooseum Center for
Contemporary Art, Malmö, Photo:
Vegar Moen

* * *

SKETCH AND FRESCO, 2001
2 Cibachrome
je / each 130 x 106 cm, gerahmt / framed
Ed. 6 + 1 AP

Nach / After:
Links / Left: Richard Evans, *Ganymed
Feeding the Eagle,* 1836
Öl auf Leinwand / Oil on canvas,
58,4 x 41,4 cm
Victoria & Albert Museum, London

Rechts / Right: Richard Evans, *Ganymed
Feeding the Eagle,* 1836
Fresko / Fresco, 61 x 49,5 cm
Victoria & Albert Museum, London

Courtesy Andréhn-Schiptjenko, Stockholm

S. / pp. 146–147, Badischer Kunstverein,
Karlsruhe, 2007, Photo: Thorsten Hallscheidt
S. / pp. 148–149, *Catalogue of British Oil
Paintings 1820–1860* (hrsg. von / ed. Ronald
Parkingson, H.M.S.O.: London 1990),
Victoria & Albert Museum, London
Photo: Per Hüttner

* * *

*THE SHEPHERDS, 1998
Temporäre Installation mit Sitzbank und
3 Gemälden aus dem Kunstmuseum Liechtenstein, Vaduz / Temporary installation with
bench and 3 paintings from the Kunstmuseum
Liechtenstein, Vaduz

Sitzbank / Bench: 40 x 200 x 58,2 cm

Gemälde von links nach rechts /
Paintings from left to right:

Frans Hals (zugeschrieben / attributed),
Flötespielender Jüngling / Boy Playing Flute,
1645–1650
Öl auf Leinwand / Oil on canvas,
60,5 x 54,5 cm

Bernardino Licinio da Pordenone, *Porträt
eines jungen Mannes / Portrait of a Young Man,*
Anfang 16. Jh. / early 16th century
Öl auf Leinwand / Oil on canvas, 42,5 x 33,5 cm

Jan de Bray, *Porträt eines Mannes /
Portait of a Man,* nach / after 1670
Öl auf Leinwand / Oil on canvas,
59 x 47 cm (oval)

Kunstmuseum Liechtenstein, Vaduz

S. / pp. 152–153, Kunstmuseum Liechtenstein,
Photo: Kunstmuseum Liechtenstein, Vaduz

* * *

*CRUISING WITH NICOLAS
POUSSIN (MADE AFTER
NICOLAS POUSSIN'S SPRING
OR THE EARTHLY PARADISE,
1662–1664), 1996–2001

Kalk, Kohle und Pastellkreide auf Fußboden /
Chalk, charcoal and soft pastel on floor,
180 x 240 cm

S. / pp. 154–155, Centre Régional d'Art
Contemporain Languedoc-Roussillon, Sète,
2000, Photo: François Lagarde

* * *

RETURNED, 1997–1998

Returned, Hampstead Heath, London, 1997
C-Print
40,5 x 55,5 cm, gerahmt / framed
Ed. 3 + 2 AP

Returned, The Ramble, Central Park,
New York, 1997
C-Print
40,5 x 55,5 cm, gerahmt / framed
Ed. 3 + 2 AP

Returned, Park K. Marcinkowskiego, Poznań,
1998
C-Print
40,5 x 55,5 cm, gerahmt / framed
Ed. 3 + 2 AP

Returned, Parc Mont Royal, Montréal, 1998
C-Print
40,5 x 55,5 cm, gerahmt / framed
Ed. 3 + 2 AP

Returned, Frescati, Stockholm, 1998
C-Print
40,5 x 55,5 cm, gerahmt / framed
Ed. 3 + 2 AP

Malmö Konstmuseum

*THE MEETING OR BONJOUR
MONSIEUR COURBET (AIRE DE
SAINT AUNÈS, WEST), 1999–2000
Installation mit 4 C-Prints, 4 freistehenden
Wänden und Scheinwerfern / Installation with
4 C-prints, 4 free standing walls and floodlights
je / each 170,4 x 206,1 cm, gerahmt / framed
Ed. 6 + 1 AP

Dunkers Kulturhus, Helsingborg

S. / pp. 162–165, Rooseum Center for
Contemporary Art, Malmö, Photo:
Vegar Moen

* * *

VIEW (PAPAGO PARK), 2007
9 C-Prints
je / each 32 x 38 cm, gerahmt / framed

Courtesy Andréhn-Schiptjenko, Stockholm

MATTS LEIDERSTAM

1956
Geboren / Born in Göteborg
Lebt / Lives in Stockholm

AUSBILDUNG / EDUCATION

2002–2006 Promotion in Bildender Kunst /
Ph.D. in Fine Arts, Konsthögskolan,
Malmö, Lunds universitet
1984–1989 M.A. in Bildender Kunst / M.A.
in Fine Arts, Konsthögskolan Valand,
Göteborgs universitet
1986 The Printmaking Department,
Royal College of Art, London
1977–1981 B.A. in Kunsterziehung / B.A. in
Art Education, Konstfack – University
College of Arts, Crafts and Design,
Stockholm
1974–1977 Ausbildung in einer Töpferei /
Pottery apprentice, Rörstrands AB,
Lidköping

RESIDENZEN / RESIDENCIES

2006 International Residency, Couvent
des Récollets, Paris
2005 Cove Park, Scotland
2004–2005 IASPIS's Studio, Stockholm
2001 CEPA Gallery, Buffalo
2000 NIFCA, Helsinki
1999 Villa Saint-Clair, Sète
1996–1997 IASPIS's Studio, London
1992 The Swedish Arts Grants Committee's
Studio Residency, Montréal

PREISE UND STIPENDIEN
AWARDS AND SCHOLARSHIPS

2008–2009 Arbeitsstipendium / Working Grant,
The Swedish Arts Grants Committee
2008 Längmanska Kulturfonden
2000 Edstranska Stiftelsens
Konstnärsstipendium
1999 Projektstipendium / Project Grant,
The Swedish Arts Grants Committee
1995–1996 Arbeitsstipendium / Working Grant,
The Swedish Arts Grants Committee
1993 BUS – Bildkonstnärernas
Upphovsrättsfond
1993 Projektstipendium / Project Grant,
The Swedish Arts Grants Committee
1991 Arbeitsstipendium / Working Grant,
The Swedish Arts Grants Committee
1987 Längmanska Kulturfonden

WERKE IN ÖFFENTLICHEN
SAMMLUNGEN / WORKS IN PUBLIC
COLLECTIONS

Albright-Knox Art Gallery, Buffalo
Eskilstuna Konstmuseum
Bonnier Foundation, Stockholm
Dunkers Kulturhus, Helsingborg
Göteborgs Konstmuseum
Iziko – South African National Gallery,
Cape Town
Kunstmuseum Liechtenstein, Vaduz
Linköping, Umeå and Solna City Council
Collections
Magasin 3 Stockholm Konsthall
Malmö Konstmuseum
Moderna Museet, Stockholm
MoCAB – Museum of Contemporary Art,
Belgrade
Norrköpings Konstmuseum
Seattle Art Museum
Statens konstråd, Stockholm
Stockholms Landsting
Sundsvalls Konstmuseum

EINZELAUSSTELLUNGEN (AUSWAHL)
SOLO EXHIBITIONS (SELECTION)

2008 Gallery Kalhama & Piippo
Contemporary, Helsinki*
Salon MoCAB – Museum of
Contemporary Art, Belgrade
Wilfried Lentz Rotterdam*
2007 Andréhn-Schiptjenko, Stockholm*
Verkligheten, Umeå
Badischer Kunstverein, Karlsruhe
2006 Kunstmuseum Liechtenstein, Vaduz
2005 Göteborgs Konsthall
DCA – Dundee Contemporary Arts
Magasin 3 Stockholm Konsthall
2004 Minetta Brook at Cedar Grove,
The Thomas Cole National Historic Site,
Catskill, New York
2002 Rooseum Center for Contemporary
Art, Malmö (mit / with João Penalva)
2001 Andréhn-Schiptjenko, Stockholm*
Klemens Gasser & Tanja Grunert, Inc.,
New York*
CRAC – Centre Régional d'Art
Contemporain, Languedoc-Roussillon,
Sète
2000 INOVA – Institute of Visual Arts,
University of Wisconsin, Milwaukee
1999 Moderna Museet bei / at Centre culturel
suédois, Paris
1998 Andréhn-Schiptjenko, Stockholm*
Arkepilag, The Royal Coin Cabinet,
Stockholm
Optica – Centre for Contemporary Art,
Montréal
1997 CRG Gallery, New York*
1996 Nordic Art Center, Helsinki
White Columns, New York
1995 Malmö Konstmuseum
Forumgalleriet, Malmö
1994 Sandvikens Konsthall
Olle Olsson-huset, Hagalund, Stockholm
Mölndals Konsthall
1993 Galleri Mariann Ahnlund, Umeå*
1992 Galleri Krister Fahl, Stockholm*
Skövde Konsthall
1990 Galleri Krister Fahl, Stockholm*
1989 Galleri Thomas Wallner, Malmö*
1987 Sub Bau, Göteborg
Bio – Mellangatan 5, Göteborg
Galleri Ets Ets Ets, Umeå
1985 Galleri Rotor, Göteborg
Linköpings Konsthall
(mit / with Eva Brodin)

* Ausstellungen in Galerien / Gallery exhibitions
(C) mit Katalog / with catalogue

GRUPPENAUSSTELLUNGEN (AUSWAHL)
GROUP EXHIBITIONS (SELECTION)

2010 *Calling Beauty,* Bureau for Open Culture
at Columbus College of Art & Design,
Columbus, OH
2009 *Konsthall SE,* Konsthall C, Hökarängen,
Stockholm
The Mountain Show, Wilfried Lentz
Rotterdam*
Seen, Unseen, Scene, Centre d'art
Passerelle, Brest
*Romantikens kraft – på spaning efter
romantiken,* Malmö Konstmuseum
2008 *Nameless Science,* apexart, New York
The Third Guangzhou Triennial – *Farwell
to Post-Colonialism* (C)
*How to build the Mississippi River in your
own backyard by RAKETA & friends,*
Uppsala Konstmuseum
2007 *Residents,* EDF Foundation Espace
Electra, Paris (C)
Who's on First, Royal Academy Schools
Gallery, London
Art Unlimited, Art Basel
Contemporary Scandinavian Art, The
Scottsdale Museum of Contemporary Art
(mit / with The Moore Space, Miami)
2006 *Konsthögskolan i Malmö,* Lunds Konsthall
*Colección Valencia Arte Contemporáneo
(VAC),* IVAM, Institut Valencià d'Art
Modern
Icónica, Patio Herreriano Museo de Arte
Contemporáneo Español, Valladolid (C)
Again for Tomorrow, CCA Royal College
of Art, London (C)
Russia: Significant Other, Anna
Akhmatova Museum, St. Petersburg
2005 *No Painting,* Kunstihoone, Tallinn (C)
2004 *Falskt & Äkta,* Nationalmuseum,
Stockholm (C)
2003 Periferic 6 – *Prophetic Corners,* Iaşi (C)
Watershed – Hudson River Art Project,
North Dock, Bear Mountain State Park
und / and Boscobel Restoration, Garrison,
produziert von / produced by Minetta
Brook, New York (C)
Le Songe d'une nuit d'été, Magasin 3
Stockholm Konsthall bei / at Centre
culturelle suédois, Paris
Influence, Anxiety & Gratitude, MIT List
Visual Art Center, Cambridge
Nostalgic Real, müllerdechiara, Berlin*
2002 *Ocho relatos nórdicos,* Centro Galego de
Arte Contemporánea, Santiago de
Compostela (C)
Collected Contemporaries, Moderna
Museet C/O Klarabergsviadukten 61,
Stockholm
View Finder, Arnolfini, Bristol (C)
Regarding Landscape, The Koffler Gallery,
Toronto
Exchange and Transform (Arbeitstitel),
Kunstverein München (C)
2001 *Paradise in Search of a Future,* CEPA
Gallery, Buffalo; Atlanta College Gallery
*The Path of Resistance – MoMA meets
Moderna 1960–2000,* Moderna Museet,
Stockholm
*The Society for Contemporary Art,
Acquisition Finalists 2001,*
The Art Institute of Chicago

Skifte, Malmö Konstmuseum
Enduring Love, Klemens Gasser & Tanja Grunert, Inc., New York*
2000 *This Boy Could Be Me,* Teater Replica, Stockholm
Edstrandska, Rooseum Center for Contemporary Art, Malmö (C)
Carnegie Art Award 2000, Konstakademien, Stockholm; Göteborgs Konstmuseum; Kópavogur Art Museum; Helsingfors Konsthall, Helsinki; Henie Onstad Kunstsenter, Oslo; Sophienholm, København (C)
Drömmen om ett landskap, Norrköpings Konstmuseum
Painterly, 11th Vilnius Painting Triennial, Contemporary Art Centre, Vilnius
Looking Back, Bard College – Center for Curatorial Studies, Annandale on Hudson, New York
Organising Freedom, Moderna Museet, Stockholm; Charlottenborg, København (C)
1999 *The Family Show,* Uddevalla Konsthall; Passagen Linköpings Konsthall; Uppsala Konstmuseum (C)
Carnegie Art Award 1999, Konstakademien, Stockholm; Kópavogur Art Museum; Amos Andersson Konstmuseum, Helsinki; Kunstnernes Hus, Oslo; Sophienholm, København; Barbican Art Gallery, London (C)
By the Way, IASPIS, Stockholm
1998 *Touch,* Museum Narodna, Poznań
From The Corner of The Eye, Stedelijk Museum, Amsterdam (C)
Spatio temporal, Magasin 3 Stockholm Konsthall
Transpositions, Iziko – South African National Gallery, Cape Town (C)
Come Closer, Liechtensteinische Kunstsammlung, Vaduz; Nikolai Kirke, København; Ludwig Múzeum, Budapest (C)
Studio Visit, Duende und / and Museum Boijmans van Beuningen, Rotterdam (C)
A Visit from Stockholm, James van Damme Gallery, Bruxelles*
1997 *Summer Collection 1997,* South London Gallery
Deposition, Biennale di Venezia (C)
Letter and Event, apexart, New York (C)
1996 *I am Curious – These Days,* Cubitt Gallery, London (C)
Conceal/Reveal, Site Santa Fe (C)
Jurassic Technologies Revenant, 10th Biennale of Sydney (C)
See What it Feels Like!, Rooseum Center for Contemporary Art, Malmö (C)
1995 *Disneyland After Dark,* Uppsala Konstmuseum; Kunstraum Kreuzberg/Bethanien, Berlin (C)
The Hotel, Hotell Gustav Vasa, Stockholm
Hello!, Andréhn-Schiptjenko, Stockholm*
1994 *Blind Love,* Moderna Museet, Stockholm
Park, Doktor Glas, Stockholm
Rum för aktuell konst, Göteborg
1991 *Art Against Aids,* Galleri Krister Fahl, Stockholm*
Galleri Mariann Ahnlund, Umeå*

    * Ausstellungen in Galerien / Gallery exhibitions
    (C) mit Katalog / with catalogue

PROJEKTE (AUSWAHL)
PROJECTS (SELECTION)

2007 *Reflektioner av rum,* Mateuz Herczka, Mako Ishizuka und / and Martin Jacobson, Andréhn-Schiptjenko, Stockholm, Kurator / curator: Matts Leiderstam
2005 *View Finder,* Projekt für eine Zeitschrift / Project for a newspaper, in Zusammenarbeit mit / in collaboration with Borga Kanturk und / and Serkan Uzkaya, in: *Radikal (Istanbul),* 16.9.2005.
2004 *Reflections of Space – Sputnikprojekt,* Kunstverein München; Residenz Museum, München
Mirrored (look at the painting and the painting looks back), Retretti Art Centre, Finland, in Zusammenarbeit mit / in collaboration with Anders Kreuger
View – Ein Abendessen, in Zusammenarbeit mit dem Koch Dan Barber / A dinner event in collaboration with the chef Dan Barber, durchgeführt im / held at Blue Hill, Stone Barn, Pocantino Hills, New York, veranstaltet von Minetta Brook im Rahmen der Reihe / produced by Minetta Brook within the series of dinners *Watershed Tastemakers*
2006–2003 *View,* eine permanente Installation für / a permanent installation for *Watershed Hudson River Art Project,* North Dock, Bear Mountain State Park und / and Boscobel Restoration, Garrison, produziert von / produced by Minetta Brook, New York
2002 *Whiteout & F for Fake,* Ausstellung im Atelier des Künstlers / exhibition in the artist's studio mit / with Kajsa Dahlberg und / and Christian Andersson
2001 *View,* eine permanente Installation am Scaniaplatsen in Malmö / a permanent installation at the Scaniaplatsen in Malmö, produziert, von / produced by National Public Art Council; The City of Malmö, Västra Hamnen, Malmö
1995 *Kärlekstörst,* ein Projekt für die Tageszeitung / a project for the newspaper *Expressen,* Stockholm
Every Morning I Feel different – Every Night I Feel the Same, Installation von / by Mikael Elmgreen in Leiderstam's Atelier / studio, Stockholm
1994 *The Arrows of Cupid,* Ynglingagatan 1, Stockholm
Blind Love, Moderna Museet, Stockholm
Via Karin, Vanja, Staffan, Cilla, Lotta, Annika, Hans, Arne, Malin, Anders och Susanna, ein Projekt von Elin Wikström in Leiderstams Atelier und in der Stadtbücherei Stockholm / a project by Elin Wikström in Leiderstam's studio and at the Public library, Stockholm
1993 *I lustgården, en installation i min ateljé,* Installation im Atelier des Künstlers / an installation in the artist's studio, Stockholm

AKADEMISCHE TÄTIGKEIT (AUSWAHL)
ACADEMIC CAREER (SELECTION)

2009–2010 Forschungsprojekt für die Realisierung der Installation / Research position as postdoctor for the creation of the installation *Neanderthal Landscape,* Konsthögskolan, Malmö
2009 Mitglied der Jury für die Vergabe des / Member of the appraisal committee for the Research Fellowship of the Arts, Kunsthøgskolen, Oslo
Unabhängiger Berater für die Vergabe von Professuren im Bereich der Bildenden Kunst / Independent consultant for the grant of professorships in Fine Arts, Konstfack – University College of Arts, Crafts and Design, Stockholm; Konsthögskolan Valand, Göteborgs universitet
2008 Mitglied der Jury für die Vergabe des / Member of the appraisal committee for the Research Fellowship of the Arts, NTNU – Trondheim Academy of Fine Art
2007–2008 Gastdozent für studentische Betreuung in Bildender Kunst / External visiting supervisor in Fine Arts, Konsthögskolan, Malmö
2004–2005 Berater für die Vergabe von Förderungen und Stipendien / Consultant for grants in Fine Arts, Stiftelsen Framtidens Kultur, Uppsala
2003 Unabhängiger Berater für die Vergabe von Professuren im Bereich der Bildenden Kunst / Independent consultant for the grant of professorships in Fine Arts, Kungl. Konsthögskolan, Stockholm
1998–2001 Professur für Bildende Kunst / Professorship in Fine Arts, Konsthögskolan, Malmö
1997 Stellvertretender Professor in Bildender Kunst / Acting Professor in Fine Arts, Konsthögskolan, Malmö
Gastdozent für studentische Betreuung in Bildender Kunst / External visiting supervisor in Fine Arts, Konsthögskolan Valand, Göteborgs universitet
1994–1995 Kunstlehrer / Teacher in Art, Carl Malmsten – Furniture Studies, Stockholm

VORTRÄGE (AUSWAHL)
LECTURES (SELECTION)

2010 ADA at Het Gemaal, Rotterdam
2009 Symposium *Why Exhibit,* IASPIS, Stockholm
Symposium *Nameless Science,* Cooper Union, New York
2007 Badischer Kunstverein, Karlsruhe
Symposium *There is a Visitor,* Uppsala Konstmuseum; Biological Museum, Uppsala
2006 Symposium *Programma Kunstproject Panorama Zuidvieugel,* Scheltema Complex, Leiden
Symposium *The Artist as Researcher,* Kunstverein Hannover
The Swedish Research Council, Stockholm

Symposium *The Construction of an Identity in Artistic Practice,* Royal Academy of Arts, London, organisiert von / organized by Goldsmiths, University of London; Kuva – Finnish Academy of Fine Arts, Helsinki; Royal Academy of Arts, London
Symposium *Mega Artist Talk,* Magasin 3 Stockholm Konsthall
Tuesday Talk, Cornerhouse, Manchester
2005 Symposium *Konstnärliga Strategier: The Artist as Historian,* Moderna Museet, Stockholm
Kungl. Konsthögskolan, Stockholm
Konstfak – University College of Arts, Crafts and Design, Stockholm
Göteborgs Konsthall
2004 Kuva – Finnish Academy of Fine Arts, Helsinki
Nationalmuseum, Stockholm
2003 Symposium *Revisiting the Show,* Asociatia Vector, Iaşi, organisiert von / organized by Asociatia Vector, Iaşi; Centre Culturel Français; Goethe Institut; Swiss Cultural Programme Pro Helvetia
The Centre for Contemporary Art, Chisinau
Yale University, New Haven
2002 Symposium *Konstnärlig Kunskapsbildning,* Malmö Faculty of Fine and Performing Arts, Lunds universitet
Symposium *Det sköna och det sanna,* Dunkers Kulturhus, Helsingborg
Symposium *Att Forska eller inte,* IASPIS; Konstfack – University College of Arts, Crafts and Design, Stockholm
2001 Symposium, *Konferens om forskning och utvecklingsarbete inom det konstnärliga området,* Malmö Faculty of Fine and Performing Arts, Lunds universitet
2000 Northwestern University, Chicago
University of Illinois, Chicago
Symposium *Organising Freedom,* Moderna Museet, Stockholm
1999 Symposium *Svensk konst – International Konst,* IASPIS, Stockholm
Symposium *Changing the System – Artists talk about their practice,* Witte de With, Rotterdam, organisiert von / organized by Konsthögskolan, Malmö; NIFCA, Helsinki; Rijkakademie, Amsterdam; Witte de With, Rotterdam
1996 Queenslands College of Art, Griffith University, Brisbane

PROJEKTE UND KATALOGE IM INTERNET / WEB PROJECTS AND CATALOGUES

www.mattsleiderstam.com

www.seeandseen.net/dissertation
Promotion, CD-Rom und Web-Veröffentlichung / Dissertation, CD-Rom and web publication: Matts Leiderstam, *See and Seen – Seeing Landscape through Artistic Practice,* Konsthögskolan, Malmö, Lunds universitet, Malmö, 2006.

www.magasin3.com/v1/exhibitions/grandtour
Online-Katalog / Web catalogue, *Grand Tour,* Magasin 3 Stockholm Konsthall, Stockholm 2005. (Einleitung / Introduction: David Neuman, Essays: Jan Avgikos, Denise Robinson, Jan Verwoert; Interviews: Matts Leiderstam mit / with Kristoffer Arvidsson, Matts Leiderstam mit / with Friedemann Malsch)

BIBLIOGRAFIE (AUSWAHL)
BIBLIOGRAPHY (SELECTION)

MONOGRAFIEN UND KATALOGE ZU EINZELAUSSTELLUNGEN / MONOGRAPHS AND CATALOGUES OF SOLO EXHIBITIONS

Matts Leiderstam. Nachbild. Ausst. Kat. / Exh. cat. Badischer Kunstverein Karlsruhe, Berlin 2010. (Essays: Anja Casser, Wolfgang Ullrich)

Matts Leiderstam. View. Hg. / Ed. Lucy Flint, New York 2004. (Essay: Lynne Cooke, Interview: Matts Leiderstam mit / with Peggy Phelan)

Matts Leiderstam. Works 1996–2001. Hg. / Eds. Matts Leiderstam und / and Peter Samuelsson, Stockholm 2002. (Essays: Ami Barak, Charles Esche, Marilu Knode, Gertrud Sandqvist, Interview: Matts Leiderstam mit / with Peggy Phelan)

Matts Leiderstam. Selbstbildnis (Leporello). Hg. / Eds. Schack-Galerie und / and Kunstverein München, München 2002. (Essays: Søren Grammel, Herbert W. Rott)

Vy En bok till dig som bor i Västra Hamnen, 2001. A public artwork made for the National Public Art Council and The City of Malmö. (Essay: Matts Leiderstam)

Moderna Museet Projekt – Matts Leiderstam. Ausst. Kat. / Exh. cat. Moderna Museet, Stockholm 1999. (Einleitung / Introduction: Maria Lind, Essay: Denise Robinson)

Matts Leiderstam – No Difference at All. Hg. / Ed. NUNSKU – Nämnden för utställningar av nutida svensk konst i utlandet, Stockholm 1996. (Essay: Lynne Cooke)

The Shepherds, an exhibition by Matts Leiderstam. Ausst. Kat. / Exh. cat. Mölndals Konsthall; Sandvikens Konsthall; Olle Olsson-huset, Hagalund, Stockholm. Hg. / Eds. Matts Leiderstam und / and Annika Öhrner, Stockholm 1994. (Einleitung / Introduction: Isabella Nilsson, Essay: Annika Öhrner)

De fyra kardinalsafterna (artist's book). Hg. / Ed. Matts Leiderstam, Stockholm 1988.

PERIODIKA (AUSWAHL)
PERIODICALS (SELECTION)

Bernd Aulich, »Die Naturidylle ist ein Trugbild«, in: *Recklinghäuser Zeitung,* 8.4.2010.

Annette Kiehl, »Mit dem Fernglas«, in: *Westfälischer Anzeiger,* 31.3.2010.

Helga Meister, »Lehrstunde in der Kunstbetrachtung«, in: *Westdeutsche Zeitung,* 23.3.2010.

Dorothee Achenbach, »Neuer Blick auf alte Meister«, in: *Rheinische Post,* 23.3.2010.

Michael Georg Müller, »Der besondere Blick auf die Natur«, in: *Neue Rhein Zeitung,* 20.3.2010.

Anja Casser, »Nachbilder«, in: *Art Value,* No. 5, 2009.

Matts Leiderstam und / and John Rajchman, »See and Seen – Seeing Landscape through Artistic Practice«, in: *MaHKUzine – Journal of Artistic Research,* No. 7, 2009.

Anu Ulmonen, »Käsitetaiteilija tähyää Neandertalin laaksoon«, in: *Helsingin Sanomat,* 26.8.2008.

Frits de Coninck, »Leder zijn eigen landschap«, in: *Het Financieele Dagblad,* 10.5.2008.

Catrin Lorch, »Matts Leiderstam – Badischer Kunstverein«, in: *Artforum,* März / March 2008.

Michael Hauffen, »Matts Leiderstam. Nachbild«, in: *Springerin,* Februar / February 2008.

Ulrika Stahre, »Klass, krig och ägande«, in: *Aftonbladet,* 31.12.2007.

Bo Madestrand, »Konstdetektiven«, in: *Dagens Nyheter På Stan,* 29.11. – 5.12. 2007.

Klaus Heid, »Der Spröde Charme des kunstpädagogischen Archivs«, in: *Regioartline Kunstmagazin,* www.regioartline.org, 17.9.2007.

Georg Patzer, »Mit der Lupe an die Details«, in: *Badisches Tagblatt,* 14.9.2007.

Carmela Thiele, »Mehr Durchblick auf das Verborgene«, in: *BNM,* 13.9.2007.

Joanna Persman, »Rumstrippeln ger mer frågor än svar«, in: *Svenska Dagbladet,* 12.5.2007.

Margaretha Rossholm Lagerlöf, »Aesthetics meets a work of the contemporary art scene: Grand Tour by Matts Leiderstam – subversion and commitment«, in: *Word & Image,* Vol. 23, No. 2, April – Juni / April – June 2007.

Miya Yoshida, »Grand Tour, by Matts Leiderstam«, in: *BT (Bijyutsu Tecyo),* Vol. 58, No. 878, April 2006.

Sinziana Ravini, »Lek med visuella lustar«, in: *Göteborgsposten,* 10.12.2005.

Jack Mottram, »Matts Leiderstam, Dundee Contemporary Arts«, in: *Art Monthly,* No. 289, September 2005.

Liutauras Psibliskis, »Matts Leiderstam, Magasin 3«, in: *Artforum,* Sommer / summer 2005.

Ronald Jones, »Matts Leiderstam, Magasin 3, Stockholm, Sweden«, in: *Frieze,* No. 92, Juni / June – August 2005.

Ricci Neuman, »Med nya ögon«, in: *Svenska Dagbladet,* 16.2.2005.

Camilla Hammarström, »Här leker Matts med konsten – och med oss«, in: *Aftonbladet,* 20.2.2005.

Claudia Steinberg, »Und plötzlich spricht die Bank«, in: *Die Zeit,* 13.11.2003.

Jeffrey Kastner, »Watershed«, in: *Artforum,* Oktober / October 2003.

Holland Cotter, »Art Shows in the Great Indoors«, in: *New York Times, Weekend Fine Arts Leisure,* 25.7.2003.

Nancy Princenthal, »A 10-Part Hello Along the Hudson«, in: *New York Times, Art & Leisure,* Mai / May – November 2003.

Matts Leiderstam und / and Philip Metz, »Selbstbildnis – a conversation«, in: *Drucksache Kunstverein München, Fall 02,* Herbst / Fall 2002.

Christian Mayer, »Die Melancholie der Tempeldiener«, in: *Süddeutsche Zeitung,* 11./12.5.2002.

Michael Hauffen, »Exchange & Transform (Arbeitstitel) Kunstverein München«, in: *Kunstforum International,* No. 160, Juni – Juli / June – July 2002.

Maria Lind, »Exchange & Transform (Arbeitstitel)«, in: *Drucksache Kunstverein München,* Frühjahr / Spring 2002.

Gertrud Sandqvist, »Ömsesidighet«, in: *Artes – tidskrift för litteratur, konst och musik,* No. 2, 2002.

Dan Jönsson, »Dubbelplattityder och fantombilder«, in: *Dagens Nyheter,* 26.3.2002.

Matts Leiderstam und / and João Penalva, »Matts Leiderstam & João Penalva«, in: *Rooseum Provisorium,* No. 1, 2002.

Peggy Phelan, »A Lava Step at Any Time«, in: *NU – The Nordic Art Review,* No. 6, 2001.

R.M. Ryan, »Matts Leiderstam INOVA«, in: *New Art Examiner,* Mai – Juni / May – June 2001.

Heinz-Norbert Jocks, »Der Homoerotische Blick«, in: *Kunstforum,* No. 154, April – Mai / May 2001.

Denise Robinson, »Matts Leiderstam, Centre Régional d'Art Contemporain«, in: *Art Press,* Mai / May 2001.

Michel Nuridsany, »Fragile, domestiquée, la nature en dialogue«, in: *Le Figaro,* 16.3.2001.

Gregory Salzman, »Regarding Landscape«, in: *Canadian Art,* No. 3, 2000.
Bo Madestrand, »So trendy it hurts«, in: *Documents sur l'art,* No. 12, 2000.

Milou Allerholm, »Vad är egentligen en familj?«, in: *Dagens Nyheter,* 25.9.1999.

Bill Arning, »Honcho featuring Artists, Dean Sameshima, Glenn Ligon, Andriano Pedrosa, Matts Leiderstam«, in: *Honcho,* Oktober / October 1998.

Alexandra Bradley, »The poetics of ambiguity: a queer sensibility«, in: *Bulletin Stedelijk Museum Amsterdam,* No. 4, 1998.

Wilhelm Snyman, »Another look at the Arcadian gardens«, in: *Cape Times,* 26.3.1998.

Gerard Mack, »Vaduz-Kunst der 90er Jahre aus Skandinavien in der Liechtensteinischen Staatlichen Kunstsammlung«, in: *Kunst-Bulletin,* April 1998.

Bill Arning, »Top of the Pops. A roundup of 11 artists with careers on the rise«, in: *Out,* Februar / February 1998.

Daniel Birnbaum, »Where Has All The Madness Gone«, in: *Parkett,* No. 50/51, 1997.

Lena From, »Matts Leiderstam Konstnär«, in: *Göteborgs-Posten,* 3.3.1997.

Terry R. Myers, »Believed to be Seen – The Work of Matts Leiderstam«, in: *Paletten,* No. 228, 1997.

Maria Lind, »Excavating the Ideal Landscape – an interview with Matts Leidestam«, in: *Material,* No. 311, 1997.

Patrik Nyberg, »Döden i Arkadien«, in: *Huvudstadsbladet,* 31.8.1996.

Bruce Ferguson, »Matts Leiderstam: Cruising with Claude«, in: *Art + Text,* No. 54, Mai / May 1996.

Gunilla Grahn-Hinnfors, »I skuggan bland träden«, in: *Göteborgs-Posten,* 4.5.1994.

Annika Öhrner, »90 Tal presenterar Matts Leiderstam«, in: *Tidskriften 90TAL,* No. 13, 1994.

Maria Lind, »Rörande utställning där allt tycks Leva ett Dubbelliv«, in: *Svenska Dagbladet,* 3.12.1994.

Lars O. Ericsson, »Förintad Intimitet. Installation of frunstrationens kyliga helvete – Matts Leiderstam på galleri Krister Fahl«, in: *Dagens Nyheter,* 3.9.1990.

WEITERE PUBLIKATIONEN (AUSWAHL) OTHER PUBLICATIONS (SELECTION)

There's Gonna Be Some Trouble – The Five Year Rooseum Book 2001–2006. Hg. / Ed. Rooseum Center for Contemporary Art, Malmö 2007. (Essay: Charles Esche)

Konstnärlig forskning under lupp, Vetenskaprådet. Hg. / Ed. Vetenskapsrådet, Stockholm 2007. (Essay: Maria Hellström)

Gesammelte Drucksachen / Collected Newsletters. Hg. / Eds. Kunstverein München und / and Revolver, Frankfurt/Main 2005. (Autoren / authors: Ana Paula Cohen, Søren Grammel, Maria Lind, Julienne Lorz, Tessa Praun, Katharina Schlieben, Judith Schwarzbart)

Micheal Petry, *Hidden Histories – 20th Century Male Same Sex Lovers in the Visual Arts,* London 2004.

Revisiting the Show. Hg. / Ed. Asociatia Vector, Iaşi 2003. (Essay: Matts Leiderstam)

John Paul Ricco, *The Logic of the Lure,* Chicago 2002.

Konsten i Västra Hamnen. Hg. / Eds. The National Public Council und / and the City of Malmö, Malmö 2001. (Essay: Pontus Kyander)

We are All Normal (and we want our freedom) – a collection of contemporary nordic artists writings. Hg. / Eds. Katya Sander und / and Simon Sheikh, London 2001. (Interview: Matts Leiderstam und / and Peggy Phelan)

Cream – Contemporary Art in Culture. Hg. / Ed. Phaidon Press, London 1998. (Essay: Åsa Nacking)

Arkipelag, a project organized by Stockholm – Culture Capital of Europe 1998. Hg. / Eds. Karen Dimond, Mattias Givell, Tove Schalin, Anna Öhrner, Arkipelag, Stockholm 1998. (Email Interview: Matts Leiderstam und / and Friedemann Malsch)

MATTS LEIDERSTAM

SEEN HERE

FROM

SEEN HERE

Appendix   1

NO DIFFERENCE AT ALL   14
THE ERUPTION OF VESUVIUS   16
THE ARTIST IS AT NIAGARA FALLS   18
PARIS, 15-03-1999 RETURNED, PARC
DES BUTTES-CHAUMONT   24
FIRST SEEN   31
VIEW (WEST POINT), APRIL 30, 2003   36
THE SUN   38
PROVENANCE   44
MUSEUM (INSIDE/OUTSIDE)   50
PROVENIENCE   54

Matts Leiderstam – Die Wahrnehmung
der Wahrnehmung   57
Matts Leiderstam—The Perception of
Perception   58
Bettina Baumgärtel

STORYLINE (SEEN FROM HERE)   65

Die Erfindung der Natur – die Erfindung der
Landschaft: Matts Leiderstam in Düsseldorf   77
The Invention of Nature—the Invention of
the Landscape: Matts Leiderstam in Düsseldorf   78
Ulrike Groos / Gregor Jansen

NEANDERTHAL LANDSCAPE   81

E-Mail-Konversation   101
Email Conversation   102
*Matts Leiderstam, Christoph Benjamin Schulz &
Jari Ortwig*

Die historische Dimension des Sehens   113
The Historical Dimension of Sight   114
Friedemann Malsch

DURCHBLICK   121
BEFORE AND AFTER   128
SELBSTBILDNIS   130
ADOLF LUDVIG STIERNELD   132
HE AND SHE   135
VIEWING POINTS   138

Parallel worlds / Parallelwelten   141
Maria Lind

SKETCH AND FRESCO   146
THE SHEPHERDS   152
CRUISING WITH NICOLAS POUSSIN   154
RETURNED   156
THE MEETING OR BONJOUR
MONSIEUR COURBET   162
VIEW (PAPAGO PARK)   166

Der labyrinthische Blick   171
The Labyrinthine View   172
Dieter Roelstraete

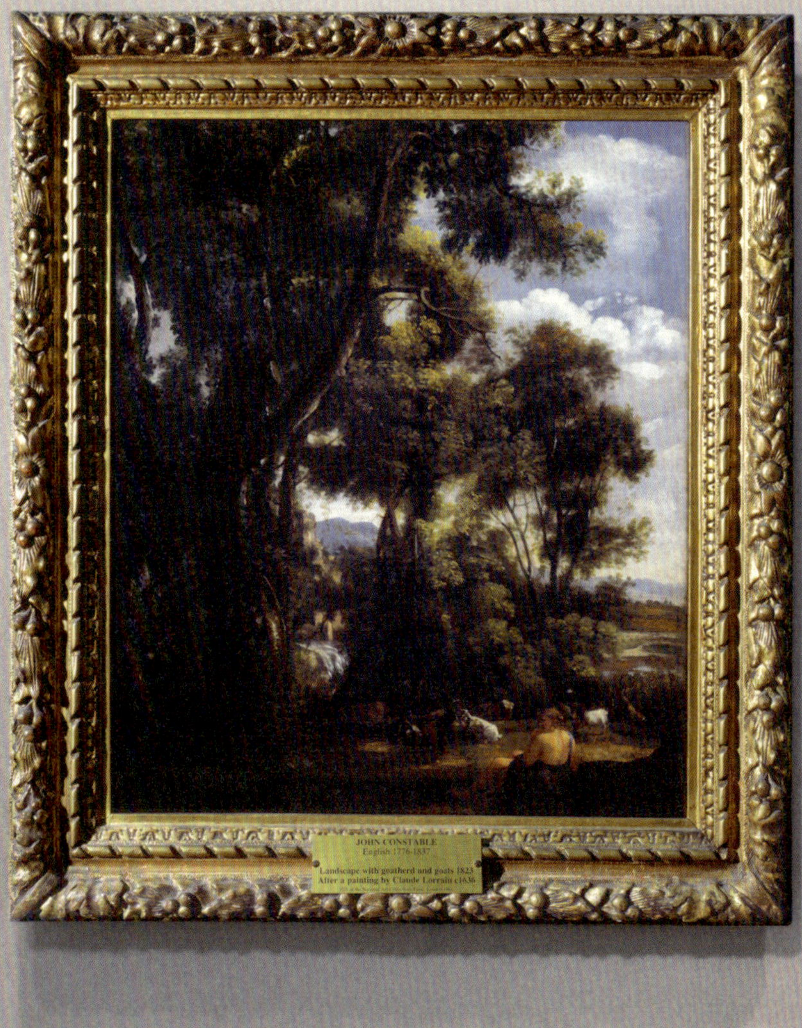

Diese Installation ist eine der ersten Arbeiten Leiderstams, in denen er die Aneignung historischer Kunstwerke, das Kopieren und Modifizieren kleiner Details, als künstlerische Strategie praktiziert und problematisiert. Die Arbeit entstand im Rahmen der 10th Biennale of Sydney als temporäre Intervention in der Art Gallery of New South Wales. Leiderstam kopierte zunächst John Constables Gemälde *Landscape with Goatherd and Goats, after Claude* (1823) – das seinerseits eine Kopie von Claude Lorrains *Paysage avec un chevrier* (1636–1637) ist – und stellte seine Fassung auf einer Staffelei direkt neben das Bild des englischen Malers. Der Titel der Installation animiert dazu, die beiden Bilder zu vergleichen und Fragen nach Originalität und Autorschaft, nach Authentizität und Täuschung, nach unbewusstem Einfluss und bewusster Bezugnahme zu stellen. Dem aufmerksamen Betrachter entgeht dabei nicht, dass der Jüngling im Vordergrund, der auf Constables Gemälde selbstversunken und in sich gekehrt wirkt, nun aufmerksam aus dem Bild heraus- und den Betrachter gezielt anzuschauen scheint.

This installation is one of Leiderstam's first works, in which he both practices and problematizes the appropriation of historic artworks—i. e. the copying and modification of small details—as a systematic artistic strategy. The work was devised as part of the 10th Biennale of Sydney, as a temporary intervention in the Art Gallery of New South Wales. Leiderstam initially copied John Constable's painting *Landscape with Goatherd and Goats, after Claude* (1823)—itself a copy of Claude Lorrain's *Paysage avec un Chevrier* (1636–1637)—and placed his version on an easel next to the painting by the English painter. The title of the installation prompts one to compare both compositions and furthermore to question notions of originality and authorship, authenticity and illusion, and subconscious influence and conscious allusion. The observant viewer cannot fail to miss the youth in the foreground who appears—in Constable's painting—to be self-preoccupied and introspective, but now seems to be looking attentively out of the painting directly at the viewer.

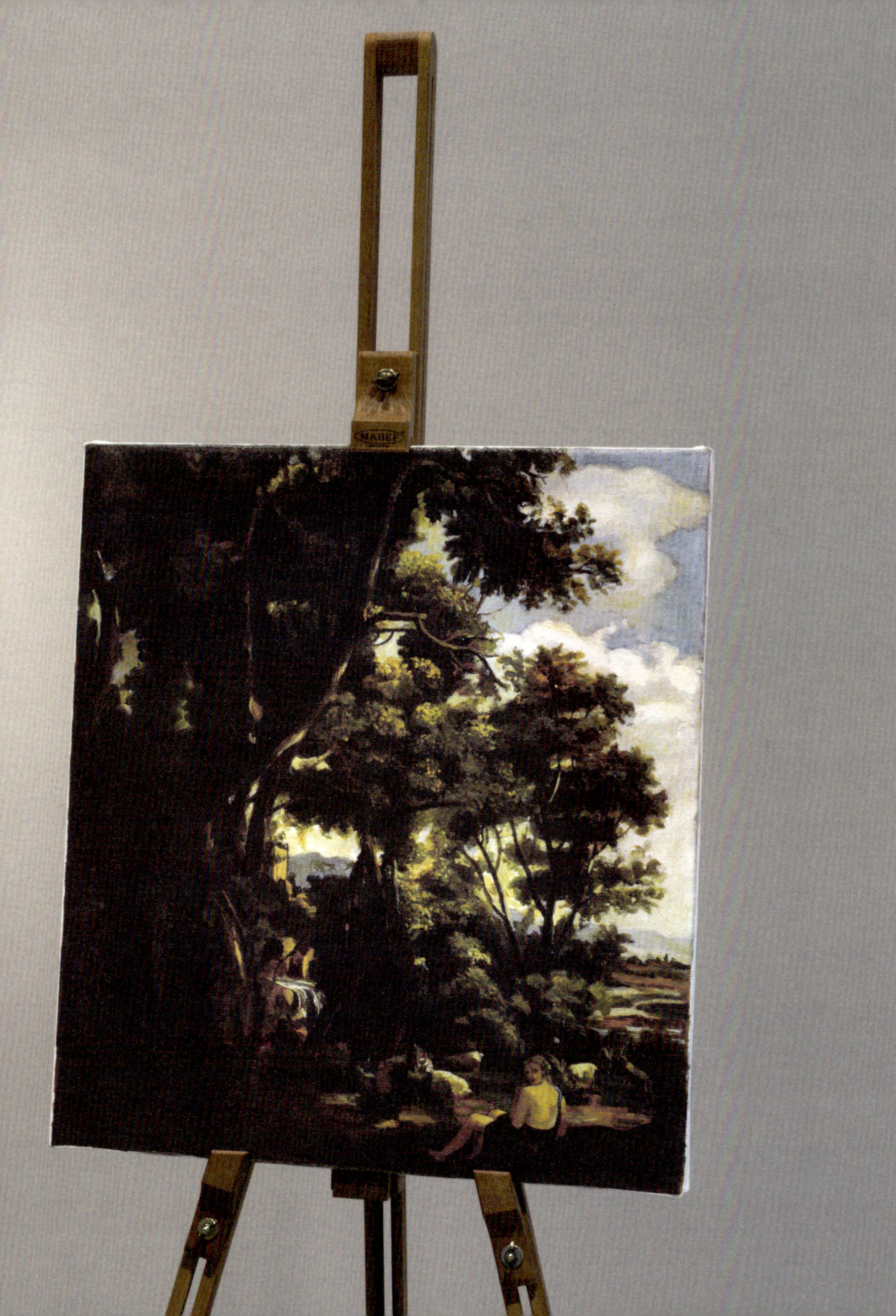

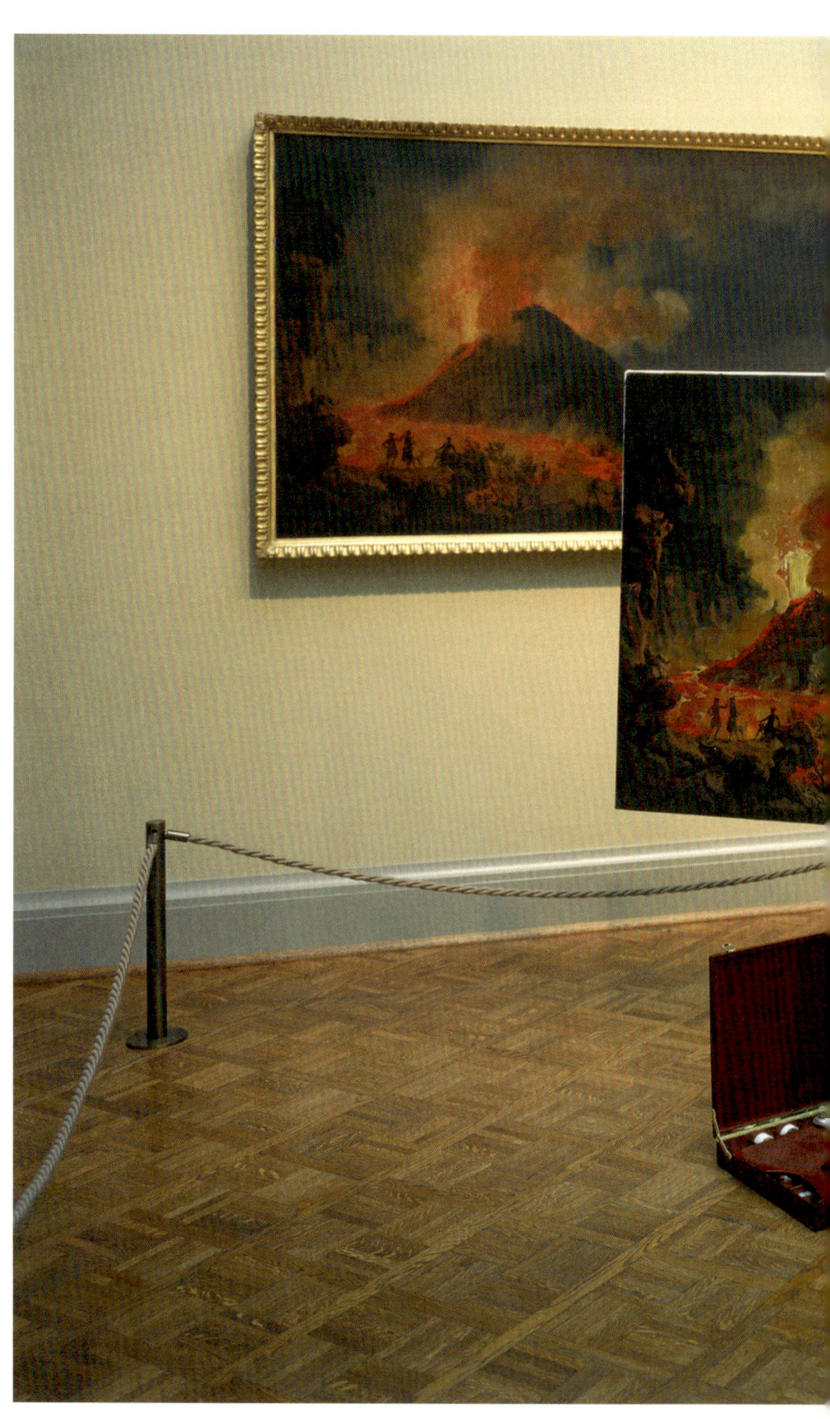

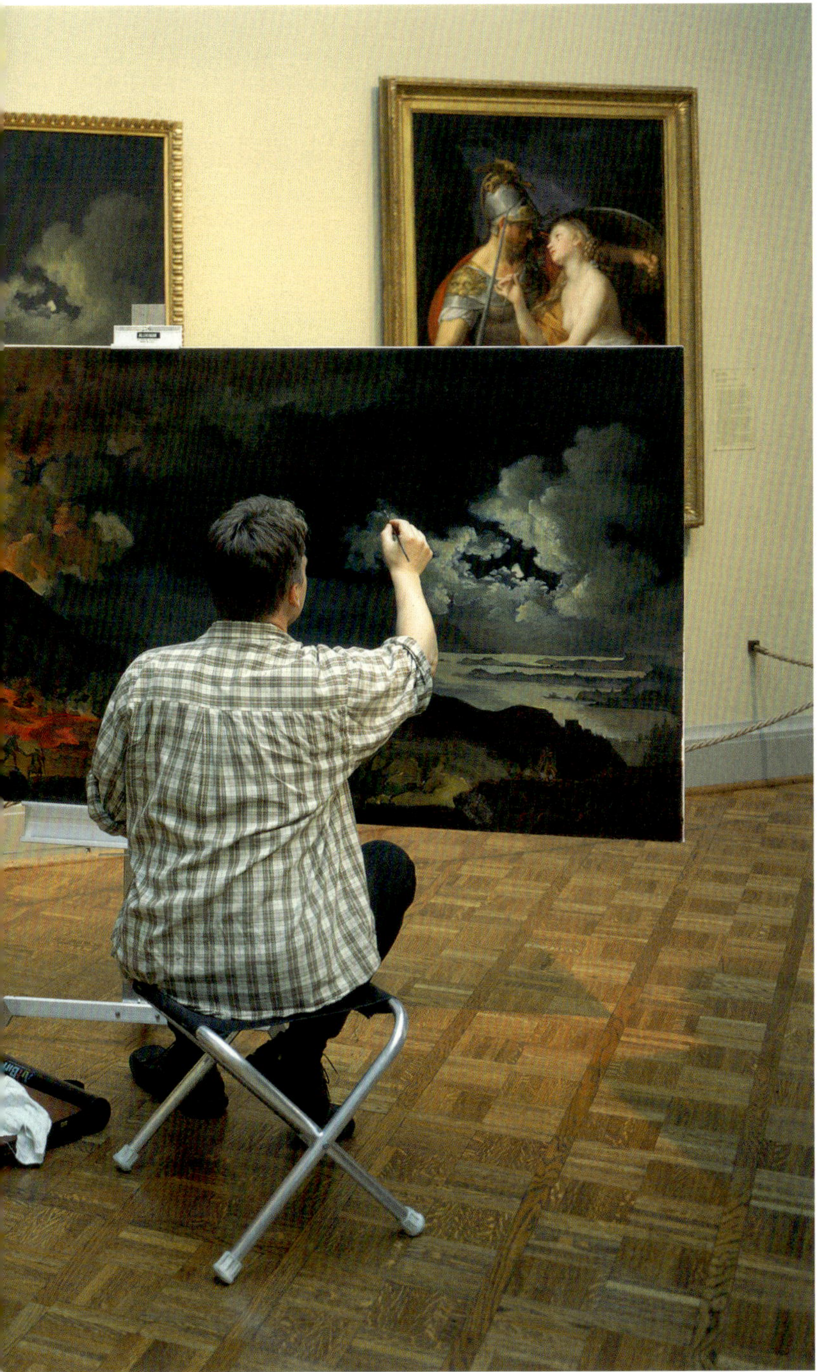

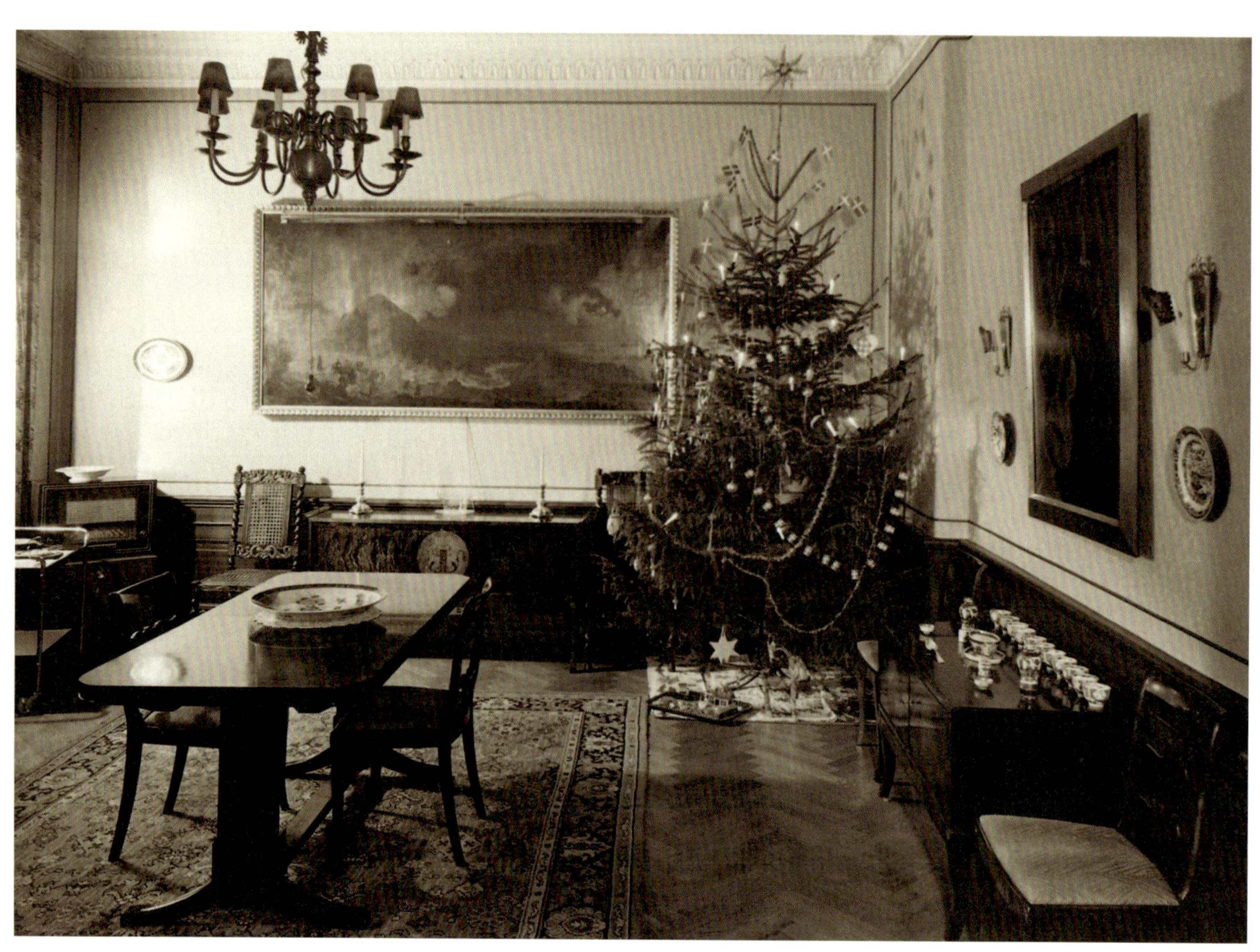

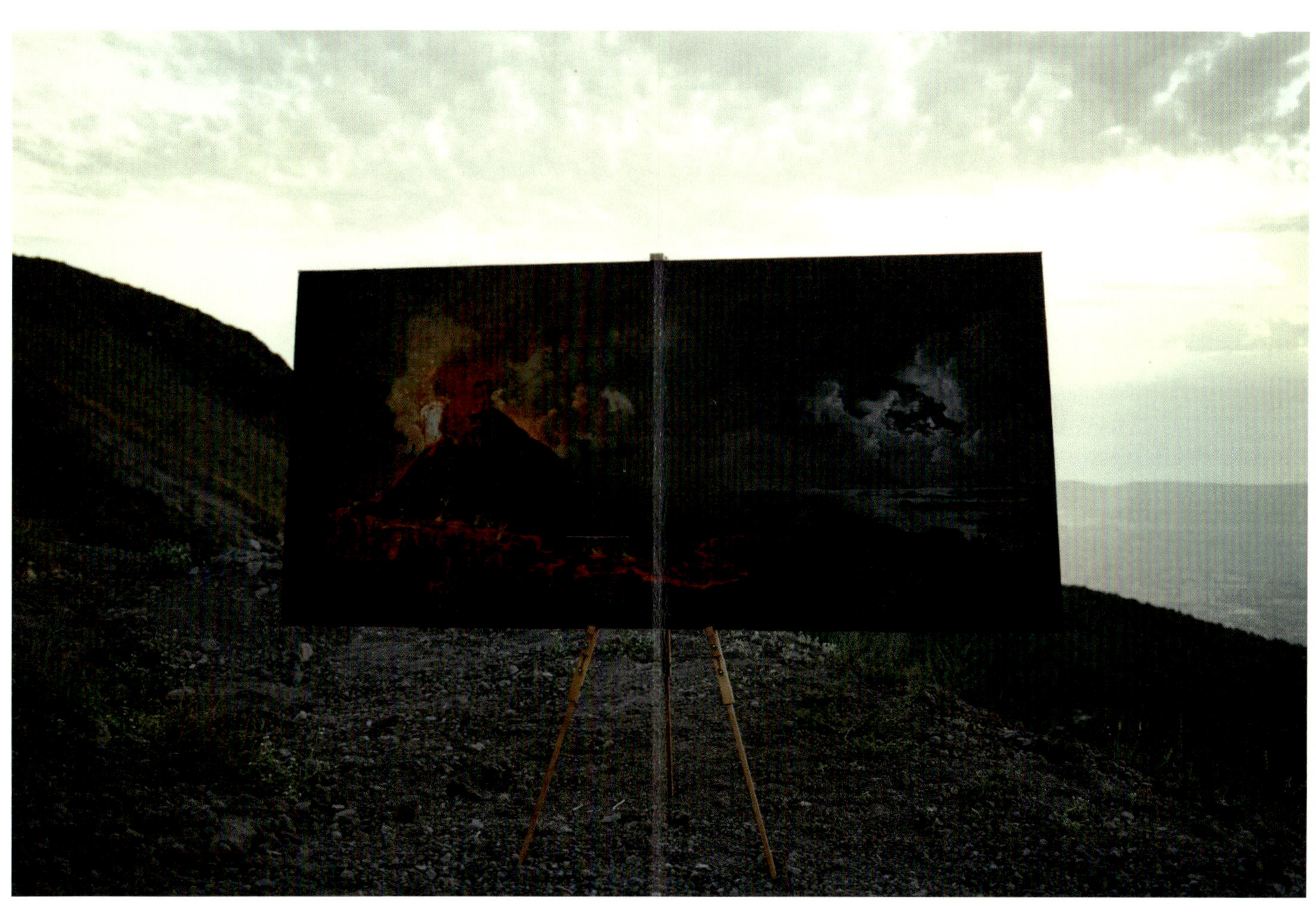

THE ERUPTION OF VESUVIUS

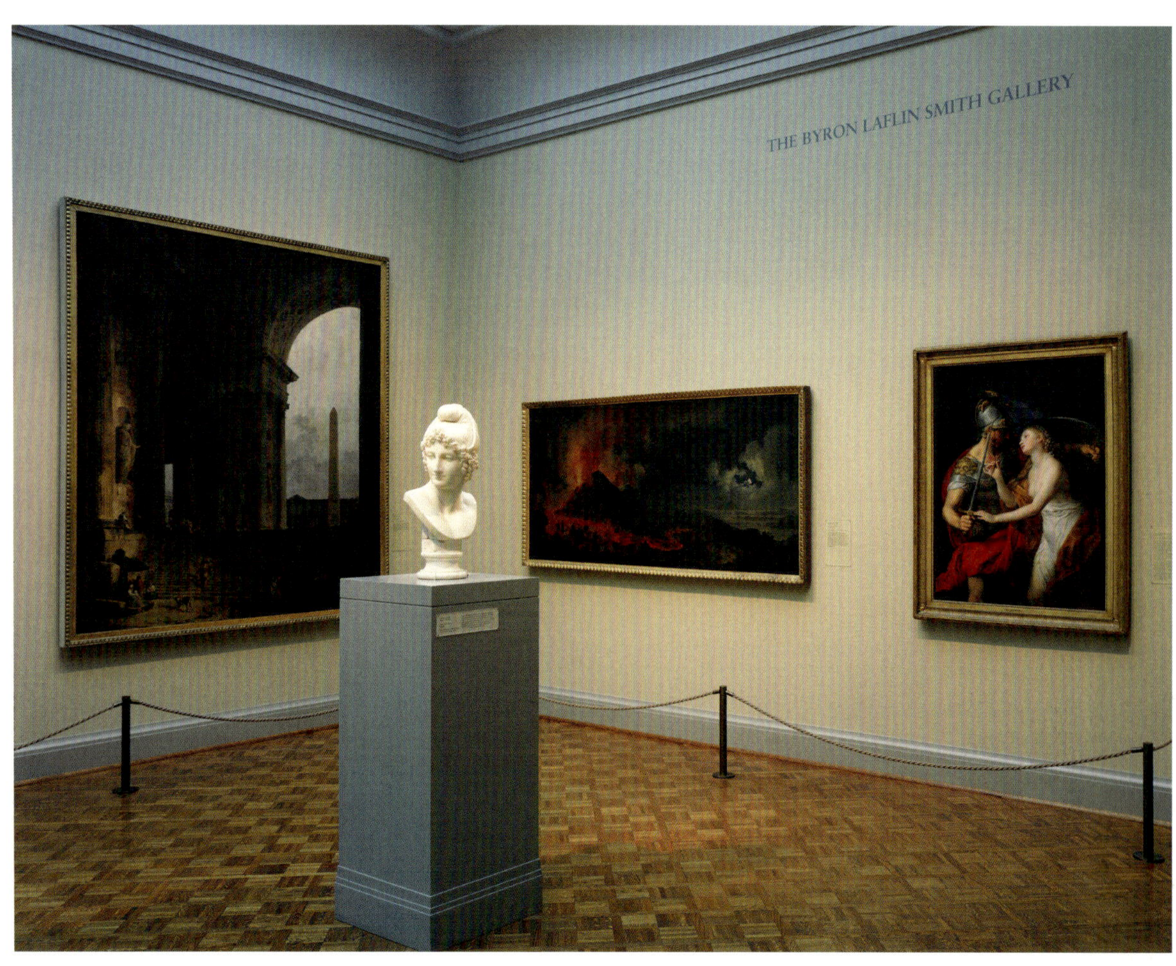
THE BYRON LAFLIN SMITH GALLERY

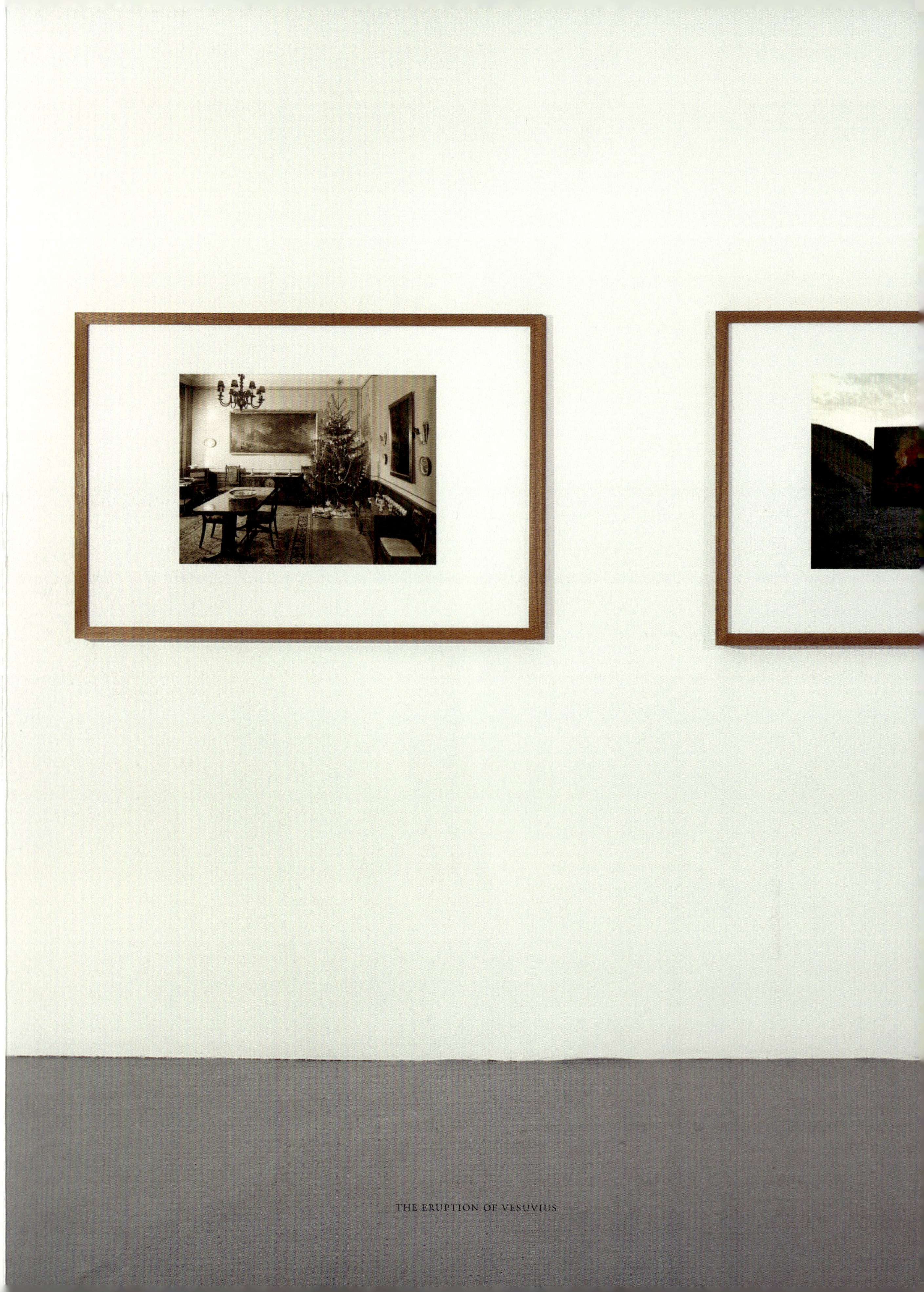

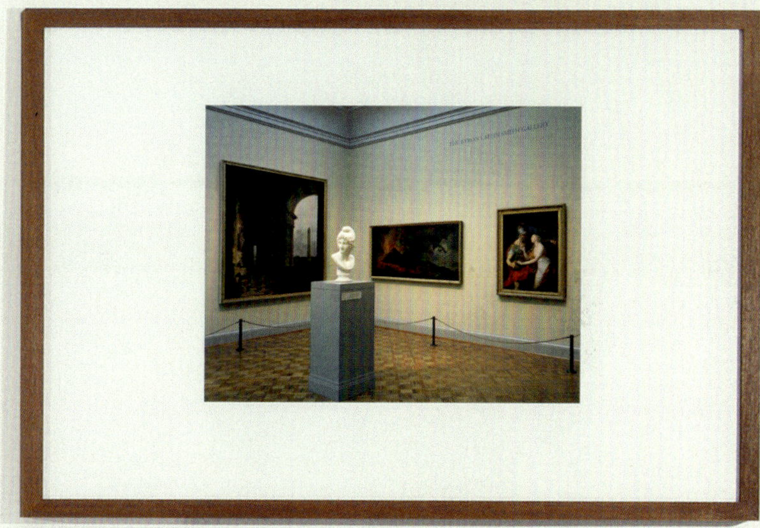

THE ERUPTION OF VESUVIUS, 2000

Im Mittelpunkt der dreiteiligen Fotoarbeit steht Pierre-Jacques-Antoine Volaires Gemälde *L'éruption du Vésuve* aus dem Jahr 1771. Im Art Institute of Chicago, wo es zwischen einer Obeliskendarstellung und einer erotischen Verführungsszene ausgestellt ist, weckte die in dieser Nachbarschaft doppeldeutig zu verstehende Darstellung einer Vulkaneruption Leiderstams Interesse. Seine Nachforschungen ergaben, dass das Werk in den 1940er Jahren im Besitz einer schwedischen Familie in Göteborg war, dem Geburtsort Leiderstams. In Chicago fertigte er eine originalgetreue Kopie des Gemäldes an und brachte diese zurück zu dem dargestellten Schauplatz. Die Fotoserie zeigt das Gemälde eingebettet in die Vulkanlandschaft, in privaten Räumen mit großbürgerlichem Interieur sowie in musealer Umgebung.

Pierre-Jacques-Antoine Volaire's painting *L'éruption du Vésuve* from 1771 forms the centerpiece for this three-part photographic work. The particular context of this intentionally ambiguous representation of a volcanic eruption—housed in the Art Institute of Chicago and positioned between the depiction of an obelisk and an erotic seduction scene—aroused Leiderstam's interest. His research revealed that during the 1940s the work belonged to a Swedish family in Göteborg, Leiderstam's birthplace. In Chicago Leiderstam prepared an exact copy of the painting and returned to the setting depicted in the original. The photo series shows the painting embedded in a volcanic landscape, in private rooms with bourgeois interiors, and in a museum context.

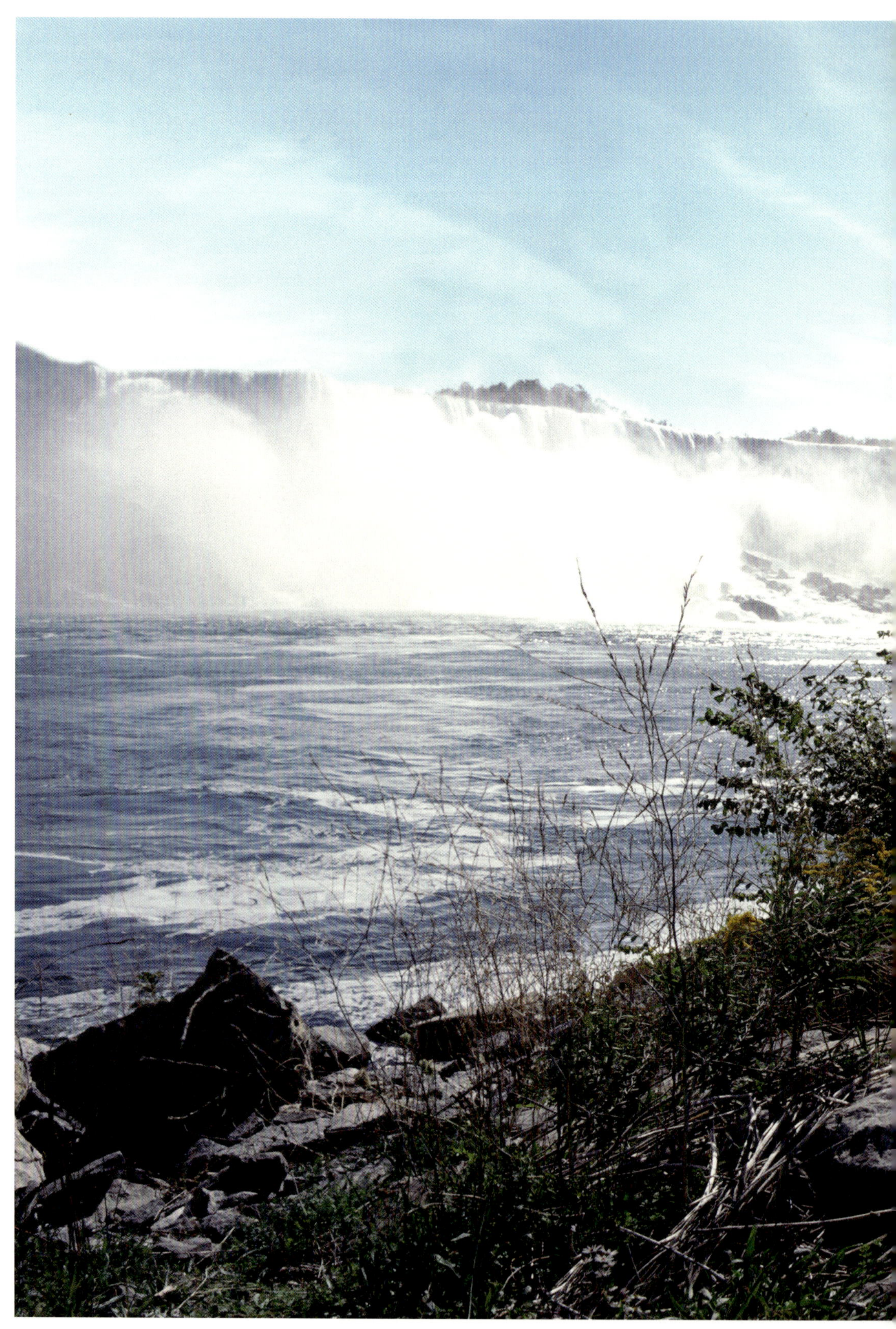

THE ARTIST IS AT NIAGARA FALLS

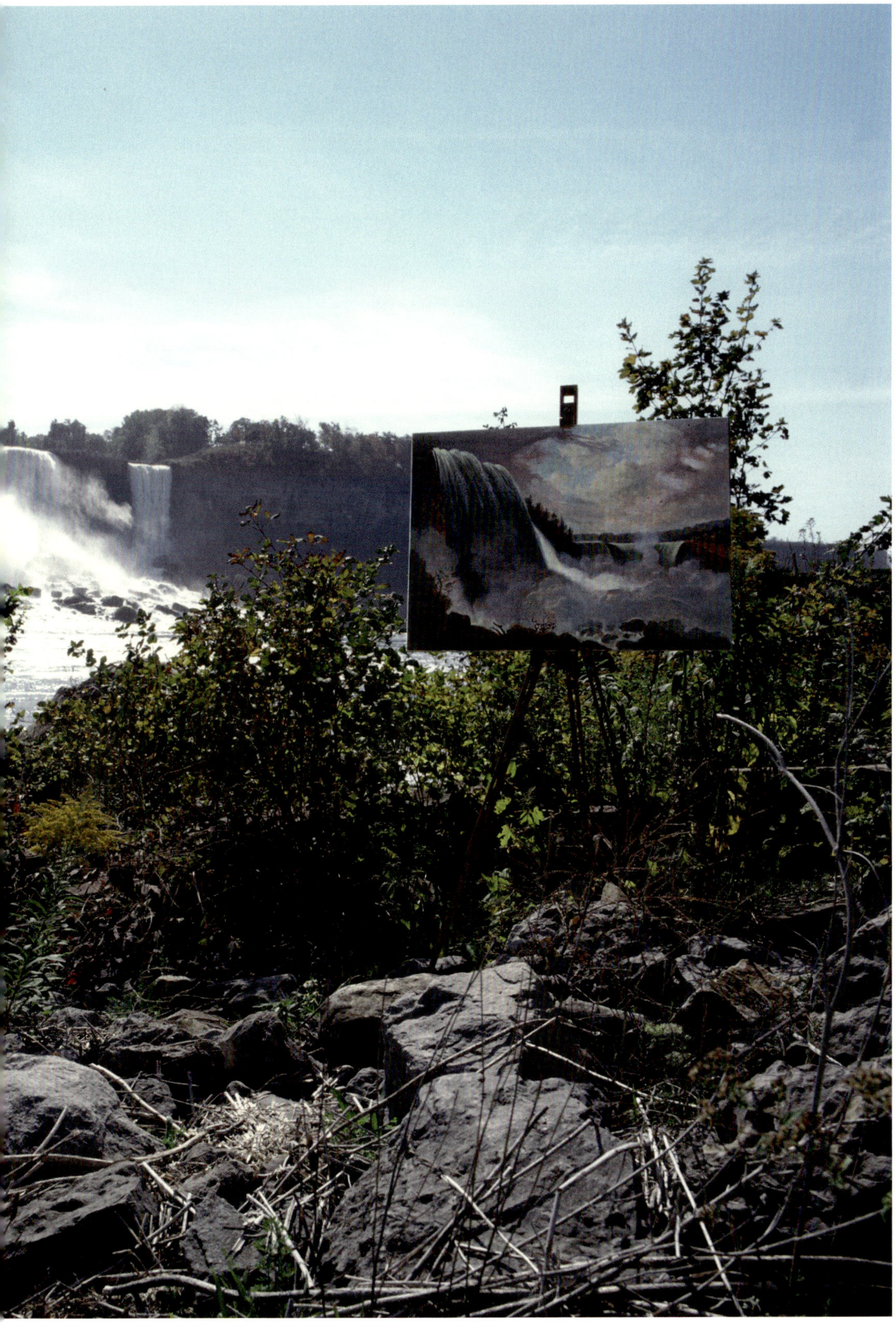

In der Albright-Knox Art Gallery im US-
amerikanischen Buffalo entdeckte Leiderstam
das Gemälde eines anonymen Künstlers aus
der ersten Hälfte des 19. Jahrhunderts, das
eine Ansicht der Niagarafälle zeigt. Er
kopierte es in Originalgröße und brachte
seine Reproduktion im Oktober 2001 an
den Ort, der auf dem Gemälde dargestellt
ist, um sie vor dem Hintergrund der Niagarafälle an der Grenze zwischen den USA und
Kanada abzulichten. Die Installation besteht
aus einer großformatigen Diaprojektion auf
eine freistehende Wand.

In the Albright-Knox Art Gallery in Buffalo,
New York, USA, Leiderstam discovered a
painting by an unknown artist from the first
half of the nineteenth century that depicts
a view of Niagara Falls. He copied it in its
original dimensions and in October 2001
returned with his reproduction to the
presumed location depicted in the painting
in order to photograph it against the background of the Falls that straddle the border
between the United States and Canada.
The installation consists of a large-scale
slide-projection onto a free standing wall.

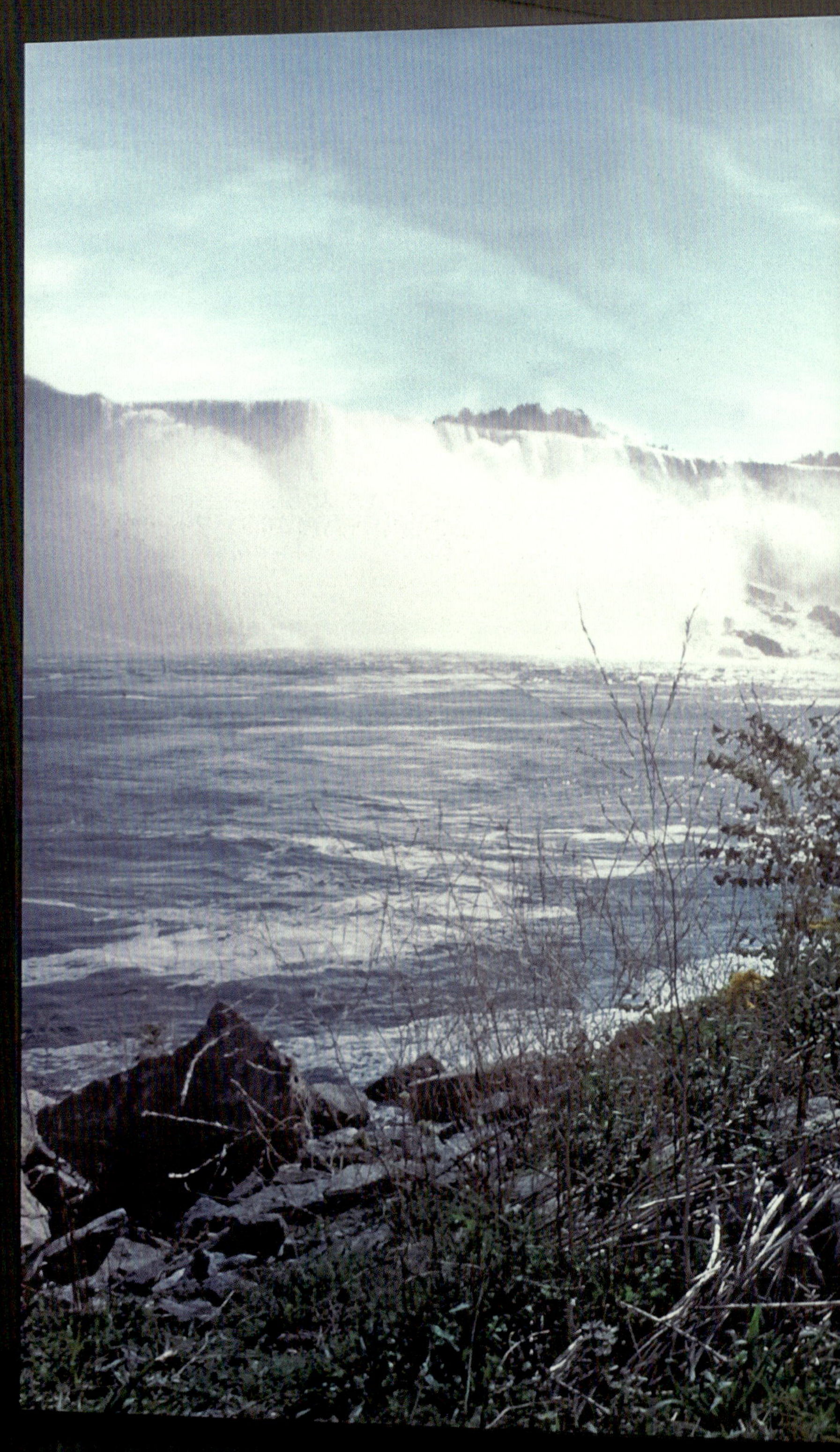

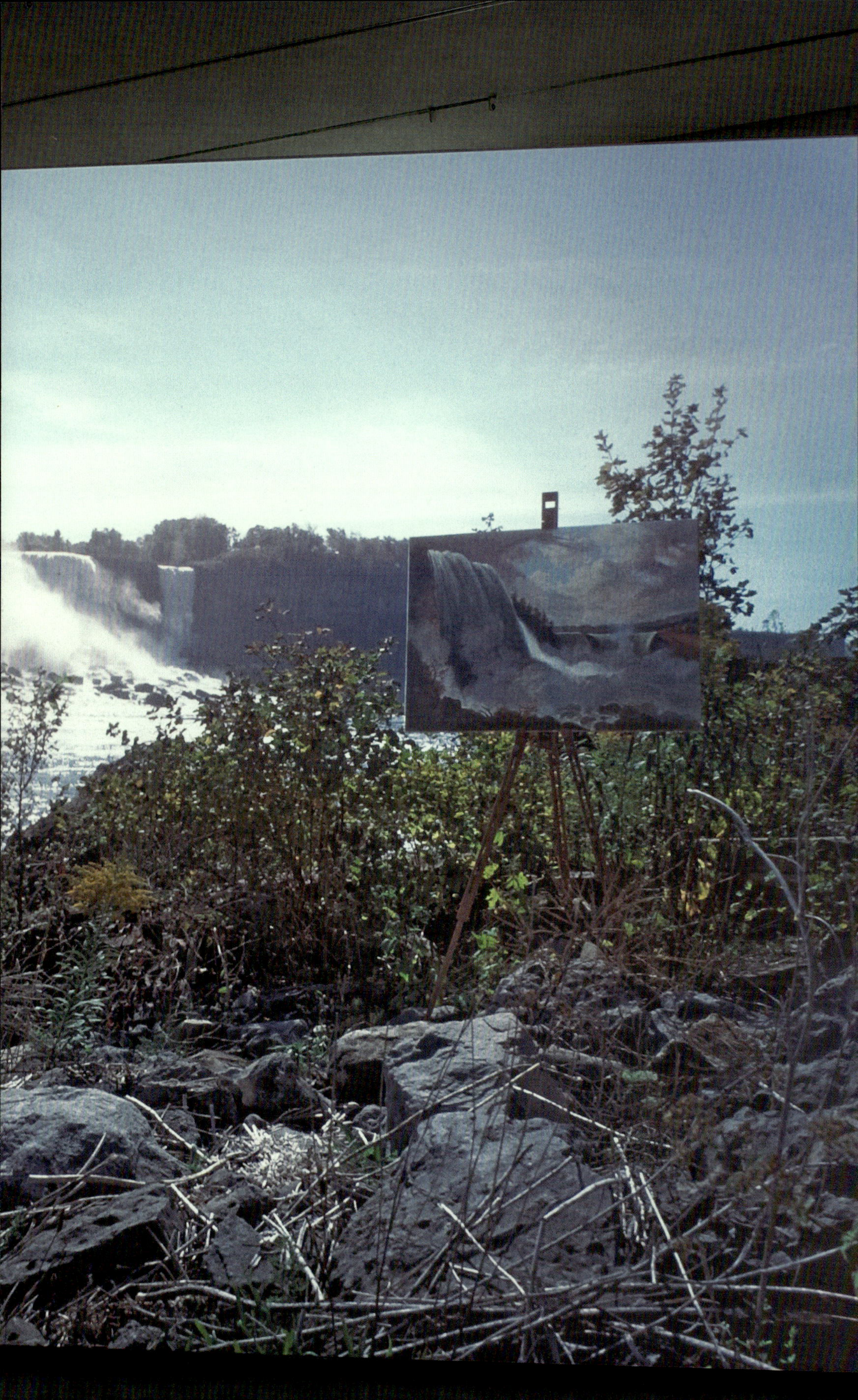

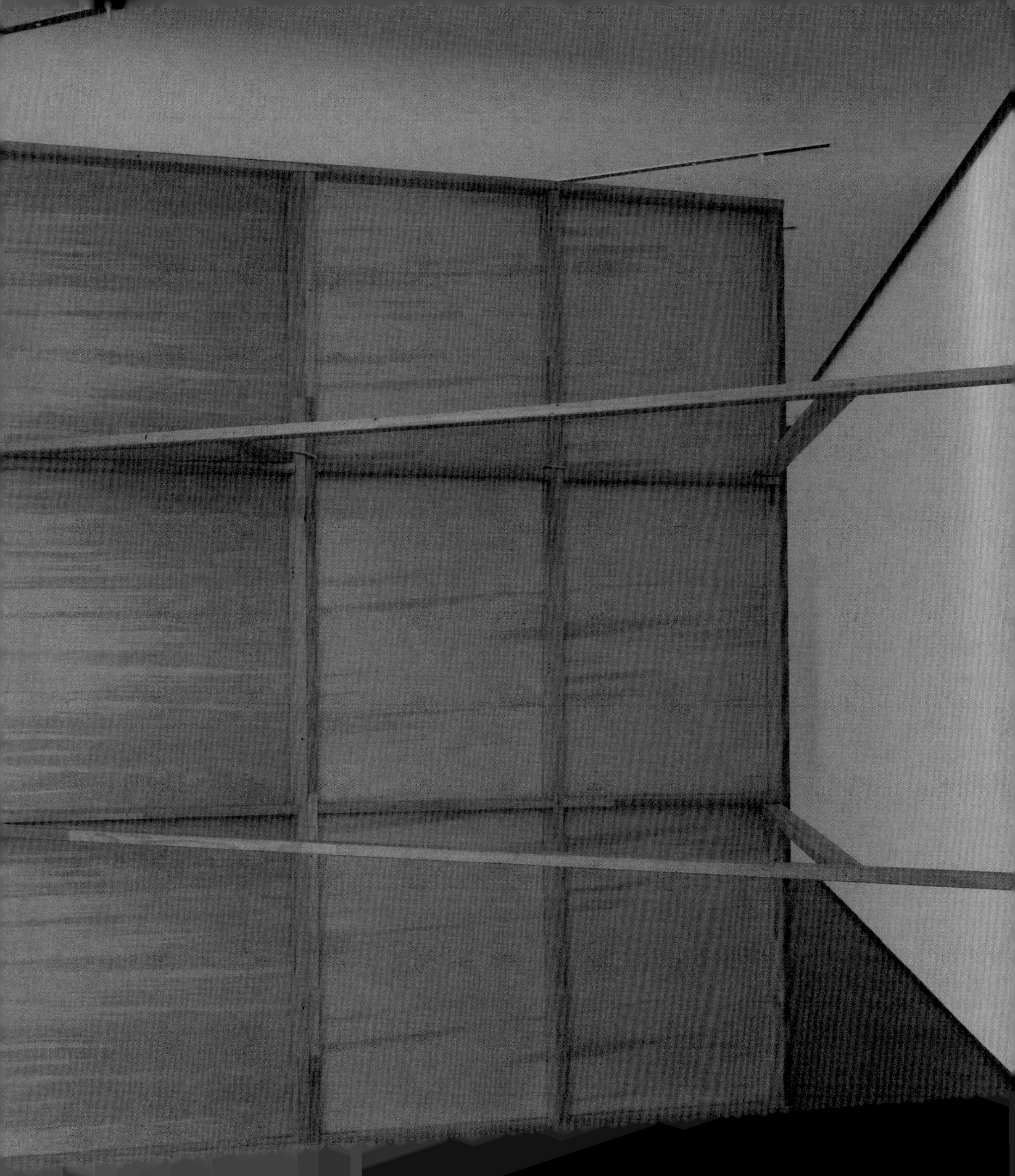

PARIS, 15-03-1999 RETURNED, PARC DES BUTTES-CHAUMONT (MADE AFTER NICOLAS POUSSIN'S SPRING OR THE EARTHLY PARADISE, ROME 1660–1664), 2000–2001

Die Arbeit *Paris, 15-03-1999 Returned, Parc des Buttes-Chaumont* beruht auf einer Fotografie aus dem Projekt *Returned* (1997–1998), die Leiderstam zu einer Diaprojektion auf einer freistehenden Wand weiterentwickelt hat. Für *Returned* hatte er mehrere Adaptionen des Gemäldes *Le Printemps ou le Paradis terrestre* (1660–1664) von Nicolas Poussin angefertigt, wobei er nur die Landschaft kopierte, auf die Figuren von Gott, Adam und Eva aber verzichtete. Seine Bilder hatte er in verschiedenen Parks, die als Crusing-Sites bekannt sind, auf Staffeleien gestellt, fotografiert und dann zurückgelassen. Für diese Installation greift er zurück auf die Aufnahme aus einer künstlichen Grotte mit Wasserfall im Pariser Landschaftspark Buttes-Chaumont, der von Georges-Eugène Haussmann und Jean-Charles Alphand anlässlich der Weltausstellung von 1867 konzipiert wurde.

The work *Paris, 15-03-1999 Returned, Parc des Buttes-Chaumont* is based on a photograph from the project *Returned* (1997–1998) that Leiderstam developed further into a slide projection on a free standing wall. He prepared several adaptations of Nicolas Poussin's painting *Le Printemps ou le Paradis terrestre* (1660–1664) for *Returned,* copying only the landscape but omitting the figures of God, Adam, and Eve. He placed his paintings on easels in different parks, which are known as crusing-sites, photographed them and left them there. For this installation, he had recourse to a photograph from an artificial grotto with a waterfall in the public gardens of Buttes-Chaumont in Paris, designed by Georges-Eugène Haussmann and Jean-Charles Alphand for the World Exposition in 1867.

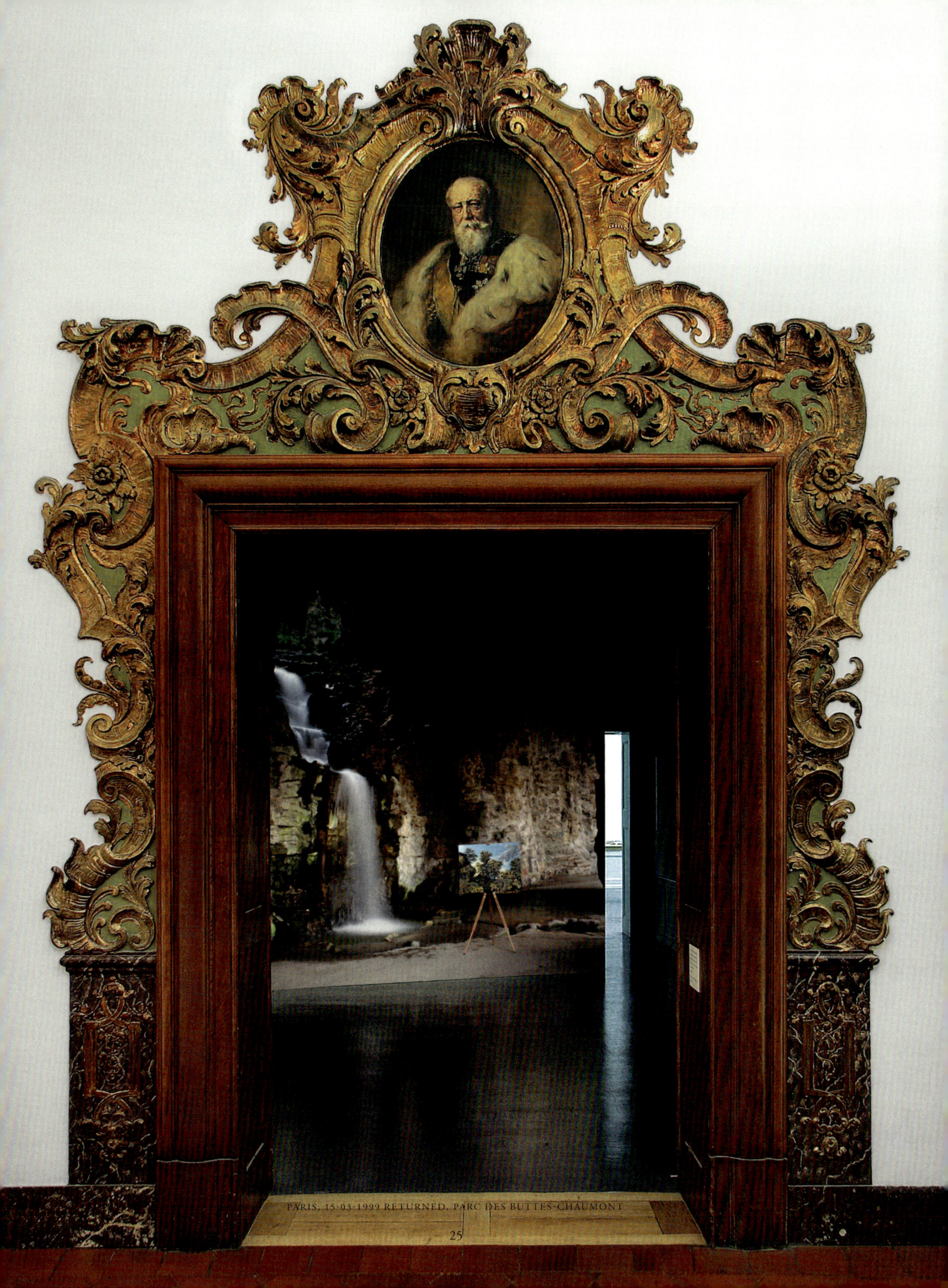

PARIS, 15-03-1999 RETURNED, PARC DES BUTTES-CHAUMONT

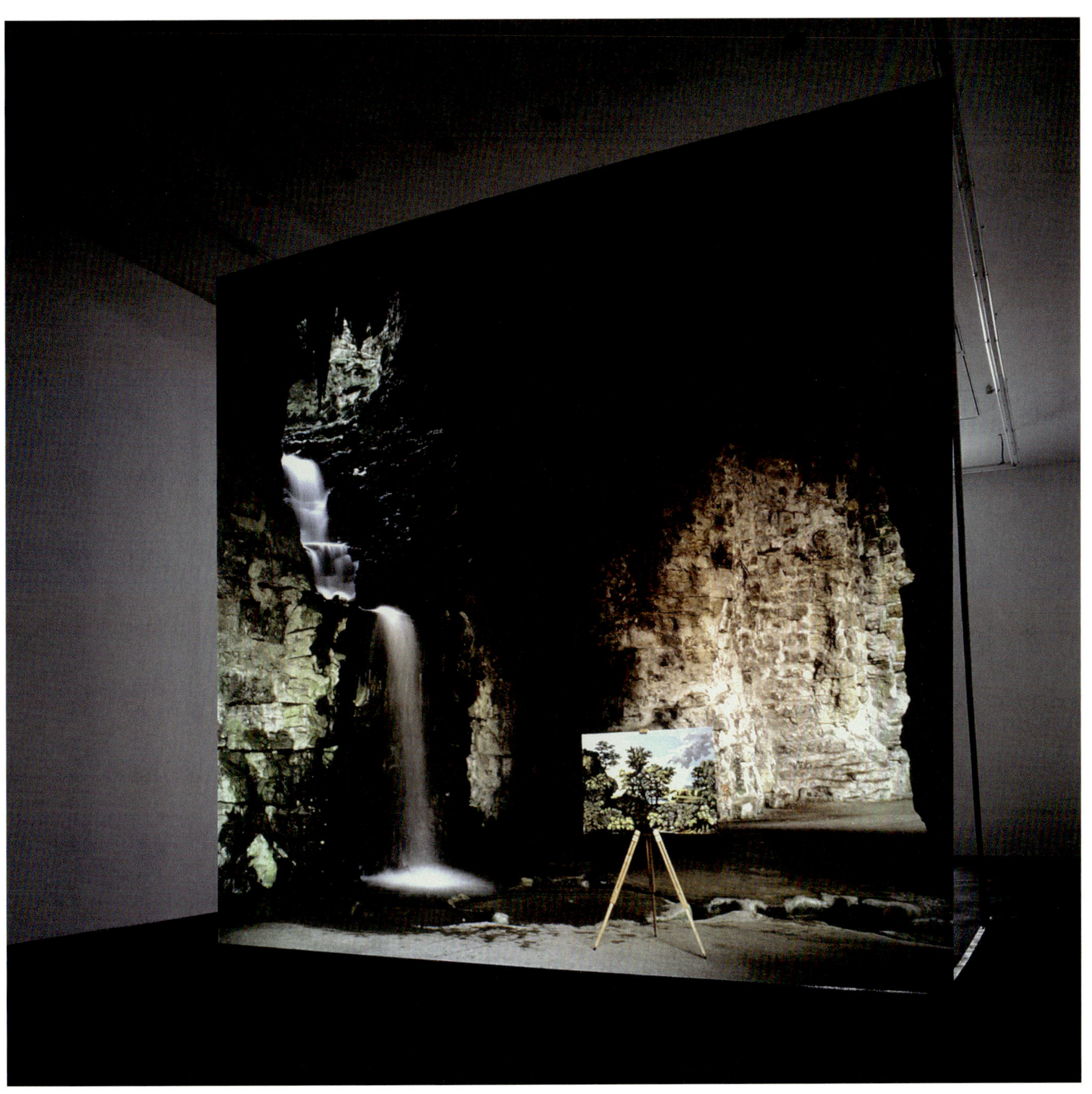

PARIS, 15-03-1999 RETURNED, PARC DES BUTTES-CHAUMONT

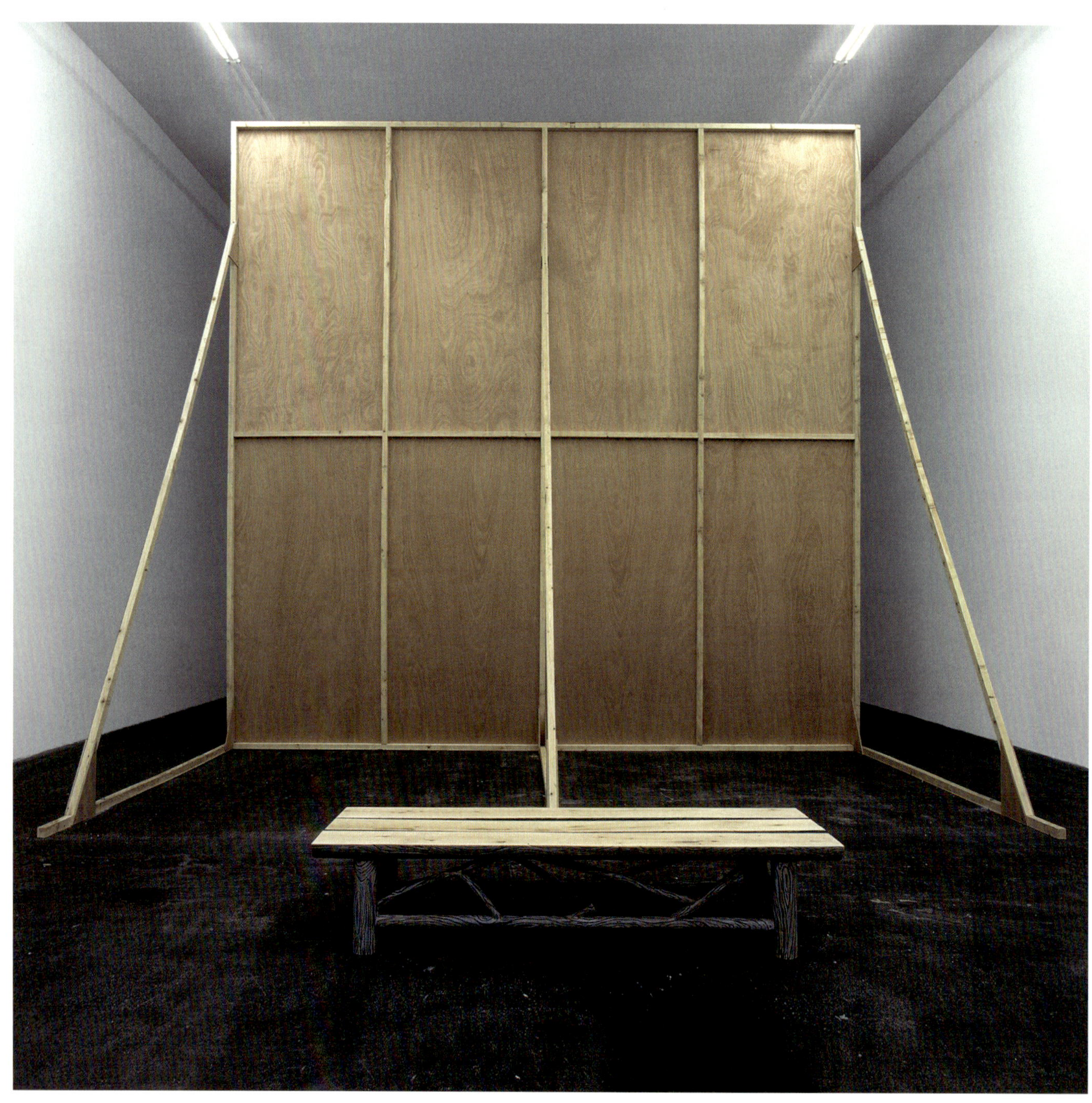

PARIS, 15-03-1999 RETURNED, PARC DES BUTTES-CHAUMONT

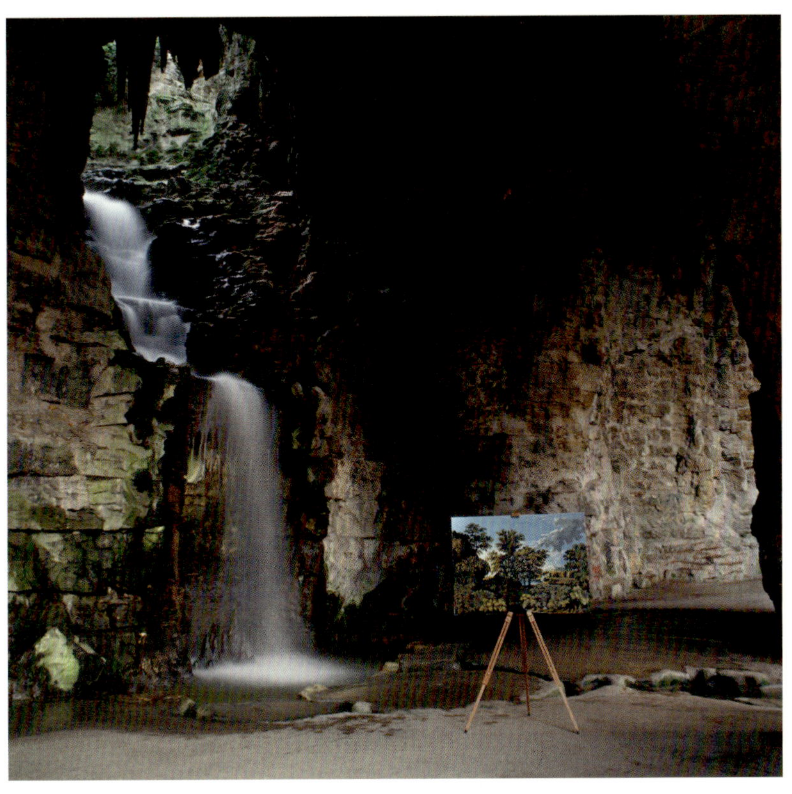

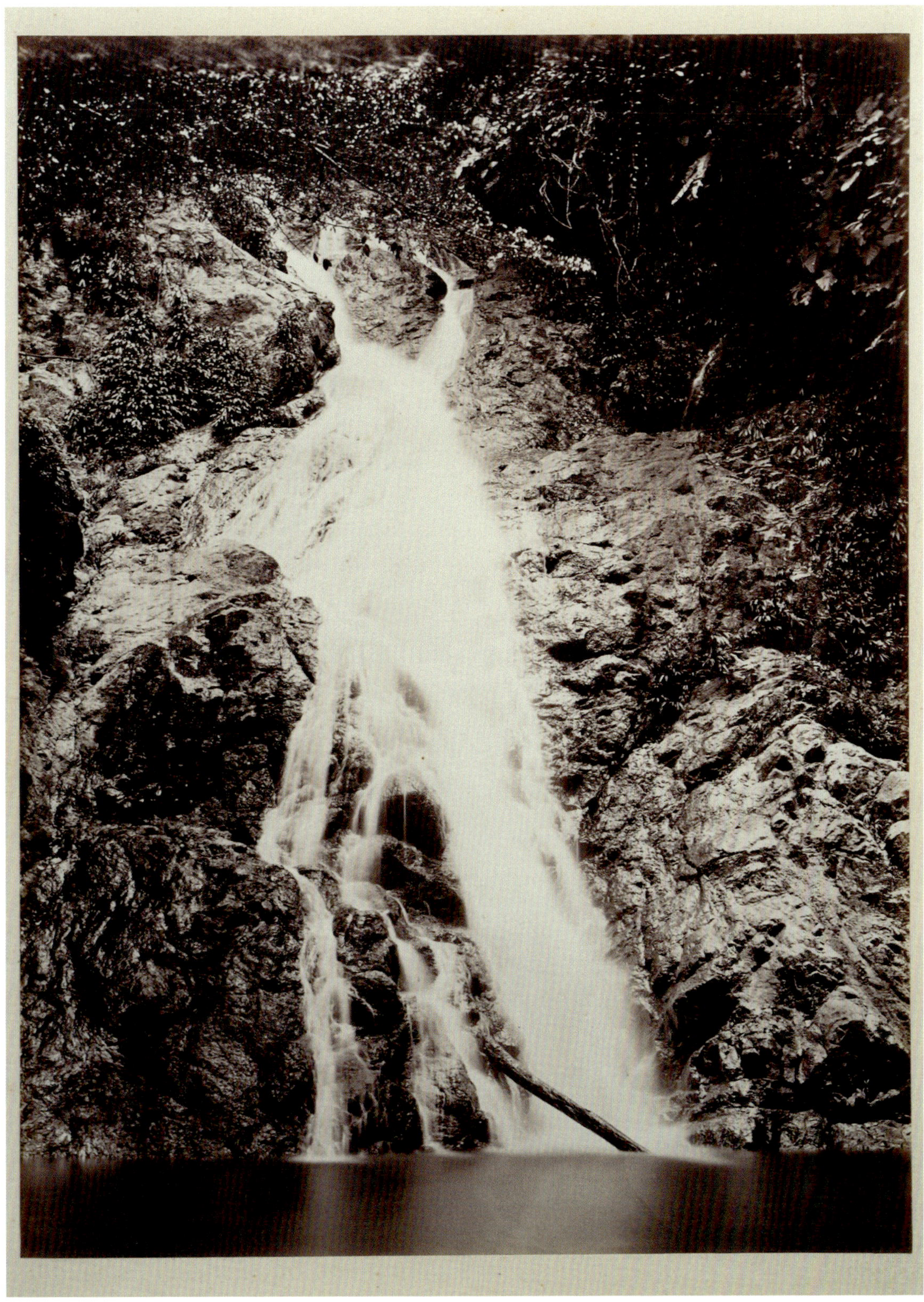

FIRST SEEN

Nachdem Wilfried Lentz, einer der Galeristen Leiderstams, einen historischen Abzug der Fotografie eines Wasserfalls des Limon River, mit der sich der Künstler im Rahmen seiner Installation *Grand Tour* (1996–1998) schon einmal beschäftigt hatte, bei einer Auktion erwerben konnte, begann dieser, die Geschichte des Fotos zu untersuchen. In *First Seen* hängt der gerahmte Vintage Print über einer aufgeschlagenen Ausgabe von James D. Horans Monografie über den Fotografen Timothy O'Sullivan (1840–1882), dem die Aufnahme ursprünglich zugeschrieben wurde. Leiderstams eigene Recherchen aber ergaben, dass das Porträt des Expeditionsfotografen, das Horan in seinem Buch als Beleg für die Autorschaft O'Sullivans anführt, nicht diesen, sondern John Moran (1831–1902) zeigt. Dem Expeditionsbericht zufolge begleitete Moran anstelle O'Sullivans die zweite der beiden sogenannten Darien-Expeditionen und muss demnach als der wahre Autor der Fotografie *The Great Falls on the Limon River* gelten. Die Ergebnisse seiner Recherche hat Leiderstam auf einer Seite zusammengefasst und in Horans Buch eingeklebt.

After Wilfried Lentz, one of Leiderstam's gallerists, managed to acquire at auction an historic print of a photograph of a waterfall on the Limon River, which the artist had already worked on in connection with his installation *Grand Tour* (1996–1998), Leiderstam began to investigate the history of the photograph. In *First Seen,* the vintage print hangs above an open edition of James D. Horan's monograph on the photographer Timothy O'Sullivan (1840–1882), to whom the photograph was originally attributed. Leiderstam's own research revealed, however, that the portrait of the expedition photographer used by Horan as proof of O'Sullivan's authorship doesn't show him, but in fact shows John Moran (1831–1902). According to the account of the expedition, Moran accompanied the second of the two so-called Darien expeditions in place of O'Sullivan and therefore must be considered the actual photographer of *The Great Falls on the Limon River.* Leiderstam summarized the results of his research in a single page and attached it to Horan's book.

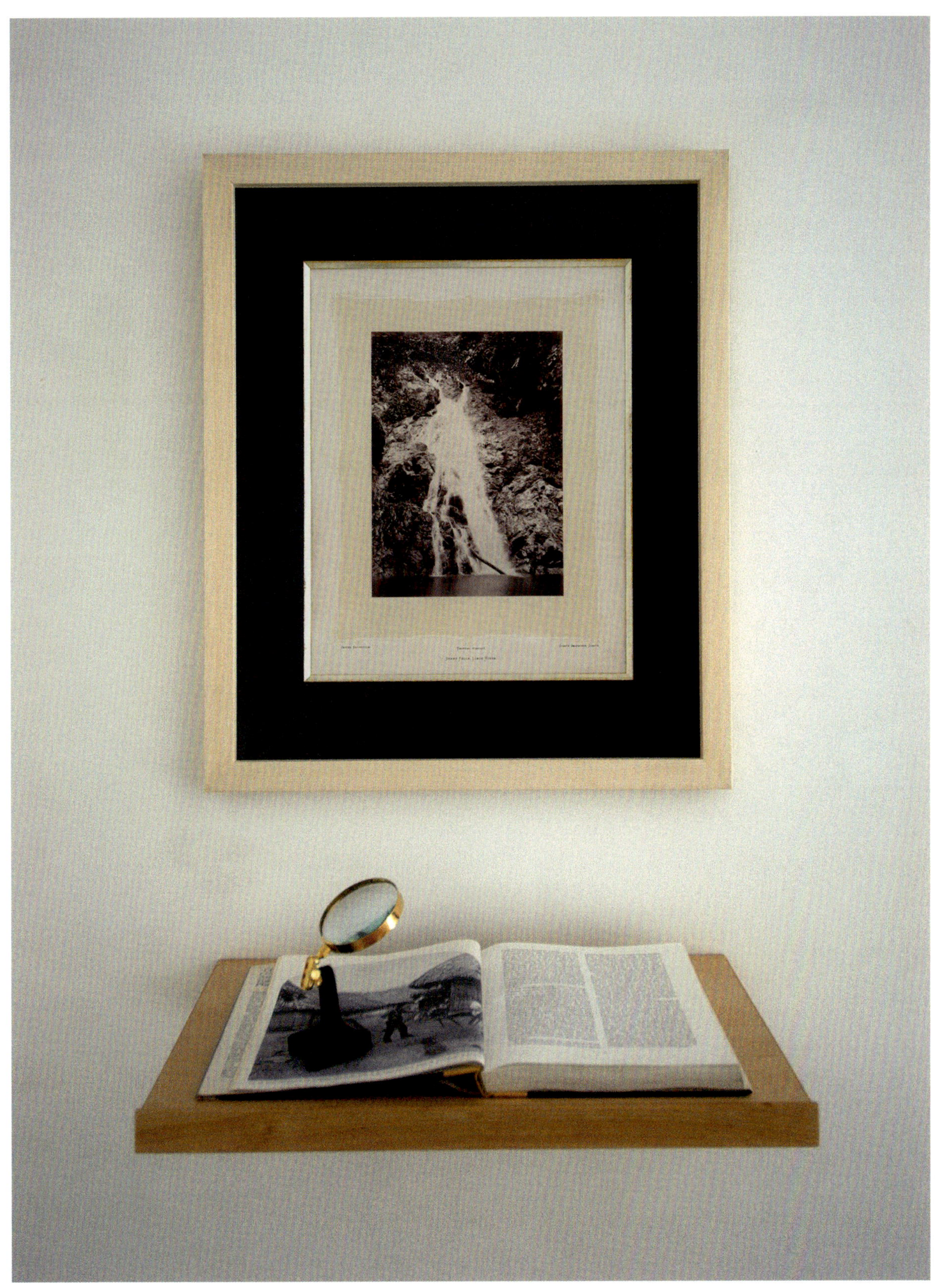

FIRST SEEN

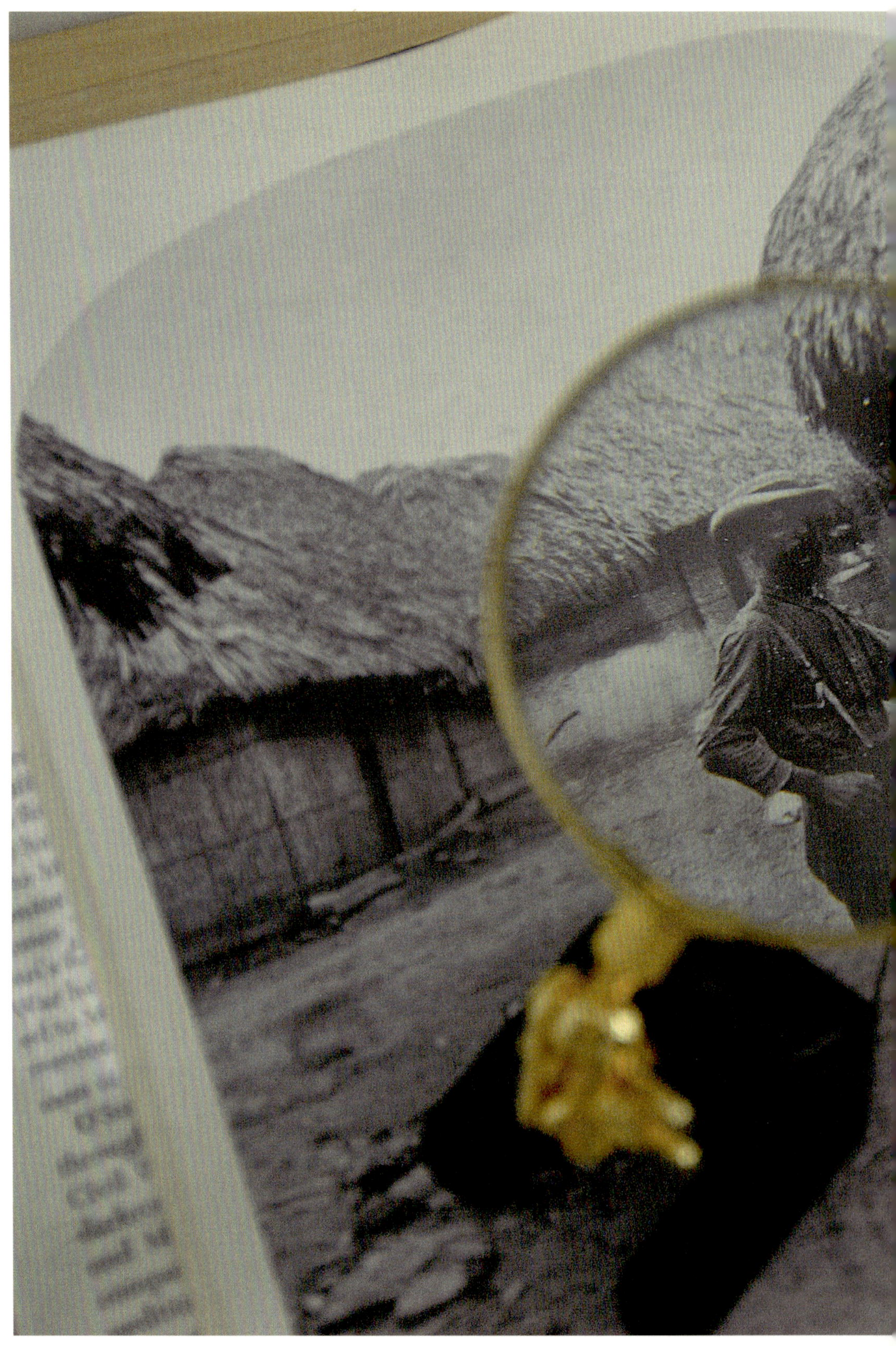

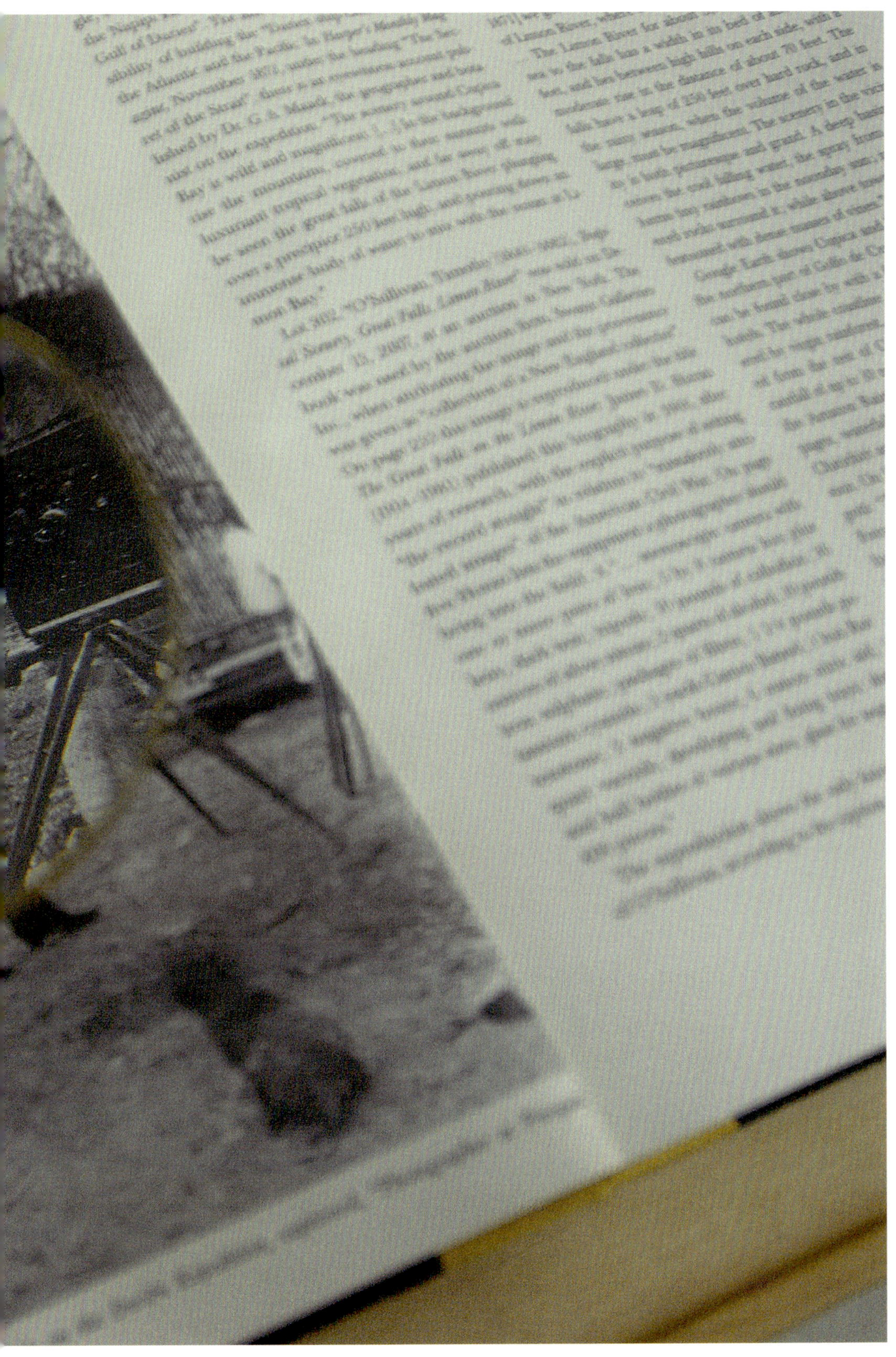

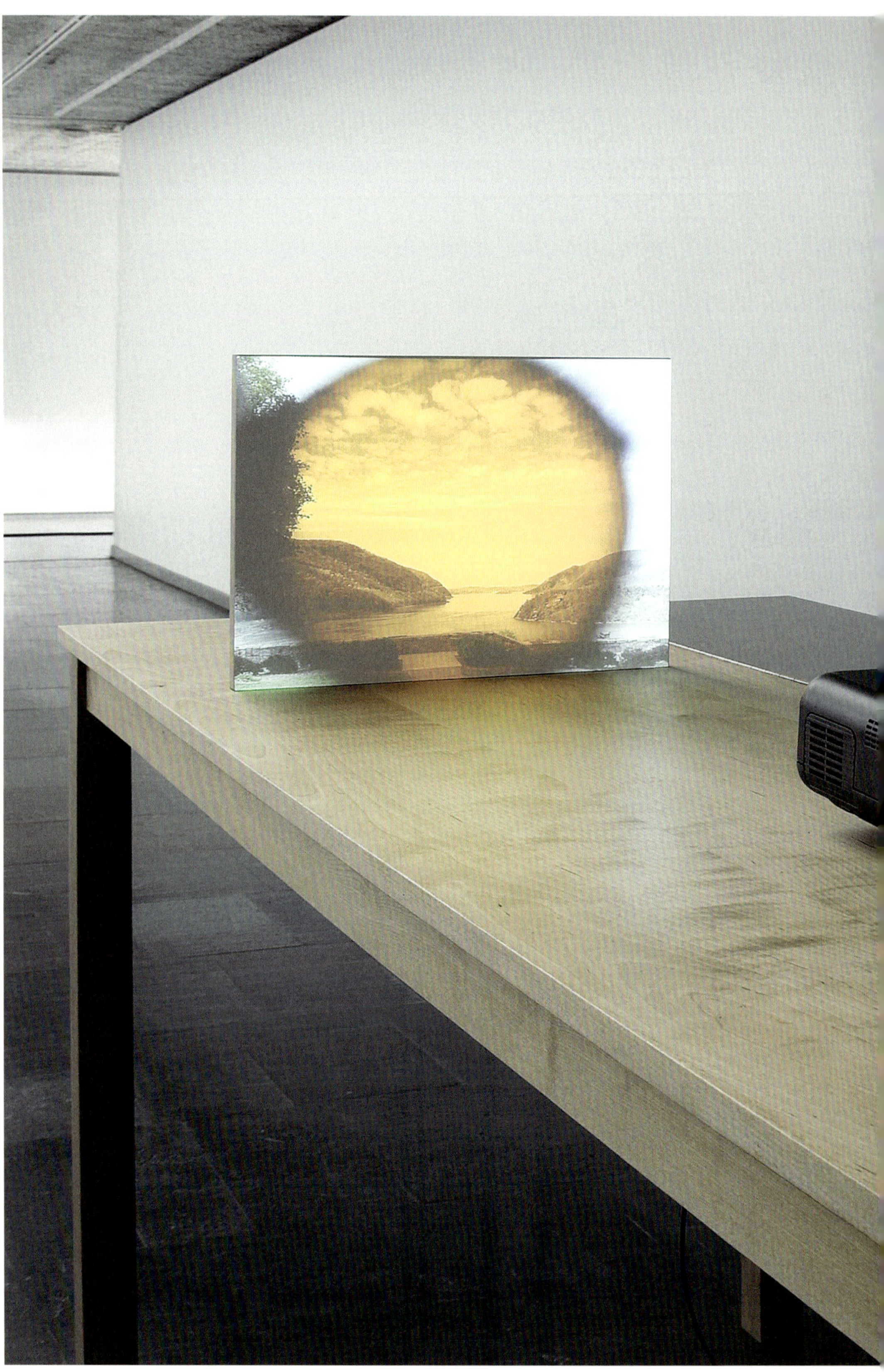

VIEW (WEST POINT), APRIL 30, 2003

Die Installation *View (West Point), April 30, 2003* ist Teil des umfangreichen Projekts *View,* das 2003 im Rahmen des *Hudson Valley Project* im US-Bundesstaat New York entstand. Das Gebiet um den Hudson River kam den Vorstellungen des 19. Jahrhunderts von einer arkadischen Ideallandschaft sehr nahe und war daher ein beliebtes Motiv der amerikanischen Landschaftsmalerei jener Zeit. Später entwickelten die Maler der Hudson River School hier ihre Vision einer originär amerikanischen Landschaft. Zur Schaffung bestimmter Blickachsen plante Leiderstam ursprünglich die Aufstellung dreier Ferngläser an unterschiedlichen Orten, darunter auch bei West Point. Da dort jedoch aufgrund militärischer Nutzung kein freier Zugang zu dem Fernglas gewährleistet gewesen wäre, entschied sich der Künstler, die Perspektive dieses Standorts in Form einer Installation zu realisieren. Die *View*-Arbeiten gehören zu den ersten Werken Leiderstams, in denen er sich auf die nach dem französischen Maler Claude Lorrain benannten Claude-Gläser bezieht und beim Fotografieren verschiedenfarbige Filter vor das Kameraobjektiv hält. Gerade in der Pleinairmalerei des 18. Jahrhunderts wurden sie dazu verwendet, unterschiedliche farbliche Stimmungen zu erzeugen. Begleitet wird die Projektion der Fotografien von einem Satz historischer Claude-Gläser.

The installation *View (West Point), April 30, 2003* is part of the extensive project *View* that arose within the framework of the *Hudson Valley Project* in New York State. The area surrounding the Hudson River closely corresponded to nineteenth-century ideas of what constitutes an Arcadian landscape and therefore became a favorite motif of American landscape painters at the time. At a later date, the painters of the Hudson River School developed their vision of original American landscape. In order to create particular visual axes, Leiderstam originally planned to set up three telescopes in different places, including one at West Point. However, since military use of the area made it impossible to guarantee free access to the binoculars, the artist decided to realize the view of this site in the form of an installation. The works comprising *View* belong to some of Leiderstam's first pieces in which he refers to Claude glasses, named after the French painter Claude Lorrain, with which different colored filters are held in front of the lens when taking photographs. The glasses were used particularly in outdoor painting during the eighteenth century, in order to create different tonal moods. The projection of the photographs is accompanied by a vintage set of Claude glasses.

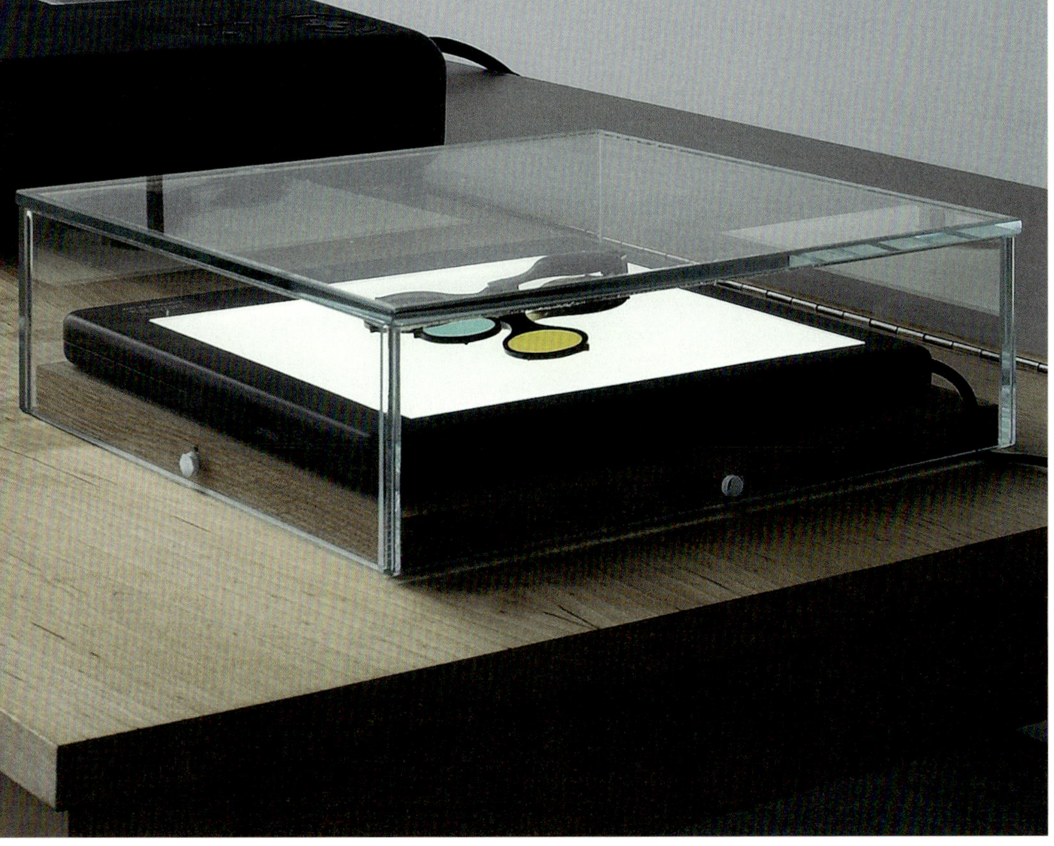

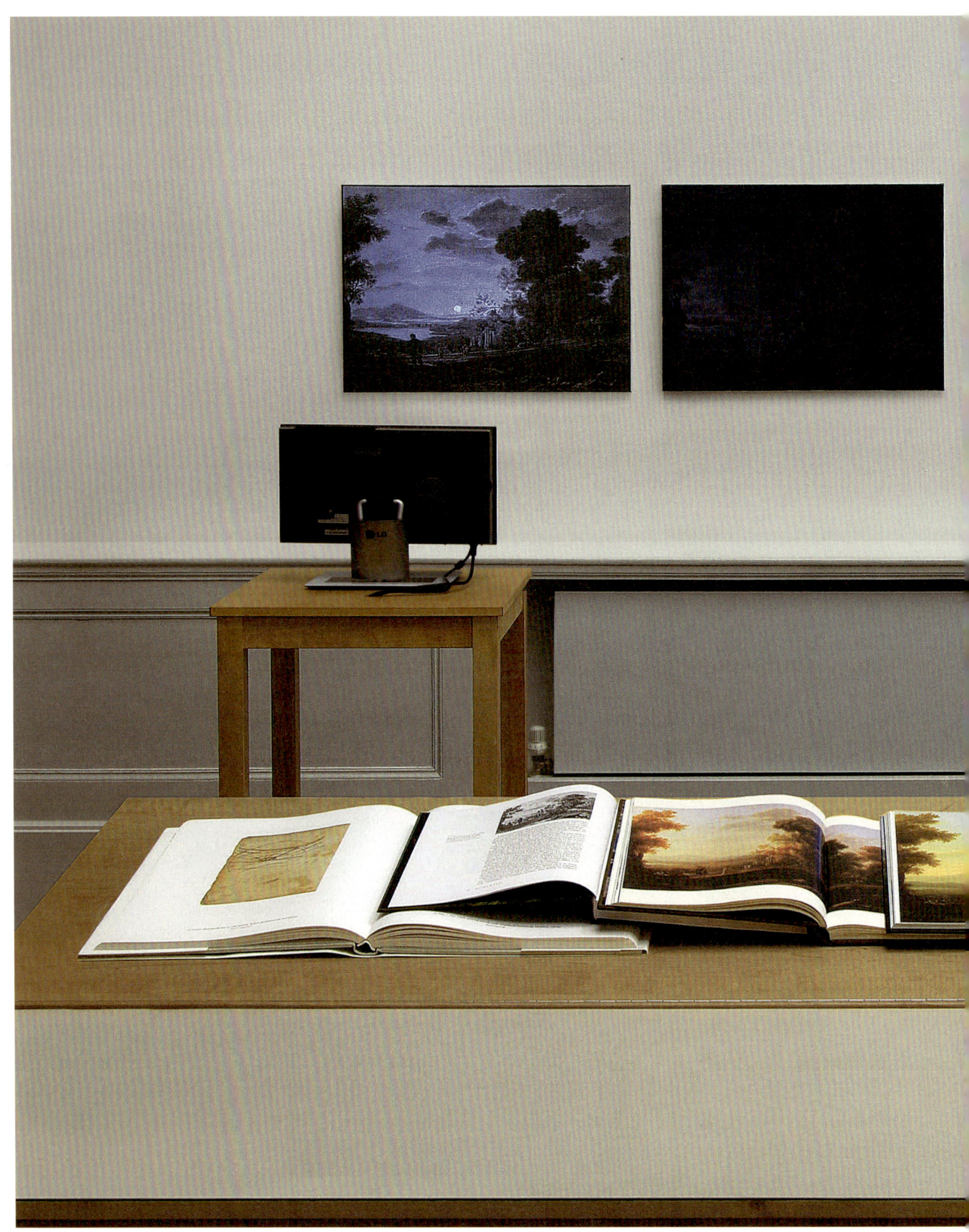

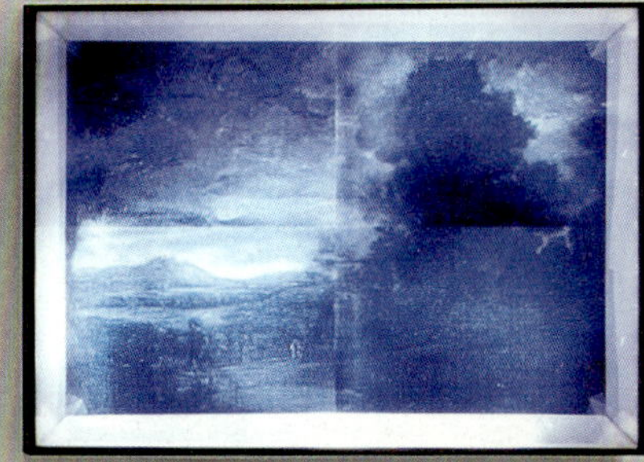

In der Installation *The Sun* beschäftigt sich
Leiderstam mit Claude Lorrains Gemälde
*Landschaft mit Rebecca, Abschied nehmend von
ihrem Vater* (1640/1641). Eine Röntgenaufnahme, die zu wissenschaftlichen Zwecken
von dem Werk Lorrains angefertigt wurde,
hatte ergeben, dass die Sonne ursprünglich
anders platziert war. Leiderstam nahm diese
Entdeckung zum Anlass, eine Kopie des Bildes anzufertigen, die er mehrfach übermalte.
Dabei vollzog er den Lauf der Sonne nach,
von ihrem Aufgang bis zum Sonnenunter-
gang. Der letzte Stand der Übermalung zeigt
die Szenerie des Lorrain-Gemäldes bei Nacht.
Die verschiedenen Etappen dieses Verlaufs
wurden fotografisch dokumentiert und
werden als Animation projiziert. Zudem ist
Leiderstams Kopie des Gemäldes im Stadium
ihrer letzten Überarbeitung zu sehen sowie
ein Leuchtkasten mit einer Röntgenaufnahme
seines Bildes. Die auf einem Tisch aufgeschlagenen Bücher zeigen verschiedene Reproduktionen des Originals von Lorrain und dessen
Röntgenbild.

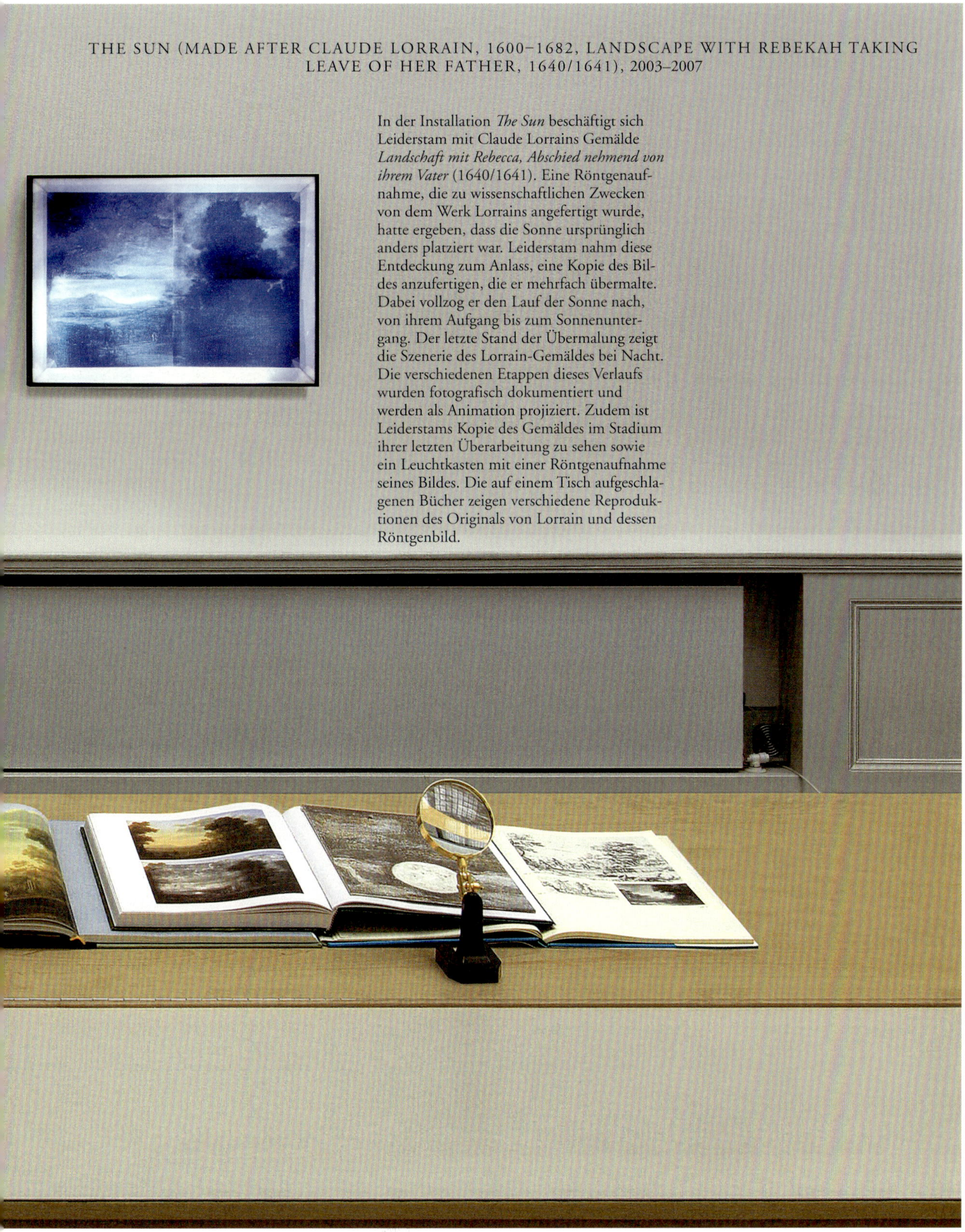

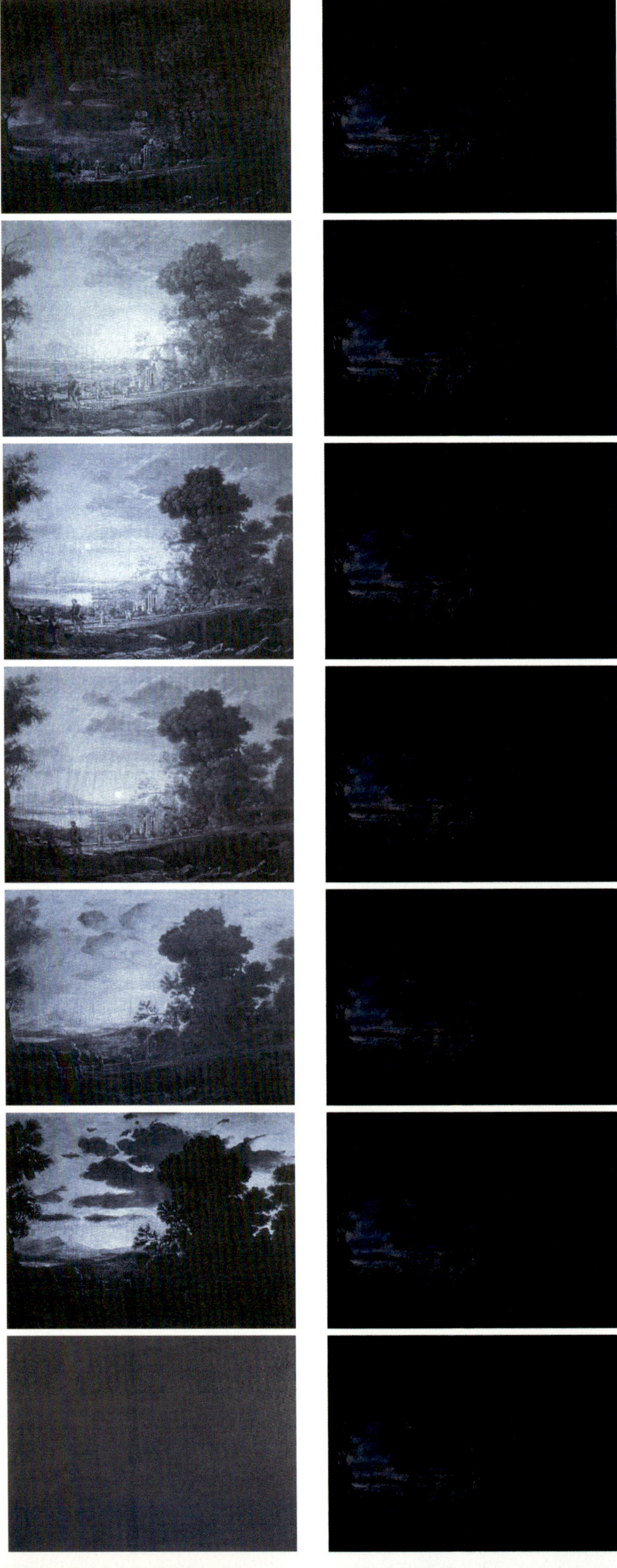

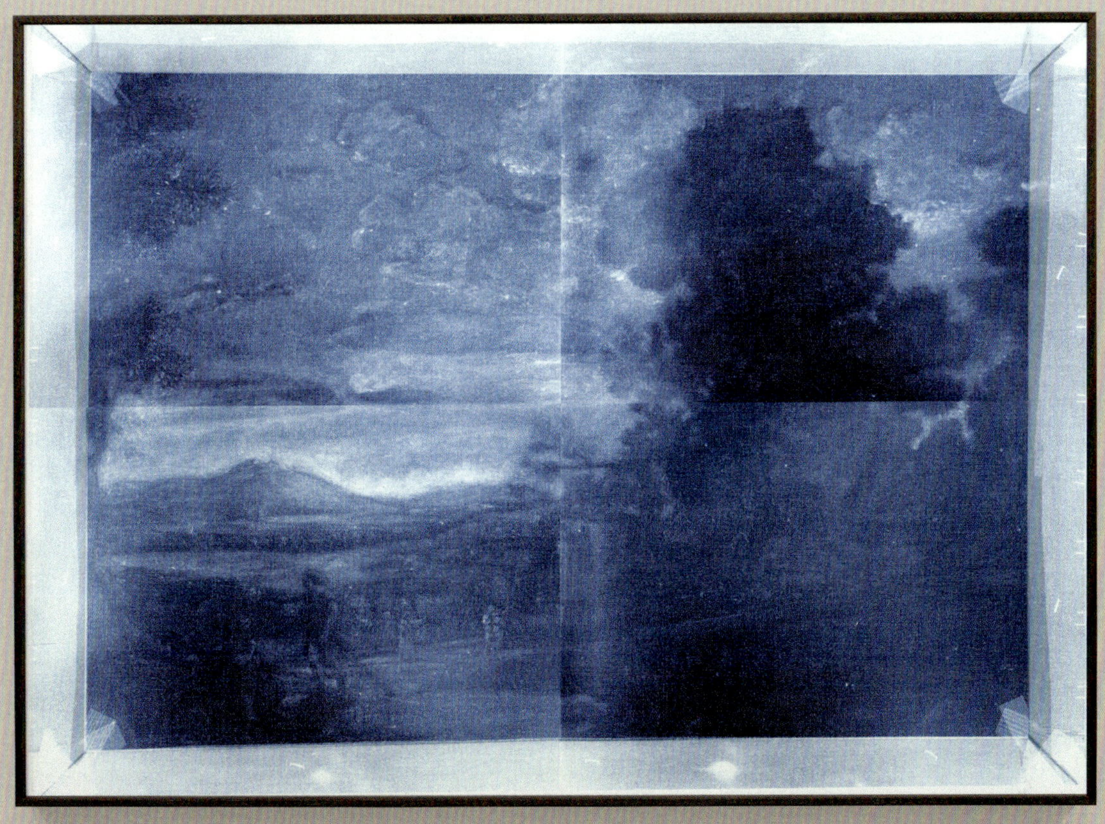

In the installation *The Sun,* Leiderstam
focuses on Claude Lorrain's painting *Landscape with Rebekah Taking Leave of her Father*
(1640/1641). A radiograph of Lorrain's work,
taken for scientific purposes, revealed that the
sun had originally been situated in a different
position. Leiderstam used this discovery as
a pretext to produce a copy of the picture,
which he then overpainted several times. In
so doing, he traced the progression of the sun
from sunrise to sunset. The last stage of the
overpainting depicts the scene in Lorrain's
painting at night. The various stages of this
process were photographically documented
and are now projected as an animation. In
addition, Leiderstam's copy of the painting
can be seen in the final stage of its reworking,
together with a light-box and a radiograph
of his painting. Open books on a table show
a reproduction of Lorrain's original and an
x-ray image of the painting.

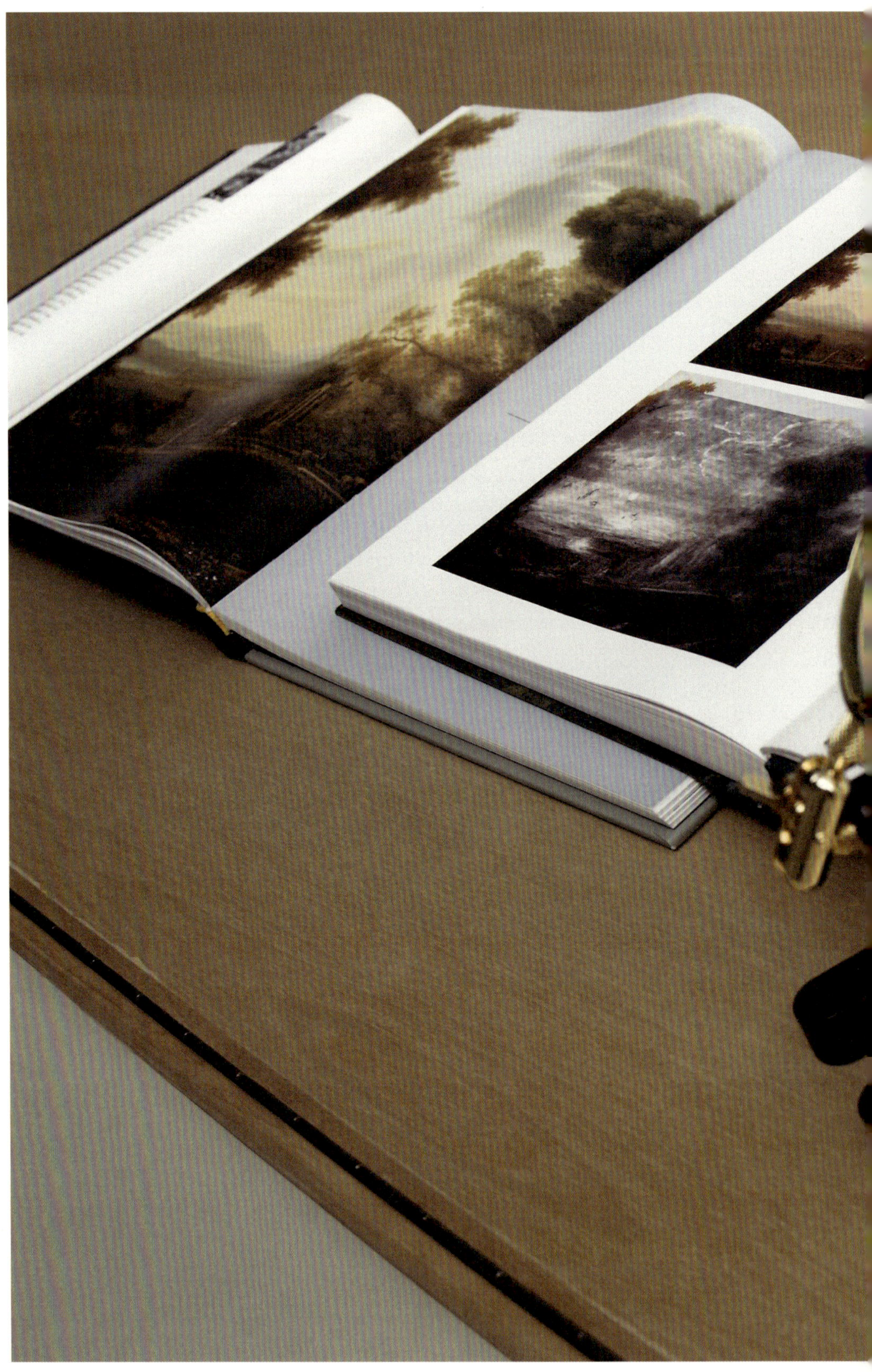

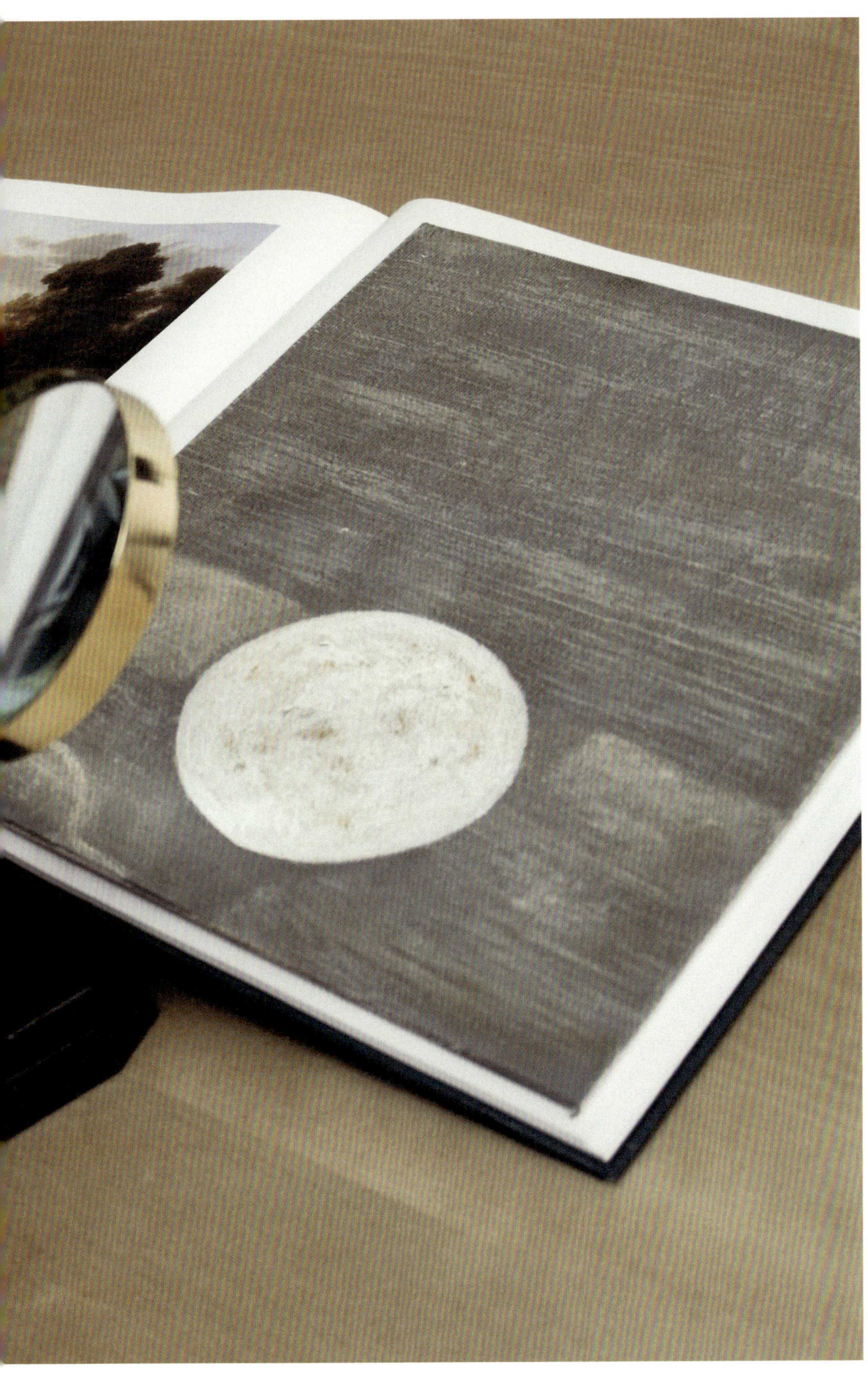

THE SUN

43

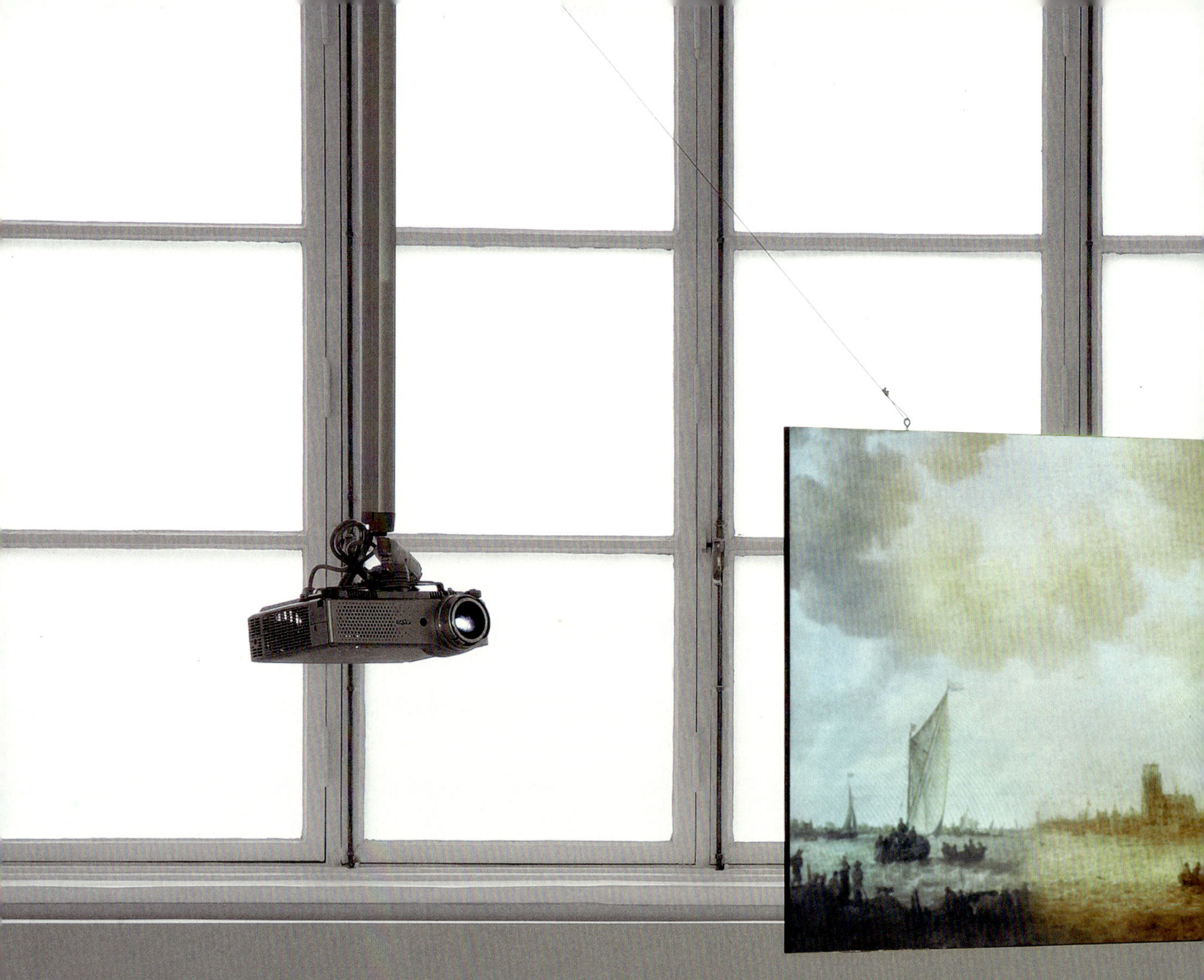

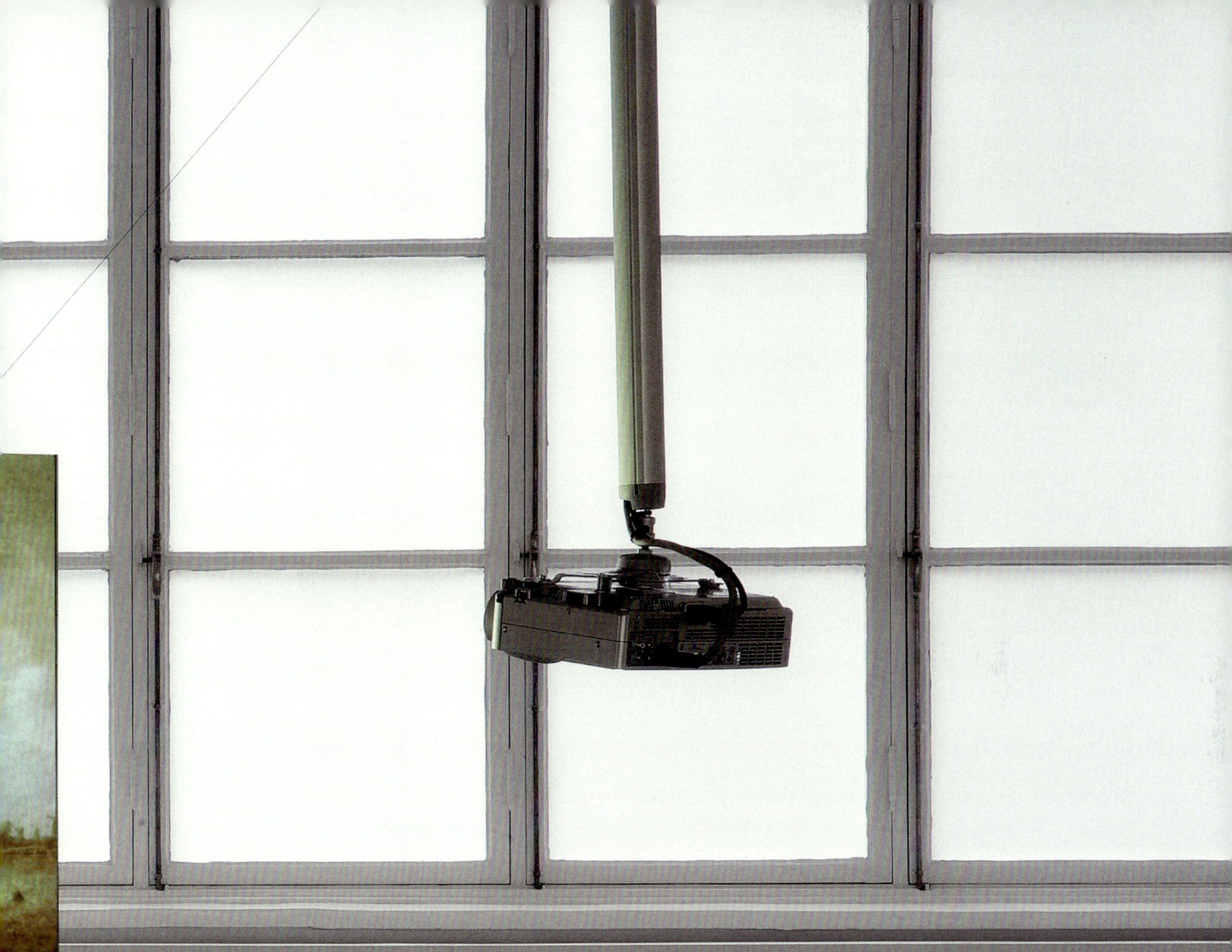

Die Doppelprojektion zeigt auf der einen Seite eine 13-minütige digital animierte Sequenz, die auf zehn Gemälden des holländischen Landschaftsmalers Jan van Goyen (1596–1656) und auf einer ihm fälschlicherweise zugeschriebenen Arbeit von Jeronymus van Diest (1631–1673) beruht. Die einzelnen Gemälde mit verschiedenen Ansichten des niederländischen Städtchens Dordrecht verschmelzen dergestalt zu einem ständig in Veränderung begriffenen »bewegten« Bild, das eine filmische Qualität suggeriert. Auf der Rückseite erscheint ein fortlaufender Text mit Informationen zu den Provenienzen der verwendeten Gemälde, die sich wie Biografien mit ihren individuellen Schicksalen und Anekdoten lesen lassen. Als Projektionsfläche dient eine Eichenholztafel, die Leiderstam in Anlehnung an van Goyens bevorzugten Maluntergrund anfertigen ließ.

The double projection shows on one side a thirteen-minute, digitally animated sequence based on ten paintings by the Dutch landscape painter Jan van Goyen (1596–1656) and one by Jeronymus van Diest (1631–1673), falsely attributed to van Goyen. The individual paintings, with different views of the Dutch town of Dordrecht, coalesce to such an extent to a perceptually changing, "moving" image that they suggest a certain filmic quality. On the back of the wall appears a continuous text imparting information about the provenance of the paintings, which can be read as biographies, with their individual histories and anecdotes. The projection surface is an oak panel that Leiderstam commissioned, in keeping with van Goyen's preferred painting ground.

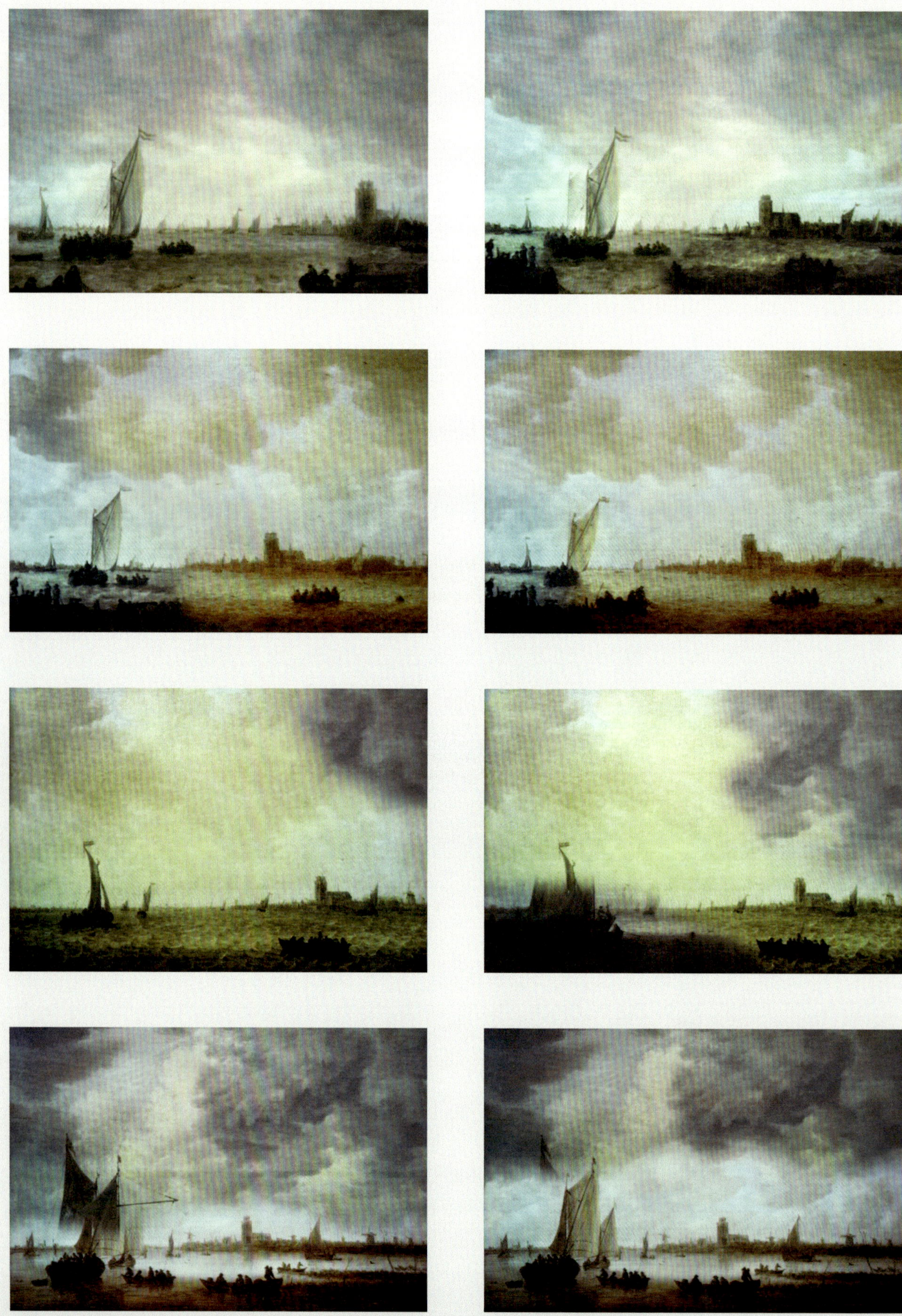

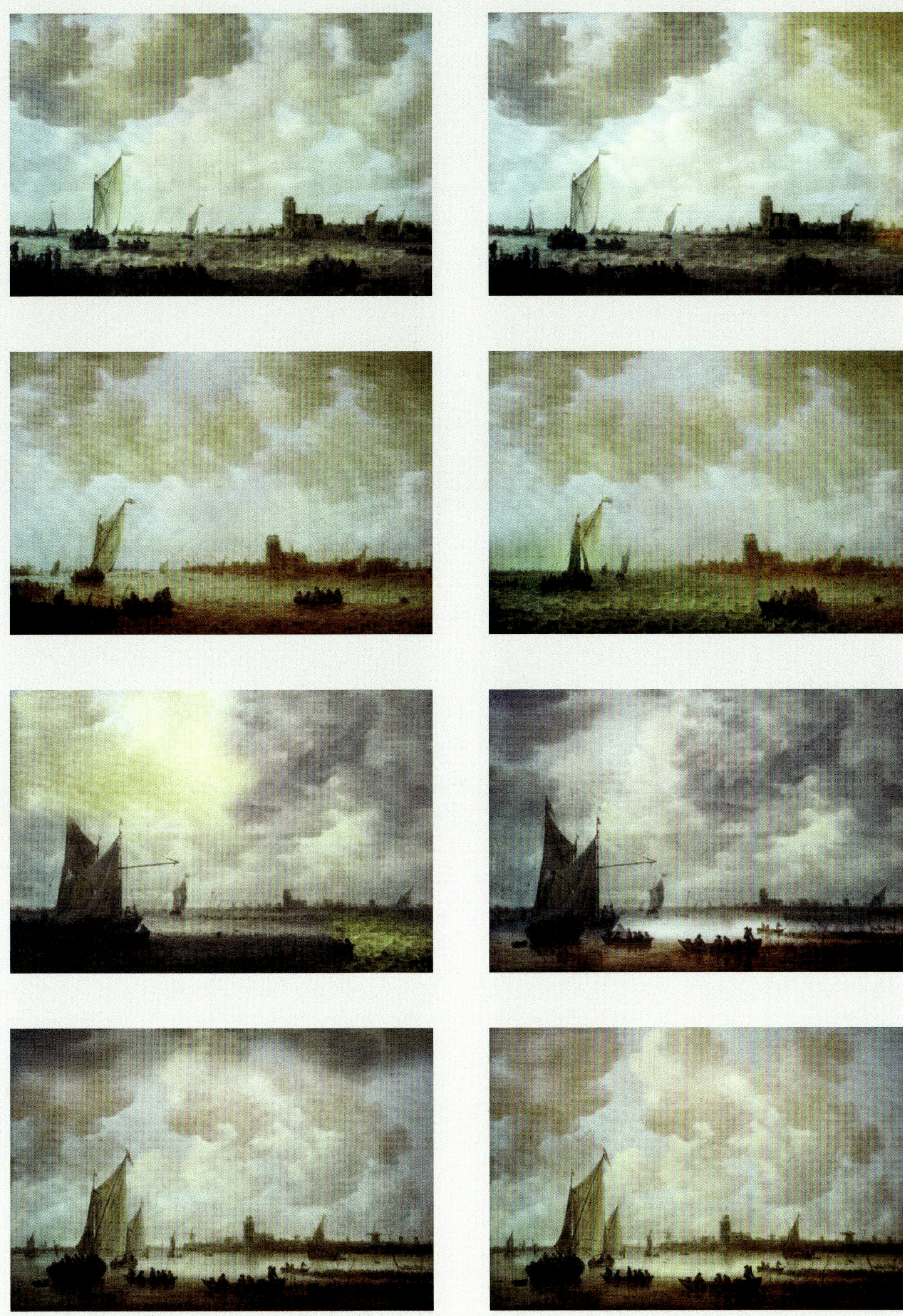

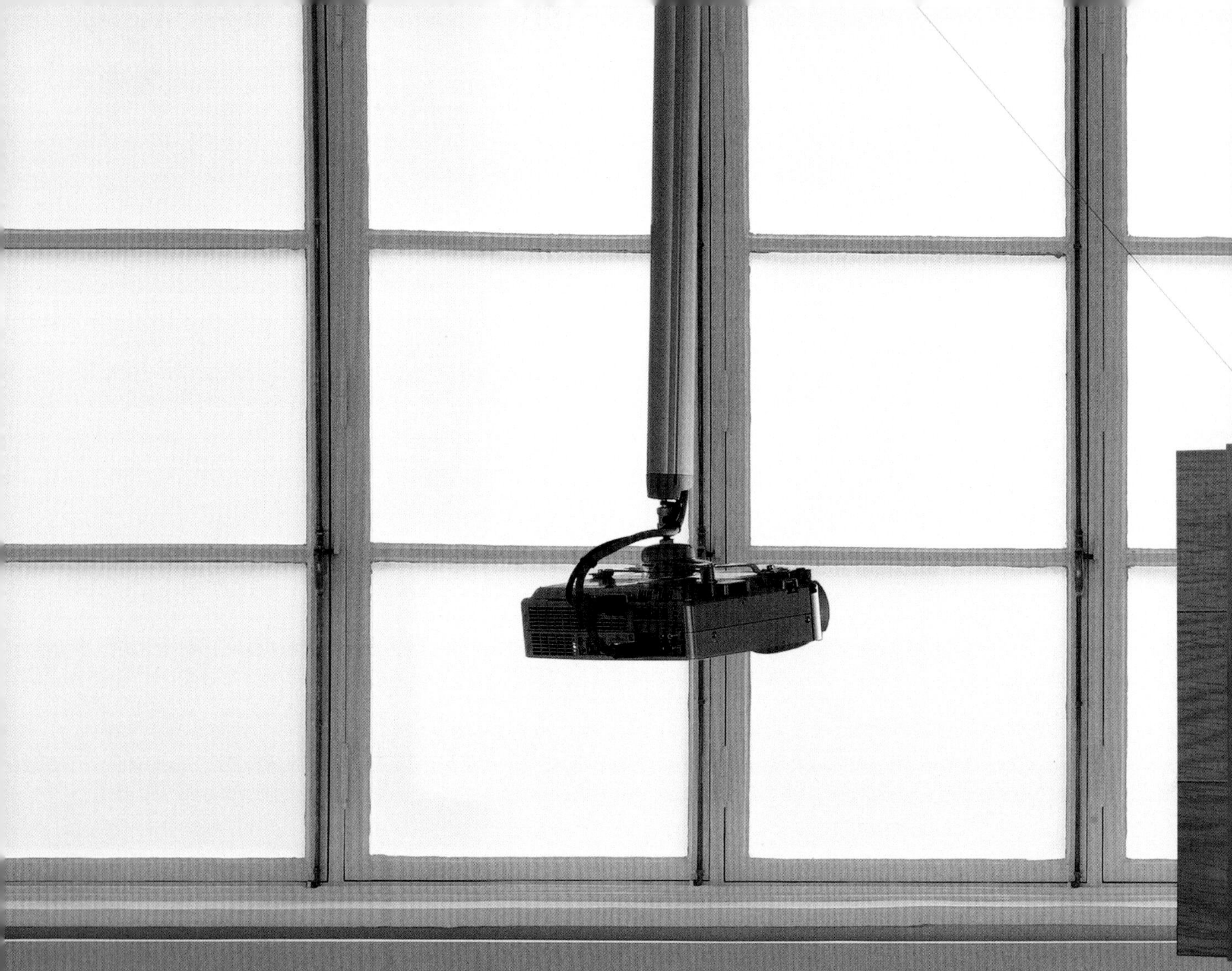

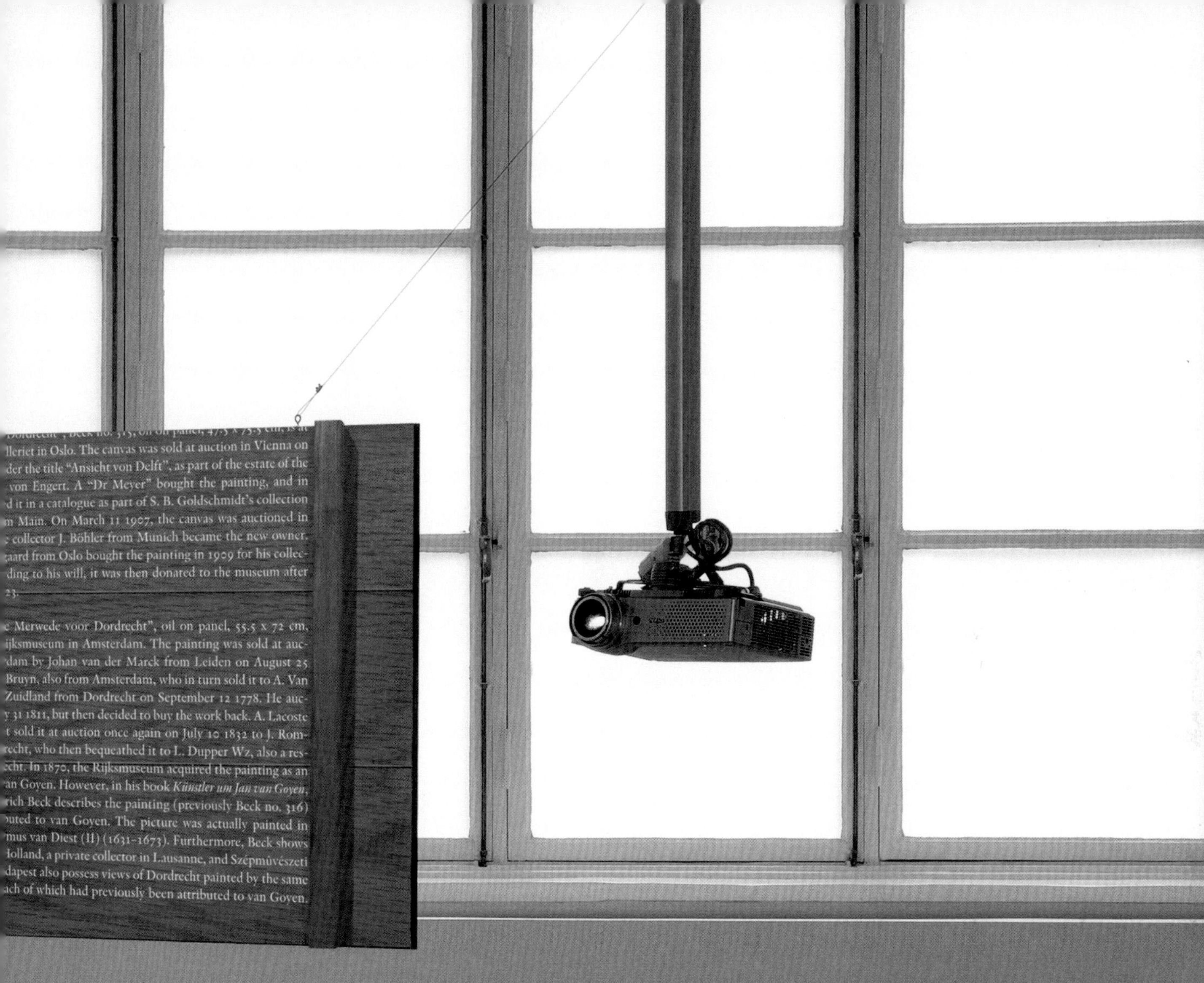

Dordrecht", Beck no. 315, oil on panel, 47.5 x 75.5 cm, is at
lleriet in Oslo. The canvas was sold at auction in Vienna on
der the title "Ansicht von Delft", as part of the estate of the
von Engert. A "Dr Meyer" bought the painting, and in
d it in a catalogue as part of S. B. Goldschmidt's collection
m Main. On March 11 1907, the canvas was auctioned in
collector J. Böhler from Munich became the new owner.
gaard from Oslo bought the painting in 1909 for his collec-
ding to his will, it was then donated to the museum after
23.

e Merwede voor Dordrecht", oil on panel, 55.5 x 72 cm,
ijksmuseum in Amsterdam. The painting was sold at auc-
dam by Johan van der Marck from Leiden on August 25
Bruyn, also from Amsterdam, who in turn sold it to A. Van
Zuidland from Dordrecht on September 12 1778. He auc-
y 31 1811, but then decided to buy the work back. A. Lacoste
t sold it at auction once again on July 10 1832 to J. Rom-
recht, who then bequeathed it to L. Dupper Wz, also a res-
echt. In 1870, the Rijksmuseum acquired the painting as an
an Goyen. However, in his book Künstler um Jan van Goyen,
rich Beck describes the painting (previously Beck no. 316)
buted to van Goyen. The picture was actually painted in
mus van Diest (II) (1631–1673). Furthermore, Beck shows
Holland, a private collector in Lausanne, and Szépmûvészeti
dapest also possess views of Dordrecht painted by the same
ach of which had previously been attributed to van Goyen.

Museum (Inside/Outside)

The Park of Friendship in New Belgrade was inaugurated in 1961, on the occasion of the first summit of the Non-Aligned Movement. Many international celebrities and officials have visited it and planted trees as a sign of eternal friendship. The Museum of Contemporary Art (Muzej savremene umetnosti) was built in 1965 close by, in the parkland of Ušće — located on the left bank of the Sava River across the Belgrade Fortress. In 1987 the building was declared a 'cultural landmark of national interest'.

Not far from the Museum is the Old Trade Fair Ground, and this area was the first major urban settlement in New Belgrade before World War II. The trade fair (sajmište) was turned by the Gestapo, the German Secret Police, into a concentration camp in December 1941 and shut down in September 1944. In the Sajmište Concentration Camp more than 40,000 Serbian and 7–8,000 Jewish victims were killed.

The area was bombed and mostly destroyed in 1944, and after the War some of the remaining pavilions were given over to artists as studios. One of the artists was the landscape painter Miloš Gvozdenović (1926–2006). In the mid-1980s Gvozdenović made a series of sketches for his paintings with views of the Museum, most often glimpsed through the parkland of Ušće. The animated film is based on eleven drawings donated to the Museum by Gvozdenović's widow.

The Museum overlooks the parkland and the river. From inside we can observe the local wildlife, visitors coming to the Museum and people strolling with their pets. Museum employees all have 'park stories' to tell, based on what they have seen through the windows.

Not so far from the Museum, about a hundred metres to the left of the concrete path, we find a few dirt paths leading into groups of trees and bushes. This site is regularly used for gay cruising, mostly by elderly gentlemen strolling with their hands behind their backs. From the Museum we may also observe a group of stray dogs. Two of the Museum's employees have been attacked, resulting in torn trousers. Pheasants have been spotted on several occasions, and we may notice a flock of wild pigeons behind the tree outside one of the office windows.

Until recently, street races were held nearby. They lasted until lampposts were put up, which made racing far too dangerous. Because of these races, the whole area used to be

MUSEUM (INSIDE/OUTSIDE), 2008

Die Installation *Museum (Inside/Outside)*, die Leiderstam 2008 anlässlich einer Einzelausstellung im Salon MoCAB – Museum of Contemporary Art in Belgrad realisierte, stellt zwei sich gegenseitig ausschließende Perspektiven einander gegenüber: Sie konfrontiert den Blick auf das Museum mit dem Blick aus dem Gebäude heraus. Auf der Basis von elf flüchtigen Skizzen des serbischen Malers Miloš Gvozdenovic (1926–2006), welche die in die Parklandschaft eingebettete Architektur zeigen, fertigte Leiderstam eine Computeranimation an, die auf einen leeren, auf einer Staffelei ruhenden Skizzenblock projiziert wird. Durch die digitale Überblendung der Zeichnungen lösen sich die einzelnen Ansichten ineinander auf. Die Sicht auf das Museum ergänzt Leiderstam durch einen Wandtext, der von den Eindrücken und Beobachtungen der Museumsangestellten beim Blick aus dem Gebäude heraus berichtet.

The installation *Museum (Inside/Outside)*, realized by Leiderstam in 2008 for a solo exhibition at the Salon MoCAB – Museum of Contemporary Art in Belgrade, juxtaposes two mutually exclusive perspectives: it places the external view of the museum in opposition to the one from inside the building. On the basis of eleven quick sketches by the Serbian painter Miloš Gvozdenovic (1926–2006), which depict the building and surrounding parkland, Leiderstam devised a computer animation that is projected onto an empty sketchpad resting on an easel. The individual views dissolve into one another by virtue of the digital superimposition of the drawings. Leiderstam supplements the view of the museum with a wall text that documents the impressions and observations of the museum employees as they look out from inside the building.

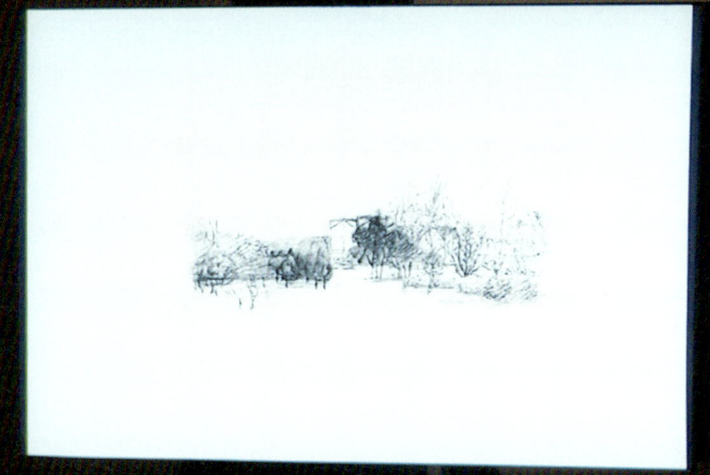

blocked off on weekends. Large audiences attended these events. On Fridays the organisers would put out old car tires to mark dangerous spots. Test drives took place on Saturdays, races on Sundays. This made it impossible to access the Museum, and it was therefore closed.

Just after Kosovo's declaration of independence, quite a big group of teenagers was seen running from one of the Museum's windows. A police vehicle was spotted driving through the park. Next to it were police with white helmets and batons. Although the events took place far away, one member of staff witnessed the police beating the teenage hooligans. After ten minutes the police drove off and the Museum park looked as if nothing had happened.

An elderly couple used to come to the park during weekends. They would park their white car under the Museum's office window. The Museum's staff realised they wanted to escape their boring everyday routine and engage in turbulent lovemaking. At first, the staff tried not to take any notice of them, but curiosity may be the most difficult thing to control. Sometimes the couple's exhibitionism would disturb the quiet work at the Museum and visually distract the entire staff, but sometimes it became just an entertainment.

The couple came more and more often. They adapted to the situation and the space with increased skill, and could no longer be ignored. The Museum staff became voluntary spectators. The natural setting, an idyllic picture with pheasants and other birds, has inspired not only those two old lovers. In no time, the pair became addicted to the park and the staff's discreet attention, which they must have been aware of. It seemed as though they wanted to show the Museum that they were still capable and willing of doing what they wanted. They started coming every day, probably because they were too impatient to wait for the weekend. They had a fixed timetable, just like the Museum. As soon as the park started to blossom, they took cover on a lawn overshadowed by a bush.

The whole story might not be as interesting had the couple been a little younger. When we see such things we become optimistic and believe life could go on forever. But every story comes to an end, and the couple have been absent for a while now. They may have found another park, or perhaps time took its toll.

Passers-by have often been seen urinating in the direction of the Museum. It is interesting that they always seem to turn towards the Museum in an attempt to avoid being seen. That kind of situation produces an uncanny sense of invisibility. How can a building like this, a building as big as this, be invisible?

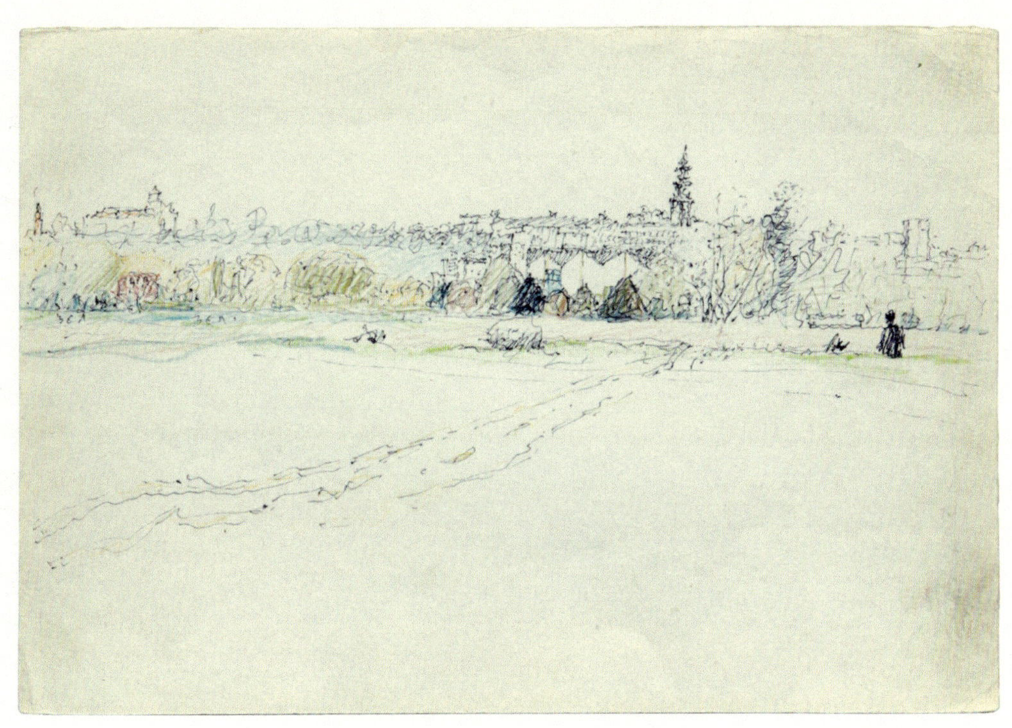

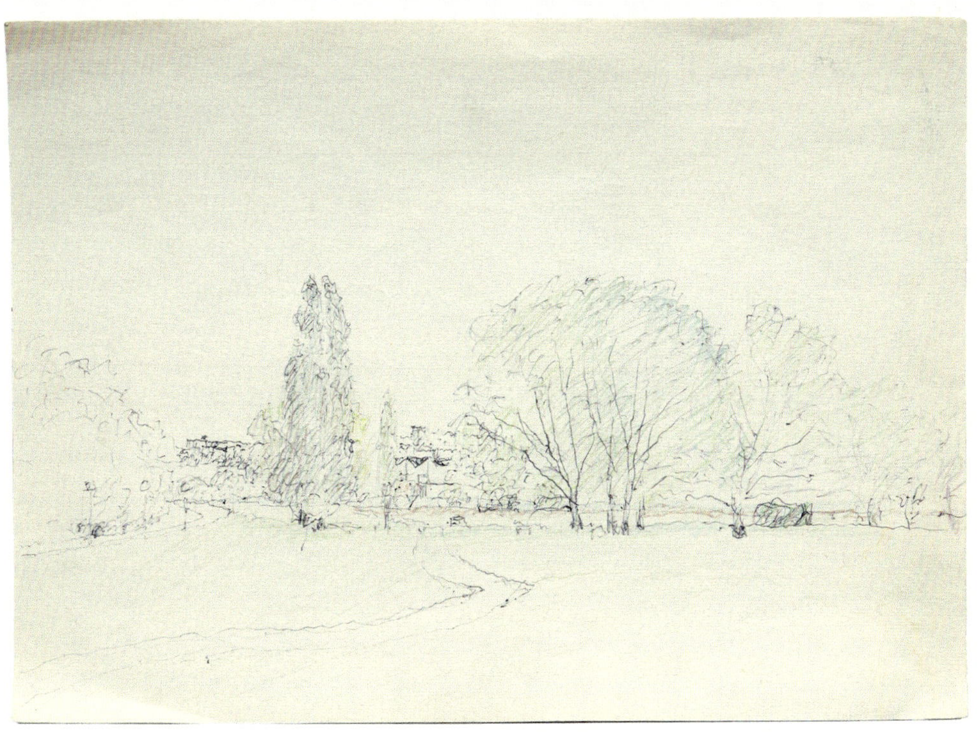

MUSEUM (INSIDE/OUTSIDE)

Die Provenienzgeschichte von Claude Lorrains Gemälde *The Ideal View of Tivoli* (1644), das sich im New Orleans Museum of Art befindet und im September 2005 vor der Zerstörung durch den Hurrikan Katrina gerettet werden konnte, ist Gegenstand der Installation *Provenience*. Auf einem Tisch liegen zwei aufgeschlagene Bücher. Ein auf die Reproduktion des Lorrain-Gemäldes gestelltes Vergrößerungsglas lenkt den Blick auf ein Detail des Werks: die Darstellung eines Mannes, der eine Frau behutsam und schützend über einen Wasserlauf trägt. Das zweite Buch ist bei einer Abbildung von Martinus Rørbyes *Blick auf die römische Campagna* (1835) aufgeschlagen. Ein von Leiderstam eingeklebter Text gibt Auskunft darüber, wie das seinerzeit anonyme Tivoli-Gemälde im Gepäck seiner jüdischen Besitzer auf der Flucht vor den Nationalsozialisten von Berlin ins schwedische Göteborg gelangte, in den 1970er Jahren mithilfe von Lorrains *Liber Veritatis* als dessen Werk identifiziert und in London zu einem respektablen Preis versteigert wurde. Die ehemaligen Besitzer stifteten einen Teil des Gewinns dem Göteborgs Konstmuseum, das dank dieser Spende das oben genannte Gemälde von Rørbye ankaufen konnte.

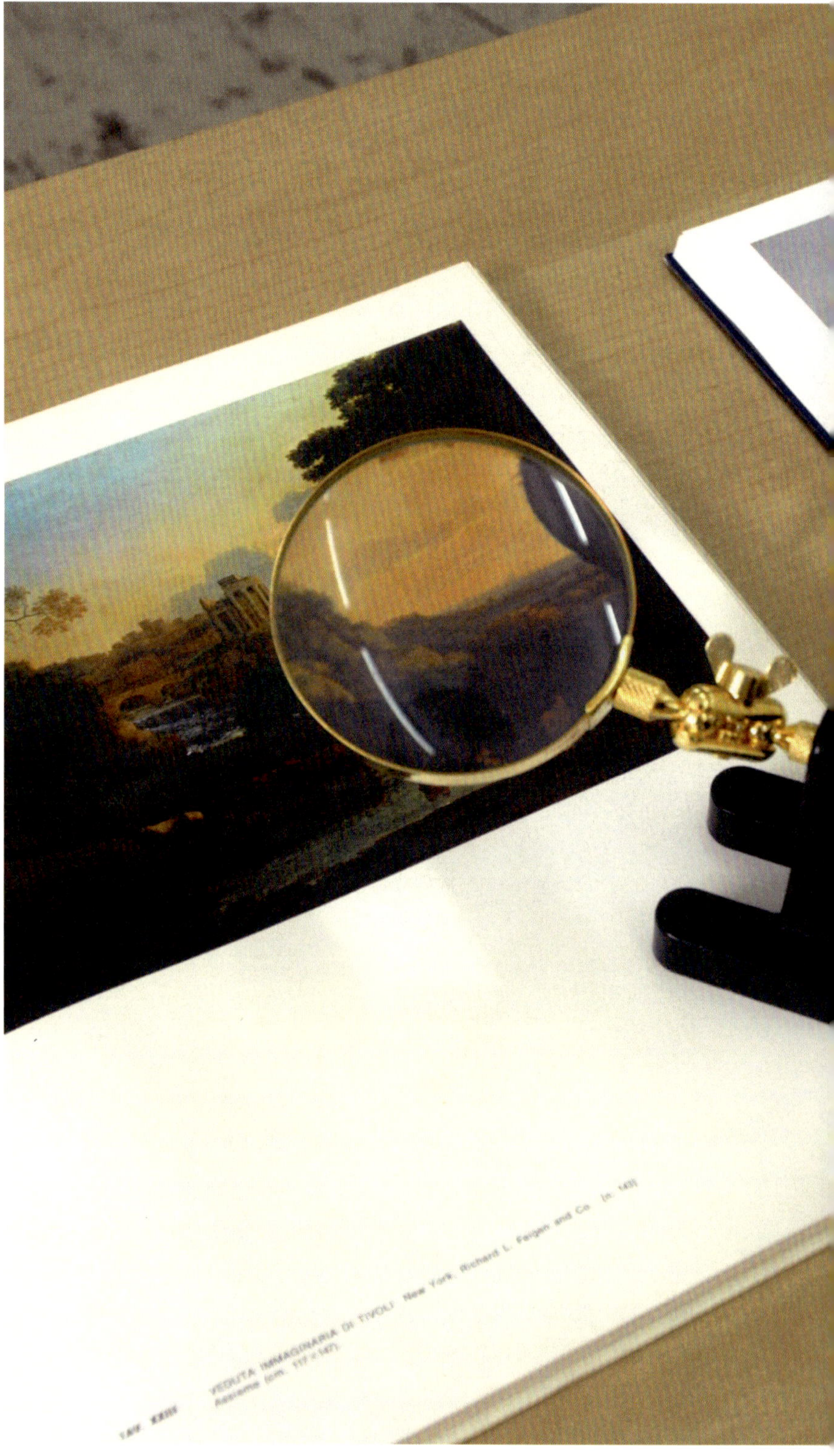

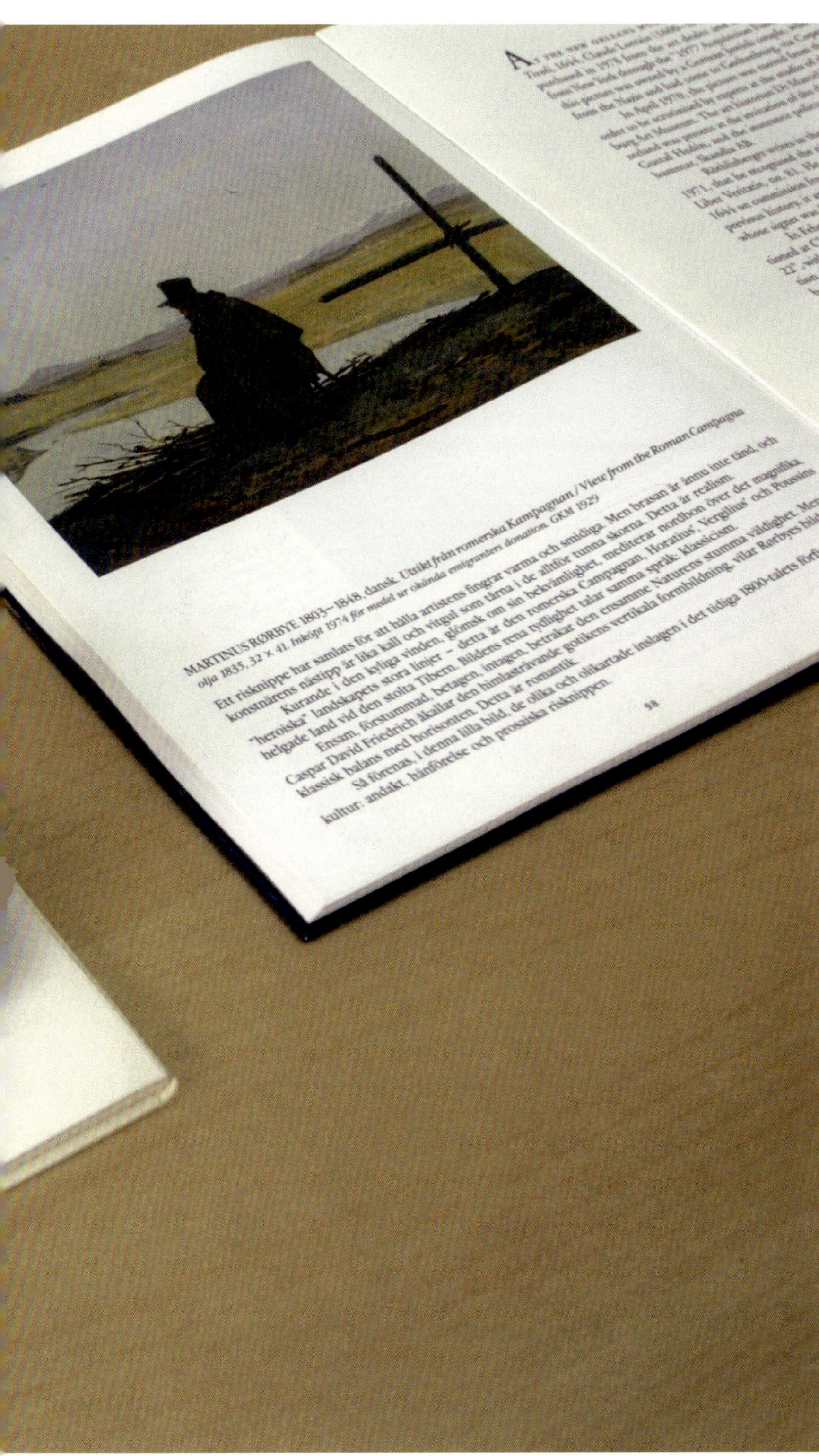

The object of the installation *Provenience* is the story about the provenance of Claude Lorrain's painting *The Ideal View of Tivoli* (1644), which is exhibited in the New Orleans Museum of Art and was successfully rescued in September 2005 from the destruction caused by Hurricane Katrina. Two open books are lying on the table. A magnifying glass placed on a reproduction of Lorrain's painting redirects the viewer's gaze towards a detail of the work: the depiction of a man who is carefully and protectively carrying a woman across a stream. The second book is open at an illustration of Martinus Rørbye's *View of the Roman Campagna* (1835). An attached text by Leiderstam provides information about how then the Tivoli painting, unattributed at the time, found its way to Gothenburg in the luggage of its Jewish owner, who was fleeing Berlin to escape from the National Socialists. It was subsequently identified in the 1970s as Lorrain's work through the latter's *Liber Veritatis* and sold at auction for a respectable price. The former owner pledged a portion of the profit to the Göteborgs Konstmuseum, which, thanks to this donation, was then able to purchase the aforementioned paining by Rørbye.

Matts Leiderstam – *Die Wahrnehmung der Wahrnehmung*

BETTINA BAUMGÄRTEL

Betrachten wir die Geschichte des Sehens und des Wahrnehmens, so zeigt sie sich uns als von jeher mit der Entwicklung optischer Werkzeuge verknüpft, die dazu dienten, die eingeschränkte Sehfähigkeit des menschlichen Auges in weit darüber hinausgehende Dimensionen zu erweitern und den Menschen in die Welt des Mikro- und Makrokosmos zu entführen. Ob durch Konvexspiegel, Reflektoren, Mikroskop, Fernrohr, Camera obscura oder in jüngerer Zeit auch durch Computersimulatoren, immer wieder haben sich Kunst und Technik, künstlerische Kreativität und praktischer Erfindergeist gegenseitig bedingt und befruchtet.[1]

Cornelis Jacobsz. Drebbel (1572–1633), ein heute längst vergessener holländischer Erfinder und Mechaniker, entwickelte schon damals unter anderem ein Perpetuum mobile sowie ein Unterseeboot, mit dem er zur Freude des englischen Hofes, für den er tätig war, in die Tiefen der Themse eintauchte. Auch wenn diese Erfindung nicht über die Testphase hinauskam, blieben andere, wie ein Mikroskop mit konvexen Linsen, nicht ohne Wirkung auf seine Mitmenschen und auf die Kunst seiner Zeit, wie im Folgenden dargelegt. Einer, der das Wagnis einging, einen Blick durch das Wundergerät zu werfen, war Constantijn Huygens (1596–1687), Sekretär zweier Statthalter der neuen holländischen Republik, Schriftsteller, Universalgelehrter und Bewunderer Drebbels. Huygens' Autobiografie überliefert die Wirkung des Mikroskops auf seine Zeitgenossen. Zwar konnte man auf den ersten Blick durch die winzigen, schlechten Linsen kaum etwas erkennen, doch nach einer Weile eröffnete sich ein erstaunliches Naturschauspiel in einer wunderbaren »Neuen Welt«: »Denn in der Tat boten sich Objekte«, so berichtet Huygens, »die bis dahin unter die Atome gerechnet wurden, da sie sich dem menschlichen Auge weithin entzogen, dem Beobachter auf einmal so deutlich dar, daß, wenn völlig unerfahrene Leute Dinge erblicken, die sie vorher nie gesehen haben, sie sich zunächst beklagen, daß sie nichts sähen, doch alsbald ausrufen, daß ihnen unglaubliche Dinge vor die Augen träten. Denn wirklich handelt es sich um ein neues Schauspiel der Natur, eine andere Welt […].« Diese Erfahrung löste bei Huygens den Wunsch aus, einen Maler dazu zu motivieren, »die winzigen Gegenstände und Insekten mit einem feinen Pinsel wiederzugeben und zu einem Büchlein zusammenzustellen, das mit dem Wort Neue Welt überschrieben wäre […].«[2]

Auf das einschneidende Seherlebnis folgte also unmittelbar der Ruf nach der Kunst, die das Gesehene, das sich mit bloßem Auge der Wahrnehmbarkeit entzieht, im Bild festhalten sollte. Das Problem dabei ist, dass ein Sehbild, so wie es auf der Netzhaut entsteht, im Grunde von niemandem gesehen und deshalb auch durch keine noch so große Kunst wiedergegeben werden kann. Denn jede Wiedergabe des Seheindrucks ist genau genommen nicht das Gesehene selbst, sondern immer etwas »Anderes«, nämlich das Ergebnis einer subjektiven Wahrnehmung.

Dieser Schwierigkeit wurde Huygens gewahr, als er wenig später durch eine von Drebbel konstruierte Camera obscura blickte, die bei ihm eine radikale Reaktion auslöste. Nun verlangte er nicht mehr nach der Kunst, im Gegenteil, nun sah er das Ende der Kunst gekommen, die durch das lebendigere Bild der Kamera abgelöst werde: »Die Kunst der Malerei ist tot, denn dies ist Leben selbst oder etwas noch Höheres, wenn wir ein Wort dafür finden können«. Die zentrale Frage, die dabei aufgeworfen wurde, war, »wozu noch Bilder mit der Hand malen, wenn sie sich von selbst in jedes Auge und in jede Camera obscura ›malen‹?«[3]

Johannes Kepler (1571–1630), einer der größten Erforscher des Sehens, lieferte quasi en passant die Ant-

1) Grundlegend dazu Martin Kemp, *The Science of Art. Optical themes in western art from Brunelleschi to Seurat,* New Haven/London 1990.

2) J. A. Worp, »Constantijn Huygens over de schilders van zijn tijd«, in: *Oud Holland,* 9, 1891, S. 106–136, hier S. 120; zit. nach Svetlana Alpers, *Kunst als Beschreibung. Holländische Malerei des 17. Jahrhunderts,* mit einem Vorwort v. Wolfgang Kemp, Köln 1985, S. 49.

3) Nach Peter Bexte, *Blinde Seher. Die Wahrnehmung von Wahrnehmung in der Kunst des 17. Jahrhunderts,* Dresden 1999, S. 25.

Matts Leiderstam—*The Perception of Perception*

BETTINA BAUMGÄRTEL

It seems that the history of seeing and perception has always been linked to the development of optical tools used to extend the limited vision of the human eye into dimensions far beyond its reach and to transport mankind into the world of microcosm and macrocosm. Be it through convex mirrors, reflectors, microscopes, telescopes, camera obscuras or, in more recent times, with the help of computer simulation, art and technology, artistic creativity and practical ingenuity have mutually determined and inspired each other repeatedly over time.[1]

Cornelis Jacobsz. Drebbel (1572–1633), a long-forgotten Dutch inventor and mechanic, was ahead of his time in inventing, among other things, a perpetual-motion machine, as well as a submarine with which he dove into the depths of the Thames to the delight of the English court, where he was employed. Although this invention never passed beyond its test phase, other contrivances, such as a microscope with convex lenses, were not without their effect on his contemporaries and the art of his day, as the following will show. One of the few who dared to look through this wonderful apparatus was Constantijn Huygens (1596–1687), secretary to two governors of the new Dutch republic, author, polymath and admirer of Drebbel's work. Huygens' autobiography testifies to the effect this optical apparatus had on his contemporaries. While at first sight not much could be seen through the tiny, poor-quality lenses, after a while an astounding natural spectacle unfolded in a wonderful "New World": "For some objects," writes Huygens, "which had hitherto been assumed to be atoms, having largely evaded the human eye, indeed suddenly appeared to the viewer so clearly that, when completely inexperienced persons saw things they had never before seen, after at first complaining about not being able to see anything at all, they soon explained that unbelievable things had come before their eyes. For it is truly a new spectacle of nature, a different world…" This experience awakened in Huygens the desire to motivate a painter to "render the tiny objects and insects with a fine brush and assemble these into a booklet entitled 'The New World'…"[2]

Thus, we see that this drastic visual experience was immediately followed by a call for an art capable of capturing that which evaded perception by the naked eye. The problem of the matter is that no human being can truly see the visual image as it develops on the retina, thus making it impossible to reproduce it through any form of art, no matter how accomplished. This is because, strictly speaking, the reproduction of a visual impression is not the visual object itself, but always something "different"—namely, the result of subjective perception.

Huygens became aware of this difficulty shortly after looking through Drebbel's camera obscura. The apparatus triggered a radical reaction in him. He now no longer called for art; on the contrary, now he saw the end of art approaching, superceded by the livelier image of the camera: "The art of painting is dead, for this is life itself or something even greater, if we could find a word for it." The central question that this prompted was "Why still paint pictures by hand, if they 'paint' themselves in every eye and in every camera obscura?"[3]

Johannes Kepler (1571–1630), one of the greatest explorers of seeing and sight, supplied the answer to this question quasi en passant: his astronomical research with the help of a camera obscura gave rise to "landscape art" as a by-product, so to speak. In a field near his house in Linz, Austria, Kepler set up a camera obscura in order to observe the rays of the sun. With the help of a 360-degree-turn of the camera's head, he traced the images produced by the apparatus, but only temporarily visible to him, on a piece of paper in such a way that a landscape picture emerged in the form of a panorama. Kepler realized it was in the landscape and with the landscape that he could best make

1) A seminal study on this subject is Martin Kemp's *The Science of Art. Optical Themes in Western Art from Brunelleschi to Seurat* (New Haven/London,1990).

2) J. A. Worp, "Constantijn Huygens over de schilders van zijn tijd," in *Oud Holland,* 9, 1891, pp. 106–136; here p. 120. Quoted from Svetlana Alpers, *Kunst als Beschreibung. Holländische Malerei des 17. Jahrhunderts,* with a preface by Wolfgang Kemp (Cologne, 1985), p. 49.

3) Cited from Peter Bexte, *Blinde Seher. Die Wahrnehmung von Wahrnehmung in der Kunst des 17. Jahrhunderts* (Dresden, 1999), p. 25.

wort auf diese Frage: Seine astronomischen Forschungen mithilfe einer Camera obscura ließen gleichsam als Nebenprodukt »Landschaftskunst« entstehen. Auf einem Feld in der Nähe seines Hauses im österreichischen Linz hatte Kepler die Camera obscura aufgestellt, um damit Sonnenstrahlen zu beobachten. Dabei zeichnete er mittels der 360-Grad-Drehung des Kamerakopfes die von diesem Apparat erzeugten, aber nur für ihn vorübergehend sichtbaren Bilder so auf ein Blatt Papier nach, dass quasi ein Landschaftsbild in Form eines Panoramas entstand. Kepler erkannte, dass er das unsichtbare Bild, das er auf der Netzhaut des Auges lokalisiert hatte, am besten in der Landschaft und mit der Landschaft sichtbar machen konnte. Seine Forschungen zur Optik und Astronomie brachten somit eine neue Form der Landschaftswiedergabe mit überdimensionalem Weitwinkel hervor. Weder Forscher noch Künstler kamen also darum herum, den wahrgenommenen Bildraum, respektive den Landschaftsraum, in die begrenzte Fläche eines Stückes Papier oder einer Leinwand zu übertragen, wenn sie die neue Seherfahrung dokumentieren oder kreativ verarbeiten wollten. Heute können digitale Medien zwar die dritte Dimension simulieren, aber allen Unkenrufen vom Ende der Kunst zum Trotz ersetzen sie nicht die Künstlerhand und das künstlerisch gestaltete Bild, ebenso wenig wie das Flugzeug je das Auto oder das Fahrrad überflüssig machen konnte. In der Kunst geht es eben nicht nur um das momentane Erkennen eines Sehbildes und dessen getreue Wiedergabe, sondern um die jeweilige Wahrnehmung und freie Gestaltung desselben.

Matts Leiderstam ist sich dieses paradoxen Spannungsverhältnisses von Seh- und Wahrnehmungsbild bewusst. In seiner für die Räume der Düsseldorfer Kunsthalle entstandenen Installation *Neanderthal Landscape* (2008–2010) gibt er deshalb die »Bildproduktion« konsequenterweise an den Betrachter weiter. Dieser allein kann (den Künstler als Betrachter eingeschlossen) authentische und einzigartige Bilder erzeugen. Indem Leiderstam ihn dazu auffordert, Perspektiv- und Standortwechsel vorzunehmen, bietet er allenfalls »Seh-Hilfen« beziehungsweise »Seh-Animationen« an. Er stellt den Betrachter vor die Wahl, entweder von der Balustrade der Empore aus die Gesamtperspektive der riesigen Wand des Kinosaals zu erfassen, auf die in freier Ordnung Landschaftsgemälde und Freilichtstudien verschiedener Künstler des 19. Jahrhunderts gehängt sind, oder mittels eines Spektivs gleichsam mikroskopisch in die malerischen Details eines einzelnen Werks einzutauchen. Der Ausstellungsbesucher erfährt sich dabei sowohl als Mensch in Aktion als auch, beim Blick durch das Spektiv, als ein in einer Art Sehstarre verharrender Beobachter. Während die weitwinklige Perspektive nicht von einem einzigen Stand- und Augenpunkt allein eingefangen werden kann, da sie sich nur dann e schließt, wenn man Augen, Kopf und Körper in Bewegung setzt, fordert die Nahsicht einen ganz anderen Körpereinsatz. Das herangezoomte Detail ist umso besser zu sehen, je bewegungsloser man den Ausschnitt einfängt.

Es kommt Leiderstam dabei nicht so sehr darauf an, wer die Urheber der Gemälde sind, die auf der Wand als großes Ensemble miteinander in Dialog treten, auch spielen weder Qualitätsmerkmale noch Datierungsfragen eine große Rolle. Vielmehr wird die Aufmerksamkeit des Betrachters hier auf seine Wahrnehmung gelenkt: Der Künstler fordert also den Betrachter von *Neanderthal Landscape* zur Wahrnehmung seiner Wahrnehmung auf, wobei er ihn zu verschiedenen Formen des Wahrnehmens, auch der eigenen Körperwahrnehmung, animiert, ihm dabei aber jede Freiheit des gestaltenden Sehens überlässt. Dies ist insofern konsequent, als dass die Wahrnehmung ein höchst individueller Vorgang ist, der sich letztlich der Darstellbarkeit entzieht.

DAS DOPPELKÖPFIGE MONSTER

Allerdings sind dem Alleingang des Betrachters auch Grenzen gesetzt: Wie schon der englische Philosoph John Locke (1632–1704) feststellte, ist der Mensch darauf angewiesen, die gleiche Perspektive wie seine Mitmenschen einnehmen zu können: »Wenn der wichtigste unserer Sinne, das Sehen, bei einem einzelnen Menschen tausend- oder auch hundertmal schärfer wäre als das beste Mikroskop, könnte er mit bloßem Auge Dinge sehen, die einige millionenmal

visible the invisible image he had localized on the retina of the eye. His research on optics and astronomy thus gave birth to a new form of rendering landscapes with the help of oversized wide angles. Thereafter, neither researchers nor artists who wanted to document or work creatively with the new visual experience could avoid transferring the perceived pictorial space, respectively the landscape, onto the limited surface of a piece of paper or a canvas. Today digital media can simulate the third dimension, but in spite of all negative predictions concerning the end of art, they cannot replace the hand of the artist nor the artistically created image, no more than airplanes or cars will ever make bicycles superfluous. For art is not simply an expression of the momentary recognition of a visual image and its faithful reproduction, but the artist's respective perception and independent composition thereof.

Matts Leiderstam is well aware of this paradoxical tension between the visual image and the perceived image. In his installation *Neanderthal Landscape* (2008–2010), conceived for the Kunsthalle Düsseldorf, he thus consequently hands the "production of the image" over to the viewer. He alone (and this also includes the artist as viewer) can create authentic and unique images. By inviting him to undertake a change of perspective and position, Leiderstam offers at best visual aids or, rather, "visual incitements." He lets the viewer choose between gazing out from a gallery balustrade onto the entirety of the gigantic wall of a cinema on which are hung, in random order, plein-air landscape paintings and sketches by various nineteenth-century artists or microscopically delving into the pictorial details of individual paintings with the help of a pair of spotting-scopes. Thus, visitors to the exhibition can experience themselves both as persona in action and, when looking through the spotting-scopes, as observers paused in a kind of visual rigor. While it remains impossible to fully grasp the wide-angle perspective from a single standpoint and position alone, since it only reveals itself when eyes, head and body are in motion, the close-up view demands a completely different type of physical activity. The less movement the viewer engages in while capturing the excerpt, the more can be seen of the details he has zoomed into.

Leiderstam is not really interested in the authors of the paintings, hanging in dialogue as a large ensemble on the wall, nor do issues of quality or questions of dating play a large role for him. Instead, he draws the viewers' attention to the nature of their own perception: the artist invites the viewer of *Neanderthal Landscape* to perceive his own perception, inciting various forms of perception, including the perception of his own body, while simultaneously allowing him all the freedoms of creative seeing. This is insofar consistent as that perception is a highly individual act that ultimately evades representation.

THE TWO-HEADED MONSTER

However, the solitary act of viewing also has its limitations: as the English philosopher John Locke (1623–1704) once aptly pointed out, human beings are dependent on being able to adopt the same perspectives as their fellow men: "Nay, if that most instructive of our senses, seeing, were in any man a thousand or a hundred thousand times more acute than it is by the best microscope, things several millions of times less than the smallest object of his sight now would then be visible to his naked eyes, and so he would come nearer to the discovery of the texture and motion of the minute parts of corporeal things …, but then he would be in a quite different world from other people: nothing would appear the same to him and others: the visible ideas of everything would be different."[4]

In order to thus make one's seeing comprehensible, respectively to be able to represent one's perception, man must, so Denis Diderot (1713–1784) in his groundbreaking "Letter on the Deaf and Mute," become a two-headed monster that is able to look itself in the eye: "They asked me … how we could have several perceptions at once. I find it difficult to grasp this, but is it easier to understand that we can only then pass judgment—meaning: be able to compare two ideas with each other, when the one is

4) John Locke, *An Essay Concerning Human Understanding* (Alexander Campbell Fraser, 1894, rpt. New York 1959), Vol. 1, p. 403.

kleiner sind als das kleinste jetzt sichtbare Objekt, und er näherte sich der Erkenntnis der Textur und Bewegung der kleinsten Teile der körperlichen Dinge [...] aber dann befände er sich in einer ganz anderen Welt als andere Menschen: nichts erschiene ihm so wie den anderen.«[4]

Um also sein Sehen verständlich zu machen, respektive seine Wahrnehmung darstellen zu können, müsste der Mensch, so Denis Diderot (1713–1784) in seinem wegweisenden »Brief über die Taubstummen«, ein doppelköpfiges Monster werden, das den eigenen Blick sehen kann: »Sie fragen mich [...], wie wir mehrere Wahrnehmungen auf einmal haben können. Es fällt mir schwer, dies zu begreifen, aber begreifen Sie etwa leichter, daß wir nur dann ein Urteil bilden – und das heißt: zwei Ideen miteinander vergleichen können, wenn uns die eine durch die Wahrnehmung und die andere durch das Gedächtnis vergegenwärtigt wird? Mir kam es so vor, als müßte man zugleich innerhalb und außerhalb seiner selbst sein und gleichzeitig die Rolle des Beobachters und die der beobachtenden Maschine spielen. Aber mit dem Geist verhält es sich wie mit dem Auge: er sieht sich selbst nicht. [...] Eine Mißgeburt mit zwei Köpfen, die auf ein und demselben Hals gewachsen sind, könnte uns vielleicht etwas Neues lehren. Wir müssen also warten, bis uns die Natur, die alles kombiniert und im Laufe der Jahrhunderte die außergewöhnlichsten Erscheinungen erzeugt, auch einmal einen zweiköpfigen Menschen darbietet, der sich selbst betrachtet und bei dem der eine Kopf Beobachtungen über den anderen anstellt.«[5] Aug in Aug mit sich selbst gäbe es also endlich jene gewünschte Wahrnehmung der Wahrnehmung.

Jedoch mahnte schon Ernst H. Gombrich, »wir dürfen nie vergessen, daß es hier um zwei Fragen geht: um die Frage, wie wir die Welt sehen, aber auch um die Frage, wie wir ein Bild wahrnehmen.«[6] Und er wies auf die bahnbrechenden wahrnehmungspsychologischen Untersuchungen von James J. Gibson hin, demnach es nicht allein um eine kurze Momentaufnahme einer Form oder Figur auf unserer Retina geht, sondern um unsere Fähigkeit, die kontinuierliche Veränderung eines Bildes in Bewegung als eine invariante Form zu erkennen. Denn Gibson konnte anhand von Simulatoren für Luft- und Raumfahrt, die das visuelle Erleben der Bewegung im Raum erzeugen, nachweisen, dass wir unsere Umgebung nicht wie eine Kamera im Schnappschussblick, sondern als dreidimensionale invariante Anordnung wahrnehmen.[7] Schon in der Landschaftsmalerei des 19. Jahrhunderts lässt sich diese Art der räumlichen Erfassung als invariante Form durchaus ablesen.

»PICTURING«

Geschult durch seine langjährige Beschäftigung mit dieser Landschaftsmalerei, hat sich Leiderstam mit sicherem Blick für die frische Unmittelbarkeit von Pleinair-Studien gerade jenem Protagonisten der Düsseldorfer Malerschule zugewandt, der zu den Pionieren der Freilichtmalerei gerechnet wird. Johann Wilhelm Schirmer (1808–1863) erhob die Landschaftsmalerei zur eigenständigen und anerkannten Gattung innerhalb der Königlich-Preußischen Kunstakademie zu Düsseldorf und wurde dort erster Professor in diesem Fach. Schon ab 1827 durchstreifte er die Umgebung Düsseldorfs und gilt seither als Entdecker des heute weitgehend zerstörten Neandertals. Im sogenannten »Gesteins« entstanden seine ersten Freilichtstudien, die sich heute in der Gemäldegalerie des museum kunst palast in Düsseldorf befinden.[8] Wie unvoreingenommen Schirmer dabei zu Werke ging, zeigt die Tatsache, dass er sich jedem noch so banalen Detail mit Staunen und liebevoller Genauigkeit zuwandte. Dabei schien es geradezu darauf anzulegen, die Distanz zu den entdeckten Sujets zu verlieren, in diese gleichsam hineinzukriechen, um sie

4) John Locke, *An Essay Concerning Human Understanding,* hrsg. von Alexander Campbell Fraser (1894), Reprint New York 1959, Bd. 1, S. 403.

5) Denis Diderot, »Brief über die Taubstummen« (1751), in: Ders., *Ästhetische Schriften,* hrsg. von Friedrich Bassenge, Berlin 1984, Bd. 1, S. 27–97, hier: S. 73.

6) Ernst H. Gombrich, *Das forschende Auge. Kunstbetrachtung und Naturwahrnehmung,* (Sonderband der Edition Pandora, hrsg. von Gennaro Ghirardelli) Frankfurt/M./New York/Paris 1994, S. 87.

7) Zuletzt James J. Gibson, *The Ecological Approach to Visual Perception,* 1979, zit. nach Gombrich, ebd., S. 88 f.

8) *Bewegte Landschaften. Die Düsseldorfer Malerschule,* hrsg. und bearb. von Bettina Baumgärtel, Ausst.-Kat. Museum der Stadt Ratingen; Neanderthal Museum Mettmann; Wilhelm-Fabry-Museum Hilden, Heidelberg 2003.

perceived through the senses and the other comprehended by the mind? It seemed to me as if one must be both within and without oneself and simultaneously play the role of the observer and that of the observing machine. But the mind behaves much like the eye: it does not see itself … . A monster with two heads, growing from one and the same neck, could perhaps teach us something new. We must therefore wait until nature itself, who combines all and has created the most unusual of phenomena over the centuries, also proffers us a two-headed human being, who can look onto himself and where the one head makes observations about the other."[5] Eye to eye with ourselves, we could finally achieve that desired perception of perception.

And yet even Ernst H. Gombrich warned in his day, "We must never forget that we have two questions here: the question of how we see the world, but also the question of how we perceive a picture."[6] And he referred to James J. Gibson's groundbreaking research in the psychology of perception, according to which perception not only involves a short snapshot of a form or figure on our retina, but rather our ability to recognize the continual alteration of an image in motion as an invariant form. Based on aerospace simulators, which create visual experiences of movement in space, Gibson was able to prove that we perceive our surroundings not via a snapshot gaze as in a camera, but as a three-dimensional invariant arrangement.[7] This manner of recognizing space as invariant form can also already be surmised from nineteenth-century landscape painting.

"PICTURING"

On the basis of this longstanding occupation with landscape painting and with a firm eye for the fresh immediacy of plein-air sketches, Leiderstam has rediscovered that protagonist of the Düsseldorf School who is considered to be one of the pioneers of outdoor painting. Johann Wilhelm Schirmer (1808–1863) raised landscape painting to an independent and recognized genre in the Royal Prussian Art Academy of Düsseldorf and became its first professor in the field. As early as 1827, he roamed the area around Düsseldorf and is since considered to be the discoverer of the Neandertal, which today is largely destroyed. His first sketches en plein-air were created in the so-called "Gesteins" and are today part of the painting gallery of the museum kunst palast in Düsseldorf.[8] How unbiased Schirmer went about his work becomes clear in how he applied himself to even the most banal of details with wonder and loving attention to the minute. He literally seemed determined to forfeit all objectivity towards his discovered subjects, to virtually crawl into them in order to fathom them in their entirety. Taking on the perspective of a Tom Thumb under the open sky, he finally and paradoxically achieved a monumentalizing of his pedestrian motifs. Not until he had undertaken this radical change of perspectives in form of oscillating in focus between extreme proximity and distance, did the entire microcosm of the flora and fauna on the ground reveal themselves to him, as well as on the other hand, the sublime vastness of the "bluish-silvery fragrance of faraway places."[9]

Schirmer's rapid shifts between close-up and far-away perspectives, precisely detailed realism and the approximation of difficult-to-grasp, invariant phenomena such as the atmosphere and the play of light, air and colors in the landscape, may be ascertained best in a series of plein-air studies from the region east of Rome, the so-called "Civitella Studies," of which most have been preserved in the painting gallery of the museum kunst palast in Düsseldorf. His method of sharpening perception by employing a radical shift of focus via movement not only of the wandering eye, but that of the entire body through

5) Denis Diderot, *Lettre sur les sourds et muets* (1751).

6) Ernst H. Gombrich, *Das forschende Auge. Kunstbetrachtung und Naturwahrnehmung,* epical edition of Edition Pandora, published by Gennaro Ghirardelli (Frankfurt/M./New York/Paris,1994), p. 87.

7) Most recently in J. J. Gibson, *The Ecological Approach to Visual Perception,* 1979, cit. in Gombrich, ibid., pp. 88 ff.

8) *Bewegte Landschaften. Die Düsseldorfer Malerschule,* exhibition catalogue, ed. Bettina Baumgärtel (Museum der Stadt Ratingen, Neanderthal Museum Mettmann, Wilhelm-Fabry-Museum Hilden, Heidelberg 2003).

9) *Bläulich silbrigen Duft der Ferne* is also the title of the simultaneous exhibition at museum kunst palast Düsseldorf for the group project "Schirmer 2010" under the general title *Johann Wilhelm Schirmer – Vom Rheinland in die Welt;* cit. in Friedrich Theodor Vischer, Briefe aus Italien (Munich, 1907), here p. 89 (5.12.1839).

vollständig zu ergründen. Durch die Däumlingsperspektive gelangte der Freilichtmaler schließlich paradoxerweise zu einer Monumentalisierung seines fußläufigen Motivs. Erst dieser radikale Wandel der Perspektiven im Blickwechsel von extremer Nähe und Ferne, offenbarte ihm einerseits den gesamten Mikrokosmos der am Boden befindlichen Pflanzen- und Tierwelt, andererseits die erhabene Weite, den »bläulich silbrigen Duft der Ferne«.[9]

Schirmers schnelle Wechsel von Nah- und Fernsichten, präzisem Detailrealismus und Annäherung an schwer greifbare, invariante Phänomene wie Atmosphäre und Licht-, Luftund Farbspiele in der Landschaft erschließen sich vielleicht am unmittelbarsten aus einer Serie von Freilichtstudien aus der Region östlich von Rom, den sogenannten »Civitella-Studien«, von denen sich die meisten in der Gemäldesammlung des museum kunst palast in Düsseldorf erhalten haben. Seine Methode, die Wahrnehmung im radikalen Blickwechsel durch die Wanderbewegung nicht nur seines Auges, sondern seines gesamten Körpers im Landschaftsraum zu schärfen, lässt sich auch in den Werken seiner Schüler aufspüren, mit denen er regelmäßig Exkursionen in die Natur als Schule des Sehens und zum Studium der Wahrnehmung durchführte.

Auch an diesem Punkt setzt Leiderstam an und beschäftigt sich zusätzlich mit der Praxis im Umgang mit solchen Landschaftsstudien sowie mit deren besonderer Präsentationsform. Schirmer und seine Schüler lebten mit ihren Arbeiten, die sie teils wandfüllend in ihren Schlafräumen aufhängten. Dies taten sie nicht allein aus praktischen Gründen, um ihre Studien trocknen zu lassen, sondern offenbar, weil sie mit ihnen eine ständige Zwiesprache halten und gleichsam im Geiste weiter an den Motiven arbeiten wollten. So berichtet Schirmer im Tagebuch seiner italienischen Reise, wie wichtig es ihm für die kreative Arbeit war, erst einmal seine Studien in seinem Zimmer an der Wand zu sehen.[10]

In seinen Pleinair-Studien konnte und wollte Schirmer kein abbildliches Verfahren der Natur verfolgen, denn in der zum Bild geronnenen Natur sah er sich in erster Linie in einem schöpferischen Prozess des Bilderfindens und damit in seiner gestalterischen Fähigkeit gefordert. Allein die Wahl des Ausschnitts und des spezifischen Blickwinkels, das Verfahren des Hinzufügens oder Weglassens verlangten vom Landschaftsmaler ein über die getreue Wiedergabe weit hinausgehendes Vermögen künstlerischer »Inventio«. Da aber Bilder neben der Wiedergabe des Wirklichen stets auch Ausdruck der nicht in der Natur existierenden Imagination sind, sind sie immer zugleich die Verbildlichung des schon Verbildlichten, des Imaginären wie des Flüchtigen. Hinzu kommt, dass ein »Bild« von der Natur immer nur ein Fragment, ein Pars pro toto sein kann, denn es erfasst allenfalls einen kleinen Sehausschnitt, obschon es als Ganzheit gedacht wird.

Wenn sich Matts Leiderstam in seiner Installation *Neanderthal Landscape* also dem Œuvre Schirmers und seiner Schüler zuwendet, so fragt er auch danach, wie ein Bild als Bild entsteht und funktioniert, genau genommen, wie das »picturing«, das heißt das Bildermachen verläuft. Dabei geht es Leiderstam offenbar weniger um die Analyse und Rezeption der ausgewählten Gemälde, als vielmehr um das aktive Bilderzeugen. Wie Svetlana Alpers schon in ihrer Schrift »Kunst als Beschreibung« dargelegt hat, ist die Kunst eben nicht die Natur selbst, sondern »representation« – die Darstellung – der Natur; entsprechend ist »picturing« – das Bildermachen – nicht einfach Sehen, sondern Sehen als aktive Einmischung in die sichtbare Welt. Somit hat auch ein Bild Schirmers nicht einfach nur Bedeutung, sondern schafft selbst Bedeutung.[11] Vor diesem Hintergrund fordert Leiderstam den Besucher dazu auf, sich selbst als »Bilderzeuger« aktiv zu beteiligen und so neue Bedeutung zu produzieren.

9) So der Titel der gleichzeitig stattfindenden Ausstellung im museum kunst palast Düsseldorf zum Verbundprojekt »Schirmer 2010« mit dem Generaltitel *Johann Wilhelm Schirmer – Vom Rheinland in die Welt;* zit. nach Friedrich Theodor Vischer, *Briefe aus Italien,* München 1907, S. 89, 5.12.1839.

10) Gabriele Ewenz (Hrsg.): *Johann Wilhelm Schirmer – Vom Rheinland in die Welt, Autobiografische Schriften,* Bd. 2, Petersberg 2010: »Civitella 24. August [1839]: […] ich denke, es wird sich geben wenn ich erst einige Sachen an der Wand [und] in der Mappe sehe, darum muthig vorwärts.«

11) Kemp, in: Alpers 1985 (wie Anm. 2), S. 16, verweist auf die Schwierigkeit, die Begriffe adäquat ins Deutsche zu übersetzen: »representation« ist ungenügend übersetzt mit Begriffen wie Darstellung, Wiedergabe oder bildliche Vorstellung.

the landscape as well, is also visible in the work of his students, which whom he conducted nature excursions on a regular basis in order to school their sight and to study perception.

This is where Leiderstam picks up the thread and, in addition, goes on to explore the practice of how such landscape studies were treated, as well as their special form of presentation. Schirmer and his students lived with their work, which they hung in their bedrooms, sometimes covering entire walls. They did this not merely for practical reasons, in order to let their studies dry, but apparently also, because they wished to constantly converse with them and continue working on the motifs in the spirit, as it were. During his travels in Italy, Schirmer thus recorded in his dairy how important it is for his creative work to first see his studies on the wall of his room.[10]

In his plein-air studies Schirmer was neither able nor did he want to produce a perfect likeness of nature. To him the consolidation of nature in a painting was first and foremost a creative process of image discovery, and this demanded artistic abilities. The choice of detail alone and the specific perspective, the process of adding or omitting, demanded of the landscape painter capabilities of artistic *invention* that went far beyond faithful reproduction. But because, aside from the reproduction of the real, these pictures are also always expressions of an imagination non-existent in nature, they are also depictions of the already depicted, of the imaginary as well as the ephemeral. Moreover, an "image" of nature can never be more than a fragment, a pars pro toto, for, although intended as a whole, it can never capture more than a small visible excerpt.

Thus, when Matts Leiderstam turns to the oeuvre of Schirmer and his students in his installation *Neanderthal Landscape,* he also inquires into how paintings are created and how they function as paintings, strictly speaking, how the "picturing"—or in other words, the creation of pictures—takes place. Leiderstam is apparently less interested in the analysis and reception of the paintings he has chosen than in the active creation of images. As Svetlana Alpers once explained in her essay "Kunst als Beschreibung" ("Art as Description"), art is not nature itself, but "representation"—the depiction—of nature; accordingly, "picturing"—the creation of images—is not simply seeing, but seeing as active intervention in the visible world. Hence a painting by Schirmer does not simply have meaning, but instead creates meaning itself.[11] Against this background, Matts Leiderstam invites viewers to actively participate as "image creators" and so produce new meaning.

10) Gabriele Ewenz (ed.), *Johann Wilhelm Schirmer – Vom Rheinland in die Welt, Autobiografische Schriften,* Vol. 2, Petersberg 2010: "Civitella 24. August [1839]: […] ich denke, es wird sich geben wenn ich erst einige Sachen an der Wand [und] in der Mappe sehe, darum muthig vorwärts." ("I believe it will pass when I've managed to see some of the things on the wall [and] in the portfolio, therefore bravely onwards.")

11) Kemp, in Alpers (see fn. 2), p. 16, points out the difficulties of translation into German: "representation" is insufficiently translated with terms like "Darstellung" (depiction), "Wiedergabe" (reproduction) or "bildliche Vorstellung" (figurative mental image).

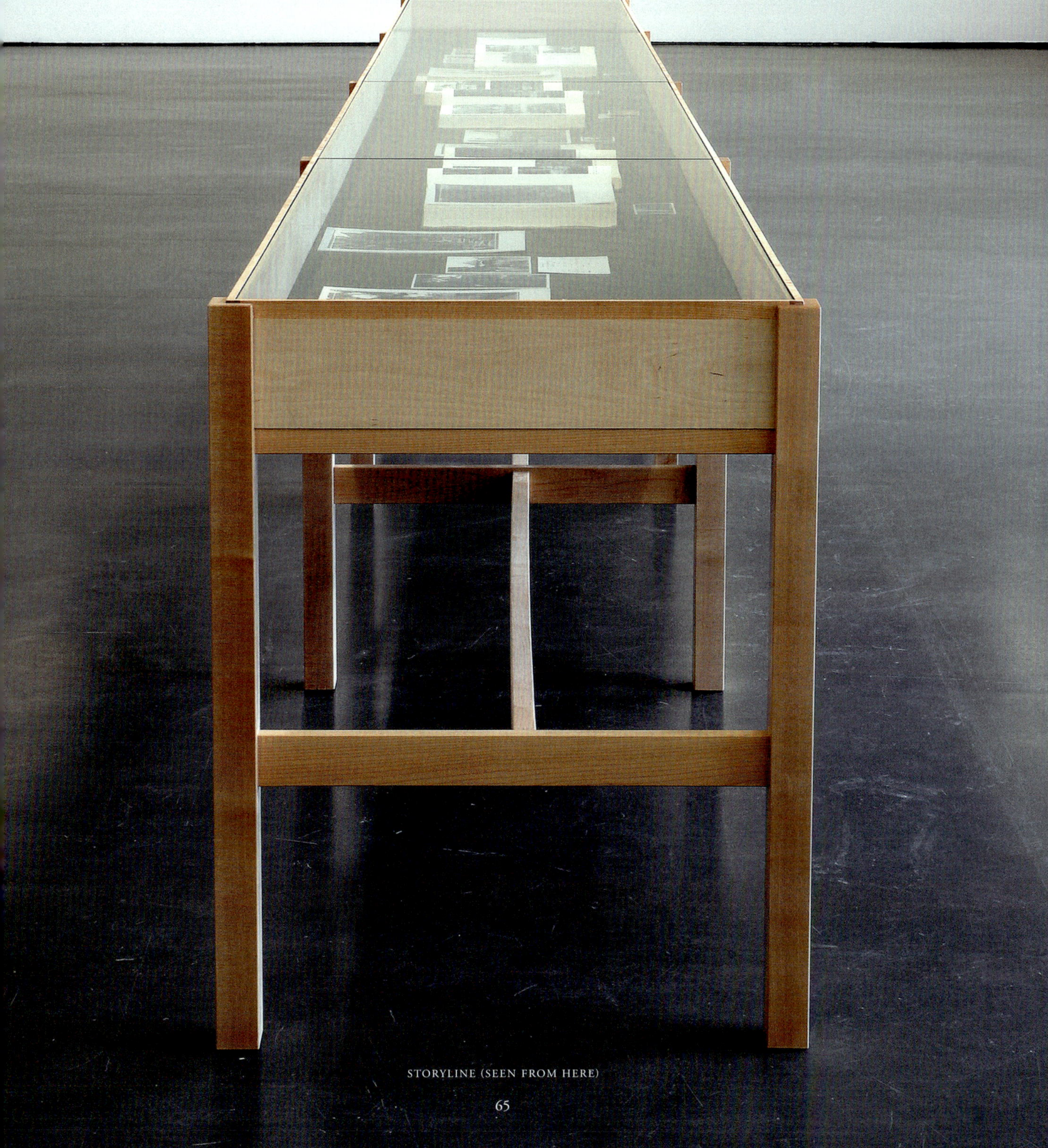

STORYLINE (SEEN FROM HERE)

Storyline (Seen from Here)

Sources:

The art historian Osvald Sirén's (1879-1966) photographs made in China between 1918-1935, and in Great Britain, France and Sweden 1946-1947, the Sirén Archive at the Museum of Far Eastern Antiquities in Stockholm.

Osvald Sirén, *Kinas trädgårdar och vad de betytt för 1700-talets Europa*, part I, *Kinas trädgårdar* and part II *Trädgårdar i Europa*, A.B. Svensk Litteratur, Stockholm 1948-1950.

Osvald Sirén, *China and Gardens of Europe in the Eighteenth Century* with an introduction by Hugh Honour, Dumbarton Oaks, Washington, D.C., 1990.

Göran Alm, *Kina Slott*, Byggförlaget, Stockholm, 2002.

Photographs made in Sweden August 2008 by the artist with assistance from photographer Hendrik Zeitler: Dragon Gate, Älvkarleby – a former road tavern and hotel by the motorway E4, now in process of becoming a Chinese culture and business centre; an 18th Century aviary used by the guides at the China House, Drottningholm, and *A Chinese Garden at Skeppsholmen*, a temporary garden up for the summer 2008 at the Museum of Far Eastern Antiquities in Stockholm.

Footnotes:

Digital images found through Google.com Image Search.

梗概（见下）

资料来源

美术史学家奥斯瓦尔德•喜仁龙（1879—1966）中国部分的照片摄于1918—1935年，英国、法国和瑞典部分的照片摄于1946—1947年。喜仁龙的档案现保存于斯德哥尔摩远东文物博物馆。

奥斯瓦尔德•喜仁龙，《中国园林及其对18世纪欧洲的影响，上卷》，《中国园林及下卷欧洲园林》，A.B. 瑞典文学，斯德哥尔摩1948—1950。

奥斯瓦尔德•喜仁龙，《中国与十八世纪的欧洲园林》，休·霍勒作序，敦巴顿橡树园，华盛顿哥伦比亚特区，1990。

Göran Alm，《中国宫殿》，Byggförlaget，斯德哥尔摩，2002。

该艺术家于2008年在摄影师亨德里克的协助下所拍摄的照片：艾尔夫卡勒比的龙门——其前身为E4高速公路上的路边酒馆兼旅店，如今正逐渐成为中国文化商业中心；德罗特宁霍尔姆的中国馆所印制导游手册中提及到的一间18世纪的鸟舍，及"斯德哥尔摩的中国凉亭"，斯德哥尔摩远东文物博物馆2008夏季展上搭建的临时庭院。

脚注：

数码图片来源于 Google.com 的图像搜索。

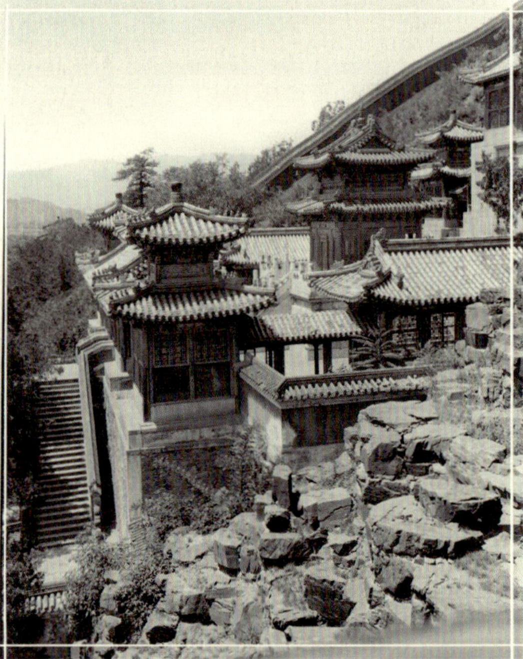

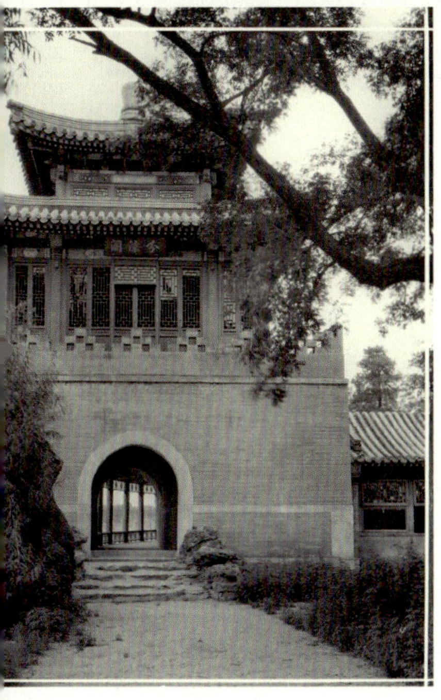

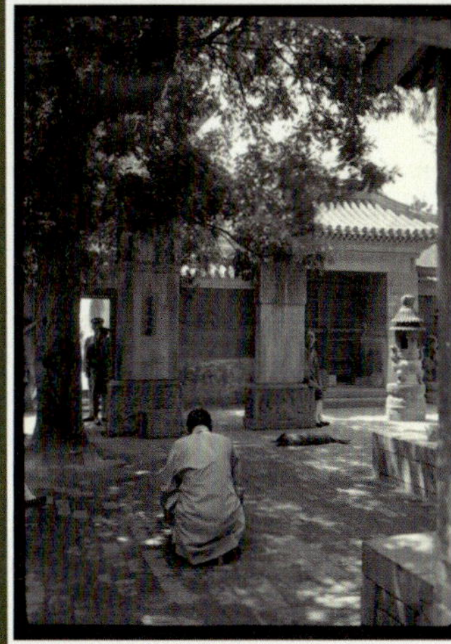

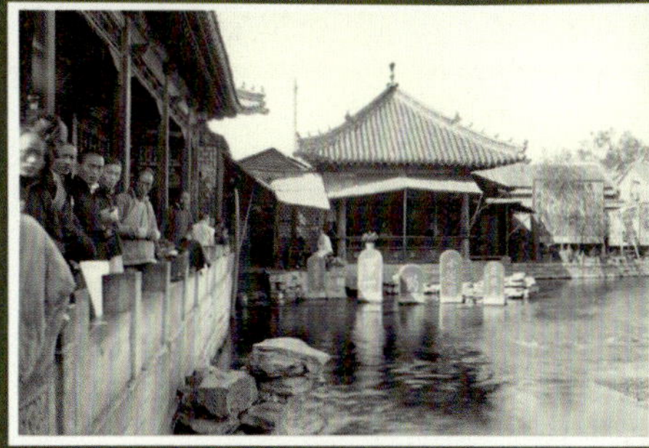

THE SIRÉN ARCHIVE
MUSEUM OF FAR EASTERN ANTIQUITIES
STOCKHOLM

SIZE

COUNTRY *China*   PROVINCE *Shantung*   PLACE *Tsinanfu*

EPOCH   ILLUSTRATED

ARCHIVE NR   NEGATIVE NR

NOTES

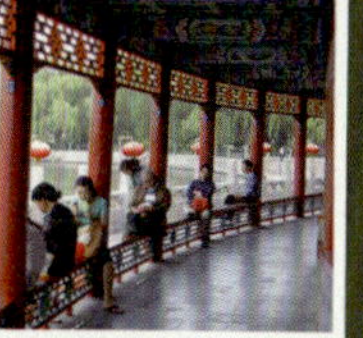

STORYLINE (SEEN FROM HERE), 2008

In der Installation *Storyline (Seen from Here)*, die für die Third Guangzhou Triennial entstanden ist, beschäftigt sich Leiderstam mit dem interkulturellen Austausch zwischen Europa und China am Beispiel der Gartengestaltung. Verschiedene Ausgaben der Bücher *Gardens of China* (1948) und *China and Gardens of Europe of the 18th Century* (1950) des schwedischen Kunsthistorikers Osvald Sirén werden zum Ausgangspunkt für die Beobachtung von Spuren der Beeinflussung, von Strategien der Aneignung und für das Nachvollziehen einer Inspiration, die stets eine Reflexion der eigenen Faszination für das Fremde und Exotische impliziert. Sirén war in den frühen 1920er Jahren für Recherchen zu seinem ersten Buch nach China gereist und hatte dort Parks und Gartenanlagen in eleganten Fotos festgehalten. Nach dem Ende des Zweiten Weltkriegs setzte er seine Forschung zur Rezeption chinesischer Garten- und Landschaftsgestaltung in Europa fort. Leiderstam ergänzt das dokumentarische Material Siréns mit eigenen Fotografien, die aktuelle Beispiele architektonischer und städteräumlicher Chinoiserien ironisch in das delikate Licht historischer Aufnahmen zu tauchen versuchen.

In the installation *Storyline (Seen from Here)*, developed for the Third Guangzhou Triennial, Leiderstam is concerned with the intellectual exchange between Europe and China as exemplified by garden landscaping and design. Different editions of the books *Gardens of China* (1948) and *China and Gardens of Europe of the 18th Century* (1950), by the Swedish art historian Osvald Sirén, form the starting point for an observation of this influence and of appropriation strategies for the retracing of an inspiration that continuously suggests a reflection of one's own fascination with the foreign and exotic. Sirén traveled to China in the early 1920s to research his first book and documented Chinese parks and garden complexes there in elegant photographs. After the Second World War, he resumed his research on the reception of Chinese landscape gardening in Europe. Leiderstam supplements Sirén's documentary material with his own photographs, which ironically attempt to immerse contemporary examples of architectural and municipal chinoiserie in the delicate light of historic photographs.

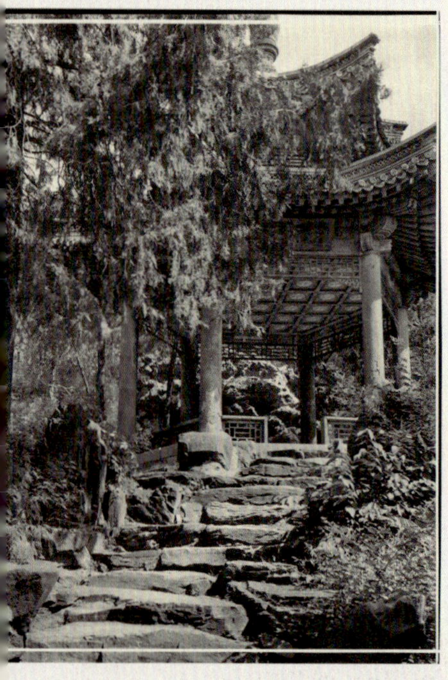

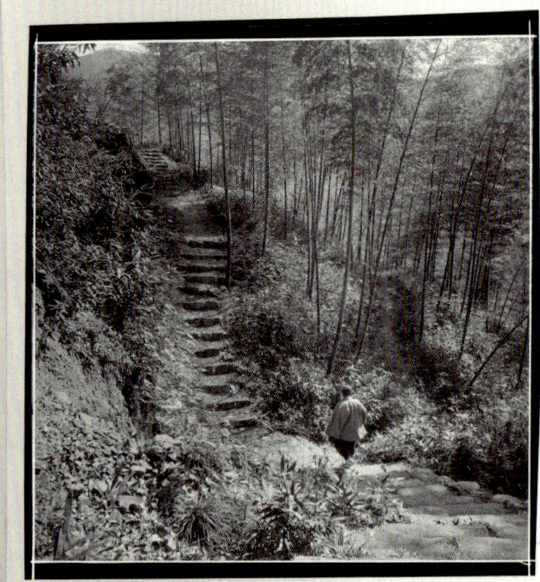

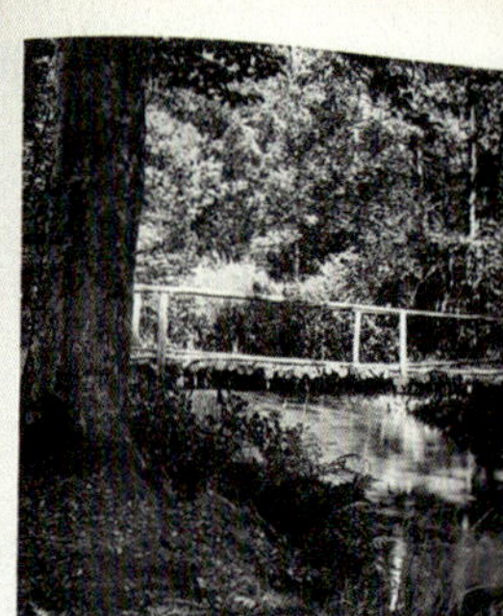

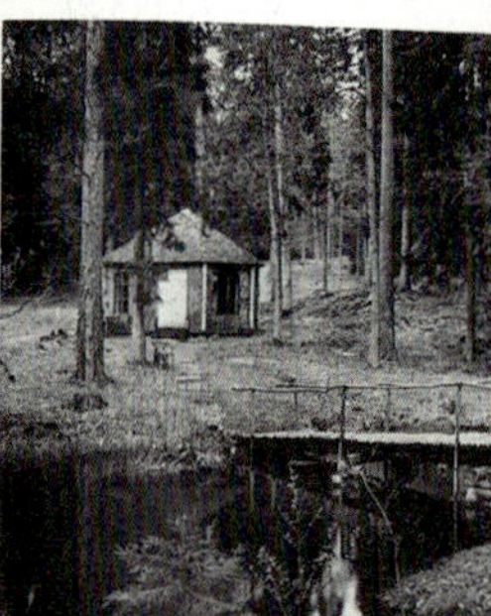

197. A. Kavelbron över bäcken nedanför eremitaget i Värnan
B. Kavelbron och eremitaget i Rydboholms-parken.

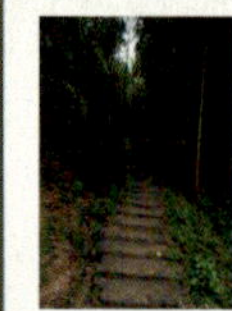

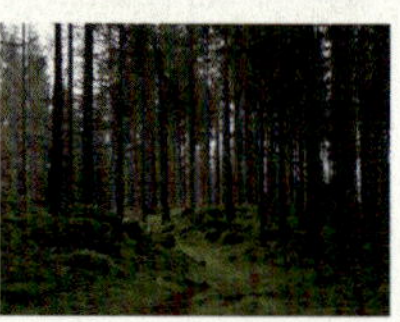

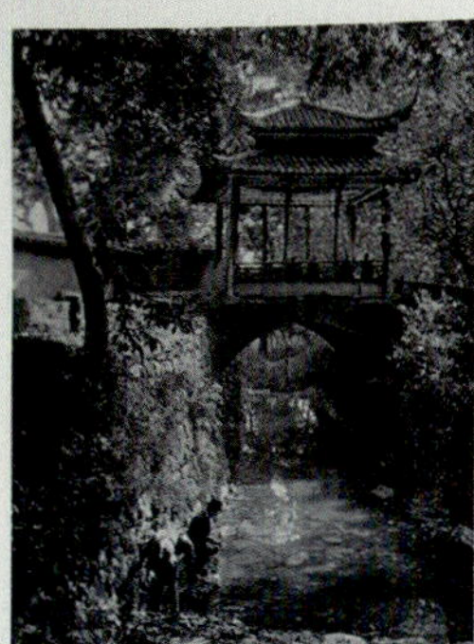

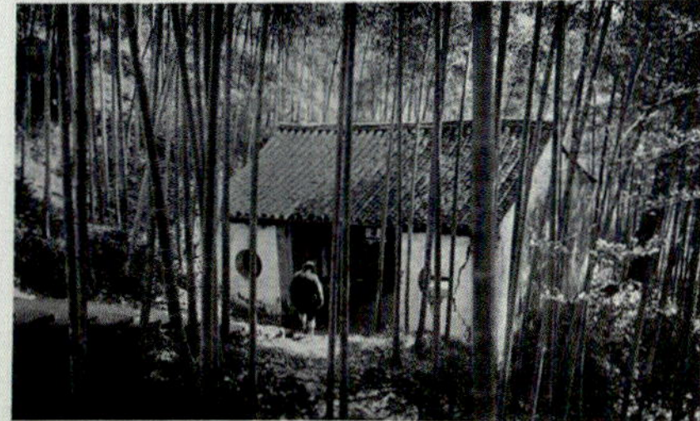

112. En paviljongkrönt bäckravin samt en bambulund vid Ling Ying Ssu, Hangchou.

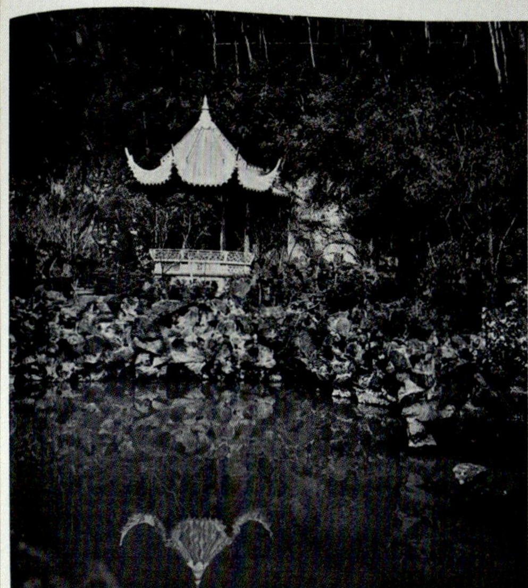

113. Paviljong i parken vid Huang Lung Ssu, Den Gula Drakens tempel, i Hangchou.

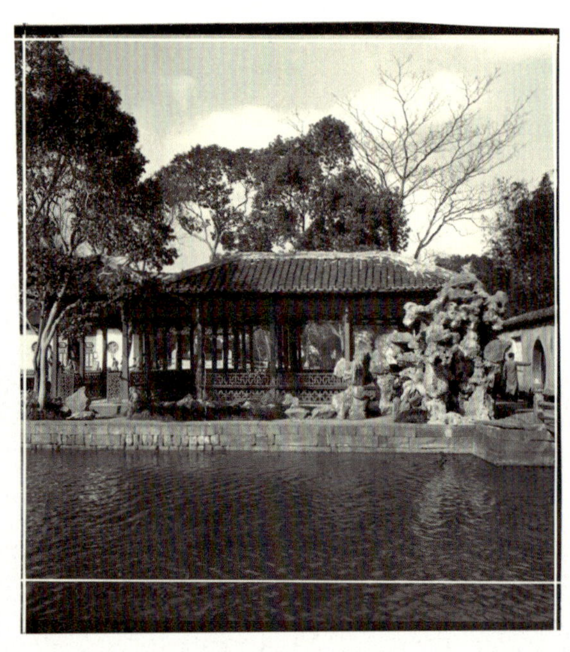

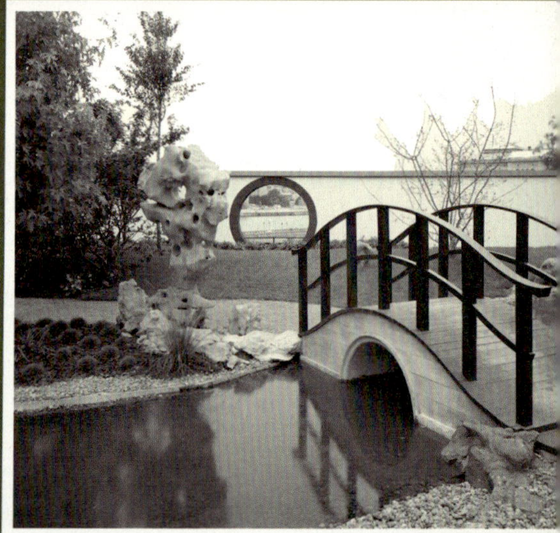

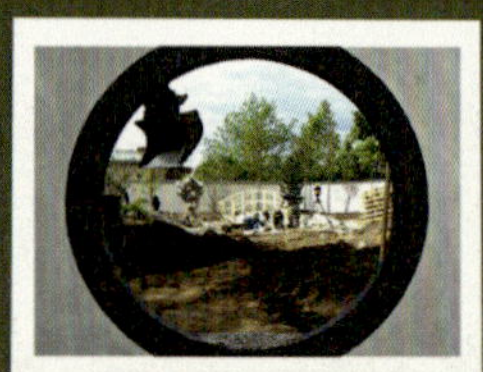

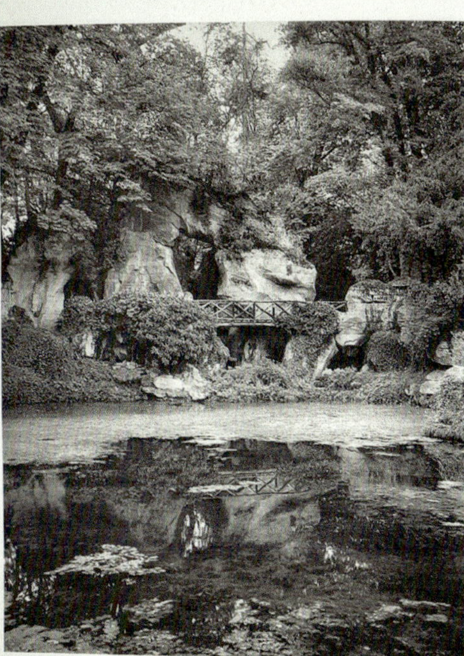

Plate 78. Hollowed rocks and palisade at the little lake in the park of Petit Trianon.

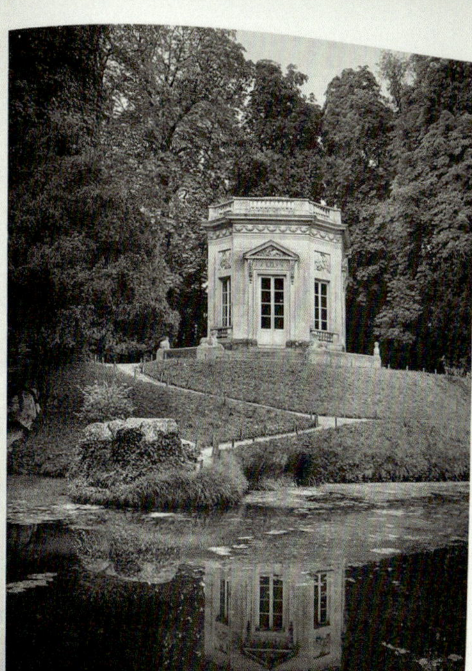

Plate 79. Belvedere or Music Pavilion built by Richard Mique at Petit Trianon.

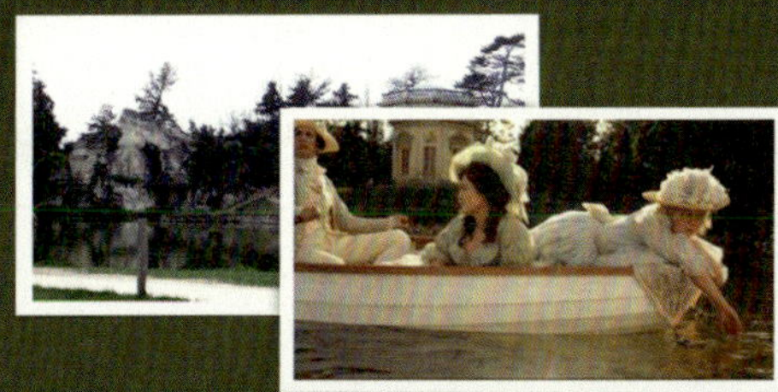

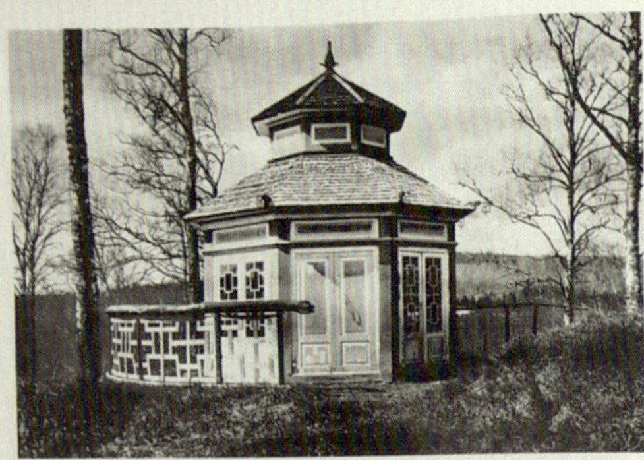

A

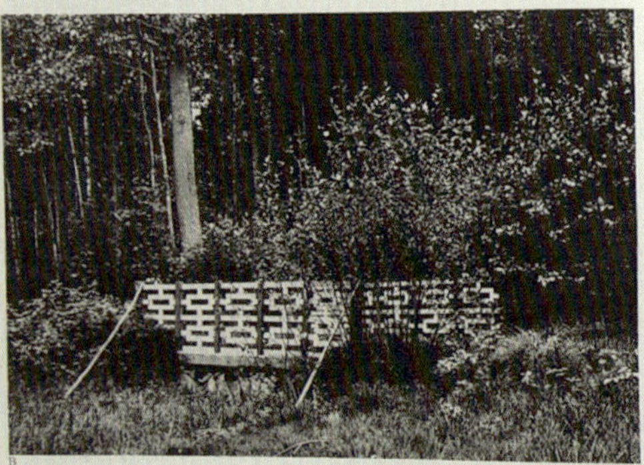

B
150. A. Det kinesiska lusthuset på Lustigkullen i Godegårds park.
B. En bro med ornamentalt räcke i Godegårds park.

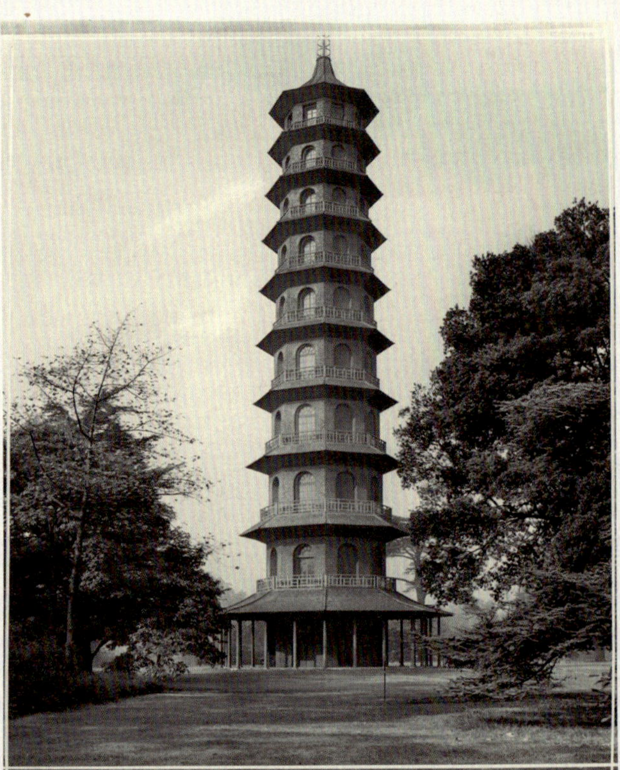

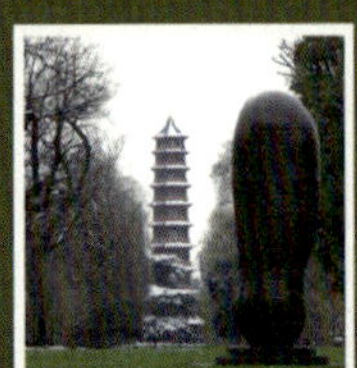

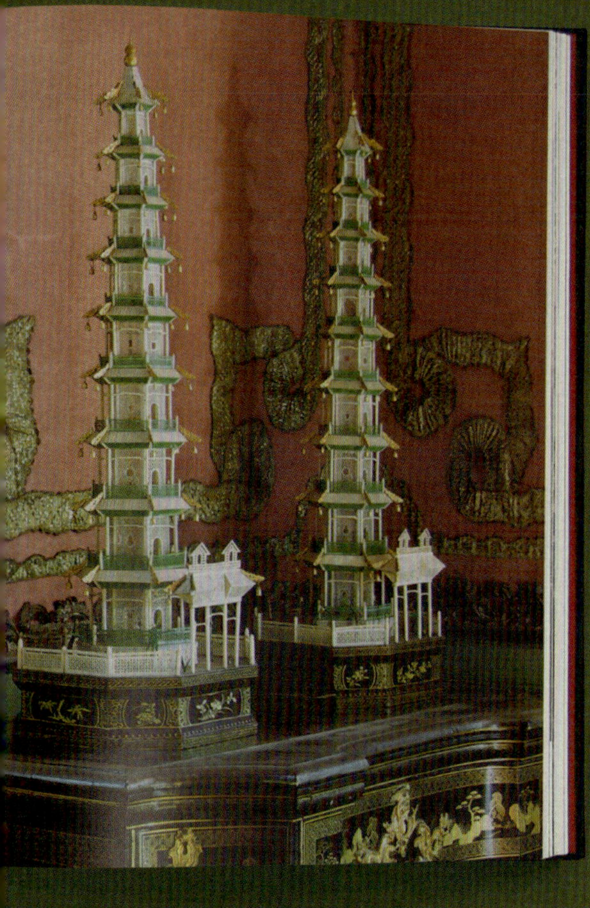

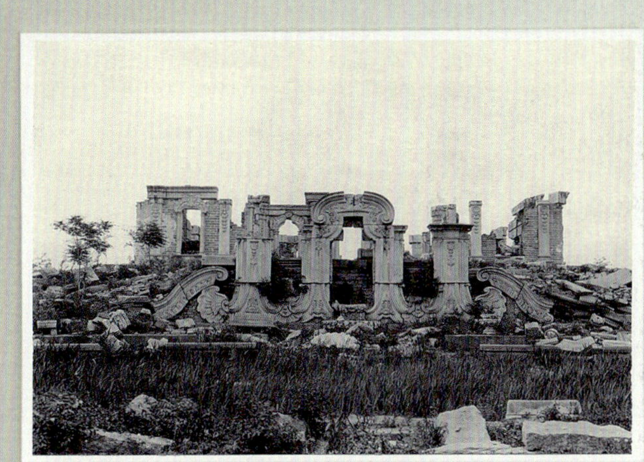

THE SIRÉN ARCHIVE
MUSEUM OF FAR EASTERN ANTIQUITIES
STOCKHOLM

Yüan Ming Yüan : Ruins

COUNTRY China   PROVINCE Hopei   PLACE Peking
SIZE
EPOCH   ILLUSTRATED
ARCHIVE NR   NEGATIVE NR
NOTES

B
Plate 133.

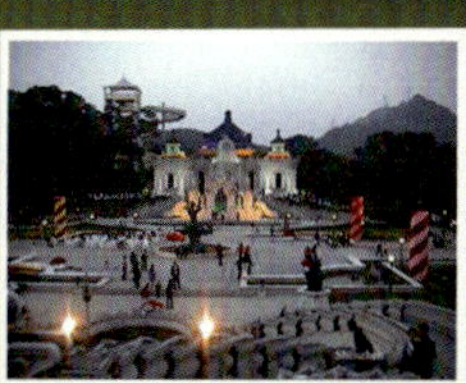

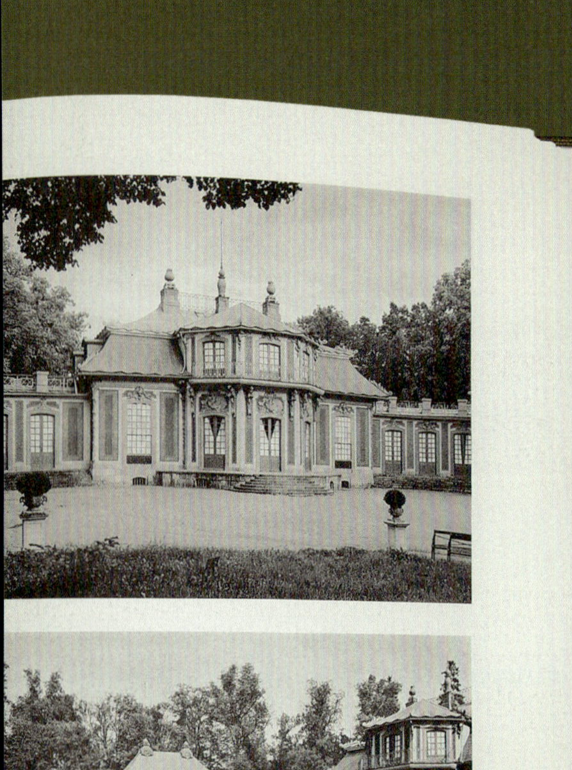

...rs of the China House at Drottningholm.

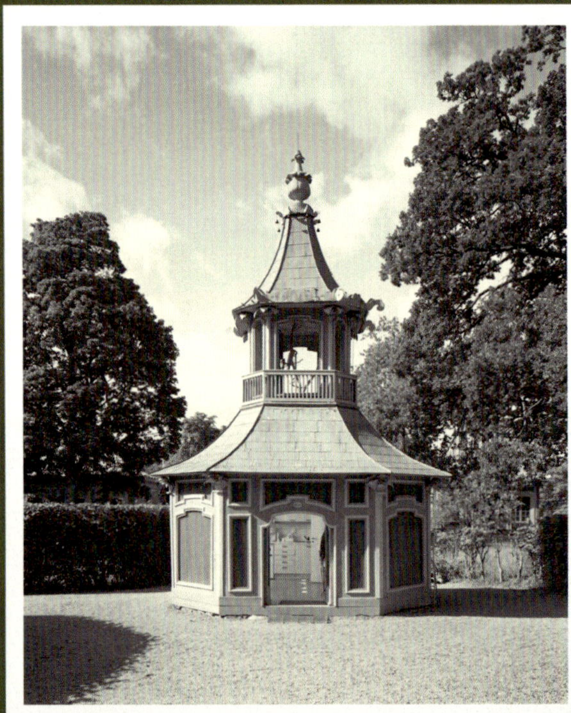

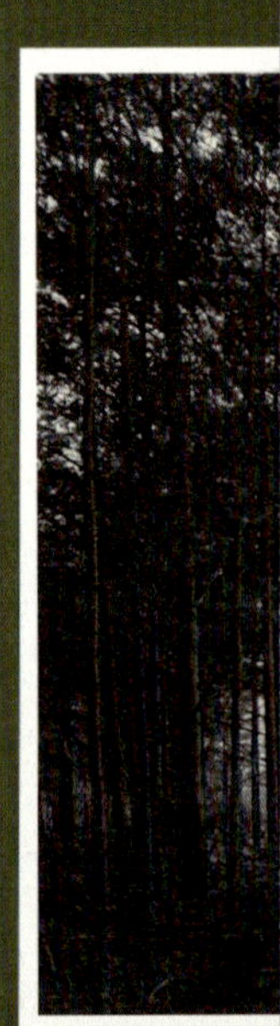

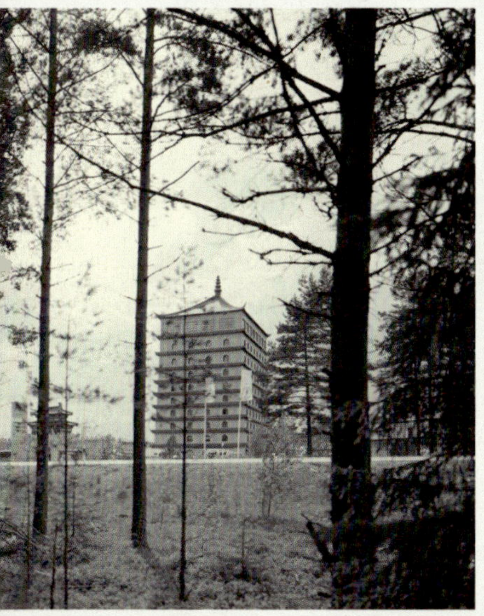

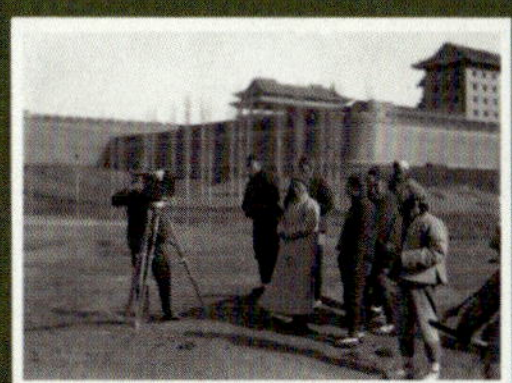

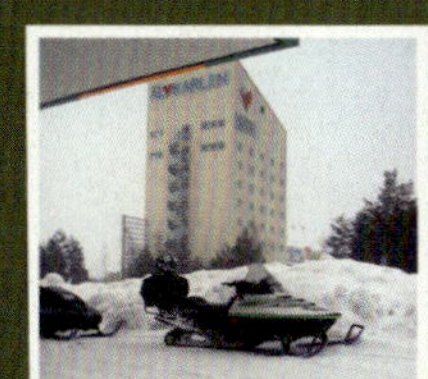

STORYLINE (Seen from Here)　　　梗概（見下）

Die Erfindung der Natur – die Erfindung der Landschaft:
Matts Leiderstam in Düsseldorf

ULRIKE GROOS / GREGOR JANSEN

Ich lernte Matts Leiderstam 1998 durch Maria Lind in Luxemburg kennen. Kurz darauf bot sich während einer Reise nach Schweden die Möglichkeit, den Künstler in seinem Stockholmer Atelier zu besuchen und ihn sowie seine Arbeit näher kennenzulernen. Ich war sofort fasziniert von der Außergewöhnlichkeit, der Vielseitigkeit und dem hohen Anspruch seiner künstlerischen Arbeitsweise: Er ist nicht nur bildender Künstler, sondern auch Kunsthistoriker und Kurator in Personalunion. Sein besonderes Interesse gilt dabei der Porträt- und Landschaftsmalerei des 18. und 19. Jahrhunderts, deren Werke er weltweit in Museen aufspürt und gezielt ihren verschlungenen und oft skurrilen Provenienzgeschichten nachgeht. Auf der Grundlage von Erkenntnissen, die auf einer fast wissenschaftlichen Herangehensweise basieren, eignet er sich die historischen Gemälde durch einen höchst kreativen Prozess der Auseinandersetzung an und macht sie zu seinem Material: Er kopiert sie, wobei er sie im Detail einfühlsam und zugleich sehr eindrücklich verfremdet, er vergleicht ihre Reproduktionen in unterschiedlichen Büchern oder fotografiert sie selbst noch einmal. Er bringt seine Kopien dahin, wo sie dem Anschein nach entstanden sind, fügt sie in die Landschaft ein und fotografiert sie erneut. Die Ergebnisse seiner Recherchen arrangiert er in komplexen Installationen, die einen unverbrauchten und unkonventionellen Blick auf kunsthistorisch vermeintlich Bekanntes und Erforschtes werfen.

Seine künstlerische Strategie verlangt ein hohes Maß an Disziplin, sie setzt intensive und zeitaufwendige Vorbereitungen voraus. Das erklärt auch den langen Vorlauf, den die Realisierung seiner neuen Installation Neanderthal Landscape *benötigte: Zwischen der Idee, der Einladung und der Eröffnung der Ausstellung vergingen nun immerhin fünf Jahre. Das ist in einem Kunstbetrieb, der gemeinhin als schnelllebig gilt, ein ungewöhnlich langer Zeitraum.*

Es freut mich immer noch sehr, dass sich Matts Leiderstam für die Idee, eine große Ausstellung in der Kunsthalle Düsseldorf zu realisieren, damals sofort begeistern konnte. Die Düsseldorfer Malerschule, die aus der von ihrem Protagonisten Johann Wilhelm Schirmer (1807–1863) an der Düsseldorfer Kunstakademie gegründeten Klasse für Landschaftsmalerei hervorging, war ihm wegen ihrer Bedeutung für die skandinavische Kunst und Kunstgeschichte natürlich seit Langem bekannt, sie interessierte ihn aber auch wegen ihres Einflusses auf die Landschaftsmalerei in anderen europäischen und außereuropäischen Ländern. Die Erkundung des Neandertals als motivischen Schwerpunkt vieler Künstler der Düsseldorfer Malerschule führte Leiderstam zu überraschenden Erkenntnissen, die auf vielschichtige Art und Weise in seine neue Installation eingeflossen sind.

Ulrike Groos, Direktorin des
Kunstmuseum Stuttgart und ehemalige
Direktorin der Kunsthalle Düsseldorf

Das gegenwärtige Interesse an der Natur, der Landschaft, ihre Wertschätzung, nicht nur als Motiv der Kunst und Gegenstand künstlerischer Reflexion, sondern auch als geografisches Phänomen und wesentliches Klimaelement der Welt, in der wir leben, ist den Menschen des 19. Jahrhunderts eher fremd gewesen. Sie mussten sich diesen positiven und bewussten Blick erst erkämpfen, ihn förmlich von der Natur abringen als Wahrnehmungserweiterung eines bis dahin immer nur skizzierten Verhältnisses zu einem nicht darstellungswürdigen Topos. Die Natur erschien im 18. Jahrhundert bei Jean-Jacques Rousseau und teils auch bei Denis Diderot als das verloren gegangene ursprünglich Gute. Der adlige Naturforscher de Buffon allerdings wertete diesen Verlust nicht als fatale Folge der Zivilisation, sondern beschrieb die unkultivierte Natur als scheußlich und bösartig und ließ nur die Umwandlung in Landschaft, in eine auf den Menschen bezogene Natur, als göttlich gerechtfertigten Auftrag gelten. Diderot behauptete schon 1767, die in den Salons hängenden Landschaftsbilder würden von den Städtern zur Kompensation ihrer Natursehnsucht dort platziert. Erst Mitte des 19. Jahrhun-

The Invention of Nature—the Invention of the Landscape:
Matts Leiderstam in Düsseldorf

ULRIKE GROOS / GREGOR JANSEN

Maria Lind introduced me to Matts Leiderstam in 1998 in Luxemburg. Shortly afterwards I had the chance to visit him in his atelier in Stockholm and get to know him and his work better. I was immediately fascinated by how extraordinary, versatile and sophisticated his artistic methods are: he is not only a visual artist, but also art historian and curator all rolled into one. He is particularly interested in portrait and landscape paintings of the eighteenth and nineteenth centuries, which he tracks down in museums worldwide, purposefully pursuing their convoluted and often bizarre provenances. On the basis of knowledge gained through an almost scientific approach, he appropriates the historical paintings in a highly creative process of involving himself with them and transforming them into his material: he copies them, both perceptively and emphatically changing them in details in the process. He compares their reproductions in various books or photographs them once more himself. He brings his copies to where the original was supposedly created, inserts them in the landscape and photographs them anew. He arranges the results of his research in complex installations that cast a fresh and unconventional eye on reputedly familiar and previously already studied material from art history.

His artistic strategy demands a maximum of discipline, for it requires intensive and time-consuming preparation. This also explains the long phase of planning needed in advance for his new installation Neanderthal Landscape: *between the initial idea, invitation and the opening of the exhibit lay at least five years. In an art scene that is still generally considered short-lived, this is an unusually long period of time.*

I am thus very glad that I was able to interest Matts Leiderstam immediately in the idea to implement a large exhibition in the Kunsthalle Düsseldorf. Of course he had already been familiar for quite some time with the Düsseldorf School of Painting, which emerged from the landscape painting class founded by its protagonist Johann Wilhelm Schirmer (1807–1863) at the Art Academy in Düsseldorf, due to its significance for Scandinavian art and art history, but he was also interested in it because of its influence on landscape painting in other European and non-European countries. The exploration of the Neandertal as a central motif of many artists in the Düsseldorf School of Painting led Leiderstam to surprising insights, which in complex ways became part of his new installation.

Ulrike Groos, Director of the Kunstmuseum Stuttgart and former Director of the Kunsthalle Düsseldorf

The current interest in nature, the landscape and its appreciation—not only as an artistic motif and object of artistic reflection, but also as geographical phenomena and fundamental climatic element of the world in which we live—was rather foreign to people in the nineteenth century. They had to struggle to gain such a positive and conscious perspective, literally wrest it from nature to broaden awareness of a hitherto only vague relationship to a topos not conceived as worthy of representation. In the eighteenth century, Jean-Jacques Rousseau and to some degree also Denis Diderot considered nature to be the original expression of the good that had been lost. However, the aristocratic scientist de Buffon regarded this loss not as a fatal result of civilization, describing uncultivated nature as hideous and malicious. Only its transformation into landscape, into nature with reference to human beings, was to him a task justified as godly. Diderot was the first to assert in 1767 that the landscape paintings hanging in the salons had only been placed there by the city folk as compensation for their desire for nature. It was not before the mid-nineteenth century that alpine tourism was pioneered by Britons into mountain ranges and territories into which previously only the foolhardy had set foot. They had only been approached from a distance and a sublime point of view.

derts setzte der durch die Briten initiierte Alpentourismus ein und erschloss ein Gebirge und Gebiet, welches zuvor nur von den Wagemutigsten betreten worden war. Eine Annäherung hatte bis dahin immer nur aus der Distanz und aus erhabener Anschauung heraus stattgefunden. Reise- und Wolkenstudien, die Darstellungen der Jahreszeiten und damit verbundener Stimmungen waren lange Zeit keine eigenständige Gattung der Malerei, sondern lediglich schmückender Rahmen für die christlichen und mythologischen Themen der klassischen Kunstgeschichte. Dies änderte sich langsam vom 16. Jahrhundert an bei Leonardo und Altdorfer, denen die ersten reinen Landschaftsdarstellungen zugeschrieben werden, und nachhaltig im 19. Jahrhundert mit besagter Landschaftsklasse Schirmers an der Düsseldorfer Kunstakademie, die sich an niederländischen Malern wie Jacob van Ruisdael oder Jan van Goyen orientierte und Studien in der freien Natur, vor allem in dem von Schirmer sehr geliebten Neandertal unternahm. Während bis Mitte des 19. Jahrhunderts die Auffassung, ein Landschaftsbild erhalte erst durch die menschlichen Figuren seine Vollendung und Bedeutung, ihre uneingeschränkte theoretische Geltung behielt, erlebte die Düsseldorfer Malerschule in den 1850er und 1860er Jahren eine Hochzeit durch einen bemerkenswerten Zulauf von ausländischen Schülern. Der Bekanntheitsgrad der Schule machte die in Düsseldorf entstandenen Werken der einheimischen wie der zugewanderten Künstler zu einem beliebten und stilprägenden Exportartikel.

Hiervon – neben zahlreichen anderen Aspekten wie dem künstlichen Wasserfall – erzählt uns Matts Leiderstam in seiner staunenswerten Installation *Neanderthal Landscape,* die seine seit 2006 hier in Düsseldorf unternommenen Forschungen bündelt. Er steht damit gewissermaßen in der Nachfolge der vielen skandinavischen Künstler, welche die Düsseldorfer Malerschule besucht und die hiesige Landschaftsdarstellung in ihre Heimat mitgenommen haben. Man darf sagen: Die Skandinavier sahen ihre Landschaft ab der Mitte des 19. Jahrhunderts mit dem Blick der Düsseldorfer oder – augenzwinkernd – mit der Brille des Neandertalers.

Die Ausstellung *Seen from Here* läuft nicht zufällig parallel zum »Schirmer Projekt 2010«, das sich dem Schaffen und der Zeit des Landschaftsmalers widmet und an dem neben dem Düsseldorfer museum kunst palast fünf weitere Institutionen der Region beteiligt sind. Über die neue Installation hinaus zeigt sie die wichtigsten Arbeiten Leiderstams aus den letzten fünfzehn Jahren und bietet somit einen repräsentativen Überblick über das außergewöhnliche Schaffen dieses Künstlers.

Unser sehr herzlicher Dank gilt Matts Leiderstam, der uns hier die Sicht des 19. Jahrhunderts auf gleichermaßen unkonventionelle wie brillante Weise in der kongenialen Form einer »Ausstellungs-Landschaft« vergegenwärtigt. Für die hervorragende Zusammenarbeit danken wir dem Künstler ebenso wie dem Kurator Christoph Benjamin Schulz, der gemeinsam mit Jari Ortwig diese komplexe und zugleich sinnliche Ausstellung realisiert hat. Wir danken Dr. Bettina Baumgärtel, Leiterin der Gemäldesammlung, museum kunst palast, Düsseldorf, Richard Bödecker, Hannah Eggerath und allen weiteren Ratgebern, die bei den Recherchen des Künstlers wertvolle Hinweise gegeben haben. Gedankt sei den Leihgebern und den Galeristen des Künstlers für ihre Unterstützung: dem Stadtmuseum der Landeshauptstadt Düsseldorf; dem Neanderthal Museum, Mettmann; dem museum kunst palast, Düsseldorf; dem Malmö Konstmuseum; dem Moderna Museet, Stockholm, dem Magasin 3 Stockholm Konsthall sowie Celine Andréhn von der Galerie Andréhn-Schiptjenko, Stockholm, und Wilfried Lentz, Rotterdam.

Die Ausstellung trägt den neu gesehenen Geist Düsseldorfs noch einmal in den Norden und wandert im Anschluss an das Malmö Konstmuseum (16.6.–22.8.2010), an das Turun Taidemuseo, Turku (1.10.2010–16.1.2011) sowie an das Kuntsi Museum of Modern Art, Vaasa (4.2. – 3.4.2011). Gedankt sei an dieser Stelle allen unseren Kooperationspartnern.

Ein besonderer Dank gilt dem Ministerpräsidenten des Landes Nordrhein-Westfalen für die großzügige finanzielle Förderung von Ausstellung und Katalog. IASPIS – International Artist Studio Programme Sweden danken wir für die finanzielle Unterstützung des Künstlers.

Nicht zuletzt möchte ich dem großartigen Team der Kunsthalle meinen ganz herzlichen Dank für die geleistete Arbeit aussprechen.

Gregor Jansen,
Künstlerischer Leiter der
Kunsthalle Düsseldorf

For quite some time, travel and cloud studies, the portrayal of the seasons and associated moods were not an independent genre of painting, but merely decorative framework for the Christian and mythological subjects of classical art history. This gradually changed from the sixteenth century onwards with Leonardo and Altdorfer, who are credited with the first depictions of only landscapes and sustainably in the nineteenth century with the aforementioned landscape class of Schirmer at the Art Academy in Düsseldorf, which took its bearings from Dutch painters such as Jacob van Ruisdael or Jan van Goyen and undertook studies en plein air, especially into the Neandertal so much admired by Schirmer. Although the notion that landscape painting was fully complete and meaningful only if it contained human figures retained its unrestricted theoretical validity until the mid-nineteenth century, the Düsseldorf School of Painting experienced a highpoint in its popularity in the 1850s and 1860s due to a remarkable afflux of foreign students. The popularity of the school transformed the artwork of both local as well as recently arrived artists into much admired and stylistically formative export articles.

It is this—in addition to numerous other aspects such as the artificial waterfall—that Matts Leiderstam recollects in his astonishing installation *Neanderthal Landscape,* which consolidates the research that he has been undertaking here in Düsseldorf since 2006. In doing so, he is to some extent stepping in the footsteps of many Scandinavian artists, who visited the Düsseldorf Academy and took the local depiction of landscapes home. We could say: the Scandinavians saw their landscape from the mid-nineteenth century onwards through the eyes of Düsseldorf or—tongue in cheek—through the glasses of a Neandertal man.

It is no coincidence that the exhibit *Seen from Here* is running parallel to the "Schirmer Projekt 2010," which is dedicated to the work and times of the landscape artist Schirmer and in which five further institutions in the region in addition to the Düsseldorf museum kunst palast are participating. Aside from the new installation, the exhibit presents Leiderstam's most important work from the last fifteen years and thus offers a representative overview of the exceptional oeuvre of this artist.

I am much obliged to Matts Leiderstam, who helped us to envision this nineteenth-century perspective in an unconventional as well as brilliant way in the congenial form of an "exhibition landscape." We wish to thank the artist for the excellent collaboration as well as curator Christoph Benjamin Schulz, who, together with Jari Ortwig, made this complex and simultaneously sensual exhibition possible. We wish to thank Dr. Bettina Baumgärtel, director of the painting gallery at the museum kunst palast, Düsseldorf; Richard Bödecker, Hannah Eggerath and all others who gave valuable advice that helped to advance the artistic research. Our sincere thanks also to the lenders and the artist's gallery for their support; the Museum of the City of Düsseldorf, the Neanderthal Museum, Mettmann; the museum kunst palast, Düsseldorf; the Malmö Konstmuseum; the Moderna Museet, Stockholm, the Magasin 3 Stockholm Konsthall as well as Celine Andréhn from the Gallery Andréhn-Schiptjenko, Stockholm, and Wilfried Lentz from Rotterdam.

The exhibit will carry the newly revived spirit of Düsseldorf once again to the North and subsequently moves on to the Malmö Konstmuseum (16.6.–22.8.2010), to the Turun Taidemuseo, Turku (1.10.2010–16.1.2011) as well as to Kuntsi Museum of Modern Art, Vaasa (4.2. – 3.4.2011). Our sincerest thanks herewith also to all our partners in this collaboration.

Special thanks goes to the prime minister of the Land Northrhine Westphalia for the generous financial funding of exhibition and catalogue. We also thank IASPIS – International Artist Studio Programme Sweden for the financial support of the artist.

Last but not least, I wish to extend my heartfelt thanks to the excellent team of the Kunsthalle for their work.

Gregor Jansen, Artistic Director of the
Kunsthalle Düsseldorf

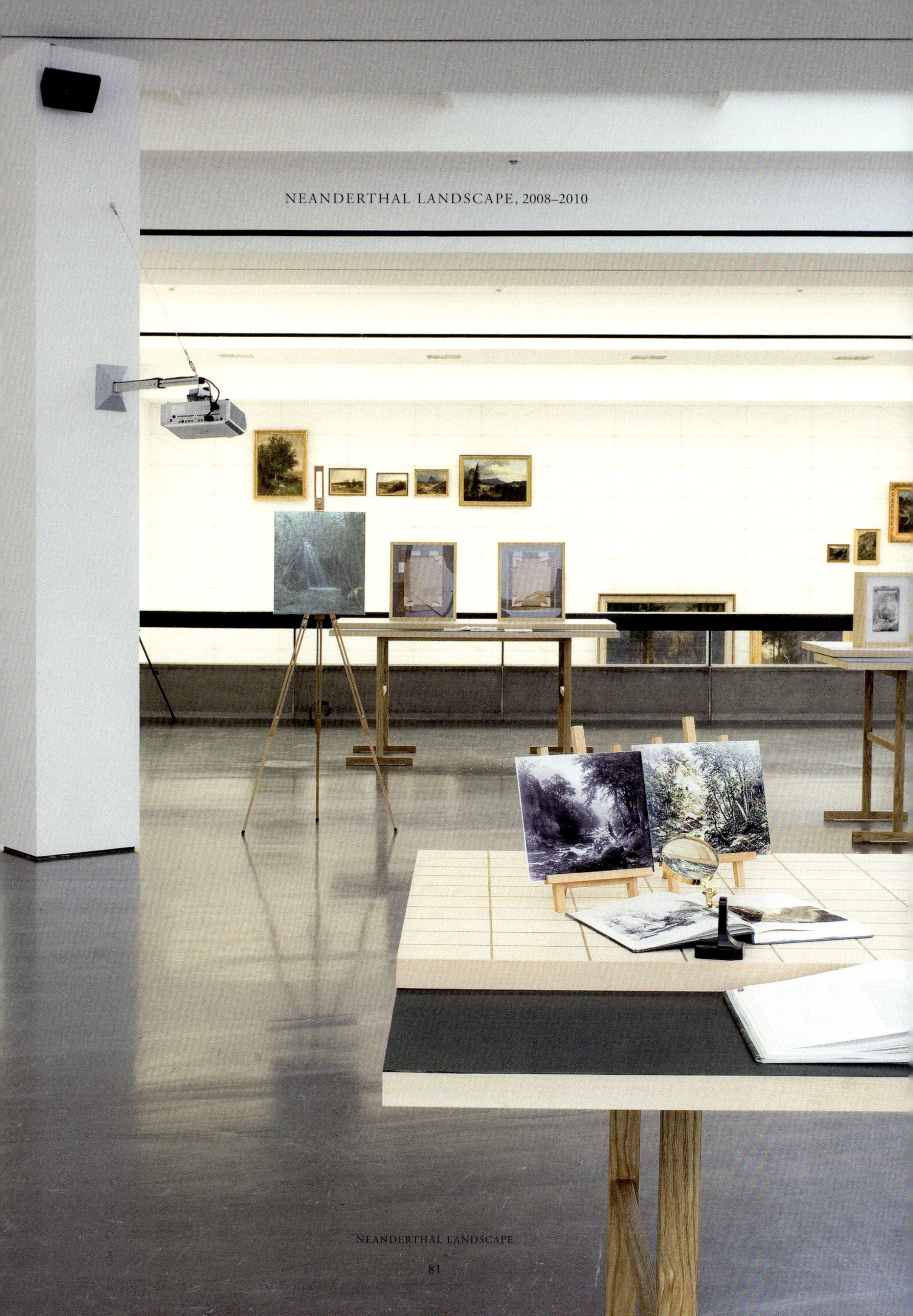

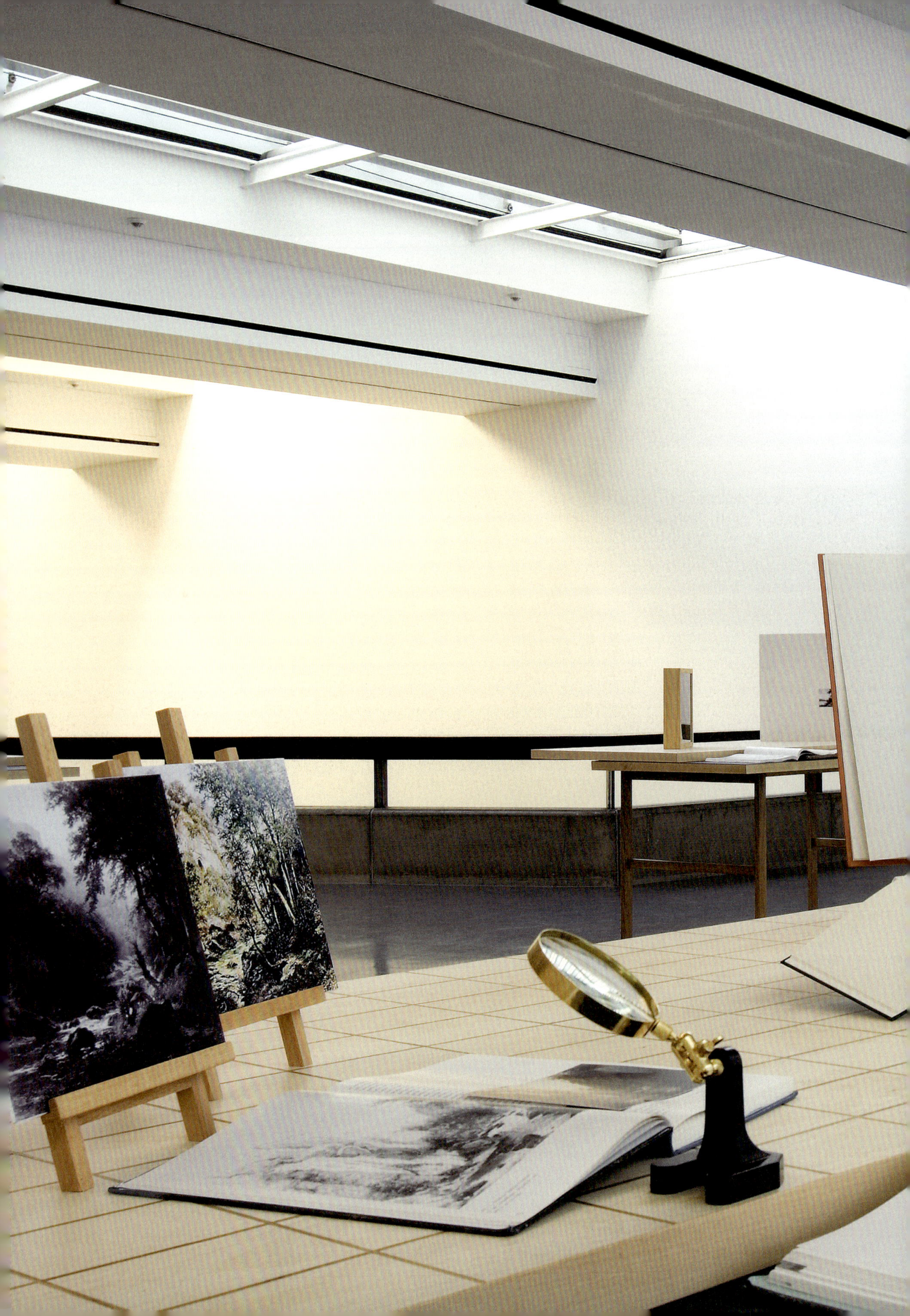

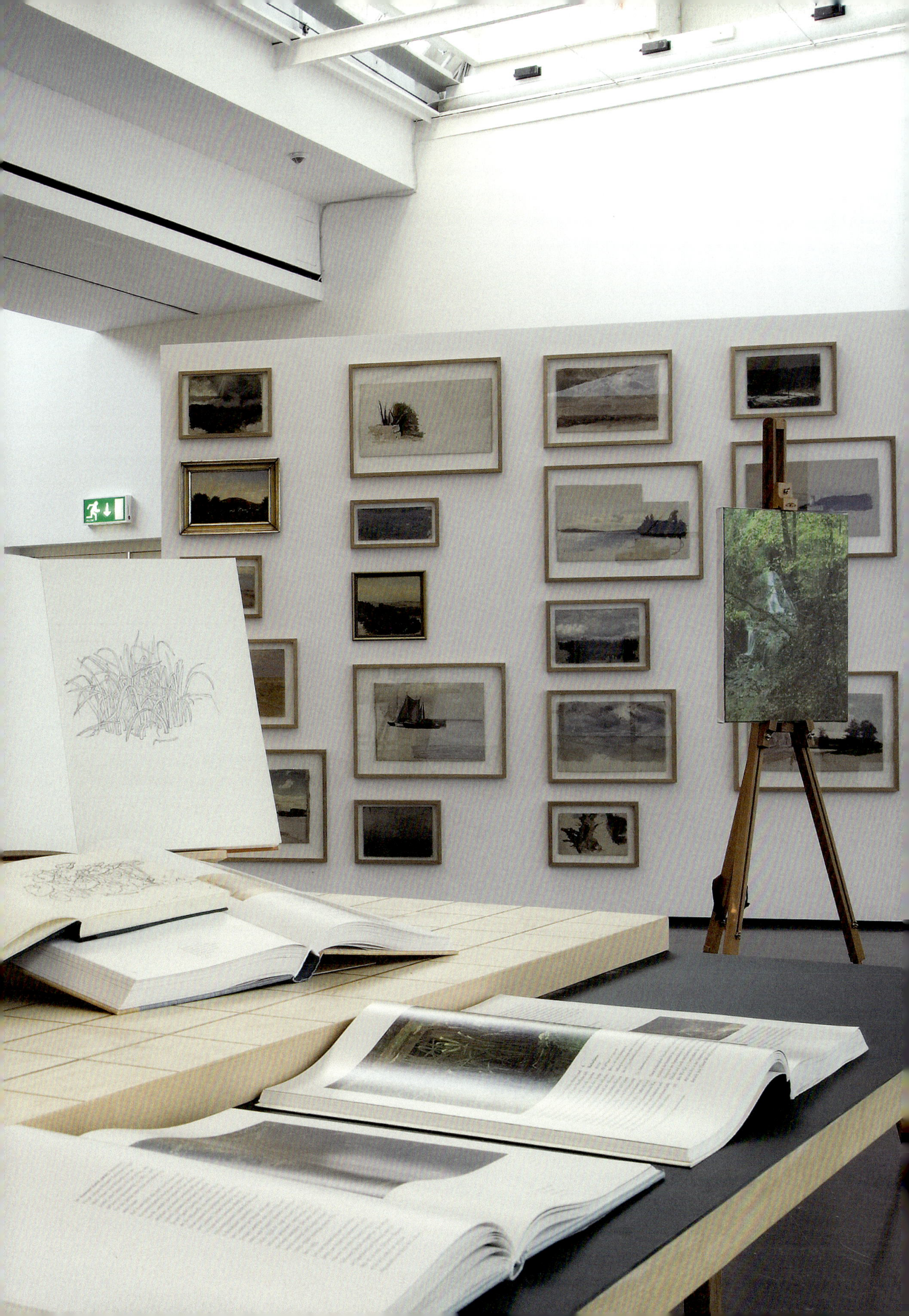

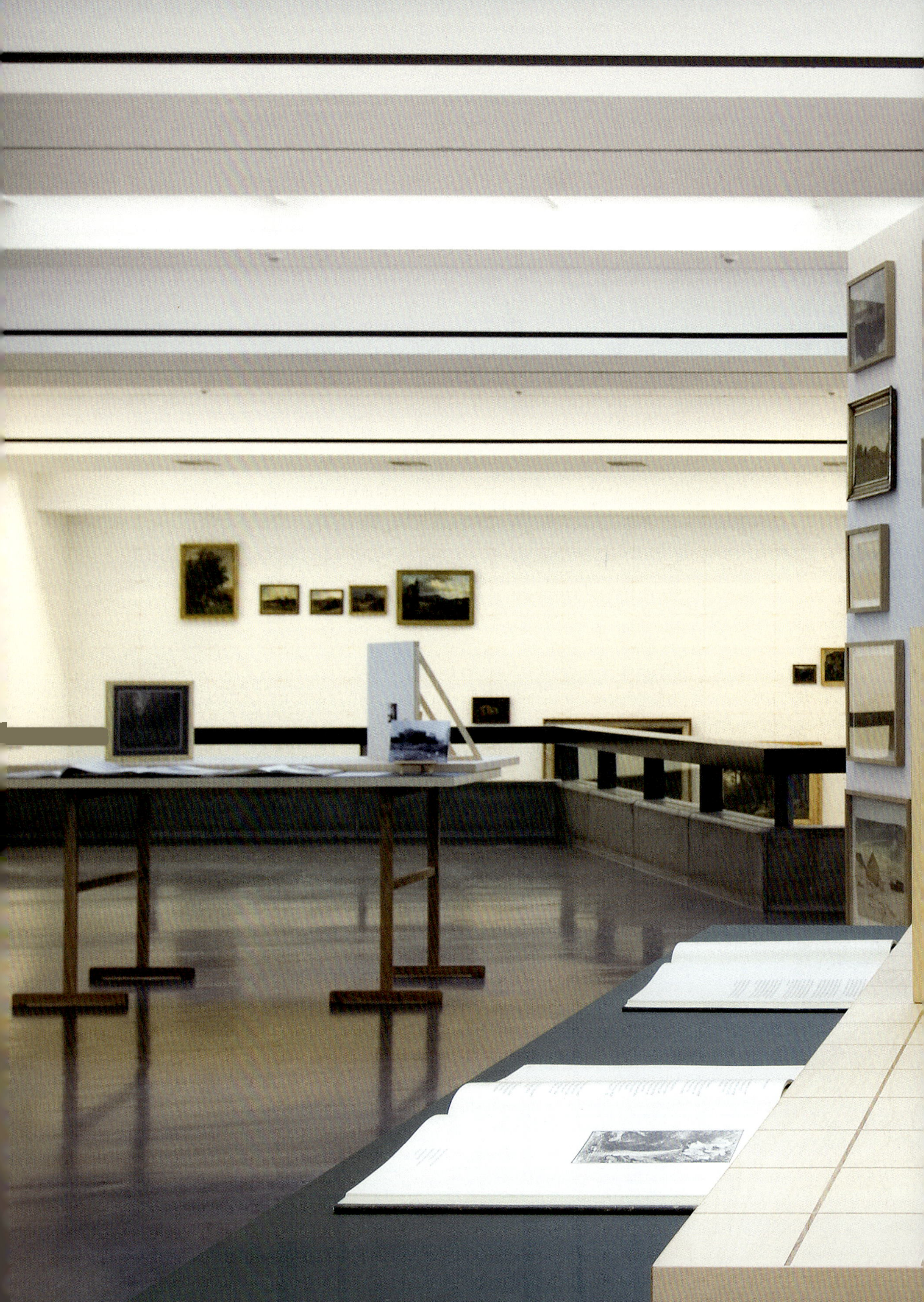

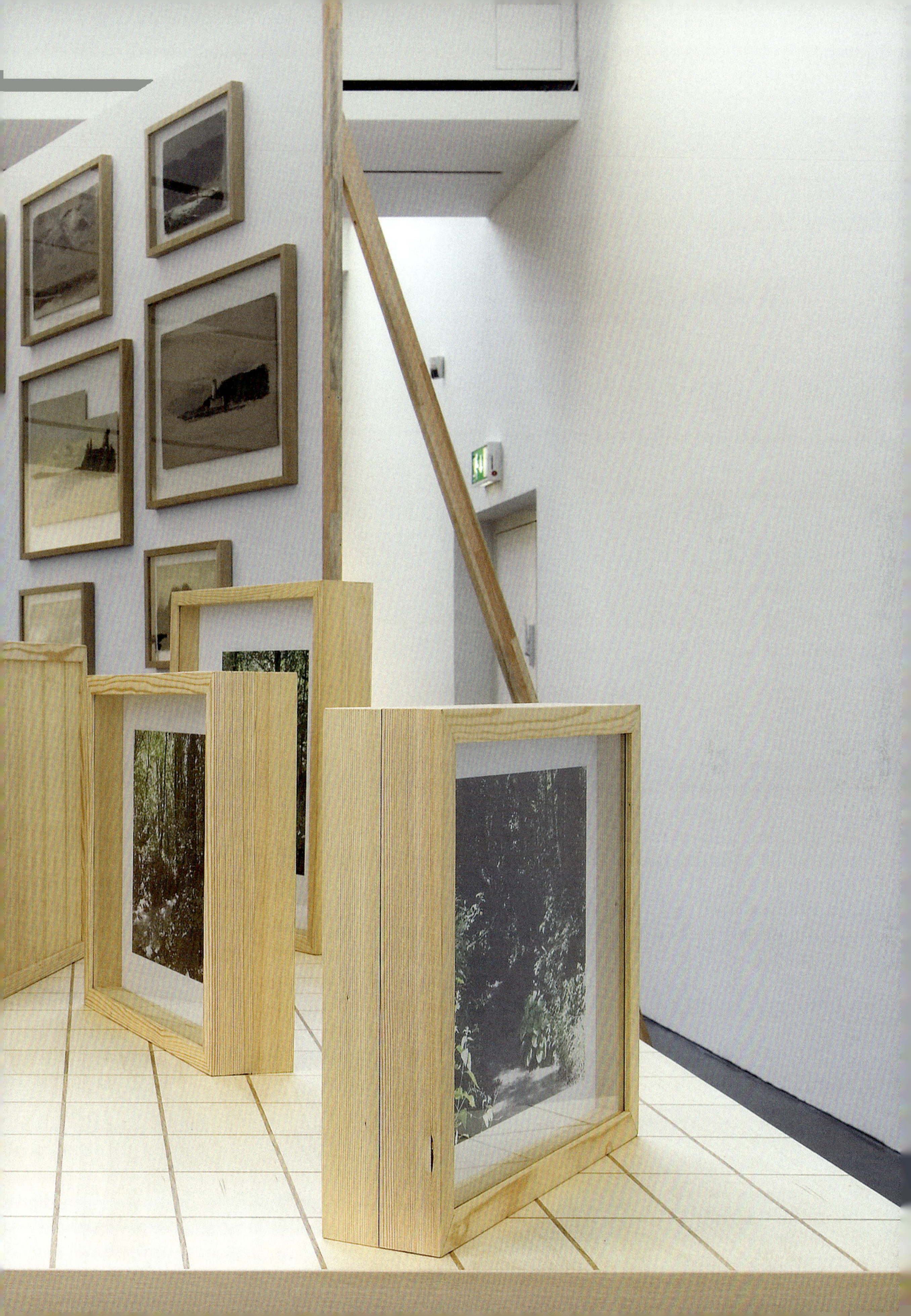

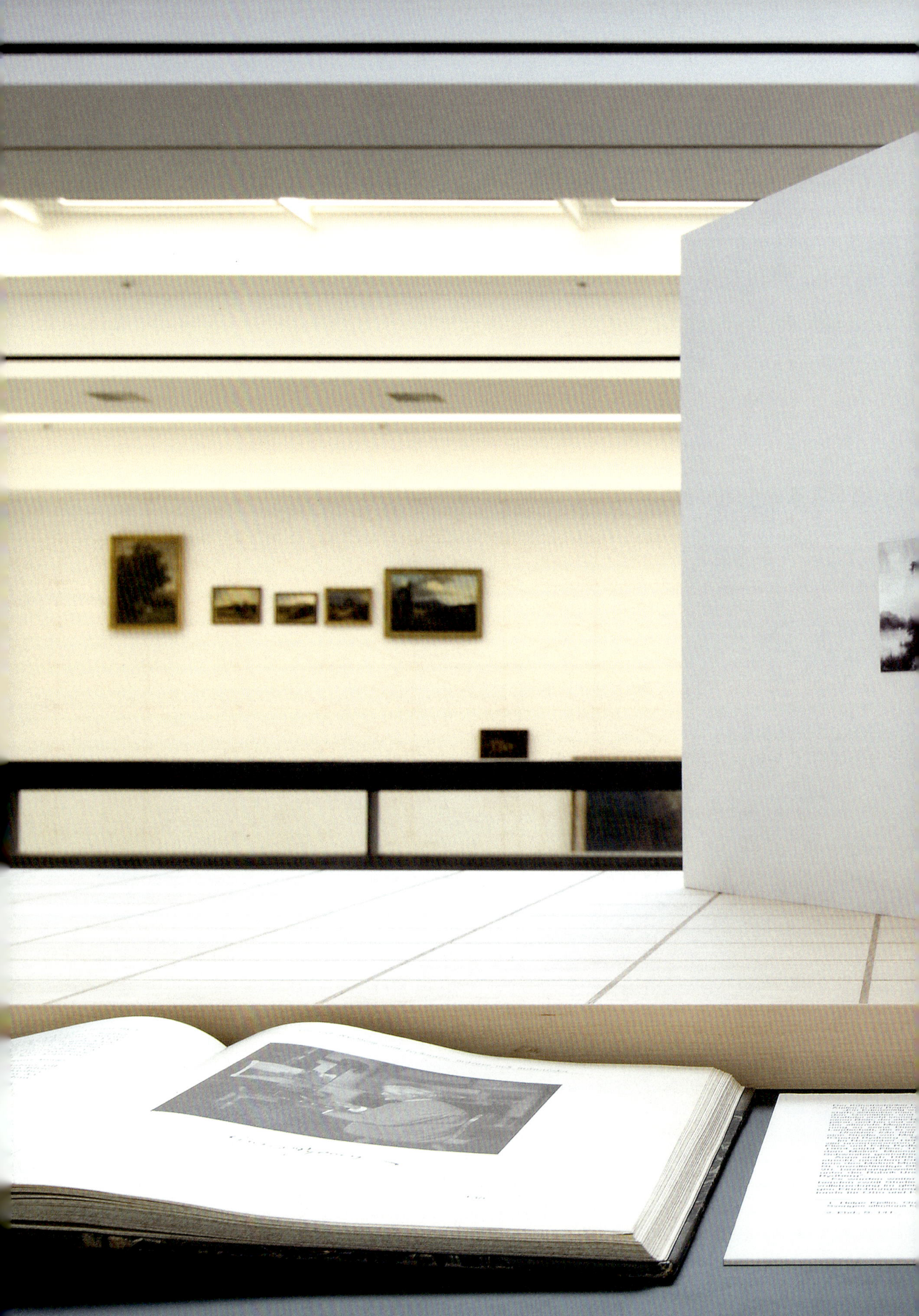

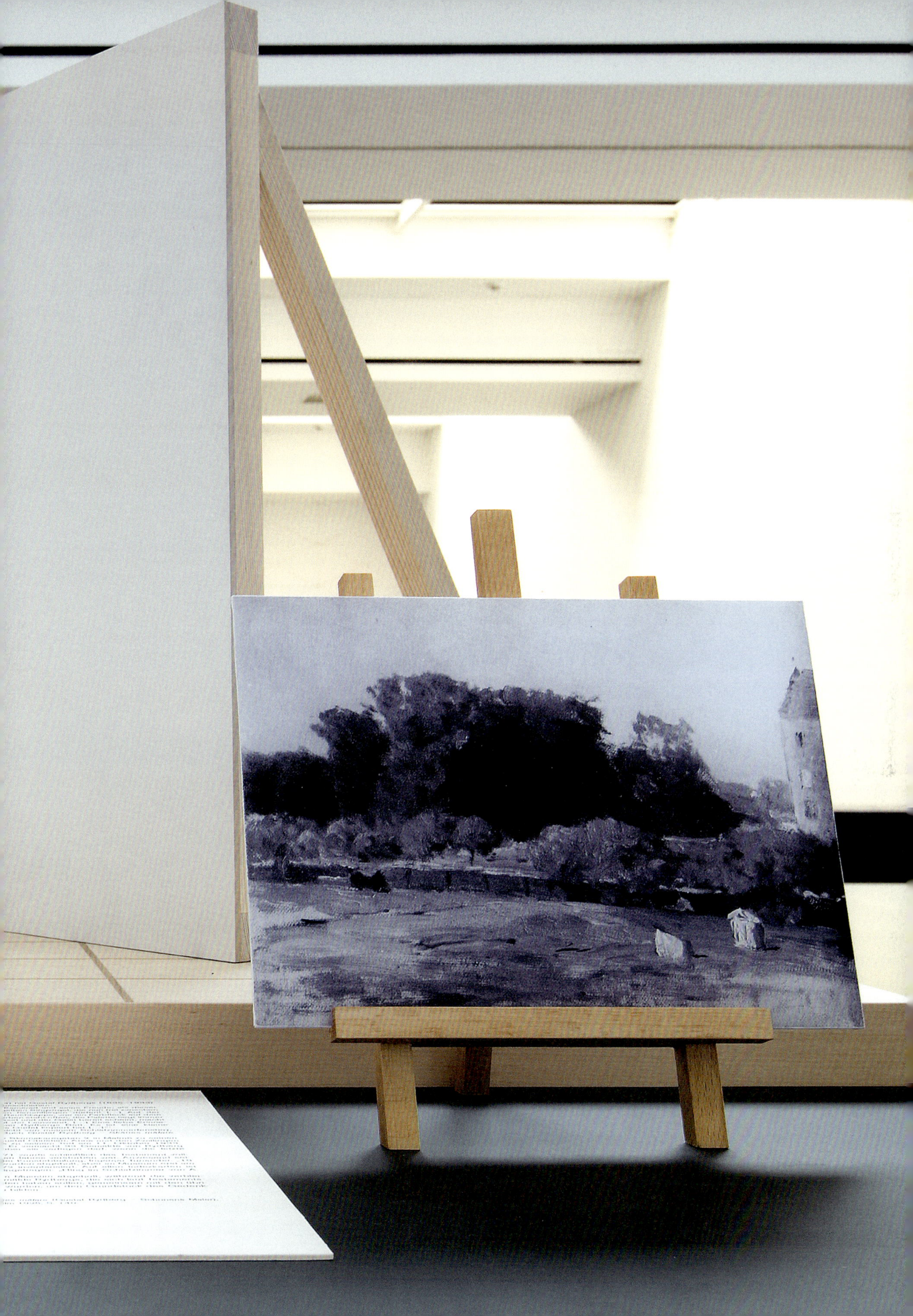

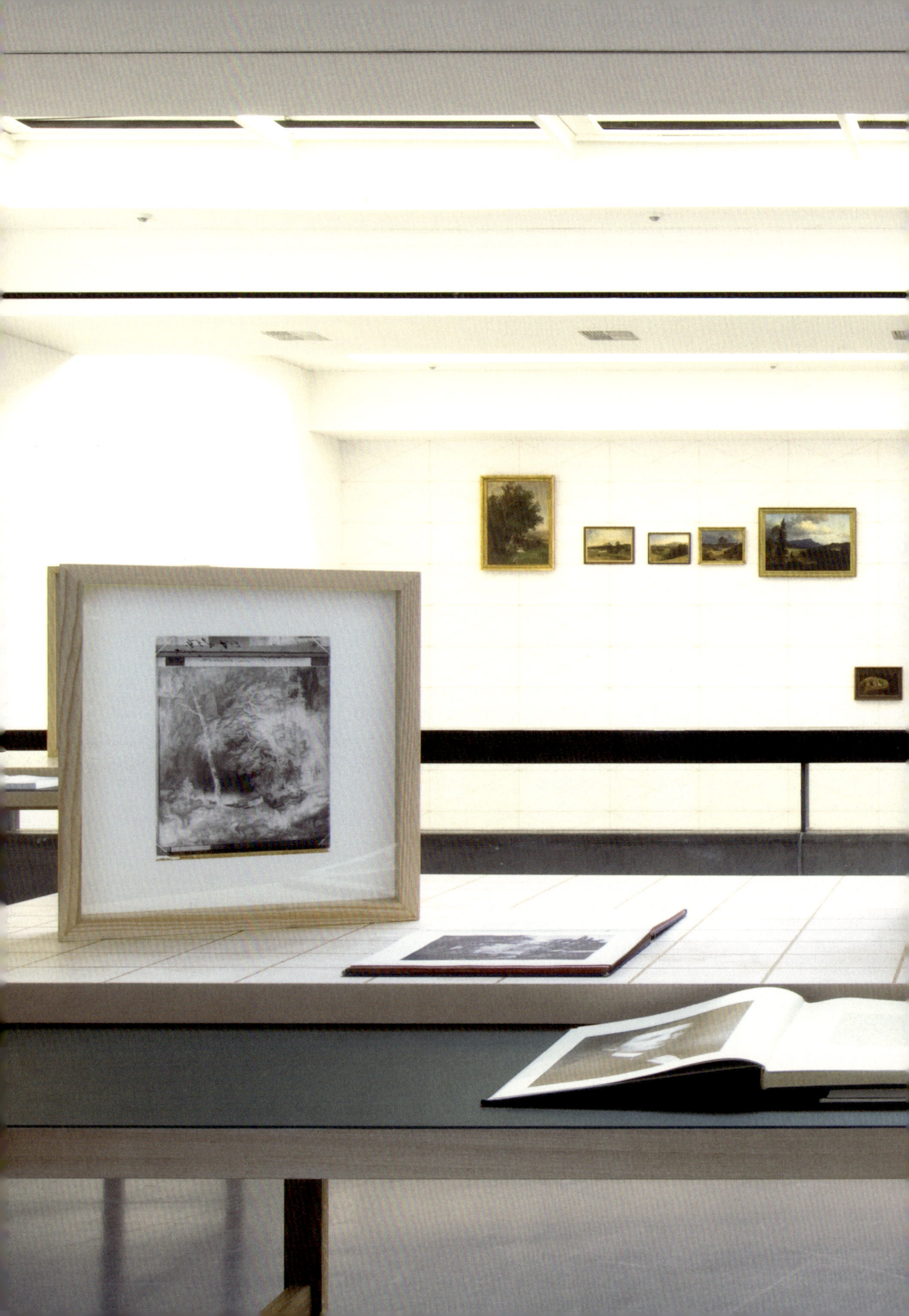

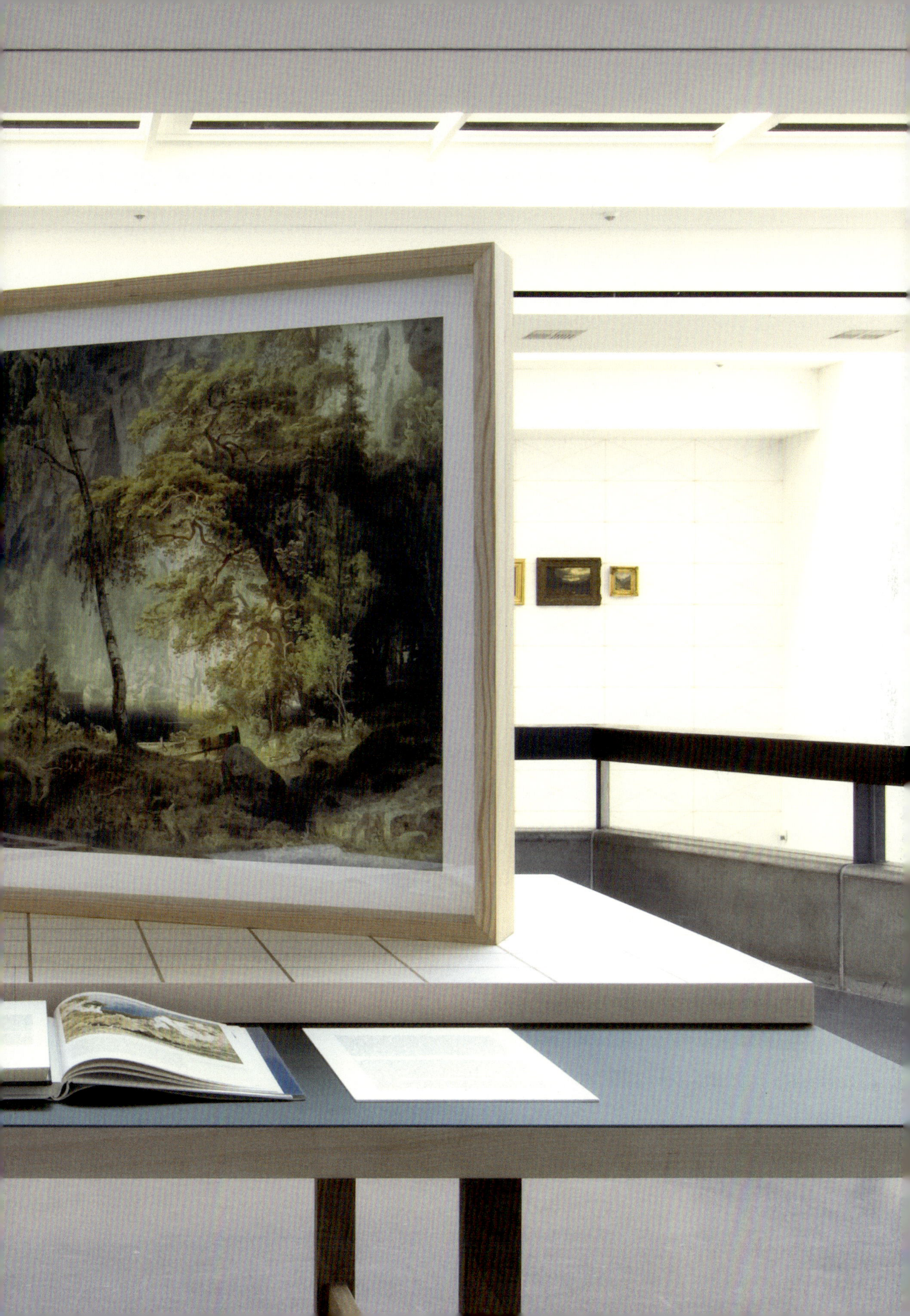

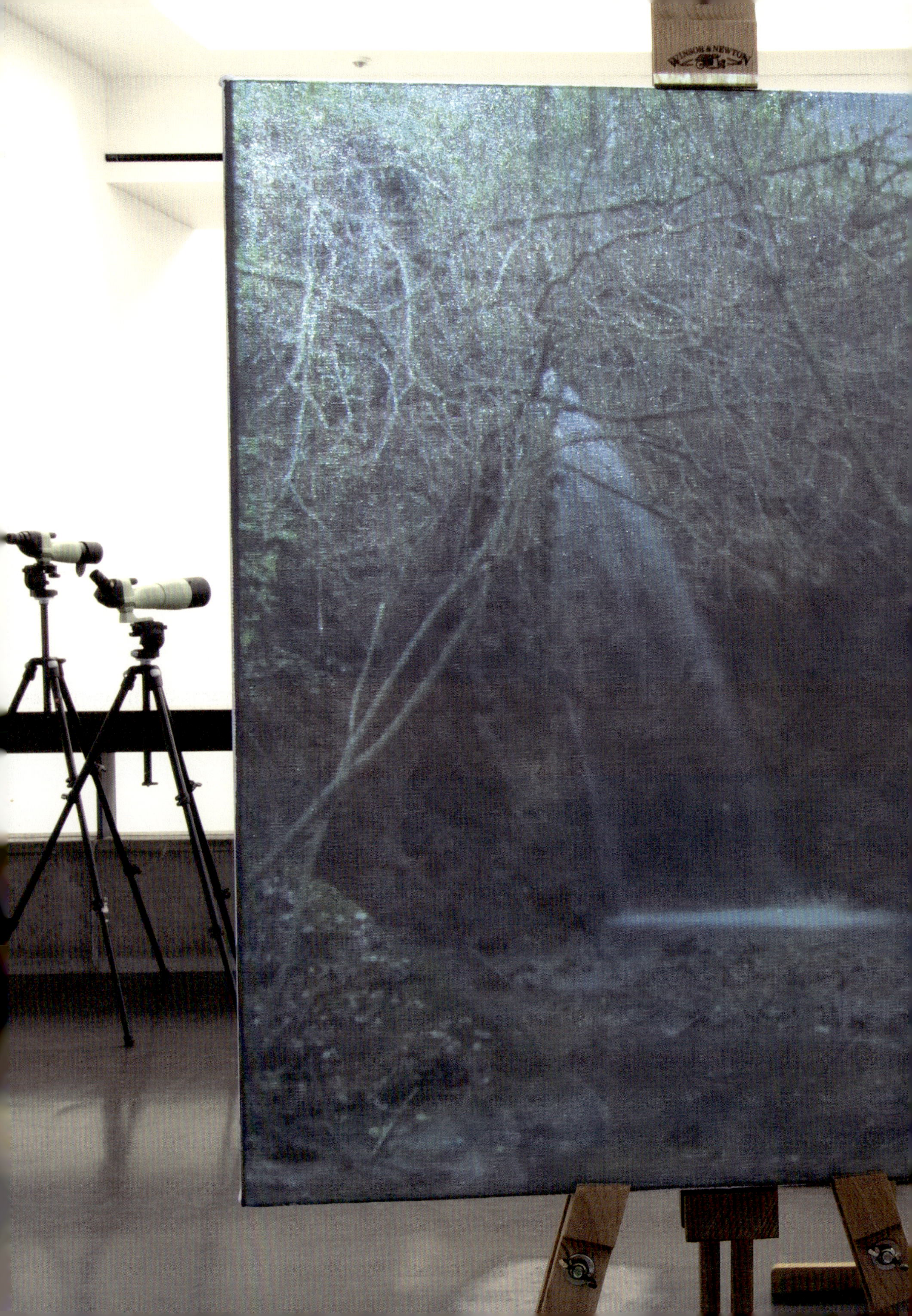

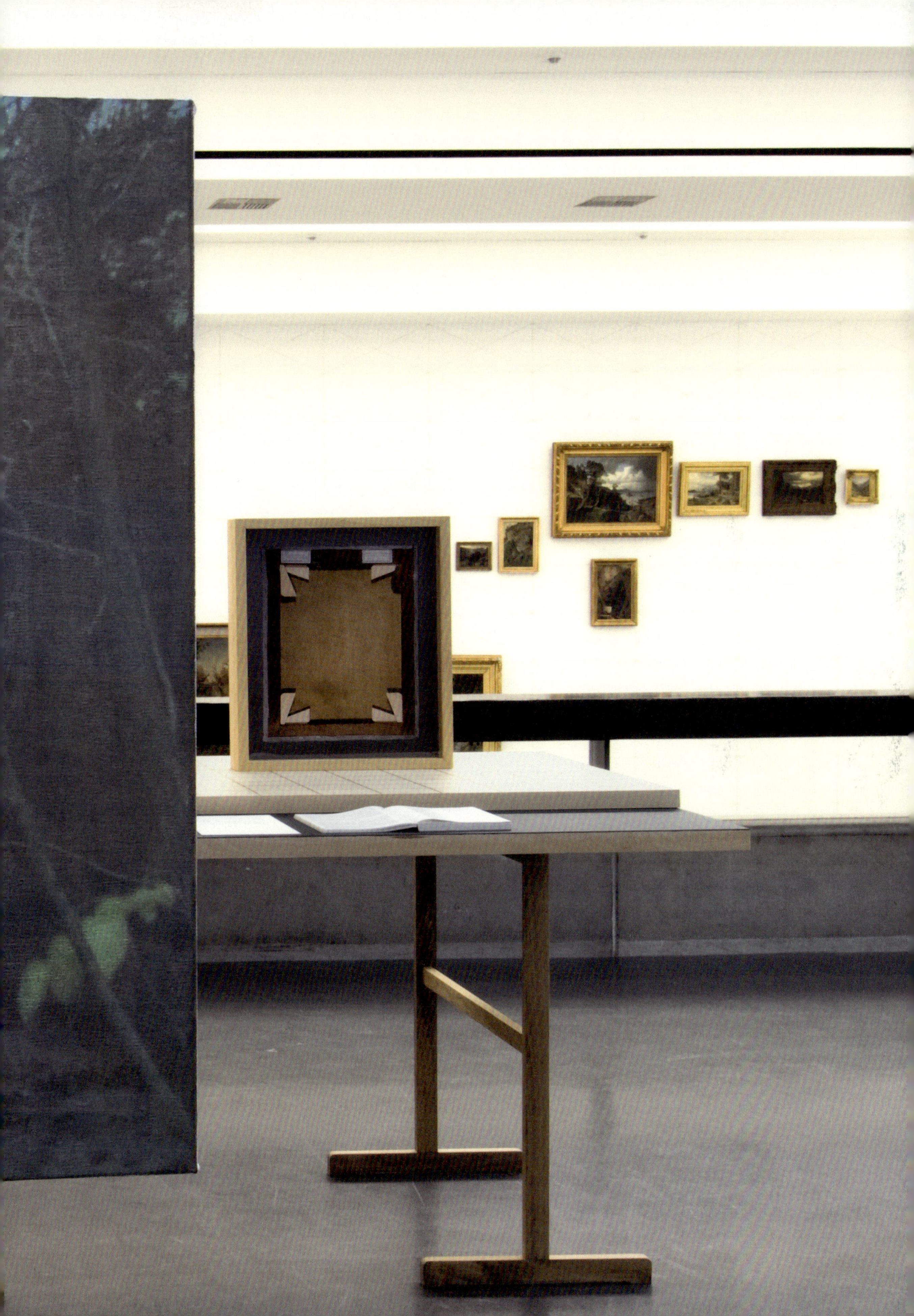

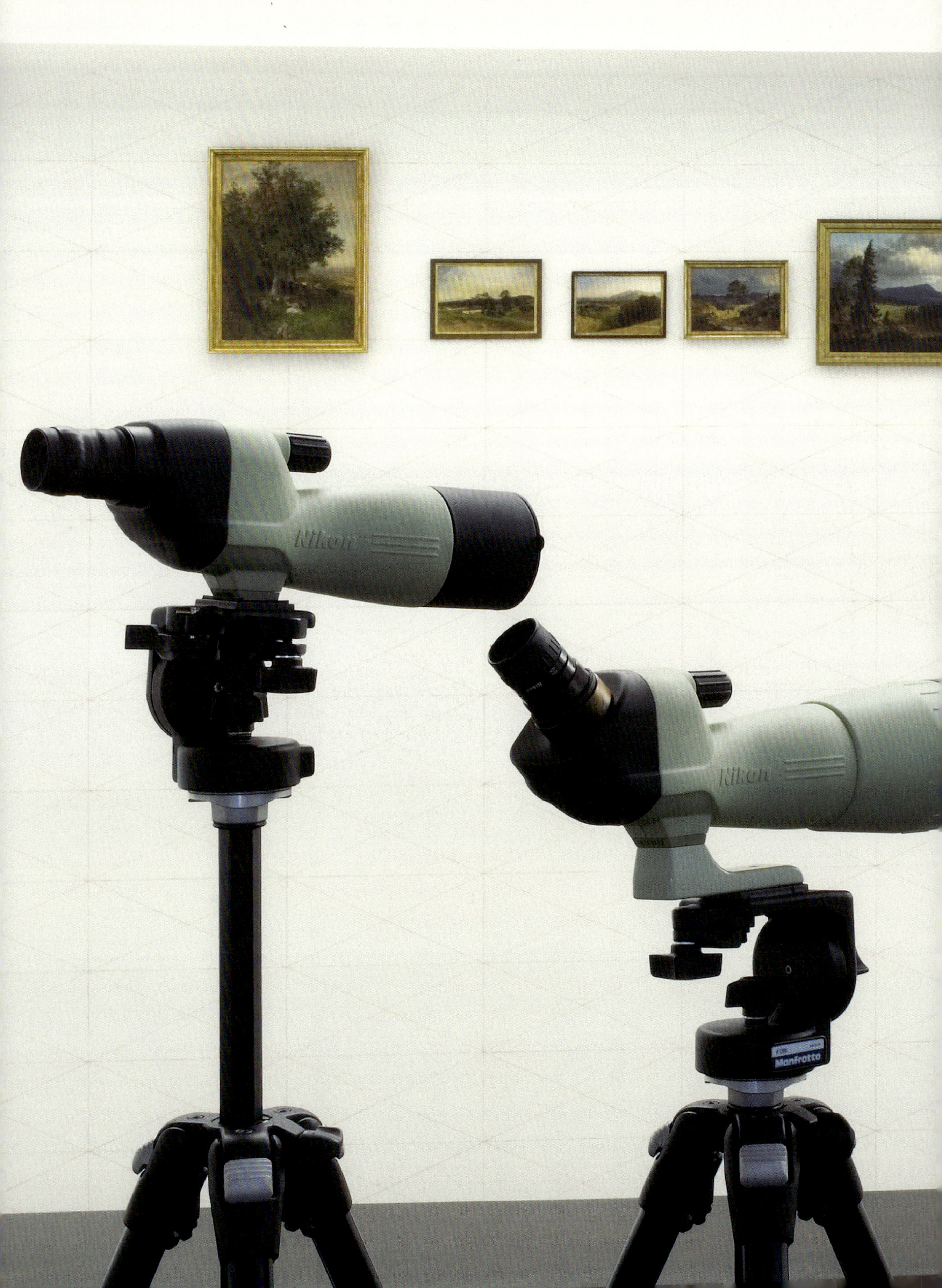

Für *Neanderthal Landscape* begab sich Matts Leiderstam auf die Spuren der Düsseldorfer Malerschule. Die weitläufige Installation in der Kunsthalle Düsseldorf umfasst zwei durch eine Empore architektonisch miteinander verbundene Räume: Der Emporensaal gleicht einem Archiv mit sieben Tischen, auf denen der Künstler mithilfe von Büchern, eigenen Texten und Fotografien, unterschiedlichen Reproduktionen historischer Gemälde und einer Computeranimation die Ergebnisse seiner Recherchen inszeniert. Auf zwei Staffeleien werden Aufnahmen der beiden Neandertaler Laubach-Wasserfälle projiziert, deren sanftes Rauschen sich im Ausstellungsraum ausbreitet. Durch Spektive auf der Empore können die Besucher ihren Blick über eine von Leiderstam komponierte »Landschaft« aus historischen Gemälden auf der großen Wand im Kinosaal schweifen lassen und sich in die Details einzelner Bilder vertiefen. Alle hier vertretenen Künstler studierten und arbeiteten einst in Düsseldorf und stehen somit in direkter oder indirekter Verbindung zur Lehre des Malers Johann Wilhelm Schirmer (1807–1863), der als Gründer der ersten Klasse für Landschaftsmalerei an der hiesigen Kunstakademie weltweit bekannt geworden ist. Die Suche nach geeigneten Motiven führte ihn und seine Studenten in das nahe gelegene Neandertal im Niederbergischen Land, wo sie ihre Freilichtstudien anfertigten. Der Einfluss der Düsseldorfer Malerschule sowie einzelner Motive insbesondere aus dem Neandertal lässt sich bis in die skandinavische, amerikanische und russische Landschaftsmalerei hinein verfolgen.

For *Neanderthal Landscape,* Matts Leiderstam set out along the trail of the Düsseldorf School of Painting. In the Kunsthalle this expansive installation comprises two rooms architecturally joined by a bridge-like gallery. The "Emporensaal" (gallery hall) resembles an archive with seven tables on which the artist displays the results of his researches with the aid of books, his own texts and photographs, various reproductions of historical paintings and a computer animation. Views of the two Laubach waterfalls in the Neanderthal are projected onto two easels, and their soft murmuring spreads throughout the exhibition space. With the aid of spotting-scopes, from the gallery visitors can let their gaze range across the "landscape" Leiderstam composed for the large wall of the "Kinosaal" (cinema hall) and become engrossed in the details of individual pictures. All the artists represented here studied and worked in Düsseldorf; they thus stand in direct or indirect relationship to the teachings of the painter Johann Wilhelm Schirmer (1807–1863), who became internationally known as the founder of the first class for landscape painting at the local art academy. The search for suitable motifs led him and his students to the nearby Neandertal in Lower Bergisches Land, to make their plein-air studies there. The influence of the Düsseldorf School of Painting, as well as individual motifs, particularly those from the Neandertal, can be traced all the way to Scandinavian, American and Russian landscape painting.

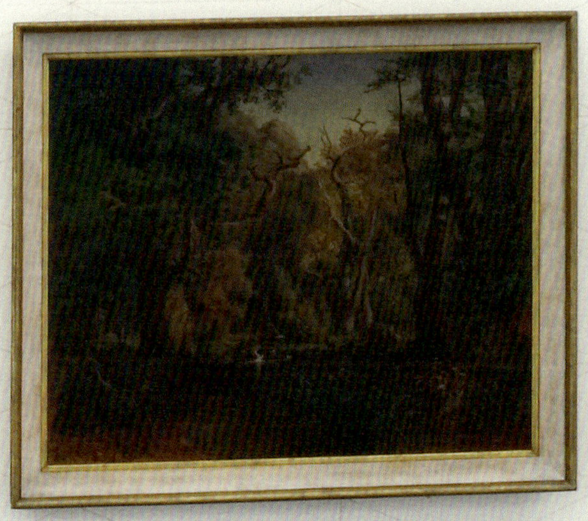

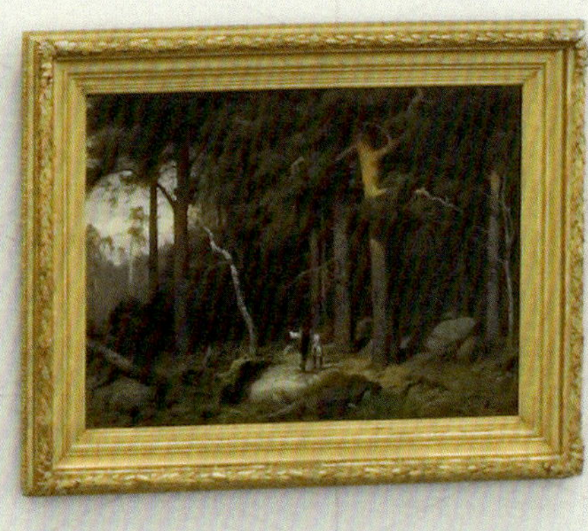

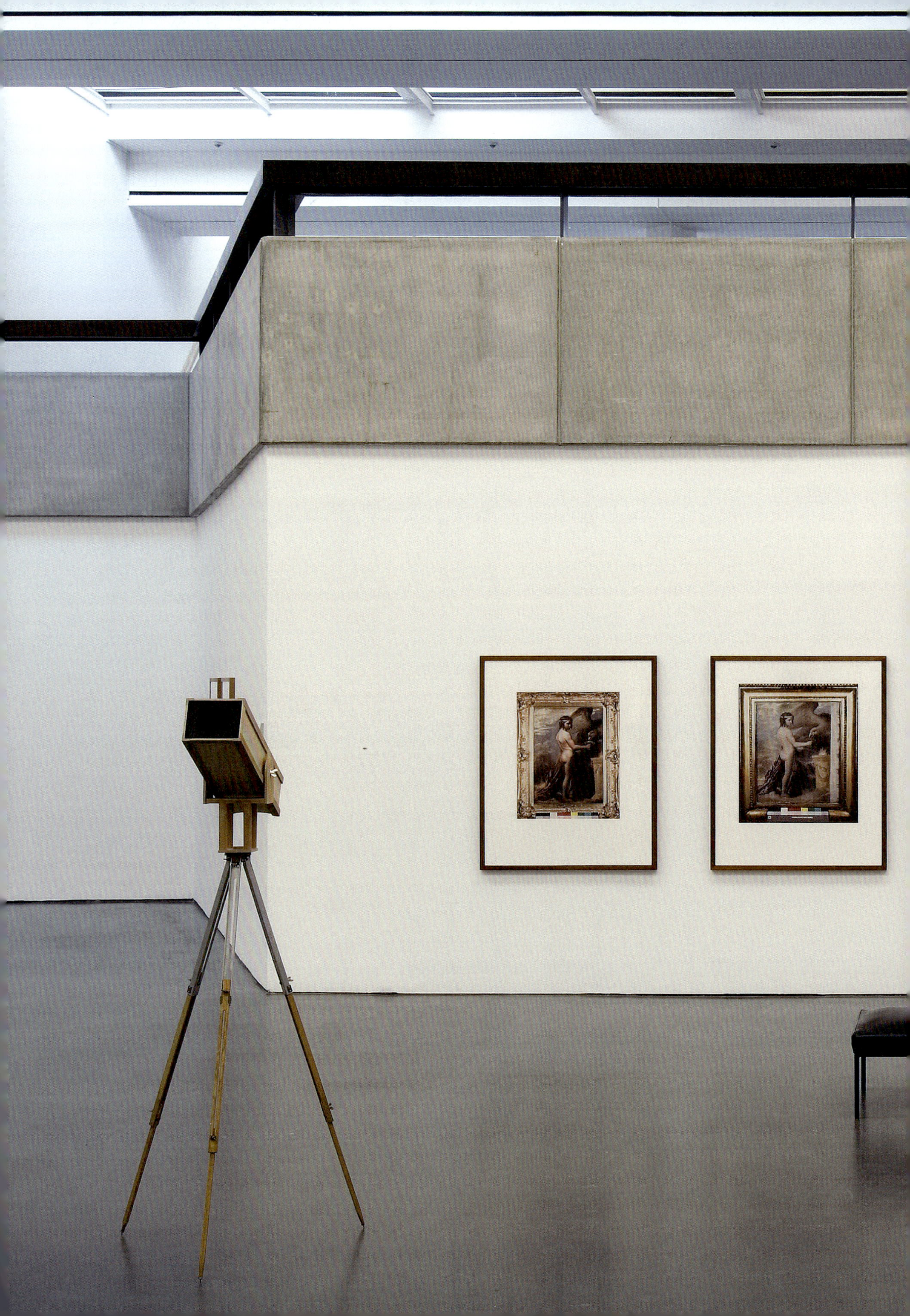

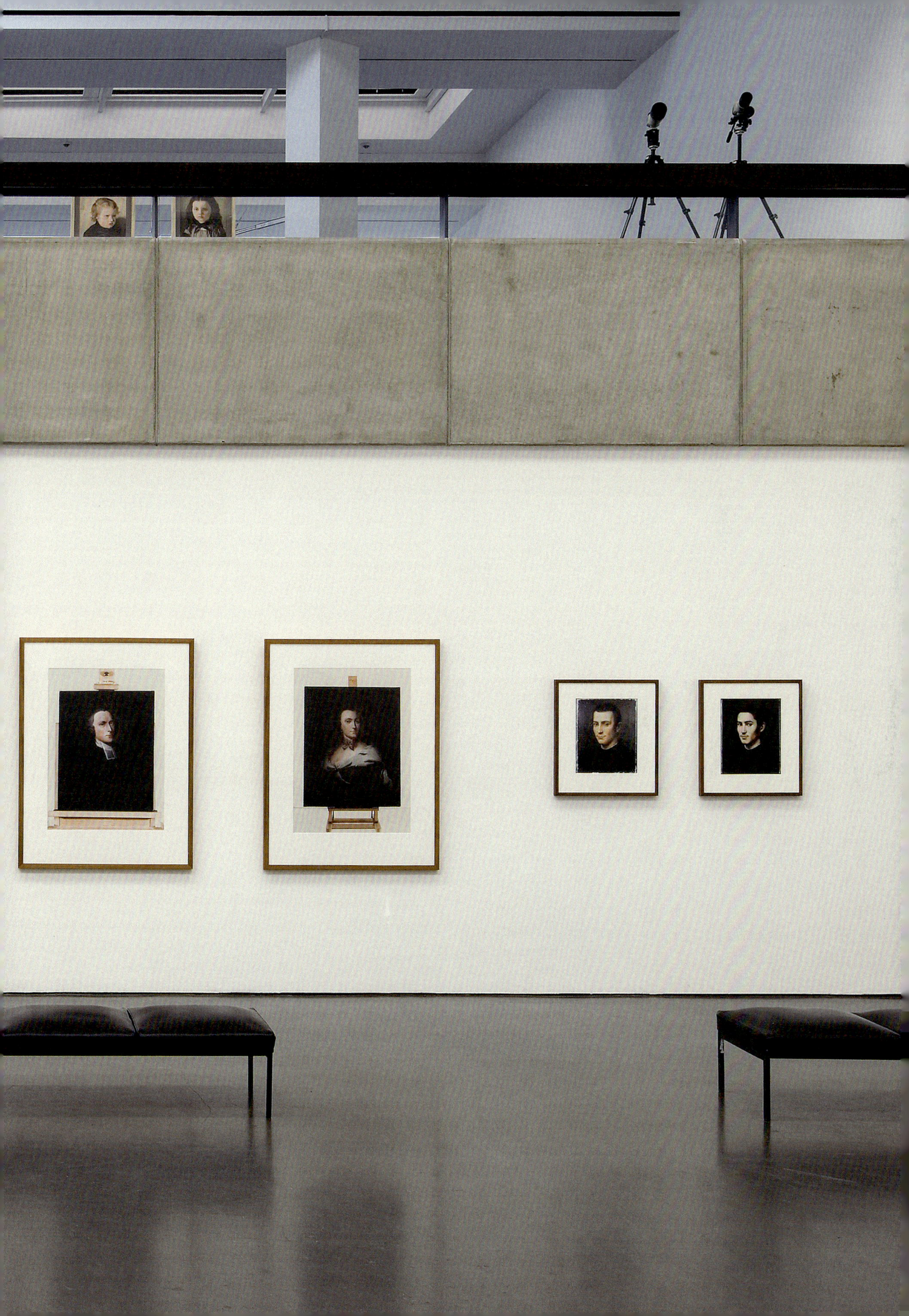

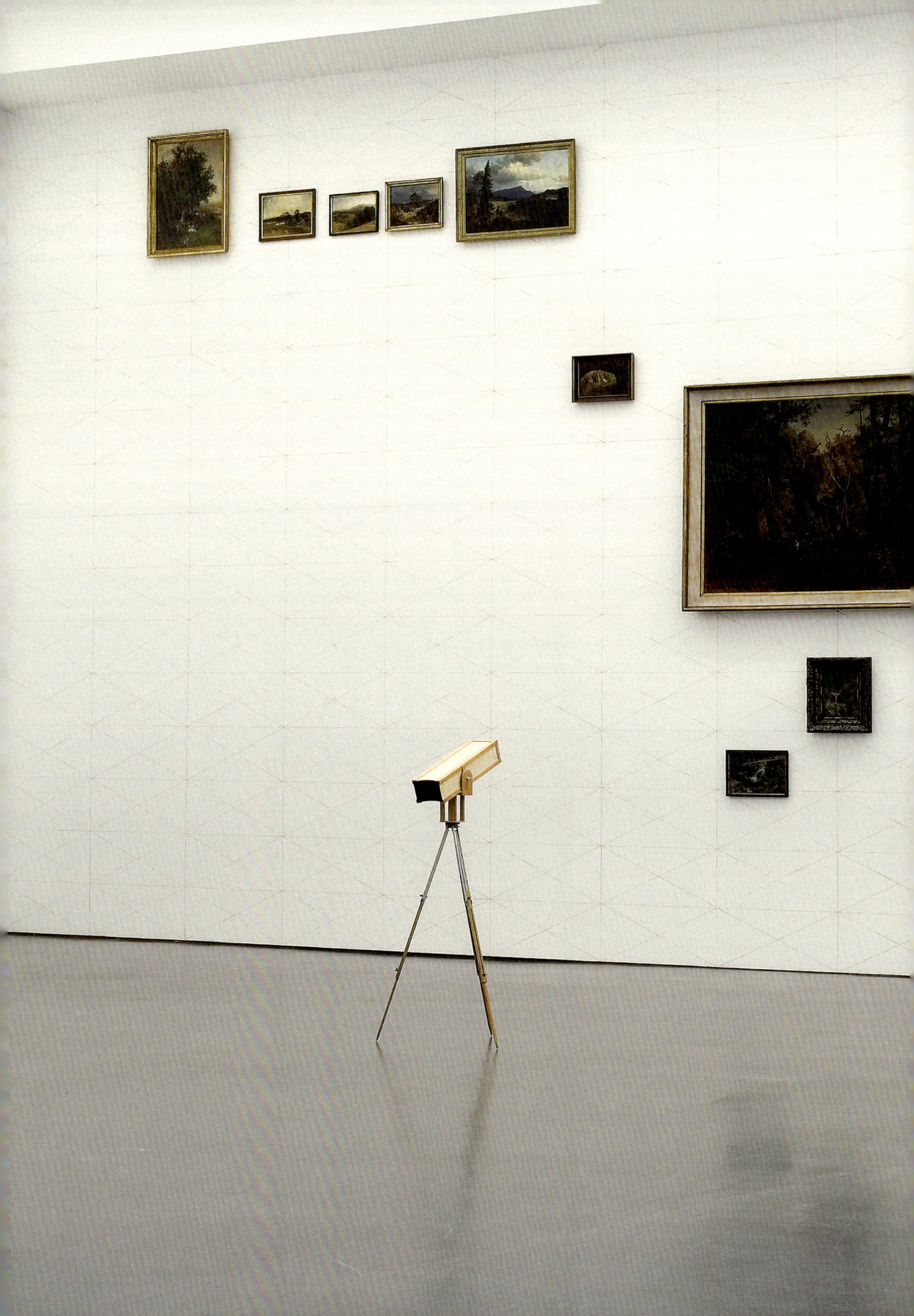

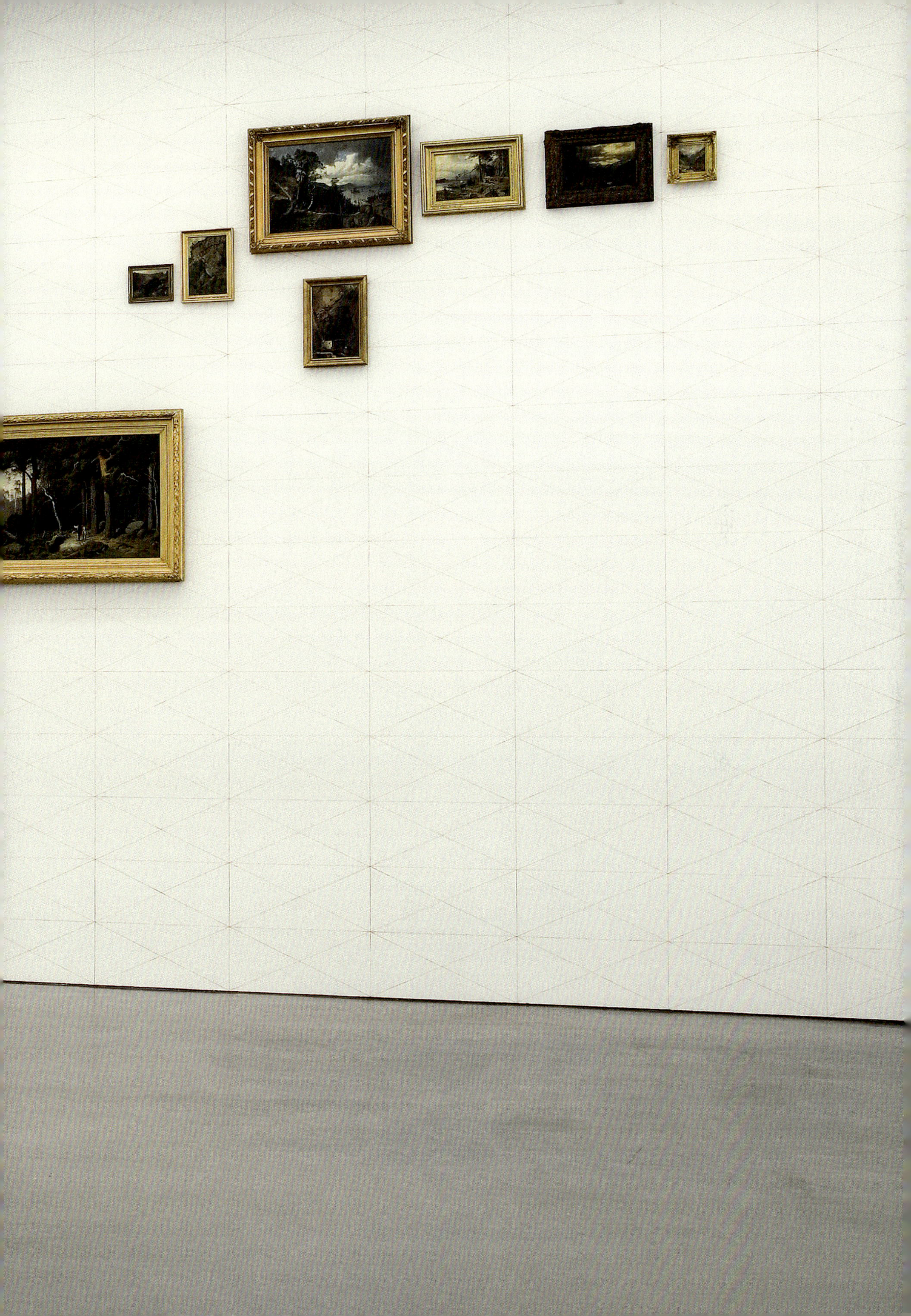

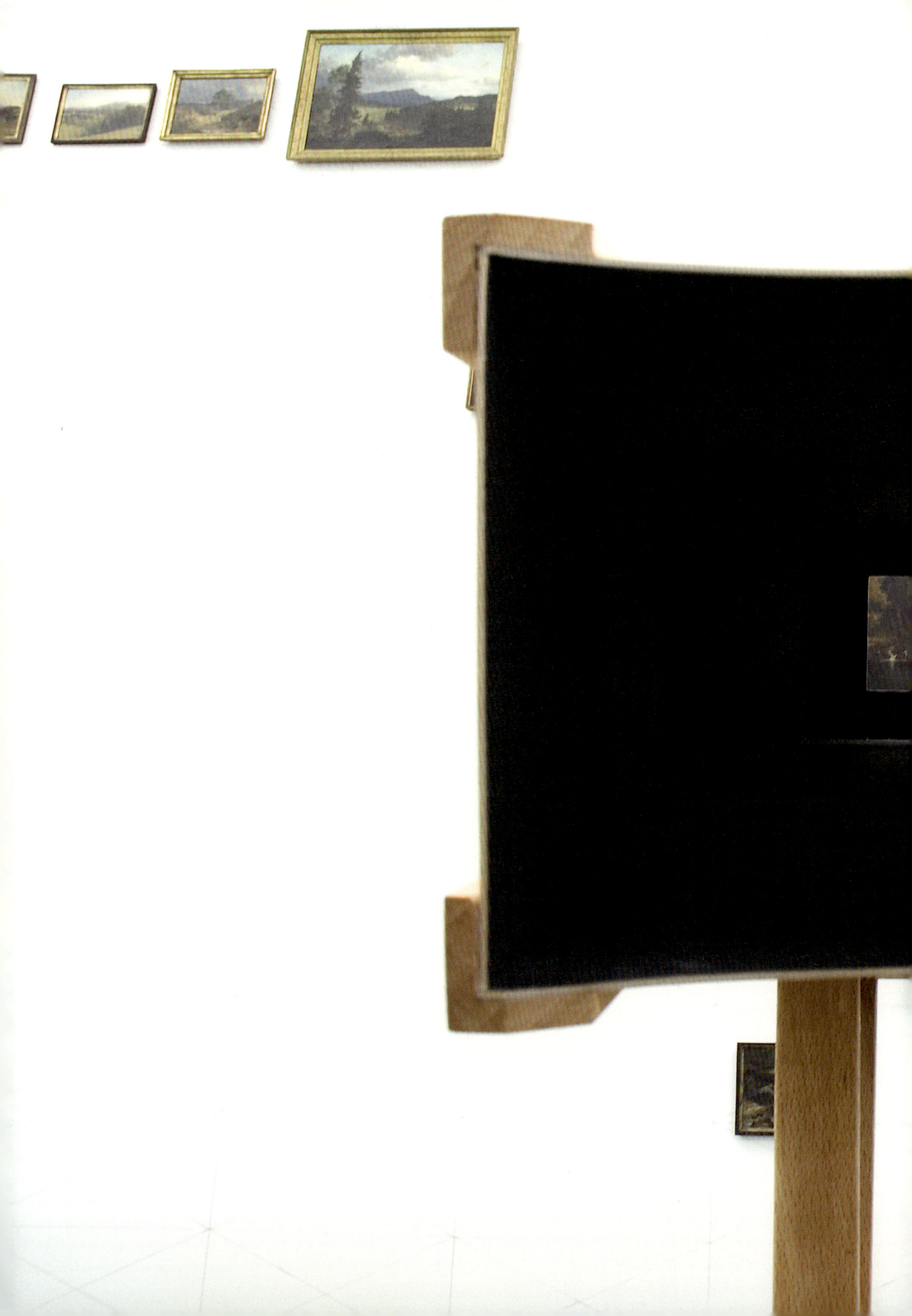

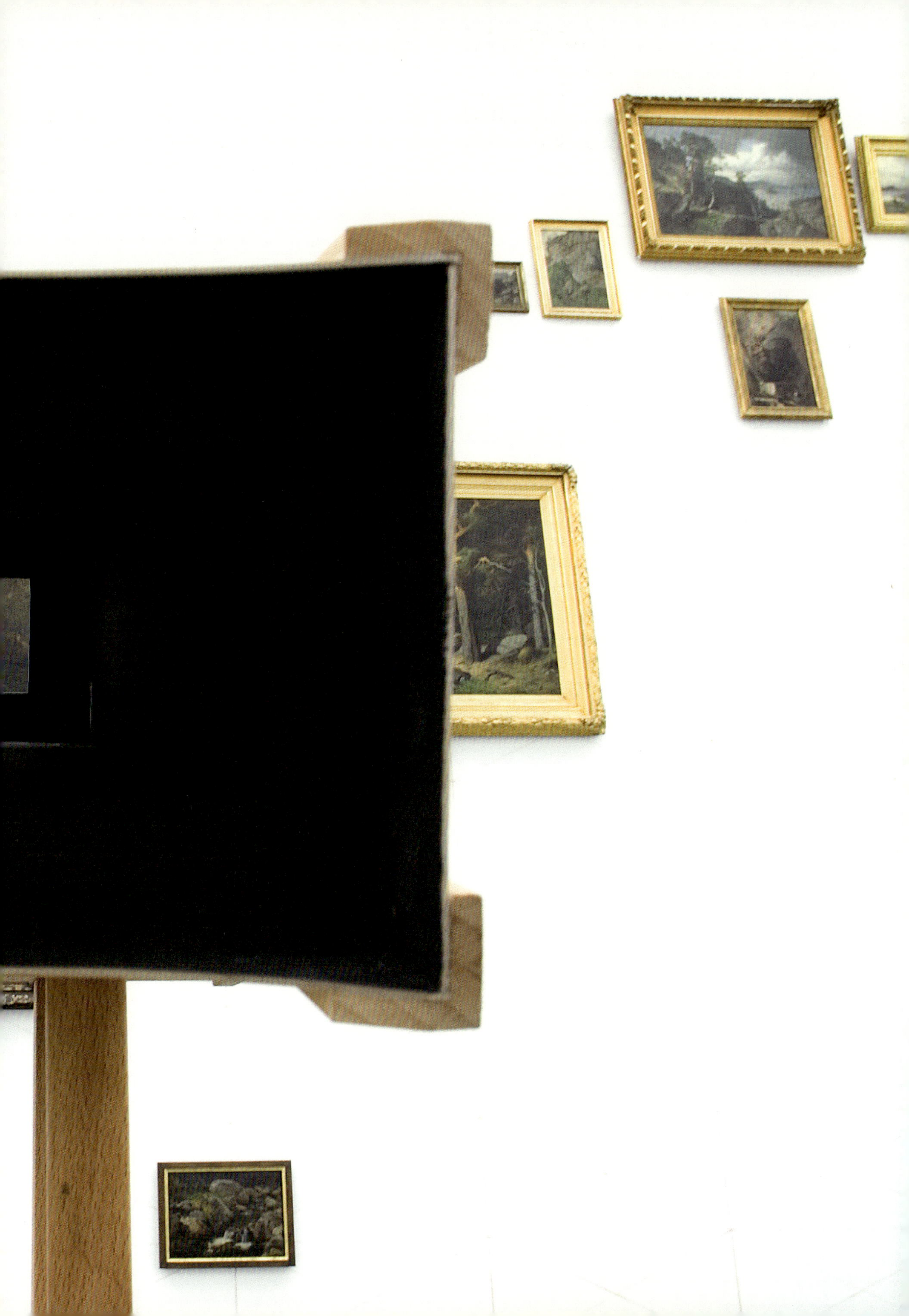

Neanderthal Landscape – Auf der Suche

Auszüge aus einer E-Mail-Konversation zwischen MATTS LEIDERSTAM, CHRISTOPH BENJAMIN SCHULZ und JARI ORTWIG während der Ausstellungsvorbereitungen

CHRISTOPH BENJAMIN SCHULZ: *Ich bin im Zentrum von Nordrhein-Westfalen aufgewachsen und erinnere mich an das Neandertal, weil ich dort mit meinen Eltern Spaziergänge gemacht habe. Die Atmosphäre war für uns aufregend und merkwürdig, denn wir wussten von den berühmten archäologischen Entdeckungen und vom »Neandertaler«, dessen Knochen dort 1856 gefunden worden waren. Die Bedeutung dieser Gegend für die Düsseldorfer Malerschule und die Landschaftsmalerei des 19. Jahrhunderts war uns allerdings nicht bewusst.*

MATTS LEIDERSTAM: Mein Weg ins Neandertal begann mit einem Besuch im museum kunst palast. Bettina Baumgärtel, Leiterin der Gemäldesammlung, führte mich in die Landschaftsbilder der Düsseldorfer Malerschule ein und wies mich auf einige Ölstudien von Johann Wilhelm Schirmer hin, die er um 1828–1830 im Neandertal gemacht hatte. Diese sorgfältig ausgeführten naturalistischen Studien beeindruckten mich sehr und warfen Fragen auf, die mich schließlich an den geografischen Ort als solchen führten. Bis dahin hatte ich nur eine ziemlich vage Idee von dieser Region gehabt, die auf dem beruhte, was wir in der Schule gelernt hatten, vielleicht in einer Stunde über Charles Darwins Evolutionstheorie – eine bildliche Vorstellung von einer idealisierten Höhle mit ausgegrabenen Knochen.

C B S: *Obwohl die archäologische Bedeutung des Neandertals in unseren Erinnerungen eine gewisse Rolle zu spielen scheint, wird sich deine Installation mit der vergleichsweise jüngeren und vorwiegend kunsthistorischen Vergangenheit des Orts beschäftigen. Dennoch scheint mir, dass die Idee oder der Vorgang, etwas auszugraben – beispielsweise aus der Kunstgeschichte –, auf der metaphorischen Ebene für deine Kunst eine wichtige Rolle spielt: Häufig bringst du vergessene oder unsichtbare Verhältnisse hinter den Fassaden der »offiziellen« Kunstgeschichte zum Vorschein.*

Ja, genau das interessiert mich. Aber im Unterschied zu einem Archäologen beschäftige ich mich nicht damit, spektakuläre Funde oder Beweise für wissenschaftliche Theorien ans Licht zu bringen. Für mich ist »Sehen« ein grundlegender Modus der Wahrnehmung, der sehr eng mit dem Prozess verknüpft ist, etwas zu erforschen, zu entdecken und schließlich auf künstlerische Weise sichtbar zu machen. Sehen ist nie eine unmittelbare Erfahrung, denn eine unmittelbare Erfahrung geht von der Annahme aus, dass alle Motivationen, Aspekte und Assoziationen durch den Akt des Sehens ausgelöscht werden. Die Zielsetzung meiner Arbeit besteht darin, aufzuzeigen, dass das, was wir sehen und wo wir in kultureller Hinsicht stehen, ein auf wechselseitigen Übereinkünften beruhendes Konstrukt ist, dass der Kontext keine unabänderliche Gegebenheit ist und daher ständig verhandelt werden muss. Der britische Kunsthistoriker Norman Bryson schrieb: »Die Tatsache, dass Kunstwerke eine andere Art von Raum einnehmen als andere Objekte in der Welt – ein Raum, der im Fall der Malerei von den vier Seiten des Rahmens begrenzt wird –, bedeutet, dass das Kunstwerk dafür geschaffen ist, sich sowohl von seinem Erzeuger als auch von seinem ursprünglichen Kontext zu entfernen, und von seinem Rahmen in andere Zeiten und an andere Orte befördert wird.« Wenn diese Gemälde also durch Zeit und Raum reisen, transportieren sie auch Geschichten – beispielsweise ihre Provenienzen, Spuren und zahlreiche Retuschen durch Restaurierungen, ebenso wie ihre Ausstellungsgeschichten. Das Werk, das wir sehen, ist nicht mehr identisch mit dem Werk, das das Atelier des Künstlers verließ.

C B S: *Das lässt mich an eine spezifische Eigenschaft deiner Arbeit denken, die ich besonders bemerkenswert finde. Obwohl es eigentlich keine etablierte »Form« der zeitgenössischen Kunst ist, sehe ich dich in gewisser Weise als Geschichtenerzähler.*

Vielleicht hast du recht. Durch meine künstlerische Praxis, in der rechercheartige Strategien eine wichtige Rolle spielen, bin ich immer wieder auf unglaubliche Geschichten gestoßen, von denen

In Search of the *Neanderthal Landscape*

Excerpts from the e-mail conversation between MATTS LEIDERSTAM, CHRISTOPH BENJAMIN SCHULZ and JARI ORTWIG during preparations for the exhibition.

CHRISTOPH BENJAMIN SCHULZ: *Having grown up in central Northrhine-Westphalia, I remember the Neandertal from walks there with my parents. The atmosphere was exciting and curious for us because we knew of the famous archeological discoveries, the "Neandertaler" whose bones were found there in 1856. But of course we weren't aware of its importance for the nineteenth-century landscape painting known as the Düsseldorf School.*

MATTS LEIDERSTAM: My path into Neandertal started with a visit to the museum kunst palast. Bettina Baumgärtel, the supervisor of the painting collection, introduced me to the museum's collection of landscape paintings of the Düsseldorf School and pointed out a couple of oil studies by Johann Wilhelm Schirmer, made in the Neandertal around 1828–1830. These carefully made naturalistic studies had a strong impact on me, triggering questions that finally led me to the geographical site itself. Before this I had only a rather vague idea of the region, built on what we learned in school, perhaps during a lecture about Charles Darwin's theory of evolution—an inner image of an idealized grotto with unearthed bones.

C B S: *Although in both our memories the archaeological importance of the Neandertal seems to play a certain role, your installation will deal with the site's comparatively recent and primarily art-historical past. Still, it seems to me that the idea or process of digging into something—as for instance the history of art— plays an important role on a metaphorical level for your work: you often unearth the forgotten or invisible background behind the facades of "official" art history.*

Yes, that's exactly what I'm interested in, but unlike an archaeologist I'm not concerned with bringing to light spectacular discoveries or evidence for scientific theories. To me, "Seeing" is an essential mode of perception, very much connected to the process of researching, discovering and finally making something visible in an artistic way. Seeing is never a direct experience, for a direct experience assumes that all motivations, aspects and associations would be erased from the act of seeing. Through my work I aim to point out that what we see, and who we are on a cultural level, is a construction based on mutual agreements, that the context is not given and therefore has to be negotiated constantly. The British art historian Norman Bryson has written, "The fact that works of art occupy a different kind of space from the space of other objects in the world—a space which in the case of painting is marked by the four sides of the frame—means that the work is built to travel away both from its maker and from its original context, carried by the frame into different times and places." Hence, these paintings carry stories with them when traveling through space and time—like their provenances, marks and multiple touchups from restorations, as well as their exhibition histories. The work we see is not the same as the one that left the artist's studio.

C B S: *This makes me think of a specific quality of your work that I find particularly striking. Although this isn't really an established "form" in contemporary art, I see you in a way as a storyteller.*

Maybe you're right. Through my artistic practice, where research-like strategies play an important role, I've more than once stumbled onto incredible stories that I feel should be told. Significant for many of these stories is that they leak into the present, creating a link between historical works of art and ourselves as contemporary viewers. I also see an exhibition, or an installation, as a form of narrative that carries its own drama. If paintings are shown at a respectful distance from each other, they are isolated. But installed in such a way that they refer to each other, they create a kind of narration. Then, stories informed by the visitors' fantasies can develop. The hanging of the landscape paintings on the big wall in the Kinosaal "tells" us that, although these works show different national landscapes, the Düsseldorf School shaped a common manner and a tradition of seeing landscape. They look like they were all painted from the same palette. Normally these paintings would

ich finde, dass sie erzählt werden sollten. Es ist bezeichnend für viele dieser Geschichten, dass sie bis in die Gegenwart hineinwirken und eine Beziehung zwischen historischen Kunstwerken und uns als zeitgenössischen Betrachtern herstellen. Und ich betrachte auch eine Ausstellung oder eine Installation als eine Form von Erzählung, die ihr eigenes Drama in sich trägt. Wenn Gemälde mit einem respektvollen Abstand zueinander gezeigt werden, wirken sie isoliert. Wenn man sie jedoch so installiert, dass sie sich aufeinander beziehen, dann erzeugen sie eine Art Erzählung. Dann können sich Geschichten entwickeln, die von den Fantasien der Besucher beeinflusst werden. Die Hängung der Landschaftsdarstellungen auf der großen Wand des Kinosaals »sagt« uns, dass die Düsseldorfer Malerschule – obwohl diese Bilder verschiedene nationale Landschaften zeigen – eine gemeinsame Darstellungsweise und eine Tradition der Anschauung von Landschaft geprägt hat. Sie sehen aus, als seien alle mit derselben Palette gemalt worden. Normalerweise würde man diese Gemälde auf eine Weise präsentieren, die den Blick oder den besonderen Stil der einzelnen Künstler betont. Durch meine Hängung scheinen sie zu einer fiktiven Landschaft – oder zu einer Geschichte – zu gehören.

C B S : *In diesem Zusammenhang erscheinen mir all die geöffneten Bücher interessant, die du in vielen deiner Arbeiten verwendest. Sie geben Hinweise darauf, dass diese sich aus einem Lektüreprozess heraus entwickelt haben und dass sie – im doppelten Sinne des Wortes – gelesen werden müssen und zur Lektüre zurückführen. Kannst du uns eine Vorstellung von der narrativen Dramaturgie der Präsentation von* Neanderthal Landscape *geben – und von den Geschichten, die der Installation zugrunde liegen?*

Bücher sind für mich Träger von Wissen, die kunsthistorische Daten und Fakten sowie Reproduktionen von Gemälden enthalten. In *Neanderthal Landscape* werden sie auf Tischen mit zwei verschiedenen Ebenen gezeigt: Die eine hat eine Oberfläche aus Linoleum, auf der die meisten geöffneten Bücher ausgelegt werden, damit man sie eingehend betrachten und lesen kann; die zweite, darüber liegende, die die untere teilweise überdeckt, hat eine Holzoberfläche mit einem Intarsien-Raster, auf dem andere, eher visuelle Materialien präsentiert werden. Jeder der sieben Tische wird einer anderen »Geschichte« gewidmet sein, die sich auf verschiedene Stränge meiner Recherche beziehen. Die Dramaturgie dieser Präsentation beruht vorwiegend auf Aussichtspunkten im Raum, von denen ich annehme, dass die Betrachter sie in der Installation wieder einnehmen werden.

C B S : *Die Tatsache, dass du dich für die individuelle Geschichte eines Kunstwerks interessierst, aber auch verschiedene Formen von Appropriation einsetzt, erinnert mich an eine Überlegung Walter Benjamins zur Übersetzung eines literarischen Werks von einer Sprache in eine andere: Er versteht das gut übersetzte Werk oder seine Lektüre nicht als etwas Defizitäres, sondern argumentiert im Gegenteil, dass die Übersetzung dem Werk zusätzliche Bedeutung verleiht und dem Leser daher etwas bietet, was das Original nicht besaß. Erscheint dir diese Vorstellung vertraut?*

Ja, in der Tat. Ich arbeite oft mit Nebeneinanderstellungen, um unterschiedliche Stadien eines Schaffensprozesses zu zeigen, manchmal aber auch, um verschiedene Stadien meiner Auseinandersetzung mit einem bestimmten Thema sichtbar zu machen, das ich recherchiere. Manchmal schließt das auch den Vergleich zwischen mehreren, voneinander abweichenden Reproduktionen eines Originals ein – etwa ein historisches Negativ oder eine Röntgenaufnahme eines Werks, das übermalt wurde. Der amerikanische Professor für neue Medien Henry Jenkins behauptet, dass wir gerade Benjamins »Zeitalter der technischen Reproduzierbarkeit« hinter uns lassen, um in einer globalen »Konvergenz-Kultur« zu leben, wo wir alle an einem »transmedialen Geschichtenerzählen« beteiligt sind, das sich über verschiedene Medien – darunter Bücher, Fernsehen und Internet – erstreckt. Es ist ein neuartiger Aneignungsprozess entstanden, der ungefähr so aussieht: Ich lade ein Internet-Bild aus einem bestimmten Kontext herunter, um es in einem anderen Zusammenhang zu verwenden. Dann wird es wieder hochgeladen, und der Prozess geht weiter. Es ist wie ein Stille-Post-Spiel mit Bildern, die sich mit jeder Übertragung verändern.

C B S : *Deine Arbeiten, vor allem deine Installationen, beziehen sich stets auf den Raum, in dem sie gezeigt werden. Sie reflektieren seine Proportionen, seine Grundfläche und sein Volumen. Die Architektur der Kunsthalle, die 1967 von den Architekten Beckmann und Brockes gebaut wurde, ist sehr speziell. Es würde mich interessieren, wie du mit dem Raum arbeiten und der Architektur Rechnung tragen willst.*

be presented in a way that emphasizes the individual artist's view or a particular style. Through my hanging they seem to belong to one fictive landscape—or one story.

C B S: In this context I find the opened books interesting that are used in many of your works. They offer hints that the works have developed from a process of reading, that they have to be read—in the double sense of the word—and they lead us back to reading. Can you give us an idea of the narrative dramaturgy of the display in Neanderthal Landscape—*and the storyline that underlies the installation?*

For me, books are containers of knowledge that carry facts and figures of art history as well as reproductions of paintings. In *Neanderthal Landscape,* they will be displayed on tables with two different levels: one with a linoleum surface, on which most of the opened books are laid out for a closer reading and a second one above, partly covering the one underneath, that has a wooden surface with an intarsia grid on which other visual material will be presented. Each of the seven tables will be dedicated to a different "story" relating to different tracks of my research. The dramaturgy of the display is mostly built on viewing points in the space that I presume the viewer will assume again in the installation.

C B S: The fact that you're interested in the individual history of an artwork but also employ various forms of appropriation reminds me of an idea Walter Benjamin expressed about the translation of a literary work from one language to another: he doesn't see the translated work or its reading as a diminishment. On the contrary, he argues that it brings additional meaning to the work and thus offers something to the reader that the original doesn't have. Does this idea seem familiar?

Yes, it does. I often use juxtapositions in order to show different stages of a process of creation, but sometimes also to show different states of my engagement with a certain subject during my research. And sometimes this also implies the comparison of various divergent reproductions of an original—an historic negative, for example, or an x-ray of a work that has been painted over. The American new-media professor Henry Jenkins suggests that we are presently leaving what Benjamin called "The Age of Mechanical Reproduction" to live in a global "Convergence Culture" where we are all involved in "transmedia storytelling" that spreads across various media, including books, television and the Internet. A new kind of appropriation process has been developed that may look like this: I download an Internet image from one context to use it for another context. Then it's uploaded yet again and the process goes on. It's like a whispering game with images that permanently change when being transferred.

C B S: Your work, and in particular your installations, always refer to the room in which they are shown. They reflect its proportions, the floor space and its volume. The architecture of the Kunsthalle by the architects Beckmann and Brockes (1967) is a very specific one. I'm curious to know how you intend to work with the space and take account of its architecture.

Seeing for me is first of all a bodily experience. So the architecture of a museum plays a significant role as it gives me directions I can work with, or against. The big wall in the so-called Kinosaal of the Kunsthalle is the core of the space installation. There are two important points to see it from: one is located just inside the doorway at the entrance of the room (S. 96–97), and the other, more spectacular one is located at the balcony in the Emporensaal (S. 92–93). There's no way one can avoid this particular experience of seeing built into the space. It's particularly great to work with this spatial disposition and the view the Emporensaal offers, as this experience mimics the way of seeing a central formation in a landscape—like standing on a lookout point in front of a waterfall or a mountain. In the center of the wall I'm planning to hang a large-format anonymous painting from around 1850, *Das alte Neandertal,* from the collection of the Neanderthal Museum. I'll then group other Düsseldorf School landscapes around this piece to form a landscape of landscape paintings. In the Emporensaal the spectator will find an archive-like installation consisting of seven display-tables. On and around this group of tables, I'll present, among other material, books on art, sketchbooks, photographs, paintings, films and texts mostly relating to the Düsseldorf School of landscape painting. I invite the viewers to view things with the aid of various optical instruments like magnifying glasses, spectives and a skiascope.

Sehen ist für mich vor allem eine körperliche Erfahrung. Die Architektur eines Museums spielt also eine wichtige Rolle, da sie mir Richtungen vorgibt, in die oder gegen die ich arbeiten kann. Die große Wand im sogenannten Kinosaal der Kunsthalle ist das Kernstück der Rauminstallation. Es gibt zwei wichtige Punkte, von denen aus man sie sehen kann: Der eine befindet sich im Eingangsbereich des Kinosaals (S. 96–97), und der andere, spektakulärere, auf dem Balkon des Emporensaals (S. 92–93). Man kann diese spezifische Erfahrung des in den Raum eingebauten Sehens nicht ausschalten. Es ist einfach großartig, mit dieser räumlichen Vorgabe und dem Blick zu arbeiten, den der Emporensaal bietet, weil dies die Erfahrung nachahmt, eine zentrale Formation in einer Landschaft zu betrachten – als stünde man an einem Aussichtspunkt vor einem Berg oder vor einem Wasserfall. Ich habe vor, in der Mitte der Wand ein großformatiges anonymes Gemälde aus der Zeit um 1850, *Das alte Neandertal,* zu hängen, das aus der Sammlung des Neanderthal Museums stammt. Um diese Arbeit werde ich andere Landschaften der Düsseldorfer Malerschule gruppieren, um eine Landschaft aus Landschaftsbildern zu formen. Im Emporensaal werden die Betrachter eine archivähnliche Installation vorfinden, die aus sieben Präsentationstischen besteht. Auf dieser Tischgruppe und um diese herum werde ich unter anderem Kunst- und Skizzenbücher, Fotografien, Gemälde, Filme und Texte zeigen, die sich überwiegend auf die Düsseldorfer Schule der Landschaftsmalerei beziehen. Ich lade die Betrachter ein, diese Dinge mithilfe verschiedener optischer Instrumente wie Vergrößerungsgläsern, Spektiven und einem Skiaskop anzuschauen.

C B S : *Kannst du etwas zu diesem merkwürdigen Instrument sagen?*
    Benjamin Ives Gilman (1852–1933), der Kurator am Boston Museum of Fine Arts war, schreibt in seinem Buch *Museum Ideals of Purpose and Method* von 1918 über das Skiaskop: »Das Wort bedeutet ›Schattenseher‹, der Betrachter, der aus und in den Schatten sieht [...], denn um gut zu sehen, ist es wichtiger, dass die Augen ausreichend beschattet sind, als dass das Objekt ausreichend beleuchtet ist.« Dieses Instrument ist eine Art Rahmer oder Sucher, der es dem Betrachter ermöglicht, sich auf ein einziges Objekt in einer musealen Präsentation zu konzentrieren – beispielsweise, um ein bestimmtes Bild anzusehen, das Teil einer Salon- oder Petersburger Hängung ist, was im 19. Jahrhundert die übliche Praxis war.

JARI ORTWIG: *In diesem Zusammenhang denke ich an die Ölskizzen des schwedischen Künstlers Gustaf Rydberg (1835–1933). Sie sind jetzt auf eine freistehende Wand als Teil der Installation* Neanderthal Landscape *gehängt. Die Arbeiten zeigen Täler und Berge, Felsen und bewölkten Himmel, ebenso wie Seestücke – typisch skandinavische Landschaftsmotive. In welcher Beziehung stehen Rydbergs Arbeiten zur historischen Landschaftsmalerei der Düsseldorfer Schule?*
    Man bezeichnete Rydberg als »Skånes målare« (Maler von Skåne). Alle Skizzen stellen Ansichten dieser Region im äußersten Süden von Schweden dar, die mich mehr an Dänemark oder Norddeutschland erinnert. Rydberg wurde in Düsseldorf von Hans Gude, einem Schüler von Schirmer, unterrichtet. Er blieb seinem Lehrer und den in Düsseldorf vermittelten Methoden treu, wurde aber mit zunehmendem Alter in seiner Malerei viel freier. Es interessierte mich sehr, wie seine Skizzen in die Sammlung des Malmö Konstmuseum gelangt waren. Die neunzehn Studien, mit denen ich arbeite, wurden 1971 erworben, und jede war versehen mit dem Vermerk: »Hing in Annas Schlafzimmer«. Anna war Rydbergs Nichte. Ich fand es ausgesprochen merkwürdig, dass sie umgeben von einem Arrangement aus den Skizzen ihres Onkels schlief.

J O : *Wie du bereits erwähnt hast, orientierten sich nicht nur skandinavische Maler am Vorbild der Düsseldorfer Schule; auch russische Künstler schufen Gemälde, die sich explizit auf ihre Prinzipien stützten.*
    Die Russen, die im 19. Jahrhundert nach Düsseldorf kamen, unterschieden sich in ihren Zielen und künstlerischen Idealen nicht sehr von den Skandinaviern. Doch ich bin auf eine jüngere, bemerkenswerte Geschichte gestoßen, die ich gerne auf einem der Tische ausbreiten wollte: Als »neureiche« Russen Ende der 1990er Jahre begannen, russische Landschaftsdarstellungen des 19. Jahrhunderts zu kaufen, um dadurch einem neuen Gefühl nationaler Identität Ausdruck zu verleihen, stieg die Nachfrage nach historischen Gemälden so sehr, dass es nicht genug Werke gab, um den Bedarf zu decken. Einige russische Händler glichen diesen Mangel aus, indem sie auf Auktio-

C B S: *Can you say something about that curious instrument?*

Benjamin Ives Gilman (1852–1933), who used to be a curator at the Boston Museum of Fine Arts, writes about the skiascope in his book *Museum Ideals of Purpose and Method* from 1918: "The word means 'shadow-seer', the seer from and into shadows" … "for a good seeing, it is more important that the eyes should be sufficiently shaded than that the object should be abundantly lighted." This instrument is a kind of framer or viewfinder that enables the visitor to concentrate on one single object in a museum display—for example, for seeing a certain painting that is part of a "salon" or "Petersburg" hanging, which was the state of the art in the nineteenth century.

JARI ORTWIG: *In this context the oil sketches by the Swedish artist Gustaf Rydberg (1835–1933) come to my mind. They're now installed on a freestanding wall as part of the installation* Neanderthal Landscape. *The works show valleys and mountains, rocks and clouded skies, as well as seascapes—typical Scandinavian landscape motifs. How do Rydberg`s works correlate with the historical landscape painting of the Düsseldorf School?*

Rydberg was called "Skånes målare" (the painter of Scania). All the sketches depict aspects of this region in the very south of Sweden, which reminds me more of Denmark or northern Germany. Rydberg was educated in Düsseldorf by Hans Gude, a student of Schirmer's. He remained loyal to his teacher and to the methods learned in Düsseldorf but became much freer in his painting when he grew older. I became very interested in how his sketches came into the collection of Malmö Konstmuseum. The nineteen studies I am working with were acquired in 1971, and each was described as "hanging in Anna's bedroom." Anna was Rydberg's niece. I found it most curious that she was sleeping within an arrangement of her uncle's sketches.

J O: *As you mentioned before, not only Scandinavian painters were geared to the works of the Düsseldorf School, but in a quite explicit manner Russian artists also created paintings based on its principles.*

The Russians who came to Düsseldorf in the nineteenth century did not differ much from the Scandinavians in their aims and artistic ideals. But there is a more recent and striking story that I stumbled on and found worth relating on one of the tables: when so-called newly rich Russians started to acquire nineteenth-century Russian landscapes in the late 1990s as a means of proclaiming a new sense of national identity, demand for historical paintings became so great that there weren't enough works to fill the need. Some Russian art dealers compensated for the deficit by buying minor Düsseldorf paintings at auctions and "refitting" them with traditional Russian attributes—or painting over the non-Russian features. But these re-worked works didn't stay in Russia. A couple of years later the same paintings were offered by a different auction house in the West—now as being Russian. Those dealers who sold them were making a great deal of money out of these fakes before the scandal was revealed a couple of years ago. It's very interesting how easily a national landscape can be transformed into the landscape of another country. I love it when the past leaks into the present in such a curious way.

J O: *One of the recurrent motifs in many of your works is the waterfall. In the new installation the double projection of two waterfalls is particularly noticeable. What's the story behind these waterfalls in* Neanderthal Landscape?

This story starts with my becoming interested in the fact that the Neandertal once was used as a kind of test site for young artists from the Düsseldorf Academy for their training in landscape painting. Today, not much of this beautiful creek remains. After the quarrymen removed the huge limestone cliffs with their famous grottos that carried such beautiful names as "Engelskammer," "Feldhofer Kirche," "Löwengrotte," "Neanderhöhe" or "Teufelskammer," the historical site as we know it from paintings was irretrievably destroyed. Only one of these historic sites, the "Laubach-fall," remains. Hanna Eggerath, a local historian, took me to this waterfall. She lives not far from the valley and has created a register of artists who came here in the nineteenth century to study and to paint. She pointed out the art historical importance of this site, and we looked at the paintings of Caspar Scheuren (1810–1887) reproduced in her book on this topic. Standing together in front of the waterfall, we compared the view from today with that of yesterday. Later I returned on several

nen unbedeutendere Düsseldorfer Gemälde kauften und diese mit traditionellen russischen Eigenschaften »ausstatteten« – oder die nicht russischen Merkmale übermalten. Doch diese überarbeiteten Werke blieben nicht in Russland. Einige Jahre später wurden dieselben Gemälde von einem anderen Auktionshaus im Westen angeboten – und zwar nun als russische. Die Händler, die sie verkauften, machten mit diesen Fälschungen sehr viel Geld, bevor der Skandal vor ein paar Jahren aufgedeckt wurde. Es ist sehr interessant, wie leicht eine nationale Landschaft in die Landschaft eines anderen Staates transformiert werden kann. Ich finde es großartig, wenn die Vergangenheit auf eine so seltsame Weise in die Gegenwart hineinspielt.

J O: *Ein wiederkehrendes Motiv in vielen deiner Arbeiten ist der Wasserfall. In der neuen Installation ist die Doppelprojektion von zwei Wasserfällen besonders markant. Welche Geschichte steckt hinter diesen Wasserfällen in* Neanderthal Landscape?

Diese Geschichte beginnt mit meinem Interesse an der Tatsache, dass das Neandertal früher als eine Art Übungsgelände für junge Künstler diente, die an der Düsseldorfer Kunstakademie in Landschaftsmalerei ausgebildet wurden. Heute ist von dem schönen Flusstal nicht mehr viel übrig. Nachdem die Steinbrucharbeiter die riesigen Kalksteinfelsen mit ihren berühmten Grotten, die so poetische Namen wie »Engelskammer«, »Feldhofer Kirche«, »Löwengrotte«, »Neanderhöhe« oder »Teufelskammer« trugen, abgebaut hatten, war der historische Ort, den wir aus der Malerei kennen, unwiederbringlich zerstört. Nur einer dieser historischen Orte, der »Laubachfall«, existiert noch. Hanna Eggerath, eine Historikerin aus der Region, zeigte mir diesen Wasserfall. Sie lebt in der Nähe des Neandertals und hat ein Verzeichnis der Künstler erstellt, die im 19. Jahrhundert hierher kamen, um zu studieren und zu malen. Sie erläuterte die kunsthistorische Bedeutung dieses Ortes, und wir sahen uns die Gemälde von Caspar Scheuren (1810–1887) an, die in ihrem Buch zu diesem Thema reproduziert sind. Wir standen zusammen vor dem Wasserfall und verglichen den heutigen Anblick mit der historischen Ansicht. Später kam ich mehrmals zurück, um zu zeichnen und zu fotografieren, da ich eine zeitgenössische Arbeit über den historischen Wasserfall machen wollte. Eines Tages, als ich den »Laubachfall« wieder einmal besichtigte, führte er kein Wasser. Ich fragte mich noch, was passiert sein mochte, als ich das Wasser auf einmal wieder fließen hörte. Ich hob meinen Blick vom Skizzenbuch und sah, wie sich der Wasserfall wieder erholte. Es dauerte nicht länger als zehn Minuten, bis er seine ganze Kraft zurückgewonnen hatte. Das brachte mich auf die Frage, wer das Wasser kontrolliert, und sie führte mich zu einem nahe gelegenen Steinbruch, wo ich erfuhr, dass das Wasser für die Reinigung der Steine genutzt wird. Und man sagte mir auch, dass es einen weiteren »Laubachfall« in der Nähe gebe, der von demselben Bach gespeist wird wie der untere – ein Wasserfall, der 1984 nach Scheurens Gemälde des Laubachfalls von 1842 rekonstruiert wurde.

C B S: *Jetzt, wo die Installation aufgebaut ist, wird ihre Eigenschaft als ein erweitertes Landschaftsbild, das die Besucher betreten und in dem sie umhergehen können, für mich sehr offenkundig.*

Die Beziehung zwischen dem Bildraum eines Gemäldes und dem physischen Raum, in dem es betrachtet wird, gehört seit Leon Battista Albertis wegweisendem Traktat »Über die Malkunst«, das 1435–1436 entstand, zu den zentralen Themen der Kunstgeschichte. Das Gemälde ist wie ein Fenster und bildet eine Art Rahmen, durch den wir in eine andere Welt hineinschauen, behauptet Alberti. Er argumentiert, dass der Betrachter exakt gegenüber dem Fluchtpunkt des Gemäldes stehen müsse, um das Motiv richtig sehen zu können. Ein solcher »Blickpunkt« ist auch in vielen meiner Installationen angelegt, und ich versuche, dem Betrachter dies bewusst zu machen. In *Neanderthal Landscape* gibt es einen zentralen Standpunkt, von dem aus man die gesamte Installation ziemlich vollständig überblicken kann. Dieser befindet sich an der Rückwand des Emporensaals, in der Nähe des Eingangs, wo ich ein Spektiv hinter einer Holzbank platziert habe. *Seen from Here* – so der Titel der Ausstellung – und durch das Spektiv betrachtet, wird die Installation zu einem zweidimensionalen Bild. Gleichzeitig kann man sehen, dass die Raumtiefe durch die Anordnung der Tische gestaffelt wird, und man kann Leute sehen, die sich in dieser künstlerischen Landschaft hin und her bewegen.

occasions to make some drawings and take photographs, since I wanted to make a contemporary work related to the historical waterfall. One day, when I visited the "Laubachfall" again, there was no water running through it. I was still wondering what might have happened when suddenly I heard water streaming. I lifted my head from my sketchbook and witnessed the waterfall recovering itself. It took no longer than ten minutes until it had reached its full power. I then began asking questions about who controls the water, which led me to a nearby quarry where I learned the water was used for cleaning stone. I also learned that another "Laubachfall" is located nearby, connected to the same brook as the lower one—a waterfall reconstructed in 1984 from Scheuren's painting of the Laubachfall from 1842.

C B S: *Now that the installation is finally complete, its quality as an extended landscape painting that visitors can enter and in which they can take a walk becomes very apparent to me.*

The relation between the pictorial space inside a painting and the physical room in which it is seen has been one of art history's central concerns since Leon Battista Alberti's groundbreaking treatise "On Painting," written in 1435–1436. As a window, Alberti argues, a painting is a kind of frame through which we look into a different world. He argues that the viewer needs to stand exactly opposite to the vanishing point of the painting to be able to see the motif correctly. Such a "point of view" is inherent in many of my installations, and I try to make the viewer become aware of this. In *Neanderthal Landscape* I have one central viewing point from which more or less the whole installation can be overseen. This is located at the back wall of the "Emporensaal," close to the entrance of the room, where I placed a spective behind a wooden bench. *Seen from Here*—as the whole exhibition is called—and seen through this spective, the installation becomes a two-dimensional image. At the same time, one can see that the arrangement of tables sequences the depth of the room, and one can see people moving back and forth in this artistic landscape.

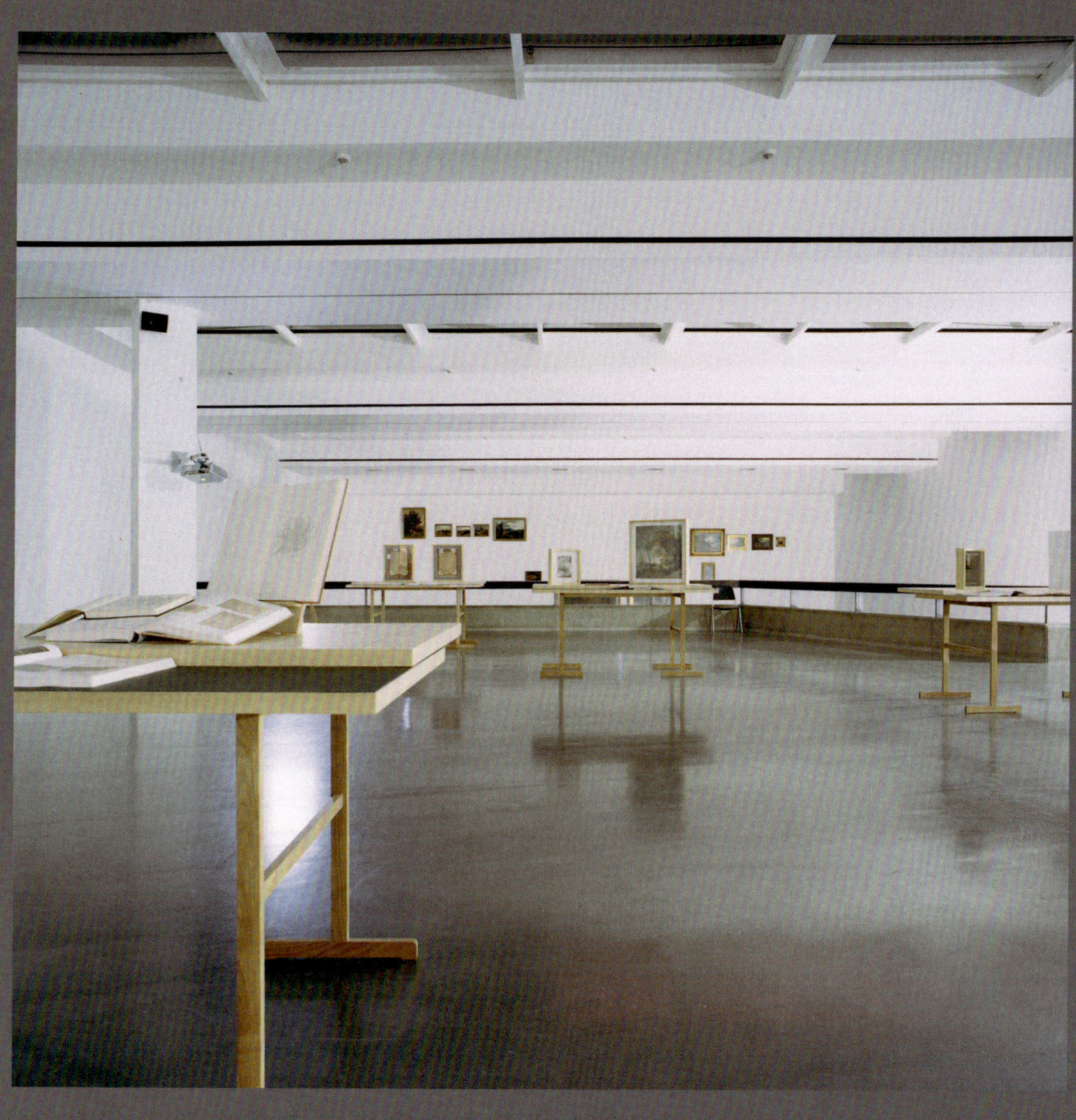

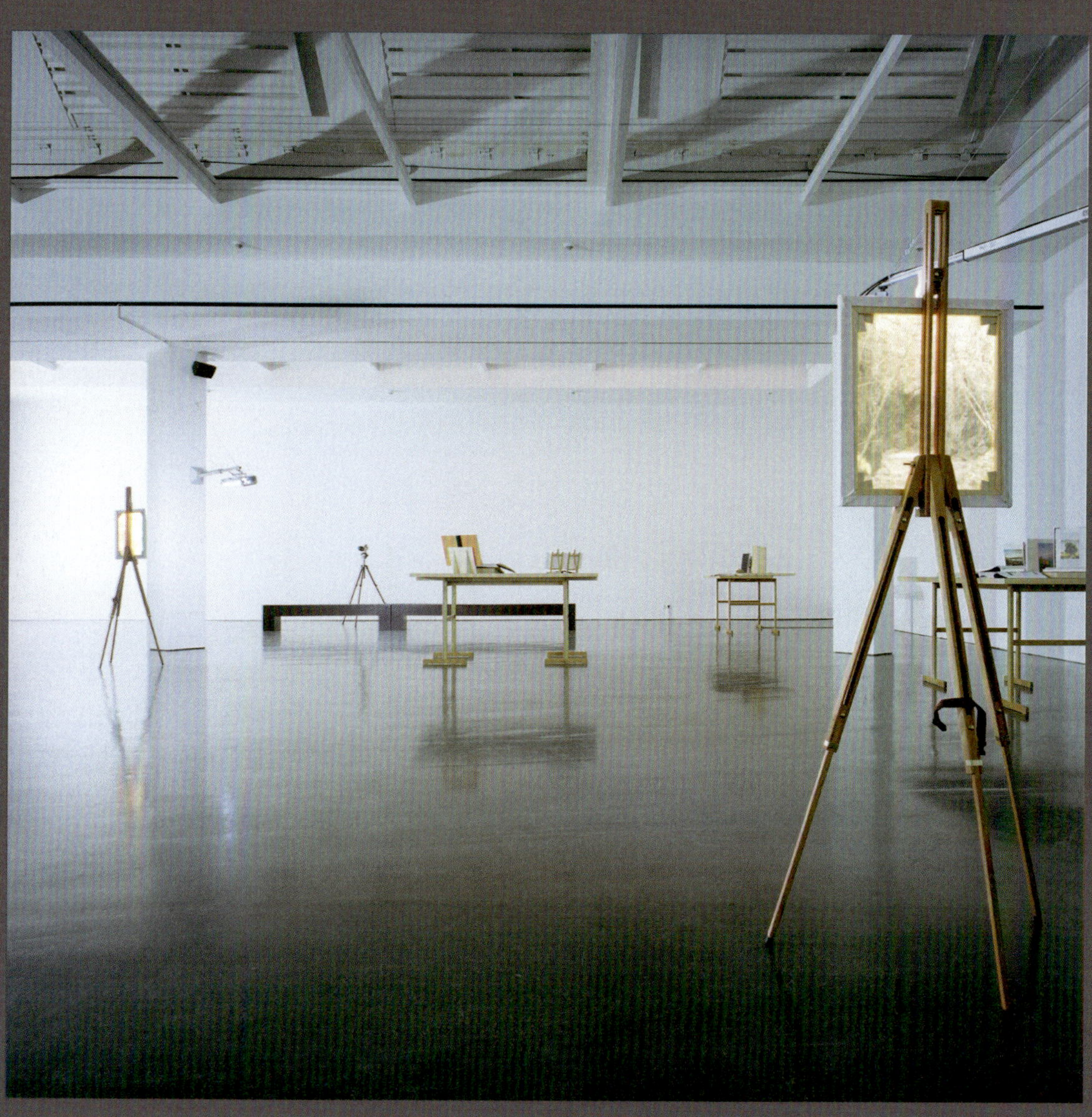

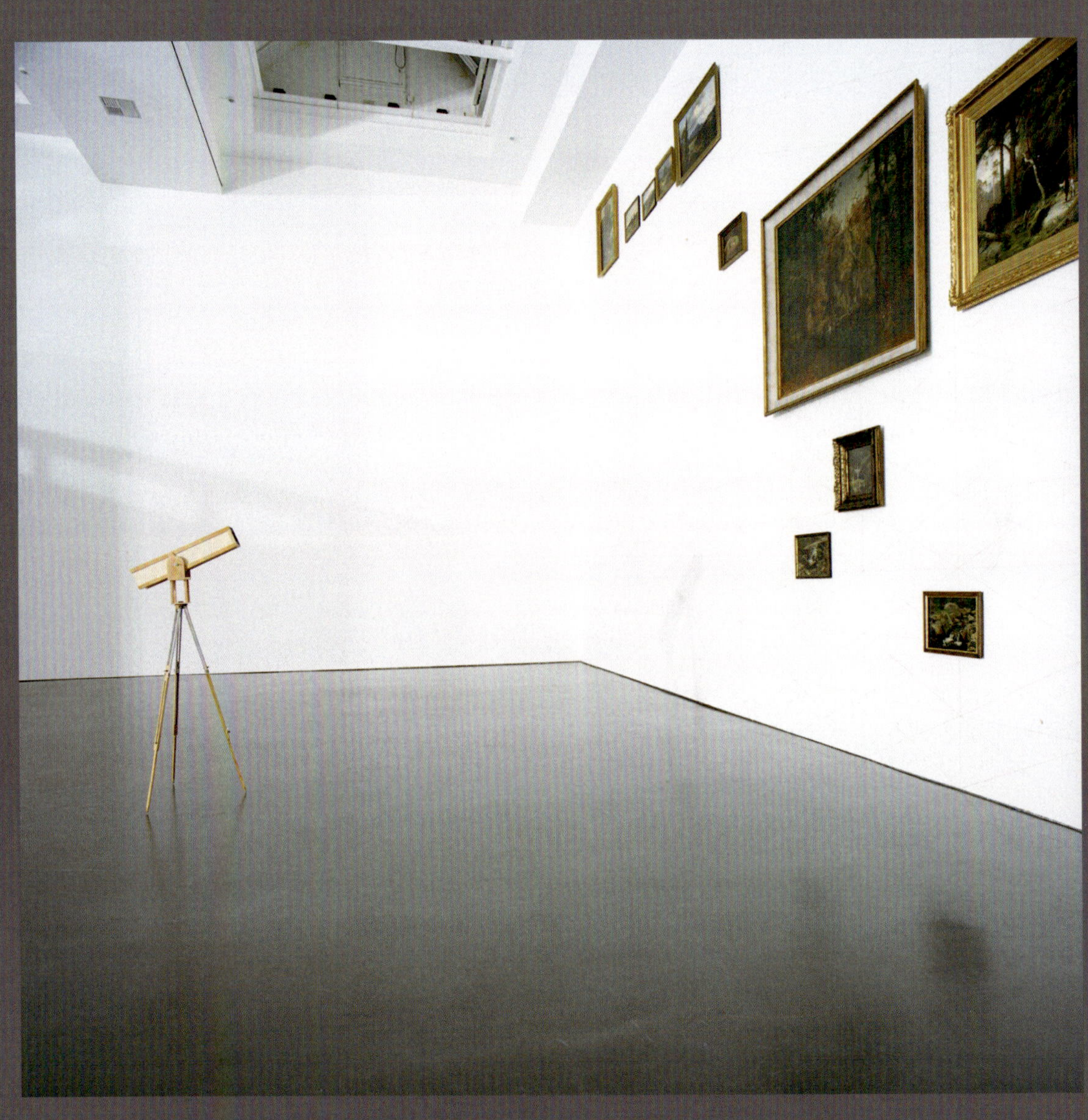

Die historische Dimension des Sehens

FRIEDEMANN MALSCH

Das Selbstverständnis der Kunstmuseen hat in den vergangenen Jahren international einen tiefgreifenden Wandel erfahren. Seinen auch für Außenstehende sichtbaren Ausdruck hat diese Entwicklung in dem 1997 eröffneten Guggenheim Museum im baskischen Bilbao gefunden, doch hatte sie bereits zwanzig Jahre früher begonnen. Mit der Eröffnung des Centre Pompidou in Paris 1977, in dem neben weiteren Kultureinrichtungen auch das Musée National d'Art Moderne untergebracht wurde, nahm eine Ausstellungspolitik ihren Anfang, die systematisch auf die Erschließung von Publikumsschichten ausgerichtet ist, die nicht zu den angestammten Museumsbesuchern gehören. Dazu bediente man sich mit Regelmäßigkeit des Formats großer und spektakulärer Ausstellungen zu übergreifenden Themen, die bis dahin stets als Sonderprojekte an zum Teil ungewöhnlichen Orten und meist zu speziellen Anlässen ausgerichtet worden waren.[1] Unter der Leitung von Pontus Hultén startete das Musée National d'Art Moderne mit einer Reihe von Großausstellungen, die insbesondere die Bedeutung von Paris im internationalen Kunstgeschehen des 20. Jahrhunderts darstellen sollten, die de facto aber zur Entdeckung der Kunst der nichtfranzösischen Avantgarden führte.[2] Damit war ein neuer Trend gesetzt, der in Deutschland vom damaligen Generaldirektor der Kölner Museen, Hugo Borger, alsbald aufgegriffen und zu einer eigentlichen Politik der Museen ausgebaut wurde. Initialzündung hierfür war die Ausstellung *Tutanchamun* in Köln 1980 im Kölnischen Stadtmuseum (!), die erstmals über eine Million Besucher anzog. Im Verlauf der 1980er Jahre entstand dann ein regelrechter Wettbewerb unter den internationalen Museen um die höchsten Besucherzahlen.

Bilbao markiert den historischen Höhepunkt der Auswirkungen dieses Wandels auf die Architektur von Kunstmuseen. Neubauten, Erweiterungen, Sanierungen – überall wurde die Architektur zum zusätzlichen Element des Spektakulären. Die Häuser entwickelten sich in zunehmendem Maße zu Veranstaltern aufsehenerregender Manifestationen. Sie taten dies teils aus freien Stücken, wurden aber angesichts eines am Publikumszulauf gemessenen Erfolges auch von ihren Trägern (meist kommunale, aber auch staatliche beziehungsweise Mischformen von öffentlichen und privaten Trägern) dazu gedrängt. Damit hat eine Kurzatmigkeit in die Museen Einzug gehalten, die sich mit anderen ihrer Aufgaben nicht verträgt. Zwei Bereiche seien hier herausgegriffen: die kontinuierliche Arbeit mit der Sammlung sowie die wissenschaftliche Beschäftigung mit Kunst. Für die Vorbereitung von Sonderausstellungen steht zunehmend weniger Zeit zur Verfügung, so dass eine sorgfältige wissenschaftliche Arbeit, deren Erkenntnisse üblicherweise erst die Begründung für eine Ausstellung liefern, innerhalb der Museen kaum noch zu leisten ist. So werden immer häufiger ausstellbare Ergebnisse umfangreicher Untersuchungen »eingekauft«. Das wissenschaftliche Personal erhält dagegen vermehrt organisatorische Aufgaben. Darunter leidet auch die Beschäftigung mit der Sammlung. Diese beschränkt sich in wachsendem Maße darauf, die bekanntesten (und bisweilen kostbarsten) Werke in stets neuen Varianten für Sonderausstellungen zu nutzen beziehungsweise zu solchen in anderen Museen auszuleihen (auch mit finanziellem Gewinn). Eine eigentliche Reflexion über die Rolle der Sammlung, ihre Besonderheiten und ihre künst-

1) So zum Beispiel seit den späten 1950er Jahren die Ausstellungen in der Villa Hügel, Essen, zu Themen der Weltkulturen. Auch noch die Ausstellung *Die Stauffer* im Württembergischen Landesmuseum, Stuttgart (1977), gehört in diese Reihe.

2) *Paris – New York* (1977), *Paris – Berlin* (1978) und *Paris – Moskau* (1979). Gleichzeitig entwickelte Götz Adriani in der Kunsthalle Tübingen sein Konzept der umfangreichen monografischen Ausstellungen zum Impressionismus, die zu großen Besuchererfolgen wurden. Werner Hofmann gelang in den 1970er Jahren in der Kunsthalle Hamburg etwas Vergleichbares mit dem Ausstellungszyklus zur Romantik (Goya, Runge, Friedrich).

The Historical Dimension of Sight   FRIEDEMANN MALSCH

In recent years a fundamental shift has taken place in what is perceived internationally as the role of the art museum. A striking example of this development, even for outsiders, is the Guggenheim Museum that opened in 1997 in the Spanish city of Bilbao, in Basque country. The beginning of this development, however, lies even further back—some twenty years earlier. The opening of the Centre Pompidou in Paris in 1977, which in addition to other cultural institutions also houses the Musée National d'Art Moderne, heralded the start of an exhibition politics systematically directed at opening itself up to a new audience who did not number among customary museum visitors. For this purpose, the format of large and spectacular exhibitions on comprehensive subjects, which had previously been organized as special projects, often in unusual locations and mostly on special occasions, was employed on a regular basis.[1] Under the direction of Pontus Hultén, the Musée National d'Art Moderne began a series of major exhibitions specially intended to depict the role of Paris in the international art context of the twentieth century, but which de facto led to the discovery of the art of the non-French avant-gardes.[2] This introduced a new trend, which was soon adopted in Germany by the general director of the Cologne museums at that time, Hugo Borger, and then expanded into effective museum politics. The initial spark was the exhibit *Tutanchamun* in Cologne in 1980 at the Museum of the City of Cologne (!), which for the first time attracted over one million visitors. Throughout the 1980s, this resulted in a outright competition among international museums for the highest numbers of visitors.

Bilbao marks the historical climax of the effects of this transformation on the architecture of art museums. New buildings, extensions, renovations—everywhere architecture has become an additional element of the spectacle. The venues have increasingly developed into presenters of startling manifestations. They have done so partly of their own accord, but have also been pressured into doing so by their funding bodies (mostly communal, but also federal or other hybrid forms of public and private funding) and in light of their success as measured in terms of visitor acceptance. This has introduced a form of breathlessness to the museums that is not consistent with their other tasks. I would like to single out two areas here: the continual work with the collection, as well as the scholarly involvement with art. Less and less time is available for the preparation of special exhibitions, so that thorough scholarly work, which usually provides the insights that act as the initial justification for an exhibition, can hardly be accomplished any longer within the museums themselves. Thus, the results of comprehensive research to determine what is suitable being exhibited are increasingly being "bought" from outside sources. The professional staff, on the other hand, has received additional organizational duties. This also impinges on their involvement with their own collections. Work with the collection is increasingly reduced to using the best-known (and occasionally most valuable) pieces for special exhibitions in constantly new variations or lending them to other museums instead (also, to be sure, with financial gain). However, true reflection of the collection's role, its distinctiveness and its artistic and substantive structures have increasingly taken a back seat. To put it bluntly: the museums have turned into event

1) An example of this tendency is the exhibition series, starting in the late 1950s, in Essen's Villa Hügel on the subject of world cultures. And even the exhibition *Die Stauffer* at the Württembergische Landesmuseum, Stuttgart (1977) belongs to this tradition.

2) *Paris – New York* (1977), *Paris – Berlin* (1978) and *Paris – Moskau* (1979). In the Kunsthalle Tübingen, Götz Adriani simultaneously developed his concept of extensive monographic exhibits on various Impressionists, which became an enormous visitor success. In the 1970's, Werner Hofmann achieved something similar in the Kunsthalle Hamburg with an exhibition series on Romanticism (Goya, Runge, Friedrich).

lerischen und inhaltlichen Strukturen tritt dagegen immer weiter in den Hintergrund. Zugespitzt formuliert: Die Museen haben sich zu Ereignisstätten gewandelt. Es bedarf deshalb heute bereits einer besonderen Anstrengung, sich des historischen Auftrags der Museen zu erinnern und diesen in die inzwischen etablierte Praxis wieder zu integrieren.

Auch Künstlerinnen und Künstler haben an dieser Entwicklung ihren Anteil gehabt. Die seit den ausgehenden 1980er Jahren wichtig gewordene Institutionskritik nahm insbesondere das Museum als Ort symbolischer Repräsentation sowie seinen Anteil an der Gestaltung des Marktes und der Selektion von Karrieren ins Visier. Ironischerweise erfolgte diese Kritik in einer Zeit, in der die Museen zusehends an Einfluss in der Kunstwelt verloren. Viele von ihnen reagierten denn auch mit einer bewussten Öffnung in Richtung des Marktes, privater Sammler und sogar für direkte künstlerische Interventionen. Für die Wiedereröffnung des Kunstmuseum Düsseldorf als »museum kunst palast« 2001 überließ die Museumsleitung – auch dies einer der Höhepunkte der Entwicklung – die Präsentation der Sammlungsbestände nicht etwa dem eigenen wissenschaftlichen Personal, sondern dem Maler Thomas Huber und dem Bildhauer Bogomir Ecker. An dieser Stelle überschnitten sich nun zwei Linien: Während die Museumsleitung eine Politik der radikalen Aktualisierung verfolgte, verbunden mit einer Unterdrückung historischer Perspektiven, beauftragte sie zwei Künstler mit der Neupräsentation der Sammlung, die sich in ihrem Werk nicht allein mit der Institution Museum auseinandersetzen (und auch nicht im Sinne der Institutionskritik), sondern die sich immer wieder auch mit der Geschichte von Bildern, von Kunstwerken und ihrer Rolle für die zeitgenössische Kunst beschäftigen.

Auch Matts Leiderstam kann zur Gruppe jener Künstler gerechnet werden, die sich in den vergangenen zwanzig Jahren auf produktive Weise mit der Rolle des Museums als strukturierendem Speicher von Zeugnissen der Kunstgeschichte auseinandergesetzt haben. Ein großer Teil seines künstlerischen Schaffens gilt Gemälden, die vor der Erfindung der Fotografie entstanden sind und sich in Museen befinden. Es ist daher nicht verwunderlich, dass Museen für Leiderstam eine wichtige Rolle spielen. Es sind vor allem Porträts, mit denen er sich beschäftigt, aber auch Landschaftsdarstellungen, die in der Regel Figurengruppen aufweisen, sei es zur Darstellung mythologischen, christlichen oder historischen Geschehens. Das die beiden Gattungen verbindende Element ist für den Künstler der »Blick«, in einem übergeordneten Sinn auch das »Sehen«. Die historische Dimension des Sehens spielt in Leiderstams Œuvre eine wichtige Rolle, weshalb er wiederholt die Rezeptionsgeschichte oder die Vita einzelner Gemälde und Topoi untersucht hat. Die Methode und die spezielle Sichtweise, mit der er in dieser Frage vorgeht, kann am Beispiel seiner Arbeiten aus der Sammlung des Kunstmuseum Liechtenstein deutlich gemacht werden.

Drei gemalte Porträts hängen an der Wand, links ein jugendlicher Flötenspieler aus der Werkstatt des Frans Hals (1645–1650), in der Mitte das Bildnis eines jungen Mannes von Bernardino Licinio da Pordenone (Oberitalien, frühes 16. Jahrhundert) und rechts das Porträt eines alten Mannes von Jan de Bray (nach 1670). Alle drei Gemälde stammen aus der Sammlung des Kunstmuseum Liechtenstein. Leiderstam hat sie für seine Installation ausgewählt und in der beschriebenen Reihenfolge verhältnismäßig tief auf die Wand hängen lassen. Vor den Bildern platzierte er eine hölzerne Bank, wie sie für schwedische Saunen typisch ist.[3] Diese lädt die Besucher dazu ein, sich hinzusetzen und in Ruhe die drei Porträts zu betrachten. Sitzend stellt man überrascht fest, dass man sich exakt auf Augenhöhe mit den dargestellten Männern befindet. Durch diesen Eingriff erreicht der Künstler eine substanzielle Veränderung in der Wahrnehmung. Gewöhnlich werden die Kunstwerke im Museum im Stehen betrachtet. Sitzmöbel erfüllen in der Regel die Aufgabe, dem vom Stehen und Flanieren ermüdeten Besucher eine Ruhepause zu ermöglichen, bevor er seinen Weg durch die Ausstellung fortsetzt. Bisweilen dienen sie auch dazu, besonders

3)   Diese Installation trug den Titel *The Shepherds* und entstand 1998 anlässlich der Beteiligung des Künstlers an der Ausstellung *COME CLOSER – Kunst der 90er Jahre aus Skandinavien und ihre Vorläufer* (19.2. – 19.4.1998), die von der Liechtensteinischen Staatlichen Kunstsammlung erarbeitet wurde und später in Budapest und Kopenhagen zu sehen war. Im Herbst desselben Jahres (16.10. – 29.11.1998) wurde eine leicht veränderte Fassung der Arbeit im Rahmen des »Arkipelag«-Programms der Stadt Stockholm anlässlich der »Kulturhauptstadt Europas 1998« im Königlichen Münzkabinett in Stockholm unter dem Titel *Blue Vision* gezeigt.

locations. Therefore, even just remembering the historical mission of today's museums and reintegrating this mission into what is meanwhile an established practice requires exceptional effort.

Artists have also contributed to this development. Institutional critique, which became important from the late 1980s onwards, targeted the museum in particular as a place of symbolic representation and questioned its role in the formation of the market and the selection of careers. Ironically, this criticism arose at a time in which the museums were noticeably losing influence on the art world. Thus, many of them reacted by consciously opening up to the market, soliciting private collectors and even allowing direct artistic interventions. For the re-opening of the Kunstmuseum Düsseldorf as "museum kunst palast" in 2001, and as one of the consequences of the aforementioned developments, the director relinquished the presentation of the collection not to his own professional staff, but to the painter Thomas Huber and the sculptor Bogomir Ecker. This is the point at which two lines intersect: by following a politics of radical renewal, combined with a suppression of historical perspectives, the museum's management commissioned a new presentation of the collection from two artists whose work not only explored the subject of the museum as an institution (yet not in terms of institutional critique) but who had previously also repeatedly dealt with the history of images, of artworks and their role in contemporary art.

Matts Leiderstam can also be considered among those artists who, over the last twenty years, have productively delved into the role of the museum as a structuring repository for the heritage of art history. A large part of his artistic work has been dedicated to paintings that were created before the invention of photography and that are now hanging in museums. It therefore comes as no surprise that museums play a key role in Leiderstam's work. In particular, it is portraits that interest him, but also depictions of landscapes, which usually feature groups of figures illustrating either mythological, Christian or historical events. For the artist, the common element in both genres is the "gaze" and, on a higher level, "seeing." The historical dimension of seeing plays an important role in Leiderstam's oeuvre, which is why he has repeatedly examined the reception history or the vita of individual paintings and topoi. His methods and the particular perspective he has adopted for this subject are best demonstrated by taking a look at his work in the collection of the Kunstmuseum Liechtenstein.

Three painted portraits hang on the wall: to the left, an adolescent flute player from the workshop of Frans Hals (1645–1650), in the middle, the likeness of a young man by Bernardino Licinio da Pordenone (Upper Italy, early sixteenth century) and to the right, the portrait of an old man by Jan de Bray (after 1670). All three paintings come from the collection of the Kunstmuseum Lichtenstein. Leiderstam chose them for his installation and let them be hung relatively low on the wall in the order described above. In front of the pictures, he placed a wooden bench of the type typical for Swedish saunas.[3] Visitors were thus invited to sit down and quietly regard the three portraits. When they sat down, viewers were surprised to discover that they were exactly at eye-level with the men portrayed. With the help of this intervention, the artist achieved a substantial change in perception. Usually, art works in a museum are looked at while standing up. Seating possibilities normally fulfill the task of providing visitors tired from standing and strolling with a break before continuing their way through the exhibition. Occasionally, they also allow for the prolonged study of especially complex paintings (which often also boast an especially large format) while sitting down. However, in these cases, the way the paintings are hung shows no consideration for the level at which the viewer is seated. On the contrary, when viewing them from below as a result of the low seating position, the paintings appear even more impressive, imposing, dominant and thus also distant.

Through his conceptual approach of hanging the paintings below the eye-level of the standing viewer, Leiderstam literally challenges the visitor to sit down and

3) This installation was entitled *The Shepherds* and created in 1998 when the artist was invited to take part in the exhibition *COME CLOSER – Art of the 90's from Scandinavia and its Predecessors* (Feb. 19–April 19,1998), compiled by the National Art Collection Liechtenstein and later shown in Budapest and Copenhagen. In the fall of the the same year (October 16- November 29). a slightly modified version of the piece was shown as part of the "Arkipelag" program of the city of Stockholm for the "European Cultural Capital 1998" at the Royal Coin Cabinet in Stockholm under the title *Blue Vision.*

komplexe Gemälde (die meist auch ein besonders großes Format aufweisen) sitzend länger betrachten zu können. In diesen Fällen aber nimmt die Hängung keine Rücksicht auf die Sitzhöhe der Betrachter. Im Gegenteil: Durch die sich aus der niedrigen Blickposition ergebende Untersicht erscheinen die Werke noch imposanter, eindrücklicher, dominanter und damit auch distanzierter.

Mit seinem konzeptuellen Ansatz, die Gemälde unterhalb der Augenhöhe der stehenden Betrachter zu hängen, fordert Leiderstam diese förmlich dazu auf, sich zu setzen, und belohnt sie dafür mit einer größeren »Nähe« zum Werk. Dank dieser Form der Inszenierung werden gleich mehrere Distanzen überwunden. Indem man den porträtierten Personen so gegenübersitzt, dass man ihnen im Wortsinne »in die Augen« schaut, wird das Gemälde einer Person, die man klassischerweise als bloßen Gegenstand eines Kunstwerks wahrnimmt und betrachtet, in das Abbild einer Person überführt, die plötzlich als ein individueller, »echter« Mensch erscheint. Dies führt zur Überwindung der zeitlichen Distanz: Wir erleben in der Individualisierung der Begegnung mit dem Gemälde die Vergegenwärtigung einer Person aus der Vergangenheit. Und daraus resultiert schließlich die Aufhebung der Distanz zum Gemälde als Kunstwerk. Auf der Bank sitzend nehmen wir nicht mehr nur ein Gemälde wahr, sondern die Präsenz der dargestellten Person.

Leiderstams Kunstgriff besteht hier also in der Re-Aktualisierung der historischen Gemälde. Seine Interventionen sind stets reziprok zu verstehen, denn er vertritt nicht etwa einen naiven Neo-Romantizismus, dessen Anliegen es wäre, die Vergangenheit unkritisch wieder aufleben zu lassen. Sein Interesse gilt vielmehr der Untersuchung jener Elemente, die für die Darstellung von menschlichen Eigenschaften nützlich sind, und hierfür eignet sich der Blick in ganz besonderer Weise. Leiderstam hat sein Werk für Vaduz nicht ohne Hintersinn *The Shepherds* (Die Hirten) genannt. Durch die Anordnung seiner Installation wird wie beschrieben ein direkter Blickkontakt zwischen dem Betrachter und den in einer weit zurückliegenden Zeit lebenden porträtierten Individuen hergestellt: eine eigentlich unmögliche Verbindung. Doch die Kunst kann, dies beweist Leiderstam mit diesem Werk, »en passant« große Zeitabstände überwinden und die Begegnung von Menschen aus unterschiedlichen Epochen möglich machen. Die Personen, mit denen die heutigen Betrachter in diesem Werk in Kontakt treten können, werden zu konkret greifbaren Ahnen, zu so etwas wie Hirten, die aus der Vergangenheit heraus ihren Blick in die Gegenwart werfen. Umgekehrt ermöglicht die Gegenwärtigkeit dieser so lebendig wirkenden Zeitzeugen dem Betrachter scheinbar eine unmittelbare Teilhabe an der Vergangenheit. Dass Leiderstam darüber hinaus Porträts von männlichen Personen verschiedener Lebensalter versammelt und damit eine große Spanne des menschlichen Lebens abdeckt, ist konzeptuell nur konsequent.

Leiderstams Untersuchungen gelten jedoch nicht der Aktualisierung oder Personalisierung historischer Prozesse, sondern vielmehr der Einmaligkeit des Ausdrucks und der Persönlichkeit der dargestellten Person sowie dem Potenzial zu deren Re-Aktualisierung. Das Gemälde des Bernardino Licinio da Pordenone ist dafür ein schlagendes Beispiel. Das Bild befand sich als Leihgabe aus Privatbesitz in der Sammlung des Vaduzer Museums und wurde diesem anlässlich der Installation von *The Shepherds* geschenkt. Da das Gemälde einen stark vergilbten Firnis aufwies und überhaupt einer Restaurierung bedurfte, wurde es zur Reinigung und Aufarbeitung einem Restaurator übergeben. Dieser entdeckte, dass das Bild etwa dreihundert Jahre nach seiner Entstehung fast vollständig übermalt worden war, um es dem Zeitgeist des Klassizismus um 1800 anzupassen. Die einzige nicht übermalte Partie waren die Augen des jungen Mannes. Die Restaurierung des Gemäldes förderte einen interessanten Chiasmus zutage: Die ursprüngliche Fassung zeigt ein ungleich jüngeres Gesicht, das zudem einen weniger »vornehmen« Gesichtsschnitt aufweist als die übermalte Version. Zugleich liegt im Blick des jungen Mannes im Original eine gemessen an seinem Alter erstaunliche Abgeklärtheit oder »Lebensweisheit«, die in der übermalten Variante zwar weiterhin vorhanden ist, im Verhältnis zum fortgeschrittenen Lebensalter des Porträtierten allerdings weniger ausgeprägt erscheint. Leiderstams Sicht auf die Gemälde zu dem Zeitpunkt, als er sie für sein eigenes Werk auswählte, hatte ihn also im Kern nicht getäuscht. Die Lebenserfahrung, die der Blick verrät, ist im Grunde

then rewards him with a greater "intimacy" with the work. Thanks to this form of orchestration, several distances are simultaneously overcome. By sitting across from the portrayed persons in such a way that we literally "look them in the eye," the person in the painting, who is typically perceived and regarded as no more than the subject of a work of art, is transformed into the person's image, which suddenly appears as an individual "real" human being. Thus, temporal distance is overcome: in the individualization of the encounter with the painting, we experience the visualization of a person from the past in the present. And this results in the suspension of our distance to the painting as art. Sitting on the bench, we perceive the presence of the represented person instead of just a painting.

Leiderstam's concept of art is therefore also one of bringing historical paintings into the here-and-now. His interventions should always be understood as reciprocal, for he does not represent a naïve neo-romanticism whose only concern is to uncritically revive the past. Instead his interest lies in the investigation of those elements useful for the depiction of human characteristics, and the gaze is well suited for this in a very special way. It is not without deeper meaning that Leiderstam named his piece for Vaduz *The Shepherds*. As described above, the composition of the installation allows for direct eye contact between the viewer and an individual who lived and was portrayed far back in time—in a sense, an impossible connection. And yet art, as Leiderstam proves with this piece, can overcome large intervals of time "en passant" and make encounters between people from different eras possible. The persons, with whom today's viewer can come into contact through this work of art, become concretely tangible ancestors, something like shepherds who gaze outwards from the past into the present. And vice versa, the presence of these seemingly living witnesses of bygone days provides the viewer with a chance to share in their past. Moreover, it is conceptually in keeping with this composition that Leiderstam has collected portraits of male personas of various ages, thus covering a large spectrum of human existence.

However, Leiderstam's investigations do not aim at updating or personalizing historical processes, but much rather seek to reveal the uniqueness of the expression and personalities of the represented persons, as well as their potential for drawing them forward into the present. The portrait of Bernardino Licinio da Pordenone is a striking example of this. The painting was previously on loan to the collection of the Vaduz museum from a private collector and was entrusted to the museum on the occasion of its use in the installation *The Shepherds*. Because the varnish on the painting had become quite yellow and the work required general restoration, it was handed over to a conservator for cleaning and refurbishing. He discovered that the painting had been almost completely painted over approximately three hundred years after its creation in order to adapt it to the zeitgeist of classicism around 1800. The only section that was not painted over was the young man's eyes. The restoration of the painting brought to light an interesting chiasmus: the original version shows a comparatively younger face, which moreover presents a less "noble" facial profile than the repainted version. At the same time, the young man's gaze in the original carries an extraordinary degree of serenity or "worldly wisdom" when measured against his age, which, although retained in the restored version, seems less pronounced in comparison to the advanced age of the figure portrayed. Basically, Leiderstam's insight into the paintings at the point in time when he chose them for his own piece thus hadn't deceived him. After all, the life experience contained in the young man's gaze is not attached to individual facial features. Leiderstam has documented the history of this painting in a photographic piece entitled *Before and After* (1999). The juxtaposition of the painting's condition before and after its restoration reveals, on the one hand, the remarkable physiognomic changes and, on the other, the unvarying intensity of the gaze, even when it differs in quality in relation to the respective facial features of the two versions.

The artworks described above illustrate Leiderstam's interest in how portrayal, on the one hand, has changed over the course of history, but also how it features certain constants that are capable of outliving historical developments. A third piece by the artist, *Selbstbildnis* (2002), examines the special relationship that a viewer can adopt towards a painting. On invitation from the Kunstverein Munich, Leiderstam created a special project in 2002 in collaboration

genommen unabhängig von den individuellen Gesichtzügen. Leiderstam hat die Geschichte dieses Gemäldes in einer fotografischen Arbeit dokumentiert, die den Titel *Before and After* (1999) trägt. In der Gegenüberstellung der Zustände des Gemäldes vor und nach seiner Restaurierung wird einerseits die frappierende physiognomische Veränderung erkennbar, andererseits aber auch die gleichbleibende Intensität des Blicks, auch wenn dieser sich im Verhältnis zu den jeweiligen Gesichtszügen der beiden Versionen in seiner Qualität erheblich unterscheidet.

Die beschriebenen Werke verdeutlichen Leiderstams Interesse dafür, wie sich die Porträtdarstellung im Laufe der Geschichte gewandelt hat, auf der anderen Seite aber auch Konstanten aufweist, die historische Entwicklungen überdauern konnten. Ein drittes Werk des Künstlers, *Selbstbildnis* (2002), beschäftigt sich mit der besonderen Beziehung, die Betrachter mit einem Gemälde eingehen können. Auf Einladung des Münchner Kunstvereins realisierte Leiderstam in Zusammenarbeit mit einem Studenten der Kunstakademie München in der Schack-Galerie, einer privaten Sammlung von Kunst des 19. Jahrhunderts, die als eigenständiges Museum betrieben wird, 2002 ein besonderes Projekt. Als Ausgangspunkt diente das in der Sammlung befindliche Selbstbildnis des späteren »Malerfürsten« Franz von Lenbach als junger Mann und Student der Malerei an der Münchner Kunstakademie. Leiderstam vereinbarte mit einem Studenten derselben Akademie, sich über einen längeren Zeitraum hinweg jeden Sonntag eine Stunde vor das besagte Gemälde zu setzen und sich für die Dauer des Projekts weder die Haare schneiden zu lassen noch zu rasieren. Aus der Aktion resultierte eine zweiteilige Fotoarbeit, die den Studenten am ersten und am letzten Tag seines Einsatzes in jeweils gleicher Perspektive in leichter Rückenansicht vor dem Selbstbildnis Lenbachs sitzend zeigt. Seine in der Zwischenzeit gewachsene Kopf- und Gesichtsbehaarung hat zu einer physiognomischen Annäherung beider geführt, doch dient dieses auf den ersten Blick erkennbare Detail lediglich dazu, auf eine grundlegendere Veränderung zu verweisen. Durch die kontinuierliche Betrachtung des Gemäldes über einen langen Zeitraum hinweg findet in der Tat eine Anverwandlung zwischen Betrachter und Gemälde statt, in diesem Fall zwischen einem Künstler und seinem älteren Vorgänger oder Vorbild. Die physiognomische Verähnlichung ist äußeres Zeichen eines inneren Prozesses.

Mit den vorgestellten Arbeiten hat Leiderstam seine Haltung gegenüber der Rolle des Kunstmuseums programmatisch formuliert. Er versteht es nicht als Archiv abgestorbener Dokumente, sondern als einen Ort, an dem sich Vergangenheit, Gegenwart und Zukunft begegnen und der gerade deshalb eine große gesellschaftliche Relevanz besitzt. Exemplarisch für die überzeitlichen Konfigurationen ist das Genre der Porträtmalerei, denn es erlaubt die Begegnung von Menschen aus unterschiedlichen Epochen. Der Blick ist in diesem Kontext von zentraler Bedeutung, ermöglicht er doch die Kontaktaufnahme, auch wenn wir uns anstrengen müssen, Blicke lesen zu können. Dafür ist das Kunstmuseum eine ideale Trainingsstätte, denn es erlaubt das Studium des Blicks in relativer Ruhe, in einer Situation der zeitlichen Entrücktheit. Eindrucksvoller und substanzieller kann ein Künstler in der heutigen Zeit kaum dem Kunstmuseum gegenüber seine Reverenz erweisen.[4] Leiderstams Werke belegen, dass Kunstmuseen auch und besonders heute eine vitale Funktion für die Herausbildung einer zeitgenössischen Identität übernehmen können. Allerdings verlangen sie auch bei jenen ein Verständnis für Zeitgenossenschaft, die für die Kunstmuseen verantwortlich sind. Es kann nicht Aufgabe der Künstler sein, die Einstellung der Museumsfachleute zu verändern, das müssen diese schon selbst leisten. Dabei können sie von Künstlern wie Matts Leiderstam nur lernen.

4)   Ähnliches gilt für die Arbeiten, in denen sich Leiderstam mit der Landschaftsmalerei beschäftigt.

with a student of the Kunstakademie München at the Schack Gallery, a private collection of nineteenth-century art, which is operated as an independent museum. The starting point for the project was a self-portrait from the collection depicting Franz von Lenbach, the late "Prince of Painters," as a young man and student of painting at the Munich Art Academy. Leiderstam arranged for a student of the same Academy to sit for an hour every Sunday in front of Lenbach's portrait over a longer period of time and neither to cut his hair nor shave for the duration of the project. The event resulted in a photographic diptych that shows the student on the first and last days of his assignment from the same slightly backwards perspective, sitting in front of Lenbach's self-portrait. The hair, which has in the meantime grown on his head and in his face, has created a physiognomic convergence of the two, but this detail, recognizable at first sight, merely serves to point out a more fundamental change. An approximation of viewer and painting has in fact taken place via the continual contemplation of the painting over a long period of time—in this case that of an artist and his older predecessor or role model. The gradual physiognomic resemblance is an outward expression of an inner process.

In these pieces, Leiderstam has programmatically formulated his position towards the role of the art museum. To him it is not an archive of dead documents but a place in which the past, the present and the future come together, thus possessing great social relevancy. The genre of portrait painting is exemplary for configurations that transcend time, for it facilitates encounters between persons from various epochs. In this context, the gaze is of central importance, as it promotes the establishment of contact even when we have to struggle in order to be able to read it. To this end, the art museum is an ideal training ground, for it allows us to study the gaze in relative peace and quiet, in a situation of temporal reverie. In today's world, an artist can hardly prove his reverence towards the art museum more impressively or substantially.[4]

Leiderstam's work proves that in this day and age art museums can also and in particular assume a vital function in the development of a contemporary identity. However, they also require that those who carry responsibility for the art museums develop an understanding of the contemporary. It cannot be the task of artists to change the attitudes of museum professionals. This is something they must do themselves. In doing so, there is much they can learn from artists such as Matts Leiderstam.

4)   The same applies to pieces in which Leiderstam explores landscape painting.

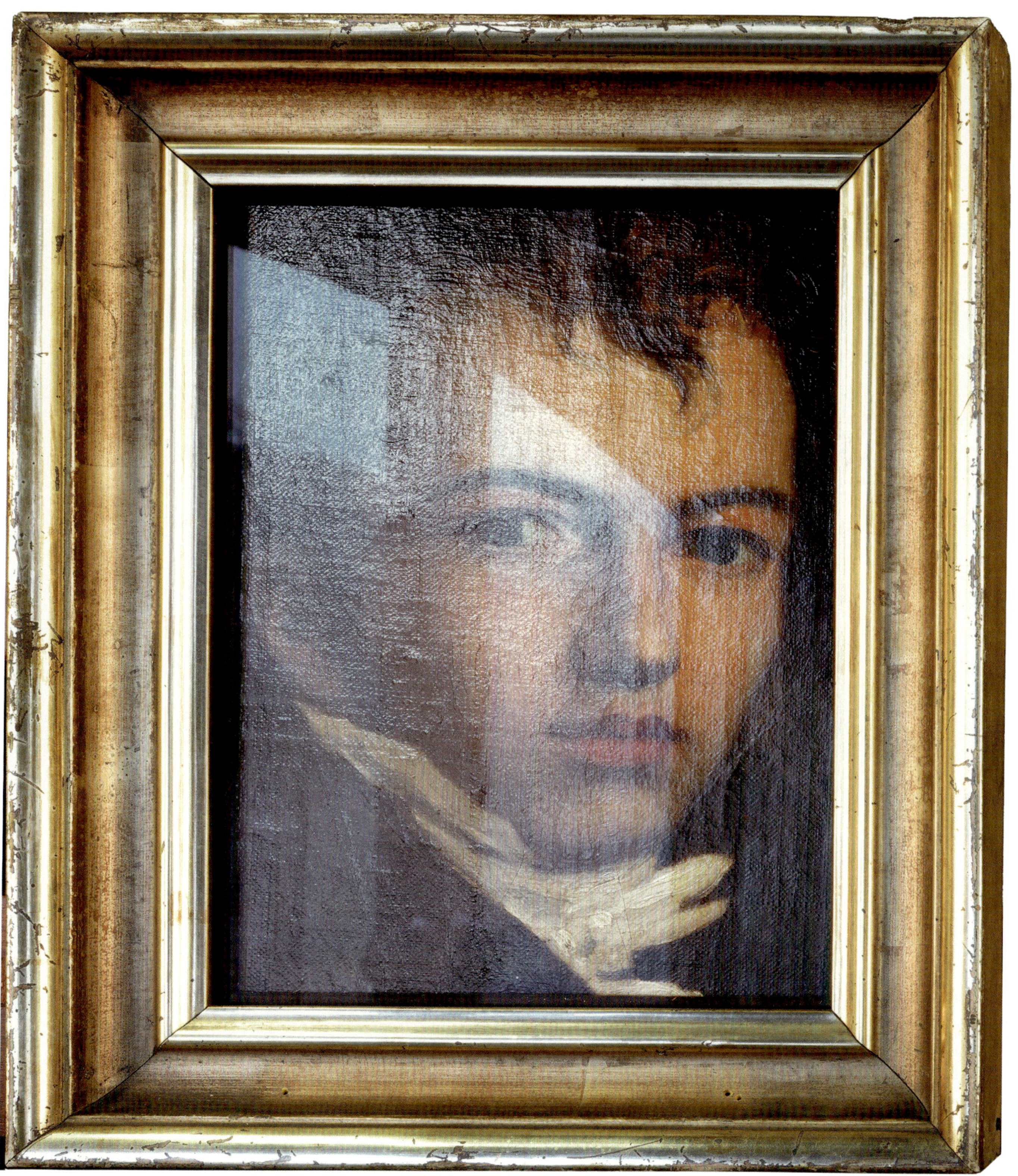

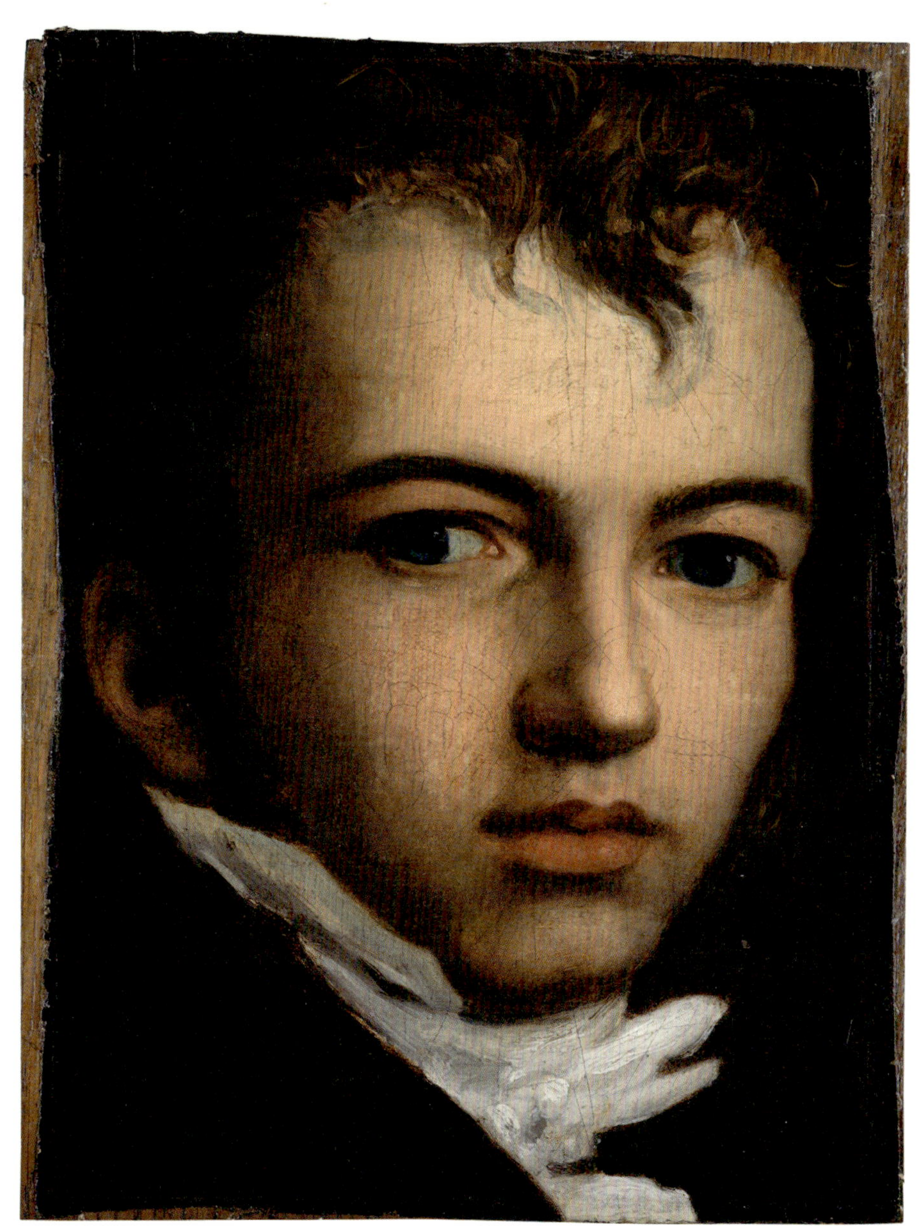

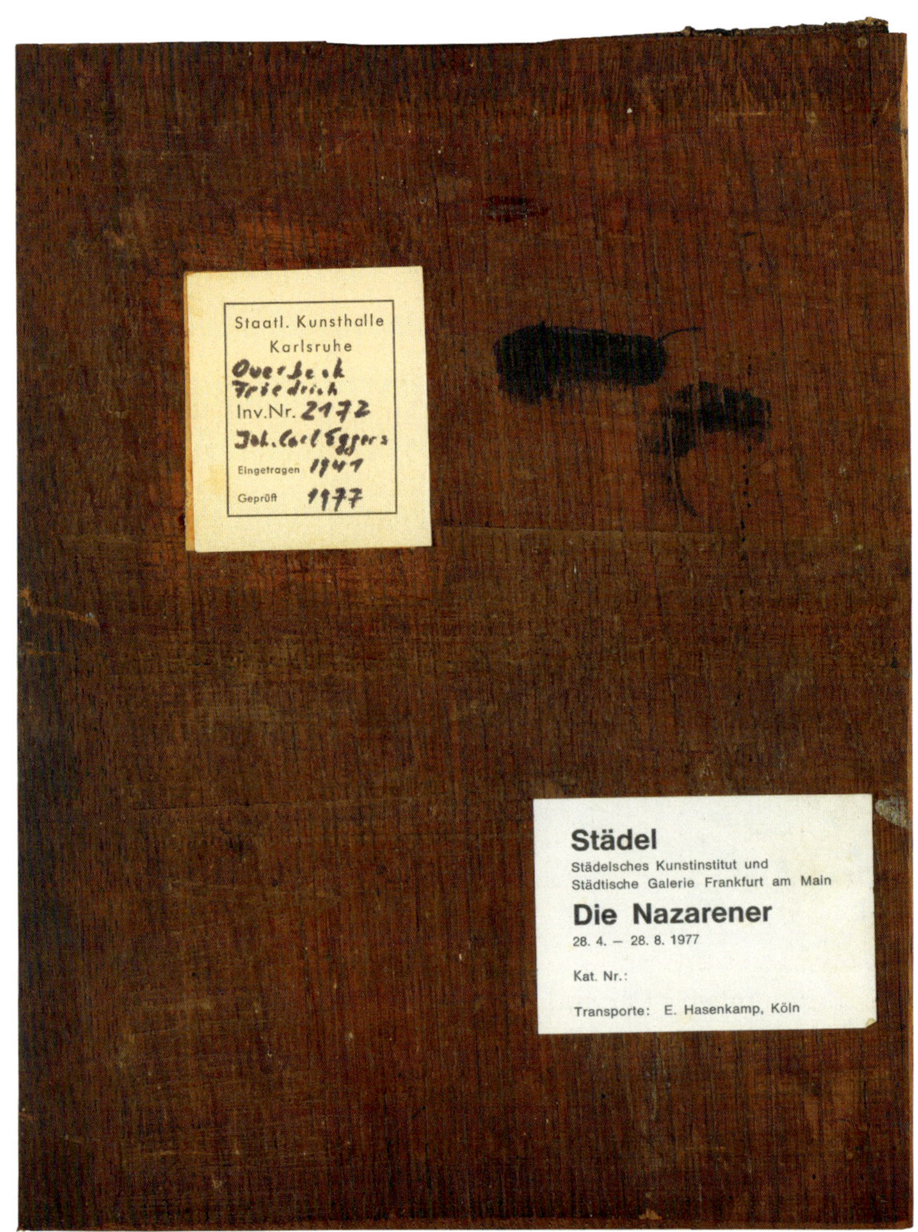

Staatl. Kunsthalle
Karlsruhe
Overbeck
Friedrich
Inv.Nr. 2172
Joh. Carl Eggers
Eingetragen 1947
Geprüft 1977

Städel
Städelsches Kunstinstitut und
Städtische Galerie Frankfurt am Main
Die Nazarener
28. 4. – 28. 8. 1977
Kat. Nr.:
Transporte: E. Hasenkamp, Köln

Durchblick (in-sight)

I.

In the archive of Staatliche Kunsthalle in Karlsruhe, a document that was sent from Bayrischen Landeskriminalamt (Bavarian Office of Criminal Investigation) on December 28, 2004 is preserved under the heading "Präventive Maßnahmen zum Schutz von Kunstwerken" (Preventive Measures for the Protection of Art Works). In this document, a person is described who, because of a court ruling, is forbidden from visiting museums, exhibition spaces, art collections, and art galleries. Several accompanying photographs taken in 1997 show an elderly man in full length as well as his head in face and in profile. He is grey-haired, 190 cm tall, weighs around 92 kg, and is known to have worn a toupee or a wig in the past. Since March 29, 1977, this man has attacked 60 works of art by spraying the surfaces of the paintings with concentrated sulfuric acid from a small bottle. The most recent assault took place on June 25, 2006 at Rijksmuseum Amsterdam.

II.

A portrait hangs at the Staatliche Kunsthalle in Karlsruhe that depicts the artist Johann Carl Eggers (1787–1863). It was painted in Rome around 1816/1820 by the artist's friend and colleague Friedrich Overbeck (1789–1869). In 1949, the museum bought the painting from one "Fräulein Cora Eggers", a granddaughter of Johann Carl Eggers who at the time lived in Karlsruhe. The medium is oil on canvas, the price was 1,200 DM, and the frame was included in the purchase. The picture was registered by the museum as number 2172 and was placed in "Sammlung Deutscher Malerei des 19. Jahrhunderts" (Collection of German Painting of the 19th century). At some point in the past, the painting was reduced unevenly and glued to a wood tablet. The painting has been cleaned by the restorers of the Staatliche Kunsthalle and small regions where layers of colour have been lost have been gently retouched. On April 23, 1987, a protective sheet of glass was mounted between the frame and the canvas. The glass is Mirogard®, 3 mm thick, manufactured by Schott AG, Grünenplan, Germany.

In *Durchblick* beschäftigt sich Leiderstam mit der Einfassung von Kunstwerken durch Rahmen und dem Schutz ihrer Oberfläche durch Glasscheiben. Insbesondere die Bedeutung des Rahmens ist dabei ambivalent, oszilliert sie doch zwischen einer pragmatischen, stabilisierenden Schutzfunktion und einer repräsentativen Funktion als architektonisch-gestalterisches Beiwerk. Für den Rahmen wie auch die Glasscheibe gilt, dass sie nicht nur Sicherheit gewährleisten, sondern auch Distanz schaffen, indem sie eine Behauptung von Schutzbedürftigkeit und Bedrohung in den Raum stellen. Am Beispiel eines Porträts des Malers Johann Carl Eggers (1787–1863), gemalt von seinem Freund und Malerkollegen Friedrich Overbeck (1789–1869), beobachtet Leiderstam, wie schutzlos das Werk wird, wenn es von seinem kleidsamen Rahmen befreit wird. Zwei Texte, einer zur Provenienz des Gemäldes, der andere zum Hintergrund präventiver Maßnahmen zum Schutz von Kunstwerken, und eine Glasscheibe stehen zwei Fotografien zur Seite, die das Gemälde in gerahmtem und ungerahmtem Zustand zeigen. Die Arbeit entstand für Leiderstams Ausstellung Im Badischen Kunstverein, Karlsruhe.

In *Durchblick,* Leiderstam is concerned with the mounting of paintings in frames and the protection of their surfaces with a sheet of glass. The significance of the frame is particularly ambivalent in this context, inasmuch as it oscillates between a pragmatic, stabilizing function and a representative function as an architectonic/design appurtenance. What holds true for both the frame and the sheet of glass is the fact that they not only guarantee security, but also create distance by raising the notion of threat and a concomitant need for protection. Using a portrait of the painter Johann Carl Eggers (1787–1863), painted by his friend and colleague Friedrich Overbeck (1789–1869), Leiderstam observes how defenseless the work is when divested of its flattering frame. Alongside a piece of glass and two texts—one on the provenance of the painting, and the other on the background to preventative measures on the protection of artworks—there are two photographs that show the painting both framed and unframed. The work was created for Leiderstam's exhibition at Badischer Kunstverein, Karlsruhe.

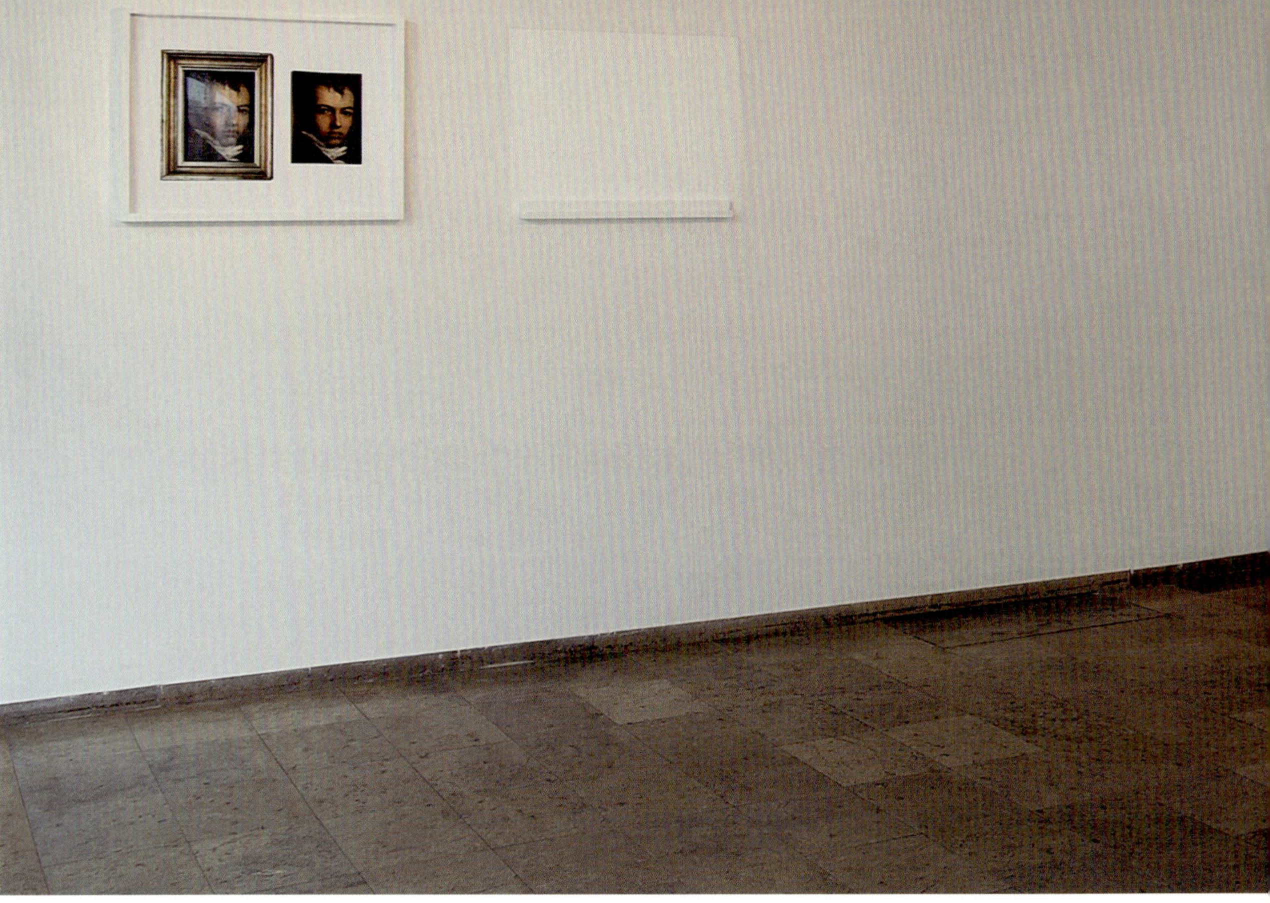

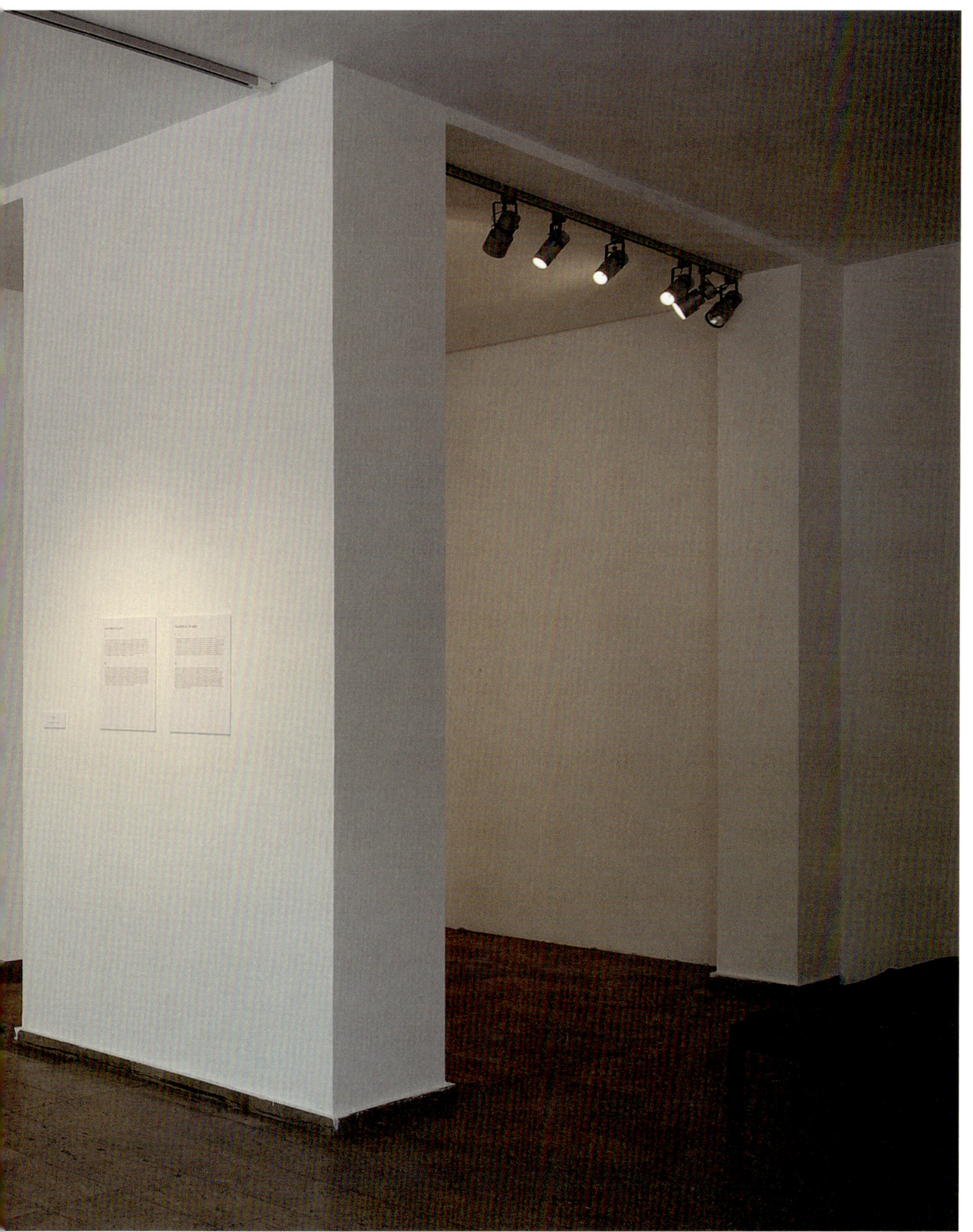

DURCHBLICK

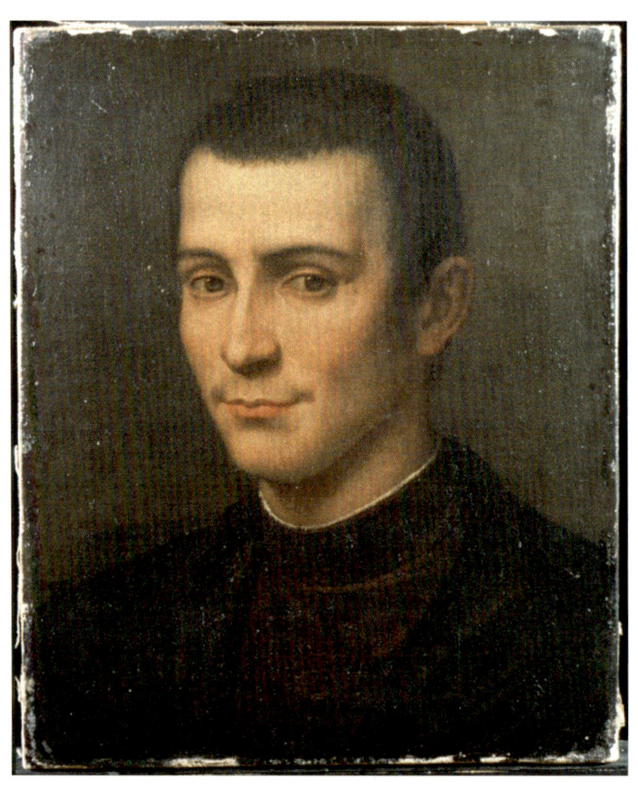

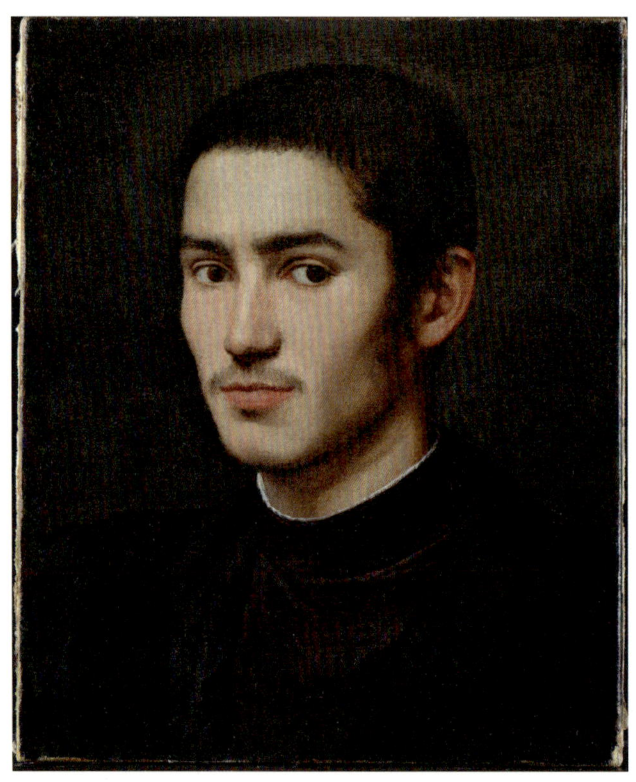

Im Zentrum der zweiteiligen Fotoarbeit steht das *Porträt eines jungen Mannes* von Bernardino Licinio da Pordenone (frühes 16. Jahrhundert) aus der Sammlung des Kunstmuseum Liechtenstein, das Leiderstam bereits in seiner Installation *The Shepherds* (1998) verwendet hat. Als er das Gemälde für eine neue Installation *(Blue Vision,* 1998) noch einmal ausleihen wollte, bestand das Museum darauf, das Werk vorher restaurieren zu lassen. Dabei stellte sich heraus, dass es im Laufe des 18. Jahrhunderts übermalt worden war. *Before and After* zeigt das Bild vor und nach der Restaurierung. Aus einem an Pier Paolo Pasolinis »Ragazzi di vita« erinnernden Jugendlichen hat die Übermalung einen erwachsenen Mann gemacht, dessen Gesichtszüge dem Schönheitsideal der italienischen Renaissance entsprechen. Indem der Künstler die beiden Fassungen nebeneinander zeigt, stellt sich die Frage nach der Funktion des Bildes für seinen Besitzer und nach dessen Motivation, es überarbeiten zu lassen.

The *Portrait of a Young Man* by Bernardino Licinio da Pordenone (early sixteenth century) from the collection at the Kunstmuseum Liechtenstein, which Leiderstam previously used in *The Shepherds* (1998), forms the centerpiece of this two-part photographic work. When the artist asked to borrow the painting again for a new installation *(Blue Vision,* 1998), the Kunstmuseum insisted on restoring the painting beforehand. In so doing, it came to light that the work had been overpainted in the course of the eighteenth century. *Before and After* shows the painting before and after the restoration. The overpainting has transformed a young man—reminiscent of Pier Paolo Pasolini's "Ragazzi di vita"—into an adult male whose features correspond to an ideal of beauty redolent of the Italian Renaissance. By juxtaposing both versions, the artist asks questions about the function the painting might have had for its owner, as well as his possible motivation for this overpainting.

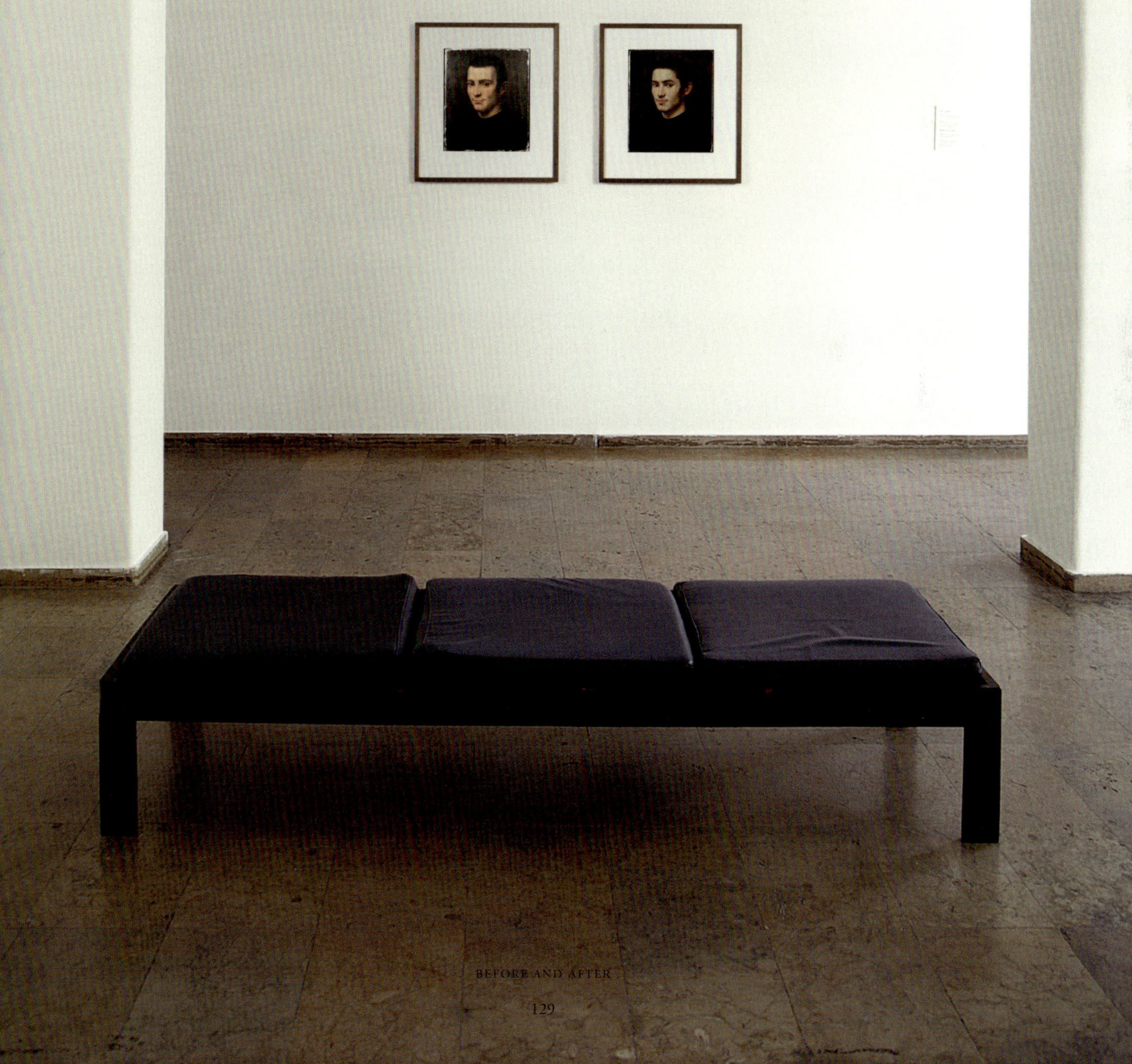

In Zusammenarbeit mit dem Kunststudenten Philip Metz, dem Kunstverein München und der Schack-Galerie realisierte Leiderstam von April bis September 2002 im Rahmen der Ausstellung *Exchange and Transform (Arbeitstitel)* ein Langzeit-Projekt. Über den Zeitraum der Ausstellung saß der junge Kunststudent jeden Sonntagnachmittag in einem von Leiderstam inszenierten Raum der Schack-Galerie mit zwei an gegenüberliegenden Wänden gehängten Bildern Franz von Lenbachs: einem Selbstporträt des Malers mit dem Titel *Jugendliches Bildnis* (1856) und dem *Bildnis eines Mannes* (1865) nach einem Gemälde von Andrea del Sarto. Auf Bitten des Künstlers betrachtete der junge Mann das Selbstbildnis Lenbachs und verzichtete darauf, sich während der Dauer des Projekts den Bart zu rasieren und die Haare schneiden zu lassen. In einer E-Mail-Konversation mit Leiderstam reflektierte der Student seine Erfahrungen während dieser intensiven Form der Bildbetrachtung. Die zweiteilige Fotoarbeit dokumentiert den Beginn und das Ende des Projekts.

From April until September 2002, in cooperation with the art student Philip Metz, the Munich Kunstverein and the Schack Gallery, Leiderstam realized a long-term project within the framework of the exhibition *Exchange and Transform (Arbeitstitel)*. Every Sunday afternoon during the course of the exhibition, the young art student sat in a room in the Schack Gallery, designed by Leiderstam, with two paintings by Franz von Lenbach hanging on the opposite wall: a self-portrait by the painter entitled *Juvenile Portrait* (1856) and *Portrait of a Man* (1865), based on a painting by Andrea del Sarto. At the artist's request, the young man regarded Lenbach's painting and refrained from cutting his hair and shaving for the duration of the project. In an e-mail exchange with Leiderstam, the student reflects upon his experience during this intensive form of viewing. The two-part photographic work documents the beginning and the end of this process.

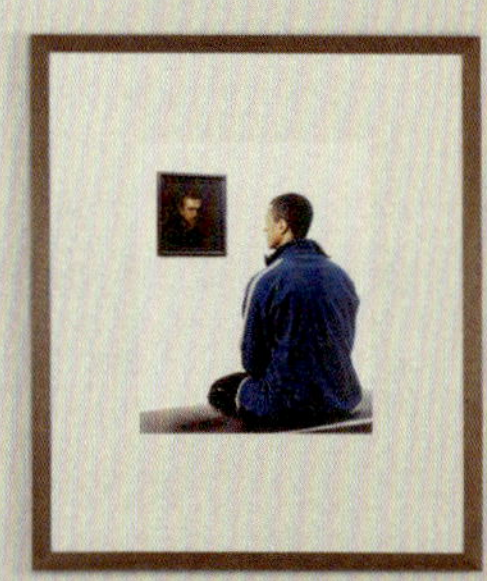 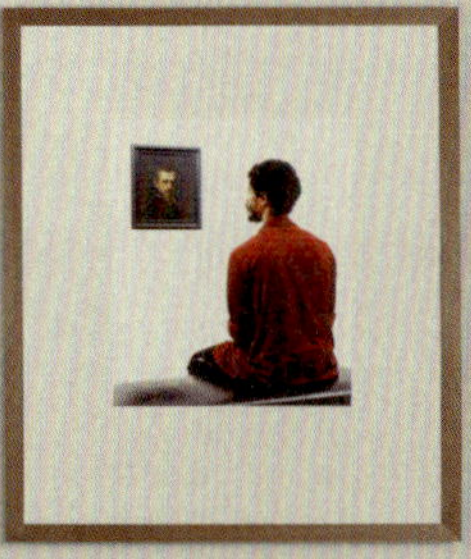

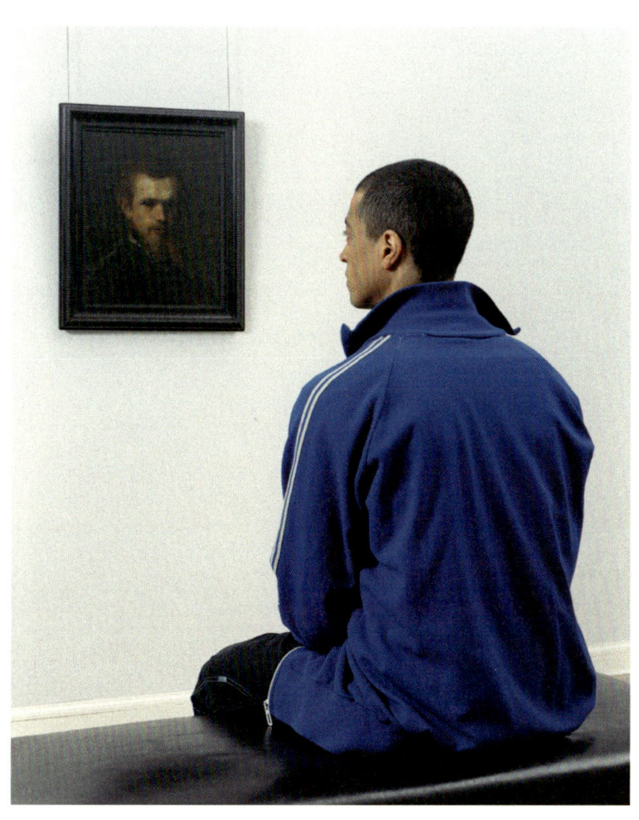

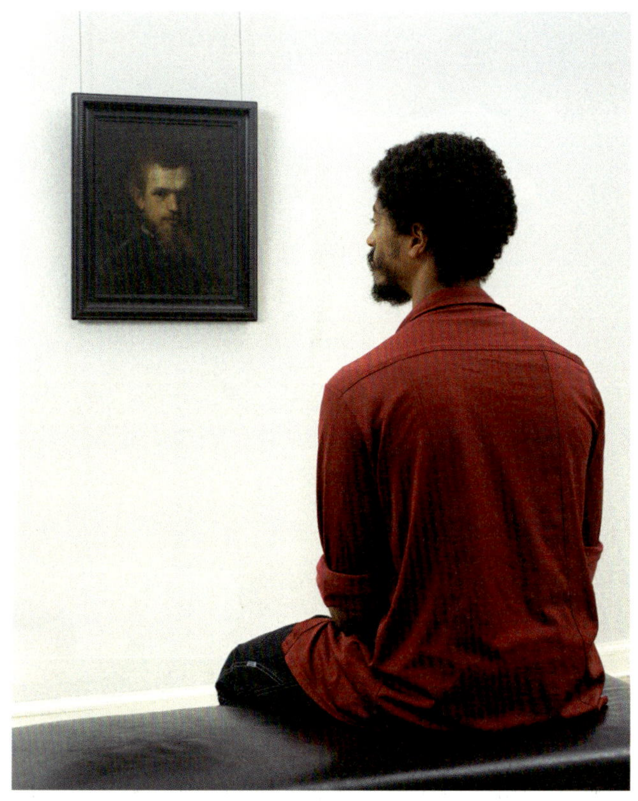

SELBSTBILDNIS

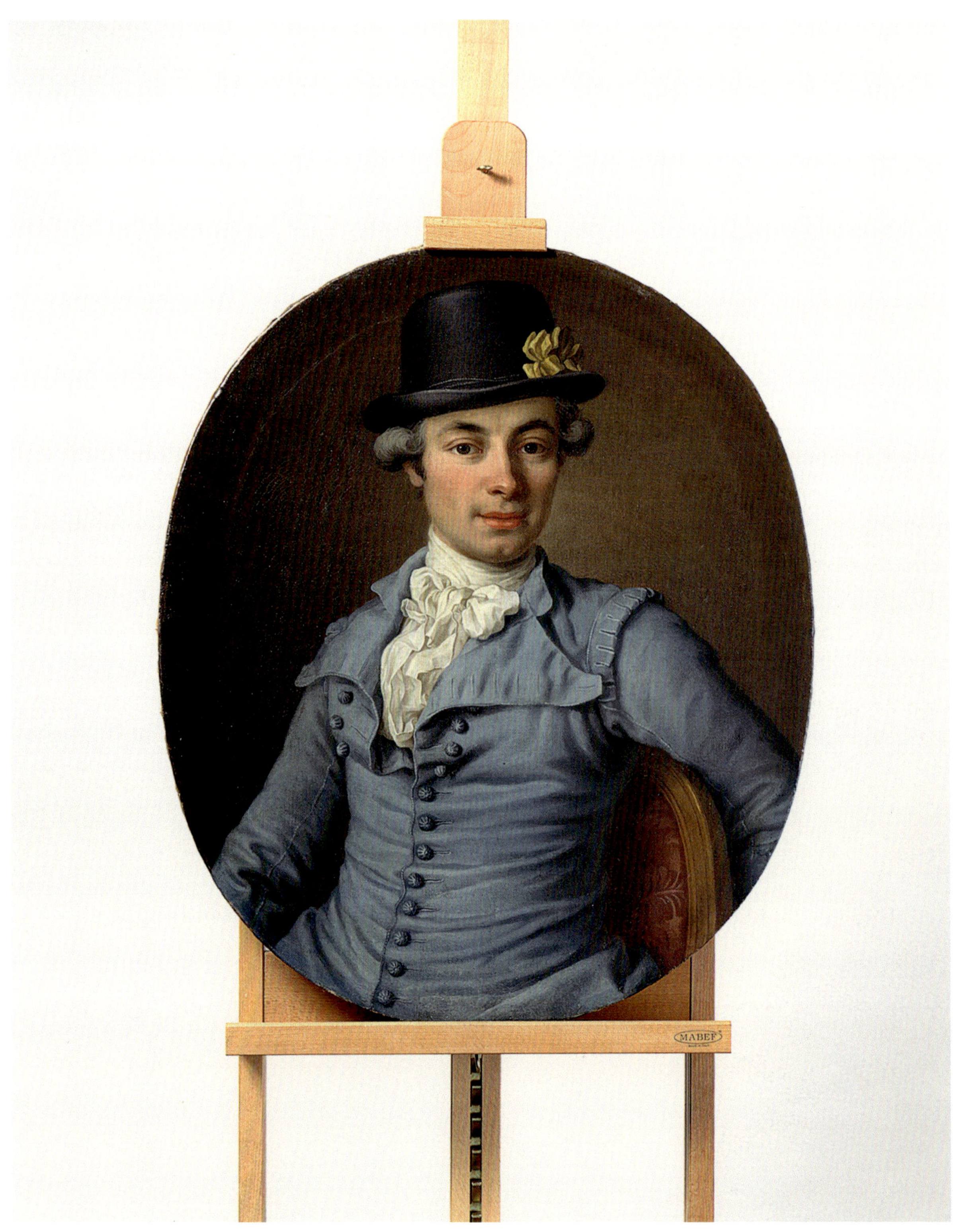

ADOLF LUDVIG STIERNELD

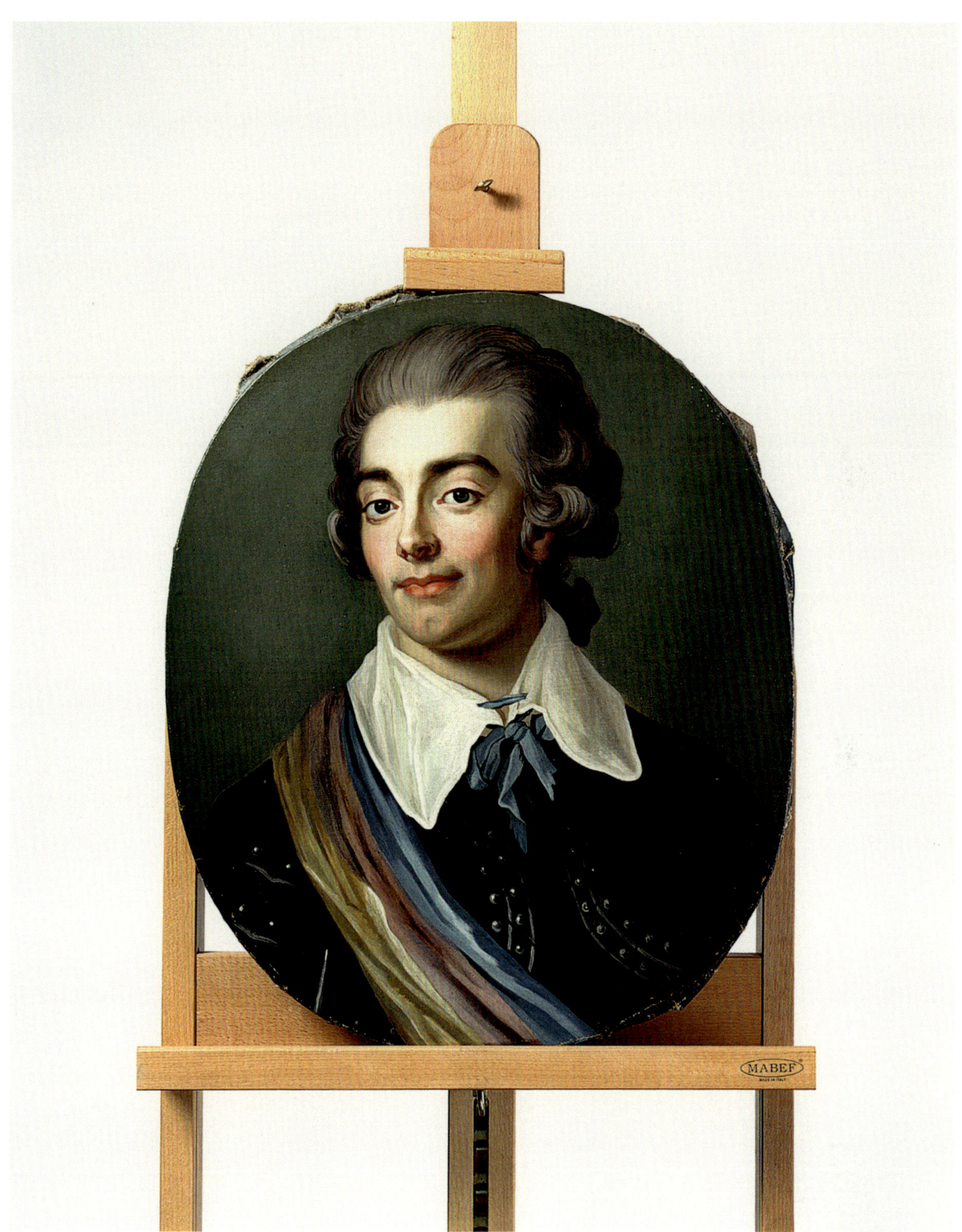

ADOLF LUDVIG STIERNELD

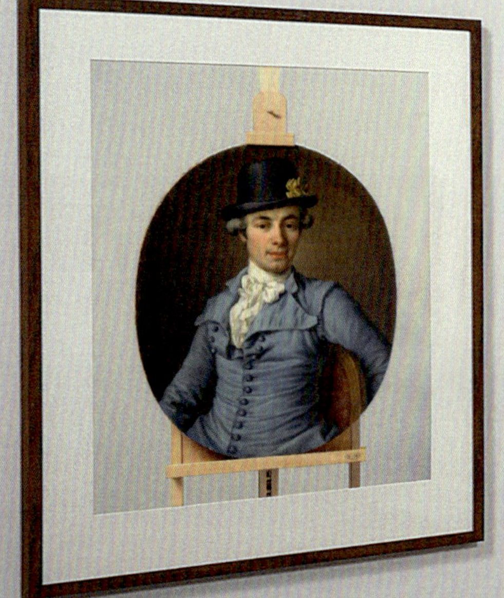

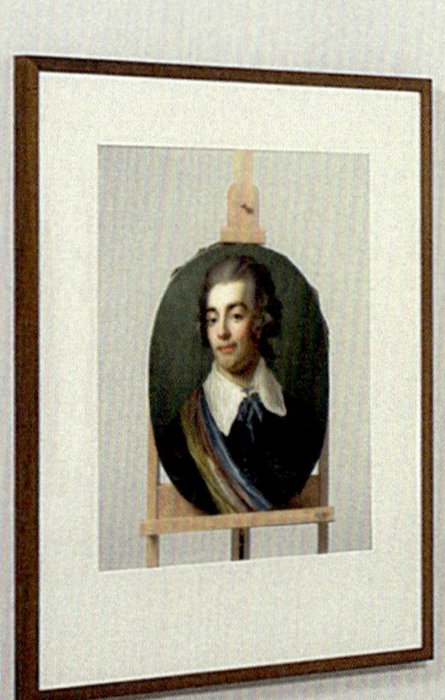

Die beiden historischen Porträts des schwedischen Freiherrn Adolf Ludvig Stierneld
(1755–1835), deren Fotografien Leiderstam
für diese zweiteilige Arbeit verwendet, sind in
einem Abstand von zwei Jahren zwischen
1780 und 1782 entstanden und befinden
sich heute im Besitz der Swedish National
Portrait Collection auf Schloss Gripsholm.
Das rechte Gemälde ist die Kopie eines Porträts des Malers Jakob Björk (1726–1793),
das linke stammt von Ulrika Pasch (1735–
1796), einer der wenigen professionellen
Künstlerinnen im Schweden des 18. Jahrhunderts. Bei der Gegenüberstellung der beiden
historischen Gemälde geht es Leiderstam
vor allem um die Beobachtung von offen-
sichtlichen Unterschieden und subtilen Codes
geschlechtsspezifischer Idealvorstellungen
und Schönheitsbilder.

Both historic portraits of the Swedish
Baron Adolf Ludvig Stierneld (1755–
1835), which Leiderstam photographed
for this two-part work, were painted two
years apart, between 1780 and 1782, and
can be found today in the Swedish National
Portrait Collection in Gripsholm Castle.
The portrait on the right is the copy of
a portrait by the painter Jakob Björk
(1726–1793), whereas the portrait on the
left was painted by Ulrika Pasch (1735–
1796), one of the few professional female
painters in Sweden during the eighteenth
century. In juxtaposing the two historical
paintings, Leiderstam is primarily interested
in the observation of obvious differences
and subtle codes of gender-specific ideals
and concepts of beauty.

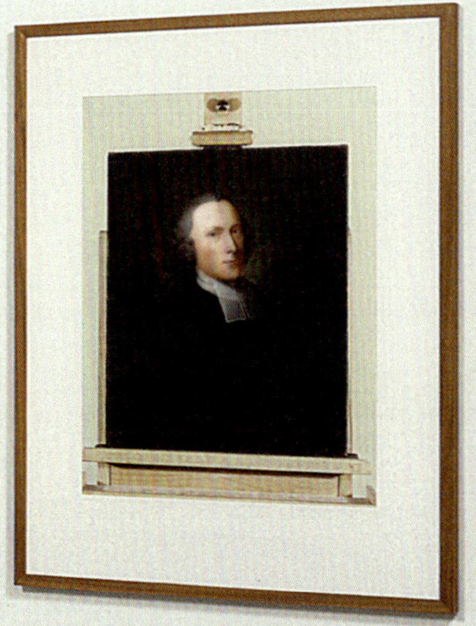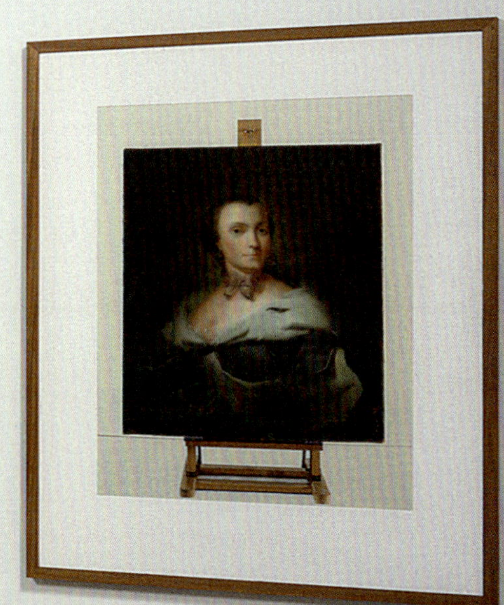

Ohne die Provenienzen explizit zu machen, stellt Leiderstam in *He and She* die Fotografien zweier historischer Porträts kommentarlos nebeneinander. Es handelt sich dabei um Gemälde des finnischen Malers Isak Wacklin (1720–1758), die den Bruder des Künstlers, den Vikar von Laihela, Samuel Wacklin, und dessen Frau Elisabeth zeigen (beide 1755). Ob die beiden Personen überhaupt in einer Beziehung zueinander stehen, lässt die Arbeit allerdings offen, und so wirft die augenfällige Ähnlichkeit der Gesichtszüge Fragen auf: Sahen sich die beiden porträtierten Personen tatsächlich derart ähnlich oder hat der Maler den Porträts sein eigenes Gesicht zugrunde gelegt? Waren »He« und »She« miteinander verwandt oder soll die äußerliche Ähnlichkeit vielmehr eine geistige Verwandtschaft zum Ausdruck bringen? Handelt es sich vielleicht sogar um ein und dieselbe Person in unterschiedlichen Kostümierungen? Ohne eine aus kunsthistorischer Sicht befriedigende Antwort zu geben, animiert Leiderstam den Betrachter, Ähnlichkeiten und Unterschiede zu studieren und verschiedene Möglichkeiten der Interpretation gegeneinander abzuwägen.

Without explicitly stating their provenance and without commentary, Leiderstam juxtaposes photographs of two historic portraits in *He and She*. We are dealing here with two paintings by the Finnish artist Isak Wacklin (1720–1758), showing the brother of the artist, Samuel Wacklin, Vicar of Laihela, and his wife Elisabeth (both 1755). Nevertheless, because this work remains open as to the precise relationship between the two persons, the obvious similarity of the facial features raises a number of questions: did the persons portrayed really have such a close resemblance, or did the painter base the portraits on his own physiognomy? Were "He" and "She" related, or is the external similarity instead intended to convey a spiritual affinity? Is it perhaps even a case of one and the same person in different costumes? Without furnishing a satisfactory art-historical answer, Leiderstam encourages the viewer to study the similarities and differences and to weigh various possible interpretations against each other.

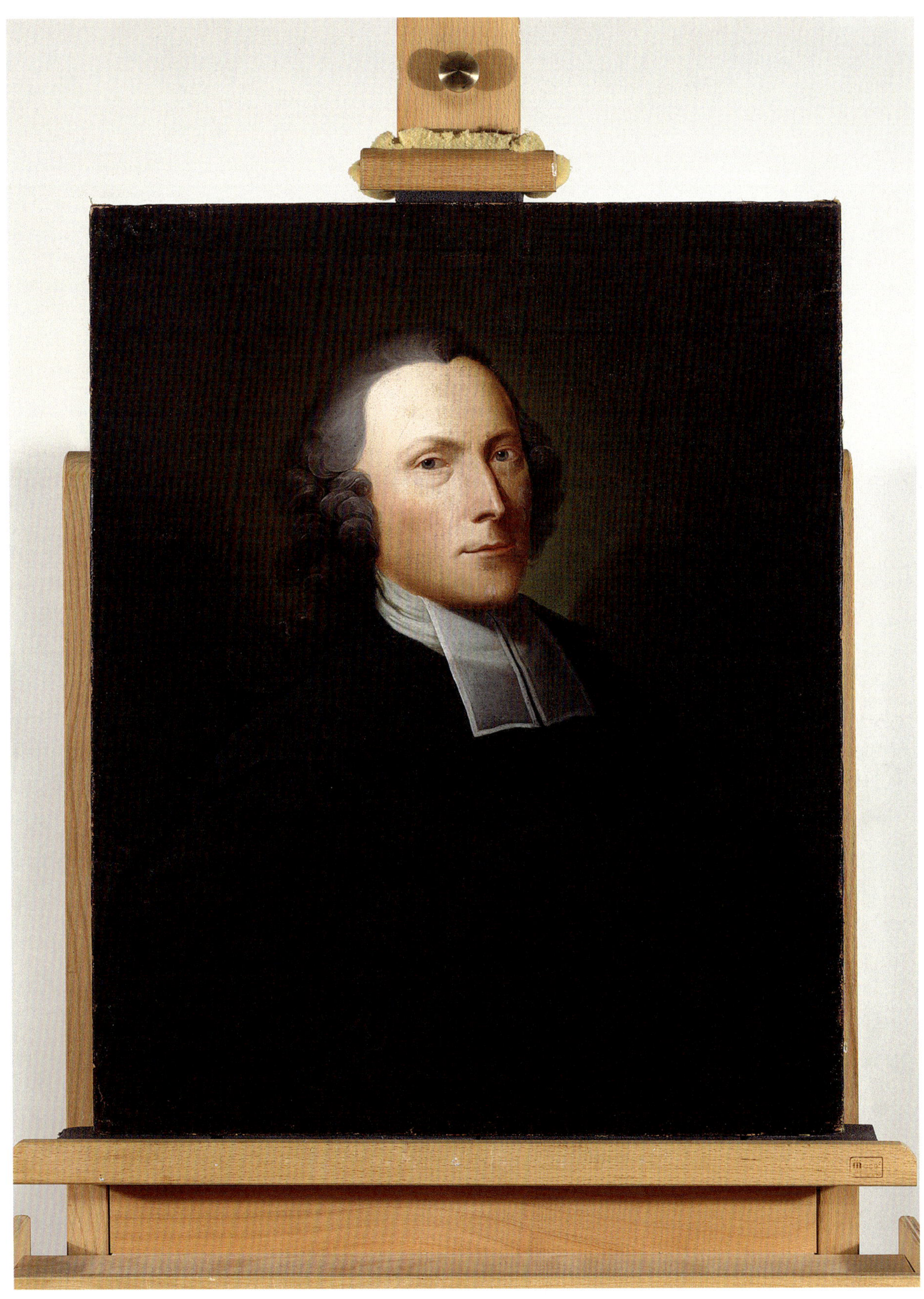

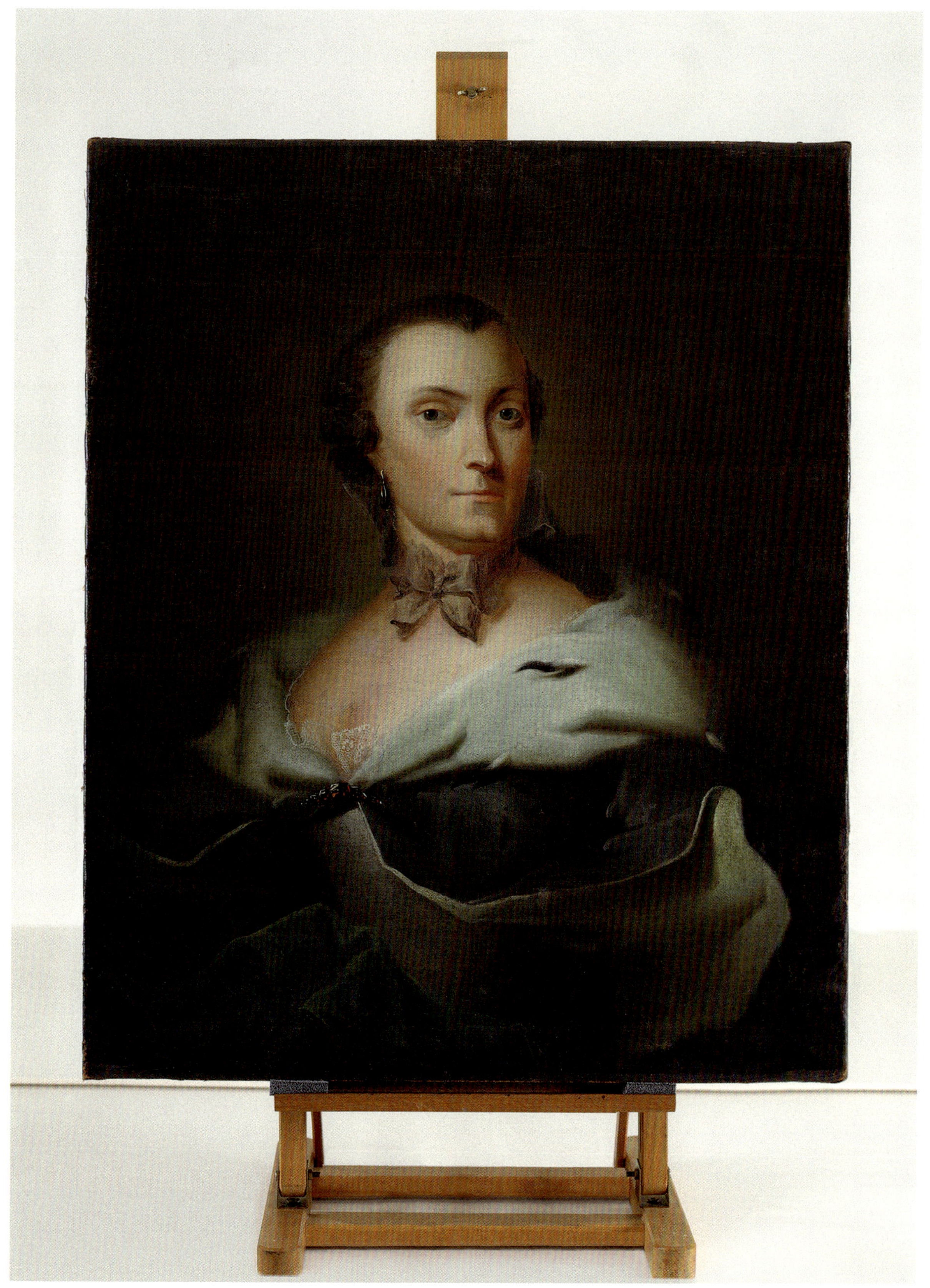

HE AND SHE

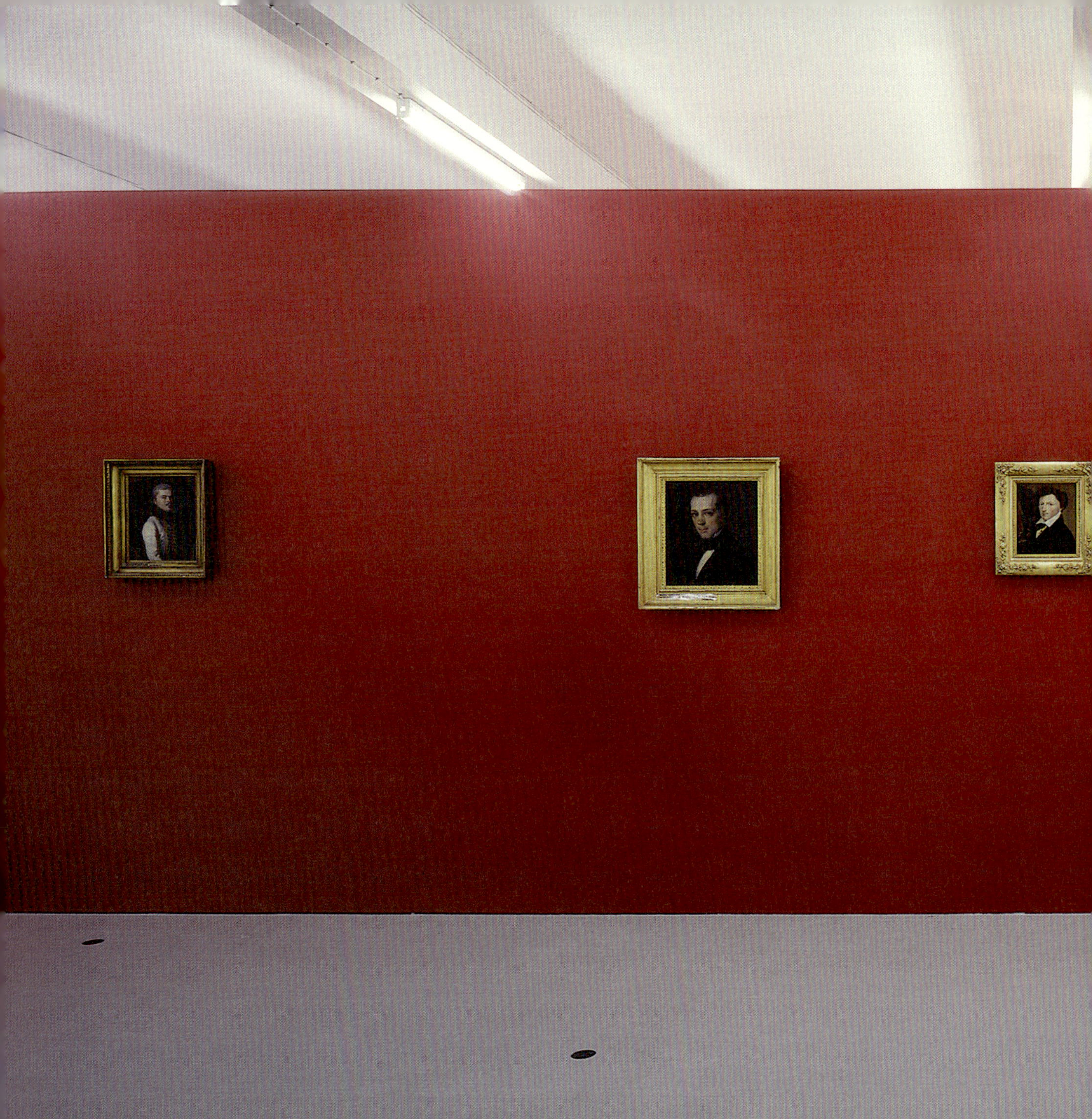

VIEWING POINTS (SHOWING THREE RECOGNIZED, TWO UNIDENTIFIED AND ONE QUESTIONED –
MADE BY TWO RECOGNIZED, ONE ATTRIBUTED AND THREE ANONYMOUS), 2002

Die temporäre Installation *Viewing Points* versammelte sechs von Leiderstam aus der ständigen Sammlung des Malmö Konstmuseum ausgewählte Porträts auf einer dunkelrot gestrichenen Wand. Auf dem Boden waren kreisförmige schwarze Markierungen angebracht, die sich den Besuchern als mögliche Stand- und Aussichtspunkte anboten. Bei den Gemälden handelte es sich zum einen um Porträts bekannter Persönlichkeiten, die von unbekannten oder anonymen Künstlern geschaffen wurden, zum anderen um Darstellungen von heute in Vergessenheit geratenen Personen, die wiederum von renommierten Künstlern stammen – eine Kombination, mit der Leiderstam ein Wechselspiel von Wissen und Unwissen, Anonymität und Vertrautheit initiierte. Gleichzeitig deutete er die unterschiedlichen Beziehungsgefüge an, die zwischen Maler und Modell, zwischen Auftraggeber und Künstler sowie nicht zuletzt auch zwischen den Porträtierten untereinander bestehen und entstehen können. Aufgrund der ungewöhnlichen Hängung zeigen sich die dargestellten Persönlichkeiten aus verschiedenen Blickwinkeln in jeweils unterschiedlichen Gruppierungen, so dass ihre realen und imaginierten Bezüge einer ständigen Bedeutungsverschiebung unterworfen sind.

The temporary Installation *Viewing Points* gathered together six portraits selected by Leiderstam from the permanent collection at the Malmö Konstmuseum and hung on a wall painted dark red. Circular black markings were positioned on the floor suggesting possible viewing or standing positions for visitors. On the one hand, the paintings were of well-known personalities created by unknown or anonymous artists; on the other hand and by contrast, there were portraits painted by renowned artists of people now forgotten—a combination Leiderstam used to initiate an interplay of knowledge and ignorance, anonymity and familiarity. At the same time, he alluded to the different existing or potential networks of relationships between the painter and model, client and artist, as well as—not least—between the portrayed figures themselves. On the basis of the unusual way the works are hung, the persons portrayed appear in different groupings when viewed from different angles, so that their real and imaginary relationships are subject to constant shifts in meaning.

Parallel worlds
With photographs by Matts Leiderstam

Parallelwelten
Mit Fotografien von Matts Leiderstam

MARIA LIND

We need to focus our gaze, long and intensively, thoroughly and thoughtfully—curiously—and contemplate what we see. We must also always be able to imagine, to compensate for vagueness and fill in gaps and omissions, to put ourselves in other, different situations. For the visual web that surrounds us is full of creases and tears, and only by accepting our shortcomings as observers can we begin to detect its width and breadth. Then, perhaps, we can approach something like insight.

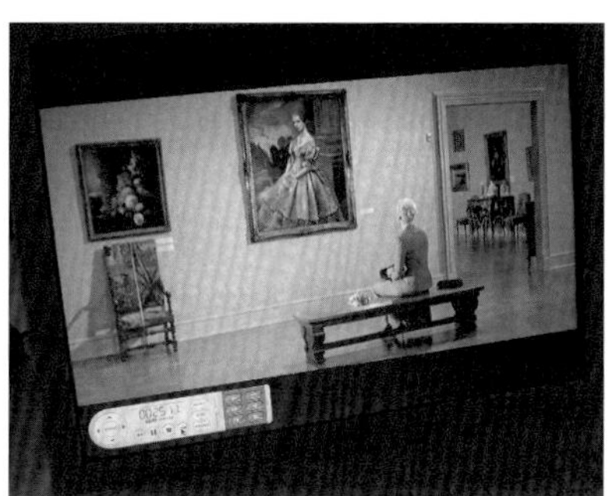

Illustration aus / from Matts Leiderstam's Dissertation / Ph.-D. Thesis (Kim Novak im / at the Museum, aus / from Alfred Hitchcock's »Vertigo«)

Wir müssen unseren Blick lange und intensiv, gründlich und nachdenklich – neugierig – fokussieren und eingehend betrachten, was wir sehen. Und wir müssen stets in der Lage sein, unsere Vorstellungskraft zu bemühen, um die Vagheiten auszugleichen, die Lücken und Auslassungen zu füllen und uns in andere, unterschiedliche Perspektiven hineinzuversetzen. Denn das visuelle Netz, das uns umgibt, ist voller Falten und Risse, und nur, wenn wir unsere Unzulänglichkeiten als Betrachter akzeptieren, können wir nach und nach seine Dimensionen erfassen. Dann können wir möglicherweise eine Art von Einblick gewinnen.

* * *

What is interesting with a copy is not its fidelity to the original but its departures. Doppelgänger and single-egg twins are other examples that capitalize on not being identical. In the same way, the distance in time from when a painting takes shape to when its successor arrives is at least as important as the visible discrepancies between the original and its recreation. Distance and the intervening gap in time and space can become the very boiling point. Disjunctures and the new fillings are the real explosives, when the production of meaning really heats up.

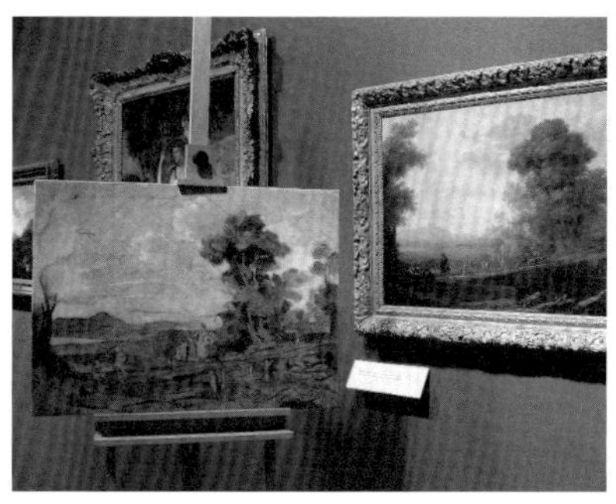

Matts Leiderstam's Kopie im / copy at the Nationalmuseum in Stockholm für / for *The Sun*, 2003

Das Interessante an einer Kopie ist nicht ihre Originaltreue, sondern es sind die Abweichungen. Doppelgänger und eineiige Zwillinge sind ebenfalls Beispiele dafür, davon zu profitieren, nicht vollständig identisch zu sein. Und so ist auch der zeitliche Abstand zwischen der Entstehung eines Gemäldes und dem Moment, in dem sein Nachfolger auftritt, mindestens ebenso wichtig wie die sichtbaren Unterschiede zwischen dem Original und seiner Neuschöpfung. Die Distanz und die zeitliche und räumliche Kluft können zum eigentlichen Brennpunkt werden. Die Lücken und ihre neuen Füllungen sind tatsächlich Sprengstoff, wenn die Bedeutungsproduktion erst einmal heißläuft.

* * *

It isn't difficult for an art historian to fall for a piece consisting of color photographs of eighteenth-century portraits on stable easels. Or for borrowed Renaissance portraits of stylish men, with sculptural gold frames, installed on a clear blue wall behind a simple wooden bench. Not to speak of a small copy of a painting of an inspired Enlightenment artist in his studio and a white archtectural model of the room in the painting. Personally, I'm enticed by *Returned,* the

Es fällt einem Kunsthistoriker nicht schwer, sich für eine Arbeit zu begeistern, die aus Farbfotografien von Porträts des 18. Jahrhunderts auf stabilen Staffeleien besteht. Oder für ausgeliehene Renaissance-Bildnisse eleganter Männer mit skulpturalen vergoldeten Rahmen, die an einer hellblauen Wand hinter einer schlichten Holzbank installiert wurden. Ganz zu schweigen von der kleinen Kopie eines Gemäldes eines genialen Künstlers der Aufklärung in sei-

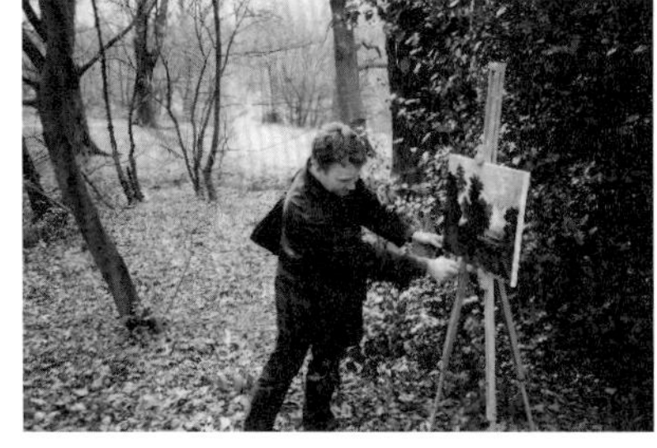

series of copies of Nicolas Poussin's painting *Le Printemps ou le Paradis terrestre,* left to their fate in homosexual meeting places mentioned in the *Spartacus* guide in a large number of parks all over the world.

nem Atelier und einem weißen Architekturmodell des Raums in dem Gemälde. Mich persönlich fasziniert *Returned,* eine Serie von Kopien nach Nicolas Poussins Gemälde *Le Printemps ou le Paradis terrestre;* diese wurden an Treffpunkten von Schwulen, die der *Spartacus*-Reiseführer erwähnt, in Parkanlagen rund um den Globus ihrem Schicksal überlassen.

Matts Leiderstam beim Abstellen seiner Kopie für / while leaving his copy for *Returned* in Hampstead Heath, London, 1997

*   *   *

The method invites recognition, even identification: the art historian's way of closely scrutinizing a painting before and after renovation; searching archives and old books for the work's provenance; scrutiny of the artist's different versions of the same motif; traveling to the sites where the work was created. It is less about the artist as ethnographer than the artist as art historian and working curator. In a broad sense, we meet the artist as researcher; the bookworm and fact-crunchers are given their allotted portion too. Add to these the semiotician and historian of ideas, as analysts and synthesizers of lines of development. This is a way of working that helps history to seep into the present so that remarkable—even absurd—coincidences arise.

Die Methode fordert dazu auf, Gesehenes zu erkennen, ja sie fordert sogar zur Identifikation auf: die gründliche Inspektion eines Gemäldes durch den Kunsthistoriker vor und nach der Restaurierung; das Durchforsten von Archiven und alten Büchern nach der Provenienz des Werks; die Untersuchung verschiedener Versionen desselben Motivs; Reisen zu den Orten, an denen das Kunstwerk entstand. Dabei geht es weniger um den Künstler als Ethnografen als um den Künstler als Kunsthistoriker und aktiven Kurator. Im weitesten Sinne begegnen wir dem Künstler als Forscher; auch als Bücherwurm und Faktenakrobat darf er in Erscheinung treten – wie nicht zuletzt als Semiotiker und Ideengeschichtler, der Entwicklungslinien analysiert und darstellt. Dies ist eine Arbeitsweise, die der Geschichte hilft, in die Gegenwart vorzudringen, so dass sich erstaunliche – und manchmal sogar absurde – Übereinstimmungen zeigen.

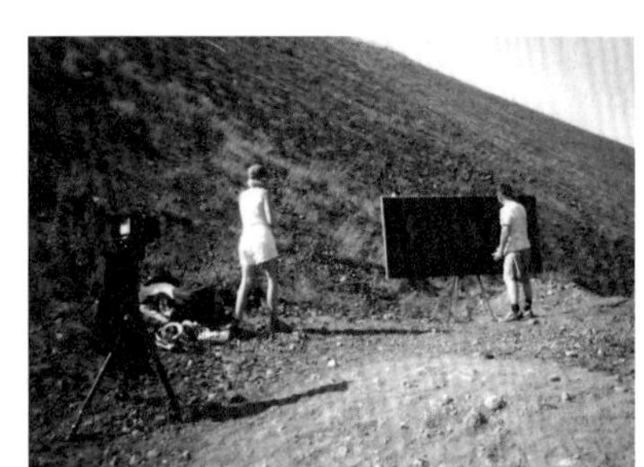

Matts Leiderstam und / and Anna Kleberg, Photo shooting für / for *The Eruption of Vesuvius,* in Neapel / Naples, 2000

*   *   *

The synergic installations are atmospheric but restrained. They aren't stirring or physically all-embracing, nor have they a high emotional temperature. Instead they are strict and decisive, clad in a rather old-fashioned scholarly guise; they do not require white coats and gloves but magnifying glasses and light boxes. Already dead or dying apparatuses and technologies like Claude glasses and slide projectors intermingle with computer screens and video projectors. The objects to

Die synergetischen Installationen sind stimmungsvoll, aber verhalten. Sie sind weder aufwühlend noch physisch vereinnahmend; auch sind sie nicht emotional aufgeladen. Sie sind vielmehr streng und bestimmt und wählen eine ziemlich altmodische wissenschaftliche Erscheinungsform; sie erfordern zwar keine weißen Kittel und Handschuhe, aber Lupen und Leuchtkästen. Bereits ausgestorbene oder überholte Apparate und Technologien wie Claude-Gläser und Diaprojektoren finden sich neben Computermonitoren und Videobeamern. Die Studienobjekte stehen zur visuellen Untersuchung bereit. Auch Blicke

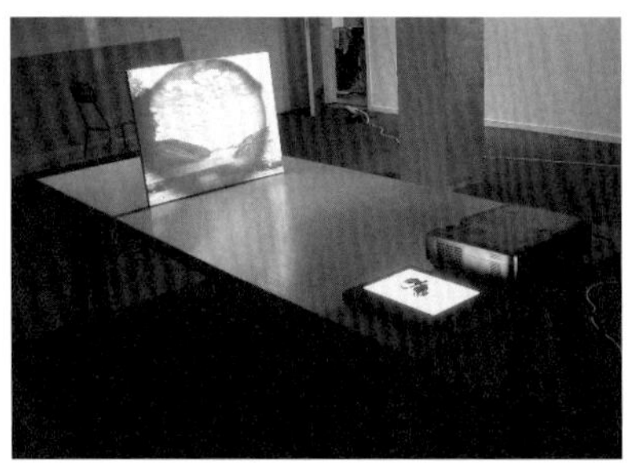

Probeaufbau / Trying out *View (West Point), April 30, 2003,* 2004

MARIA LIND »Parallel worlds / Parallelwelten«

be studied are ready for visual inspection. Views through windows and other openings contribute to the new perspectives. The potential of the space is utilized and new interventions avoided: we can fantasize about what the space can be but, true to the spirit of Brecht, it cannot be conjured away. More than extremely temporarily. Despite the transparence, it can all seem obscure—in the word's best sense—rather than eccentric.

durch Fenster und andere Öffnungen fördern neue Sichtweisen. Das Potenzial des Raums wird genutzt, neue Eingriffe werden vermieden: Wir können uns vorstellen, was der Raum sein kann, aber er lässt sich, ganz im Sinne von Brecht, nicht vollständig wegzaubern. Nur für einen extrem kurzen Moment. Trotz der Transparenz wirkt alles womöglich eher obskur (im besten Sinne des Wortes) als exzentrisch.

*   *   *

There are subtle deviations which only appear when one has spent a certain amount of time with the tables. Together, they create a direction in the room, a clear reference to where our attention should be aimed. We are instructed with mild manipulation: look here, see there, sit down here, step up there. The binoculars or telescopes can be set in a particular way, with specific filters and frames, or aimed at a carefully selected target; at other times, they can be turned in different directions.

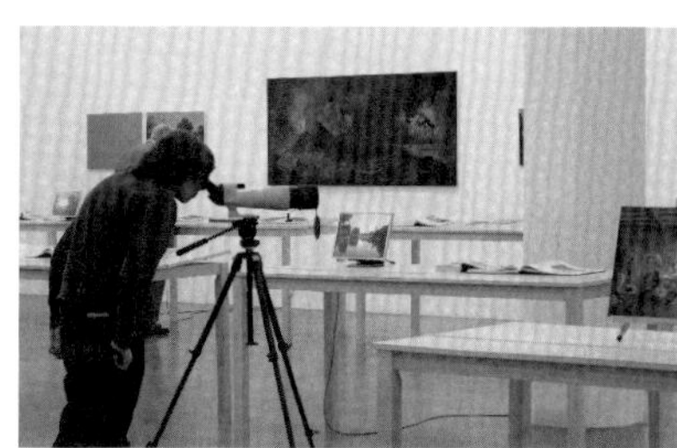

Ausstellungsbesucher / Visitors,
Grand Tour, Magasin 3 Stockholm
Konsthall, 2005

Es gibt subtile Abschweifungen, die erst erkennbar werden, wenn man eine gewisse Zeit an den Tischen verbracht hat. Zusammen erzeugen sie eine Richtung im Raum, einen deutlichen Hinweis auf das, worauf wir unsere Aufmerksamkeit lenken sollen. Wir werden mit sanftem Nachdruck instruiert: Sieh hierhin, schau dorthin, setz dich hier, geh dort hinauf. Die Binokulare oder Ferngläser können auf eine bestimmte Weise, mit speziellen Filtern und Rahmen, eingestellt oder auf ein präzise ausgewähltes Ziel gerichtet sein; in anderen Fällen lassen sie sich in verschiedene Richtungen drehen.

*   *   *

There is an element of choreography and visitor management, with planned patterns of movement and spatial limitations. In both cases, the performative is foregrounded; as visitors we participate in a production and a presentation which have a purpose, an intention. To discover something overlooked, to enjoy something previously unknown—with a sharpened gaze. We find ourselves in the middle of the "exhibitionary complex" where to see and be seen in an institution is a cornerstone in the formation of the modern subject. In the installations we look at images at the same time as we ourselves are exposed to becoming an image.

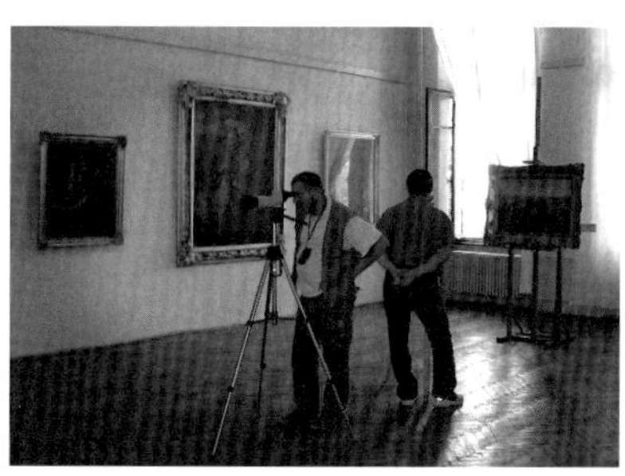

Ausstellungsbesucher / Visitors,
City of Iași in 1842 (Back to the Future),
Iași Art Museum, 2003

Es gibt ein Moment von Choreografie und Besucherführung, mit kalkulierten Bewegungsabläufen und räumlichen Begrenzungen. In beiden Fällen wird das Performative in den Vordergrund gerückt; als Betrachter sind wir an einer Produktion und einer Präsentation beteiligt, die eine Absicht, einen Zweck verfolgen: etwas zu entdecken, das bisher übersehen wurde, und sich – mit geschärftem Blick – an etwas bislang Unbekanntem zu erfreuen. Wir befinden uns inmitten des »Ausstellungskomplexes«, in dem es zu einem Grundzug in der Entwicklung des modernen Subjekts gehört, in einer Institution zu sehen und gesehen zu werden. In den Installationen betrachten wir Bilder, während wir selbst der Situation ausgesetzt sind, ein Bild zu werden.

*   *   *

Sometimes people execute a particular action in the exhibition space: for instance, copying an original painting or looking intensively at specially selected paintings for a

Manchmal führen Menschen im Ausstellungsraum ungewöhnliche Tätigkeiten aus: Sie kopieren beispielsweise ein Original oder betrachten ausgewählte Gemälde für eine

certain amount of time. All the while, the beard grows longer and longer to end up resembling the beard in the self-portrait on the wall.

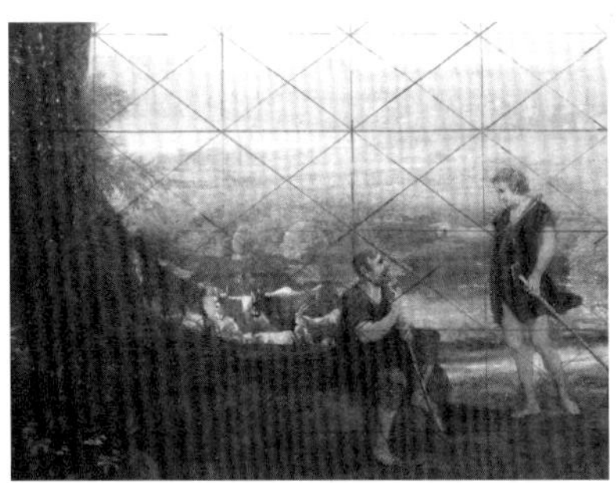

gewisse Zeit mit großer Intensität. Währenddessen wird der Bart immer länger, um schließlich dem Bart in dem Selbstbildnis an der Wand zu ähneln.

Photo shooting, *Selbstbildnis,*
Schack-Galerie München, 2002

* * *

Yet here is also something less rational, something more difficult to grasp and more driven by desire. Cruising as a way to seek and sometimes to find whatever can elicit and satisfy a certain desire. A discreet, sometimes totally hidden model for how entities are linked together in an exchange. It is here that something dry in the presentation, somewhat dusty in the expression, comes forth as a breaking point.

Doch es gibt hier auch etwas weniger Rationales, etwas, das nicht so leicht fassbar und mehr vom Begehren gesteuert ist. Ein Umherstreifen, um etwas zu suchen und manchmal auch zu finden, das ein bestimmtes Begehren wecken und befriedigen kann. Ein diskretes und manchmal vollständig verborgenes Modell dafür, wie Existenzen durch Austausch miteinander verbunden sind. Hier wird die gewisse Trockenheit der Präsentation, das leicht Staubige des Ausdrucks, als eine Bruchstelle deutlich.

Vorbereitende Studie für / Preparatory study for *The Sun,* 2003

* * *

Despite all the restraint and attention to facts, there is a fervor: eyes meet and the corners of the mouth turn up. Fingers signal and absence speaks. A dark part of the bushes in a painted copy suddenly promises secret dalliances. Correspondences of a less conventional kind are staged, and contact arises as part of an erotic game that begins with visual attraction and that can easily end with abrupt breaks, even with pain. However, the logic is the opposite of the pornographic: here things are suggested rather than expressed. References to sexuality are with an assured sense of style, albeit not polished. Equally, as in the exhibitions in general, it is about how a place is negotiated, about the transference of desire from image to person, back to image and back to person, etc. How inner and outer images fluctuate and how intense pleasure is followed by sobering, and then the process starts all over again.

Trotz aller Zurückhaltung und Konzentration auf die Fakten gibt es auch Leidenschaftlichkeit: Blicke begegnen sich, Mundwinkel heben sich. Finger geben Zeichen, das Abwesende ist vielsagend. Ein dunkler Bereich des Gebüschs in einer gemalten Kopie verheißt plötzlich heimliche Liebesspiele. Weniger konventionelle Korrespondenzen werden inszeniert, und Kontakt entsteht als Teil eines erotischen Spiels, das mit visueller Anziehungskraft beginnt und ohne Weiteres abrupt, ja sogar schmerzhaft enden kann. Die Logik ist jedoch das Gegenteil von Pornografie: Dinge werden hier eher angedeutet als ausformuliert. Hinweise auf Sexualität werden mit sicherem Stilgefühl vorgetragen, aber nicht aufpoliert. Ebenso geht es, wie in den Ausstellungen im Allgemeinen, darum, wie ein Ort verhandelt wird, wie das Begehren vom Bild auf die Person übertragen wird und wieder zurück auf das Bild und zurück auf die Person und so fort.

Wie innere und äußere Bilder sich ständig verändern und wie auf intensive Lust Ernüchterung folgt und der Vorgang wieder von vorne beginnt.

Installation von / of
Adolf Ludvig Stierneld,
Nationalmuseum in
Stockholm, 2004

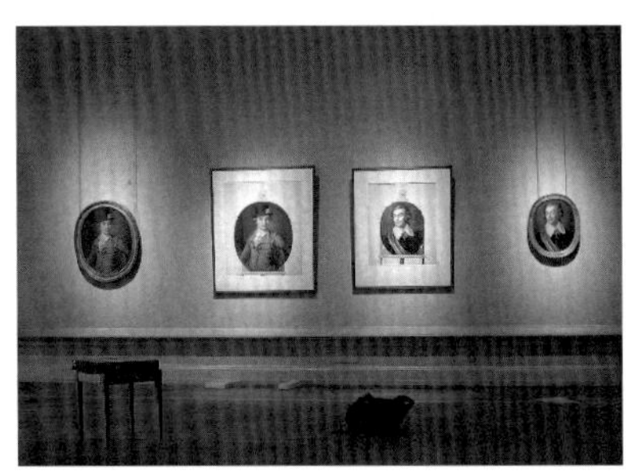

MARIA LIND »Parallel worlds / Parallelwelten«

144

* * *

If conceptual artists went from the aesthetics of administration to the administration of aesthetics, then here there is a movement from the aesthetics of research to the research of the aesthetic. The entire practice is research-based and even includes Sweden's first artist Ph.D. However, it isn't just about the regimes of art-history aesthetics in terms of high art but also the regimes of the visual in a broader sense: how we see and what we see. Doubt arises immediately: how do we know that what we see agrees with the seen? In a strict sense, not even a microscope can guarantee correct vision. Beyond the disregarded gaze and the blind spots of the majority culture lie the conscious and unconscious codes that everyone uses. So it is hardly surprising that the material can seem nerdy and uncool; even if undisputed masters figure in it, they are relegated to the category pre-modern history—in other words, more or less irrelevant.

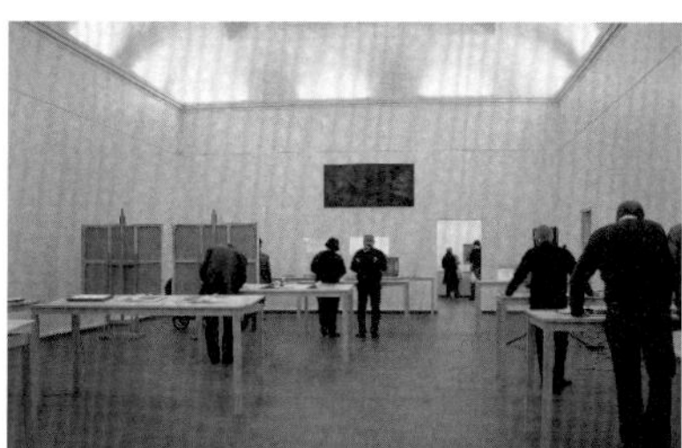

Vergrößerungsglas / Magnifying glass
in *Provenience,* 2008

Wenn Konzeptkünstler von der Ästhetik der Verwaltung zur Verwaltung der Ästhetik übergegangen sind, dann findet sich hier eine Bewegung von der Ästhetik der Forschung zur Erforschung des Ästhetischen. Die gesamte Arbeit beruht auf Recherchen und brachte den ersten künstlerisch erreichten akademischen Ph.D.-Titel Schwedens hervor. Allerdings geht es nicht nur um die Regimes kunsthistorischer Ästhetik mit Blick auf die Hochkunst, sondern auch um die Regimes des Visuellen in einem umfassenderen Sinn: wie wir sehen und was wir sehen. Sofort kommt Zweifel auf: Woher wissen wir, dass das, was wir sehen, mit dem Gesehenen übereinstimmt? Streng genommen, kann nicht einmal ein Mikroskop eine korrekte Sicht garantierten. Die bewussten und unbewussten Codes, die jeder verwendet, liegen außerhalb des unbeachteten Blicks und der blinden Flecke der Mehrheitskultur. So überrascht es kaum, dass das Material nerdig und uncool erscheinen kann; selbst wenn unbestrittene Meister darunter sind, werden sie in die Kategorie der Vormoderne verbannt – sie sind, mit anderen Worten, mehr oder weniger irrelevant.

* * *

Here there is a desire to know, but what is proposed is another model for knowing than that priviledged by the mainstream—neither purely pre-modern nor entirely modern episteme. Instead, we are offered another form for knowledge, one based on empirical eclecticism and a large dose of imagination. The pre-modern, or in other words the pre-Freudian, is paired with completely contemporary references. If modernity is our current antiquity, with an endless variation of modernist "neo-classicisms," then these pre-modern preferences are comparable to a metaphorical Middle Ages—often considered unsophisticated and irrelevant, with the wrong aesthetics, but in fact dynamic and genuinely innovative.

Grand Tour, Göteborgs Konsthall, 2005
Vorbereitung von / Preparing *Provenience,*
Stockholm, 2008

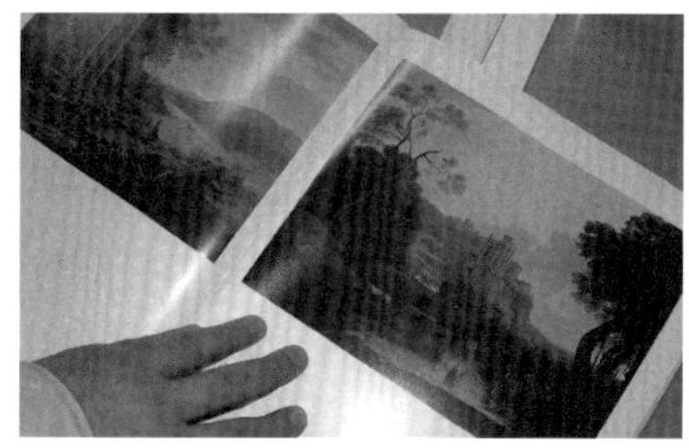

Es gibt hier einen Wunsch zu wissen, aber es wird ein anderes Modell des Wissens vorgeschlagen als das vom Mainstream bevorzugte – ein weder rein vormodernes noch gänzlich modernes Epistem. Stattdessen wird uns eine andere Form für Wissen angeboten, die auf empirischem Eklektizismus und einer großen Portion Vorstellungskraft beruht. Das Vormoderne oder, anders ausgedrückt, das Vorfreudianische, wird mit ganz und gar zeitgenössischen Referenzen gepaart. Wenn die Moderne unsere gegenwärtige Antike ist, mit ihren endlosen Variationen modernistischer »Neoklassizismen«, dann lassen sich diese vormodernen Vorlieben mit einem metaphorischen Mittelalter vergleichen – das oft für naiv und irrelevant gehalten wird und angeblich die falsche Ästhetik hatte, tatsächlich jedoch dynamisch und höchst innovativ war.

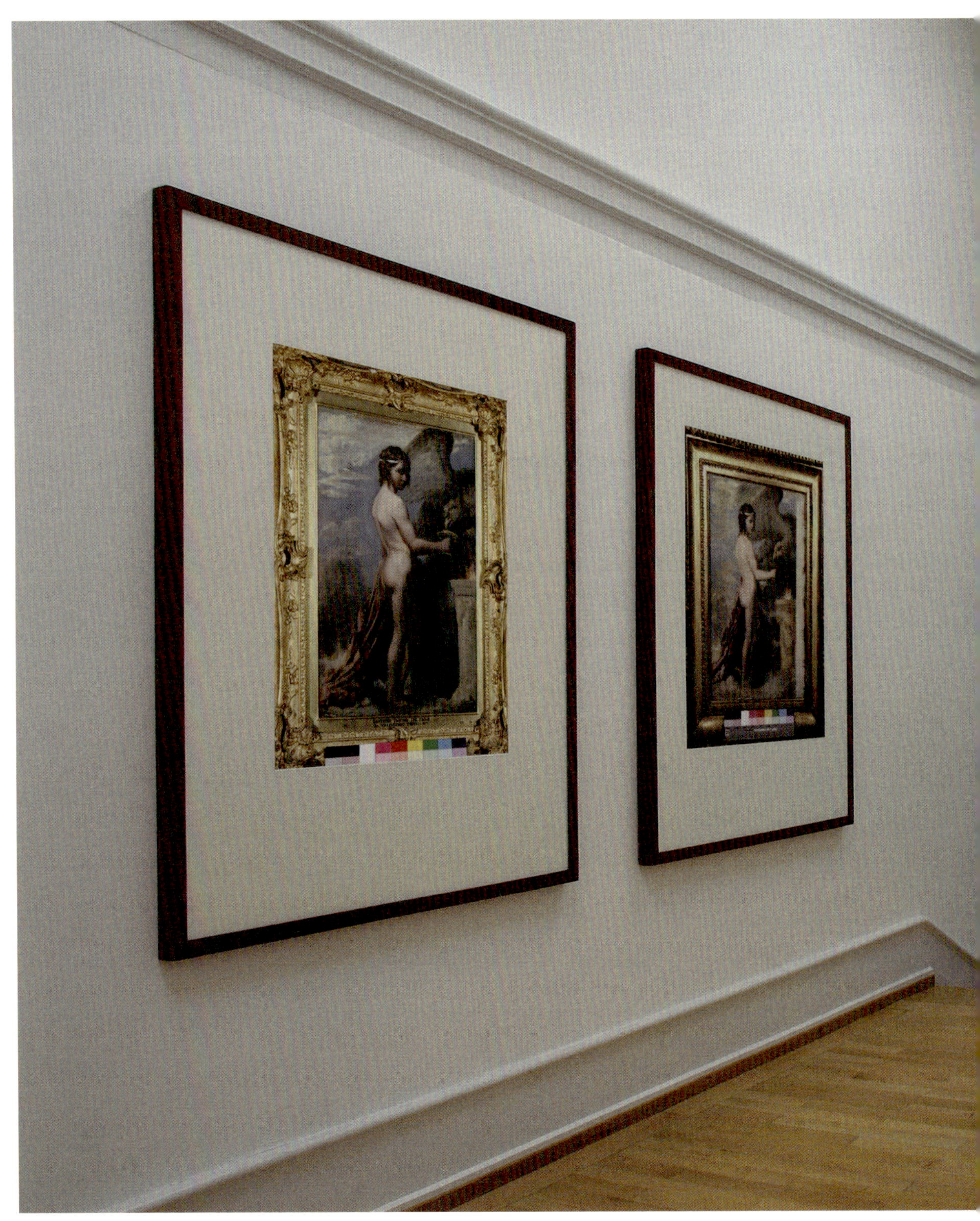

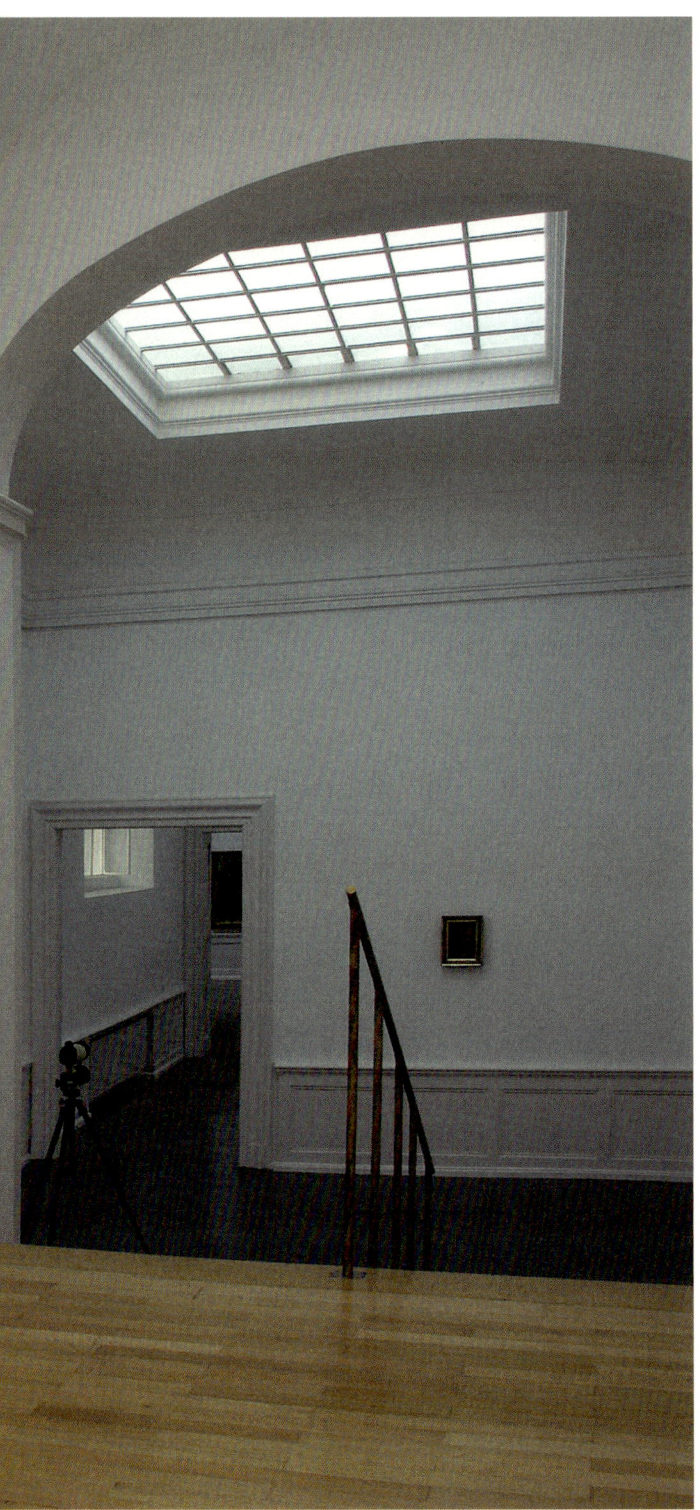

Die beiden Fotografien in *Sketch and Fresco* zeigen zwei Stadien eines Werks des englischen Malers Richard Evans (1784–1871) mit dem Titel *Ganymed Feeding the Eagle*. Als Evans die in einem dunkleren Kolorit gehaltene Ölskizze (1822) als Fresko realisierte, erfuhr das mythologische Motiv nicht nur eine Veränderung durch das malerische Verfahren, sondern auch eine deutliche atmosphärische Umwertung, die Leiderstams Aufmerksamkeit auf sich zog. Während Ganymed, der in der bildenden Kunst häufig als Projektionsfigur homoerotischer Fantasien diente, in der Studie noch kokett aus dem Bild herausschaut und der Adler bedrohlich wirkt, scheint das Fresko im Vergleich deutlich verklärter und entschärft. Darüber hinaus gilt Leiderstams Interesse auch in dieser Arbeit wieder einer Anekdote aus der Provenienzgeschichte der historischen Vorlage. Nachdem Evans mit seinem Schaffen in Rom, wo er sich nach einem Studium der italienischen Malerei niedergelassen hatte, keine befriedigenden Erfolge verbuchen konnte, gab er sein Atelier schließlich auf. Das besagte Fresko ließ er zurück. Bei einem Besuch des Kensington Museum in London einige Jahre später entdeckte er dort sein Fresko wieder, ausgestellt als antikes Original aus einer Grabstätte im Umland Roms. Nur Dank der Ölskizze, die ihm als Vorstudie für das Fresko gedient hatte, gelang es ihm, den Generaldirektor des Museums von seiner Autorschaft zu überzeugen.

The photographs in *Sketch and Fresco* show two stages of a work entitled *Ganymed Feeding the Eagle* by the English painter Richard Evans (1784–1871). When Evans realized them as frescos, with a sketch in oils (1822) held in a darker coloration, the mythological motif experienced not only an alteration by means of the painterly method, but also a marked atmospheric re-evaluation, which caught Leiderstam's attention. Whereas Ganymed, who frequently served as a focus for the projections of homoerotic fantasy in the fine arts, still gazes out coquettishly from the painting and the eagle looks menacing, the fresco, by contrast, seems significantly more blissful and defused. Over and above this, Leiderstam's interest is directed once again, in this work, to an anecdote about the provenance of the historic template. After Evans had been largely unsuccessful with his work in Rome, where he had settled following a period of study of Italian painting, he finally abandoned his studio there. He left behind the fresco in question. Some years later, on a visit to the Kensington Museum in London, he came across his fresco exhibited as an original classical exponent from a cemetery in the vicinity of Rome. Thanks to the sketch in oils that had served him as a preliminary study for the fresco, he was then able to convince the director of the museum that he was indeed the rightful painter.

EVANS, Richard (1784–1871)

Born 1784; pupil of and assistant to Sir Thomas Lawrence, painting for him drapery, backgrounds and replicas. Exhibited 42 works, mostly portraits, at the RA between 1816 and 1845 (when he is supposed to have had a dispute when his pictures were refused) and six subject pictures at the BI 1831–56. Visited Paris in 1814, copying paintings in the Louvre, and lived for many years in Rome, where he copied old masters and attempted fresco painting. He painted copies of Raphael's arabesque decorations and panels in the Vatican Loggia for the V&A which were acquired in 1843. Died Southampton, November 1871.

LIT: *Art Journal* 1872, p75 (obit); *The Times* 30 May 1958

Ganymede Feeding the Eagle
159-1865   Neg GJ5988
Fresco, 61 × 49.5 cm (24 × 19½ ins)
Given by Sir Matthew White Ridley BI 1865

According to an old label (see below), painted in Rome, in the manner of an antique Roman fresco. The *Art Journal* gave a fuller account quoting an obituary of Evans in the *Hampshire Telegraph* published late in 1871:

> During his residence in Rome he experimentally practised fresco-painting, and, on giving up his studio there, presented one of these paintings, which he did not care to take with him, to the attendant who swept out the studio. Many years afterwards, when on a visit to the Kensington Museum, he was astonished to find this identical fresco hanging up there, it having been presented by the executors of a wealthy connoisseur as a genuine piece of antique fresco-painting from a tomb the neighbourhood of Rome. He examined his original sketch of the subject [presumably 36–1870 p89], made a special journey to London, convinced Mr Redgrave, the Director-General for Art, that the fresco was really his work, and not an antique, and the picture now hangs at foot of one of the staircases in the Kensington Museum, with its real history attached to it.

The most famous modern depiction of the god Jupiter and his youthful companion and cup-bearer Ganymede is also a fresco, painted by Anton Mengs in 1758–9 in imitation of antique Herculanaeum wall-painting and intended to deceive his friend, the connoisseur Winckelmann. Evans, however, seems to base the pose of Ganymede on Michelangelo's famous marble sculpture of 'Bacchus' (Bargello, Florence). He depicts Jupiter in the traditional guise of an eagle.

The old label reads:

> Ganymede feeding the Eagle. /Fresco, painted at Rome, by Richard Evans, in the manner of the antique Roman frescoes./Presented by Sir M W Ridley, Bart, MP, with relation to the durability of modern fresco painting./This work was purchased in 1836, by the late Sir M W Ridley Bart, from Capranesi of Rome,/together with another fresco, now in the British Museum, which is a true work of antiquity./Capranesi stated that they were taken from a tomb in the Via-Appia./This fresco was however subsequently recognized by Mr R Evans, as his own work.

Sir Matthew Ridley (1807–77) gave two fresco paintings to the British Museum in 1865. Of the first, the head and torso of a man, the 1933 catalogue states: 'This fragment is said to have come from the "Baths of Ti (ie the Golden House of Nero). It is much repainted and the style and accessories are not antique in feeling'. Of the other, a flute-player, the catalogue records:

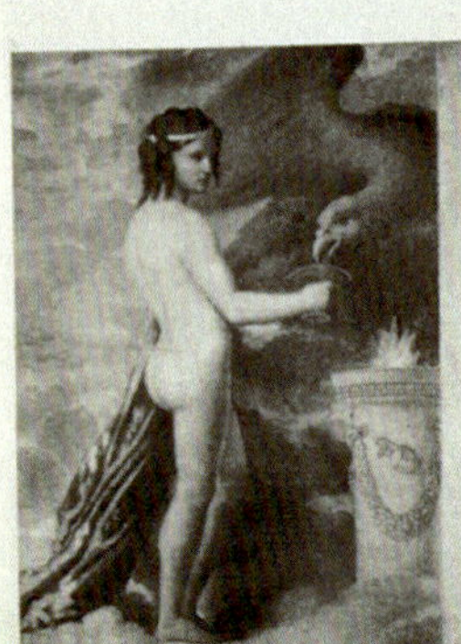

Ganymede Feeding the Eagle   159-1865

This fragment is said to have been found in a columbarium on the Via
Appia in 1823. The whole surface is so completely covered with modern
paint that no trace of ancient work is visible; and in view of the
exceptionally large scale, and the sentimental pose, it is very probable
that the whole figure is a 19th century fabrication, and not merely a
heavily restored original (A P Hinks *Catalogue of the Greek Etruscan and
Roman Paintings and Mosaics in the British Museum* 1933, p62, nos 91 and
92, repr figs 69, 70).

It seems likely that the latter painting is also the work of Richard Evans, as
there are similarities in style and mood to the present work.

LIT: *Art Journal* 1872, p75

Ganymede Feeding the Eagle
36-1870   Negs GB424, GB425 (with part of frame)
Paper on canvas, 58.4 × 42.1 cm (23 × 16⅝ ins)
Given by the artist 1870

An oil sketch, said to have been painted in 1822, for the fresco (see
59–1865, p88).

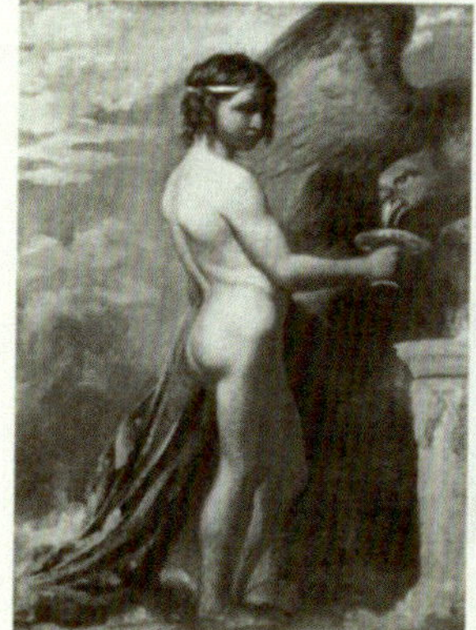

Ganymede Feeding the Eagle   36-1870

FAED, John, RSA (1819–1902)

Born Gatehouse-of-Fleet, Kirkcudbrightshire, 31 August 1819, son of a
millwright and engineer, and elder brother of the painter Thomas Faed RA.
Worked as a miniature painter by the age of nine. Moved to Edinburgh
1839/40, and studied at the RSA. Exhibited 40 works at the RA between
1855 and 1893, three at the SBA in 1879, but principally at the RSA: 234
works 1841–95 (elected ARSA 1847, RSA 1851). Early works were
miniature portraits, then, in 1850s, subjects from Shakespeare, the Bible,
Burns, Scott, and Scottish ballads, and also landscapes; achieved a
considerable reputation by 1860. Founder member of the sketching club 'The
Smashers', continued in London as 'Auld Lang Syne'. Toured Middle East
1857, moved to London 1864, retired to Gatehouse 1880. Studio sale at
Christie's 11 June 1880. Several of his works were engraved. Died Gatehouse
22 October 1902.

LIT: *Art Journal* 1871, pp237–9; *Scotsman* 23 October 1902 (obit); *DNB*;
       Wood Dict; M McKerrow *The Faeds – A Biography* 1982

The Great Hall at Haddon
104-1900
Millboard, 35.5 × 50.7 cm (14 × 20 ins)
Signed and dated '.Faed 1860.' br
Purchased 1900

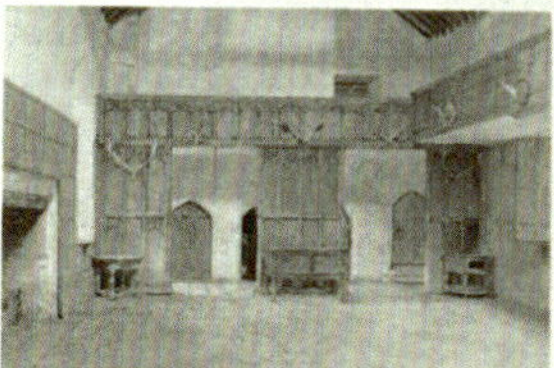

The Great Hall at Haddon   104-1900

Haddon Hall, Derbyshire, home of the Vernon family, now Dukes of
Rutland, was principally built from 1370 onwards; the great Banqueting Hall,
typically medieval in plan, is the oldest room of which the original structure
is still substantially intact. Faed shows the entrance screen with the minstrels'
gallery above (compare the photograph repr in the 1977 guide book, p12,
which shows almost the same view with some of the furniture in the same
position). Because of features such as the castellated towers, the Picturesque
aspect of Haddon Hall was much admired by painters, and – particularly in
the 19th century – used inside and outside for backgrounds for pictures (see
for example J C Horsley's 'Rival Performers', FA83 p129). In the artist's 1880
sale there were numerous sketches of Haddon; in his list of works, 'Haddon
Hall in Old Times' is given under 1865 and as bought by the dealer Gambart

89

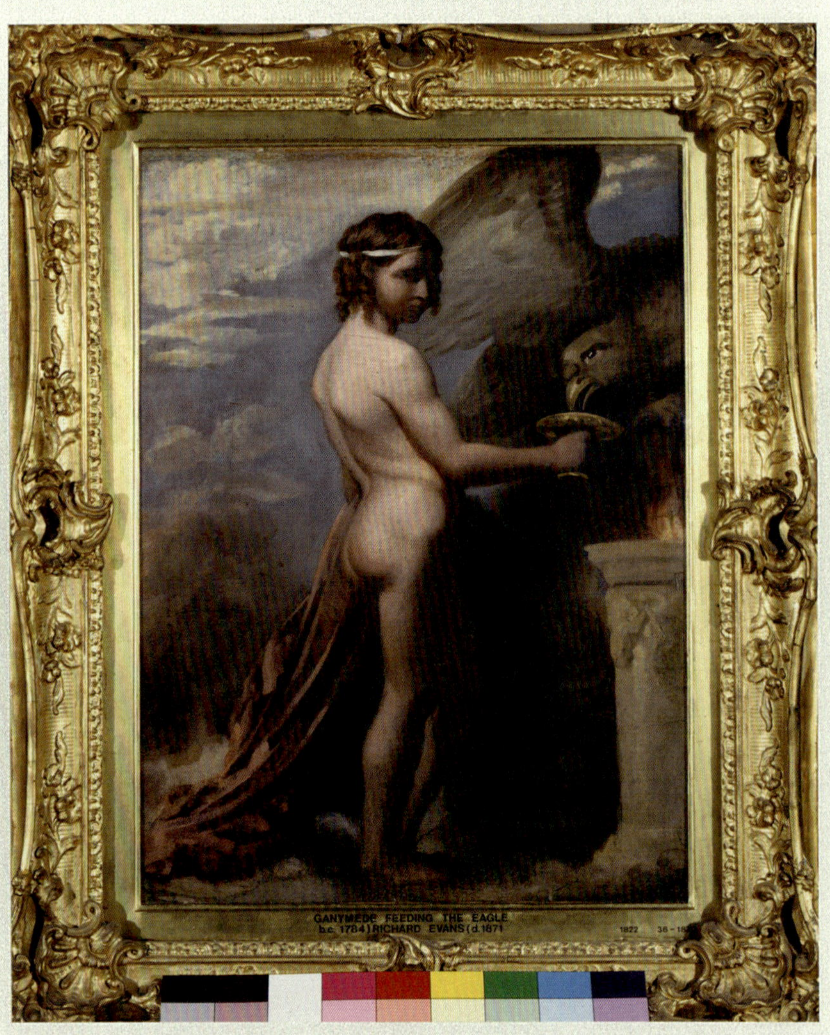

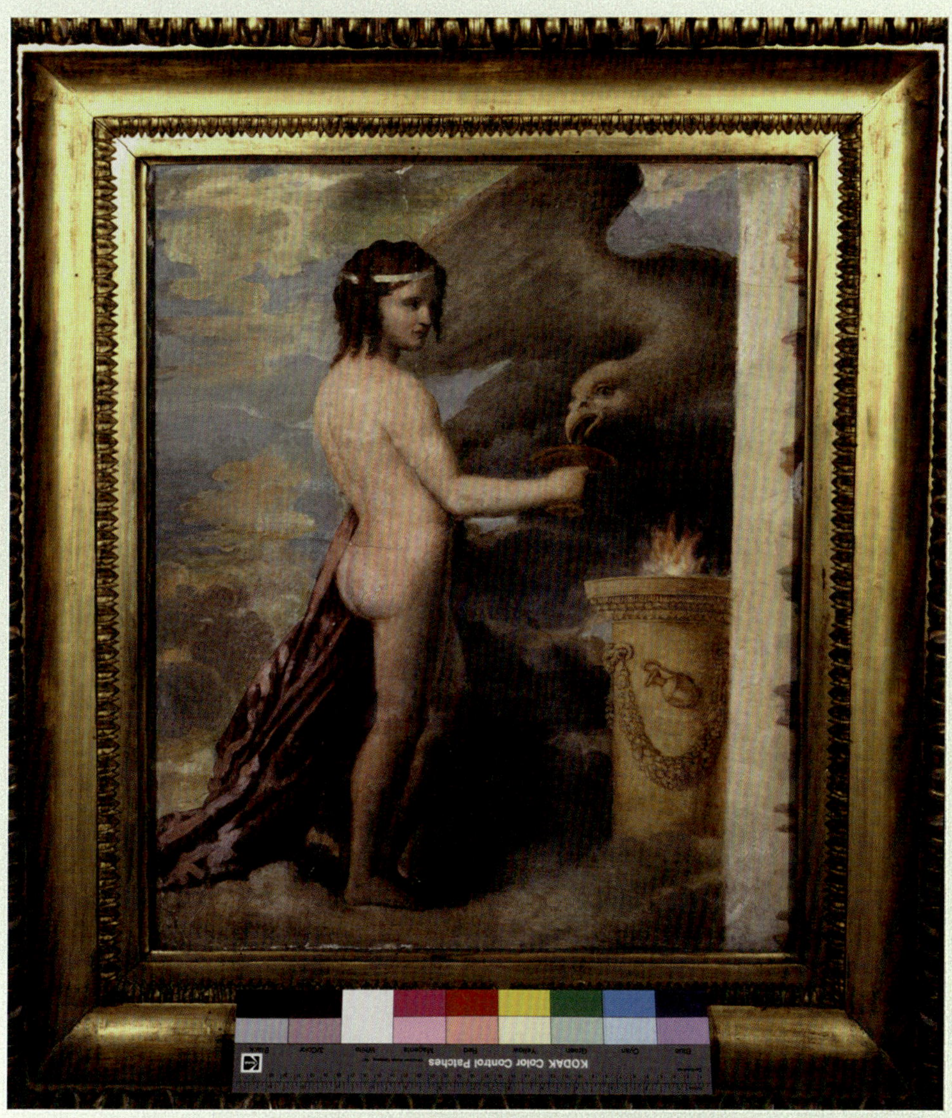

Mit der Installation dreier historischer Männerbildnisse aus der Sammlung des Kunstmuseum Liechtenstein spielt Leiderstam auf die homosexuelle Praxis des »Cruisings« an, dem flanierenden Ausschauhalten nach potenziellen Sexualpartnern in städtischen Parks oder auf Parkplätzen. Insbesondere der männliche Betrachter sieht sich hier unfreiwillig in ein imaginiertes Beziehungsgefüge eingebunden, indem er mit dem Bildnis eines flötespielenden Jünglings aus der Werkstatt von Frans Hals (1645–1650), Bernardino Licinio da Pordenones *Porträt eines jungen Mannes* aus dem frühen 16. Jahrhundert und Jan de Brays Gentleman aus dem späten 17. Jahrhundert konfrontiert wird. Die Inszenierung wirft Fragen auf, suggeriert sie doch eine für die meisten Betrachter ungewohnte Verdichtung scheinbar expliziter männlicher Blicke. Gleichzeitig bieten sich die Porträtierten dem geneigten Besucher als Zielscheibe erotischer Fantasien im Museumsraum an.

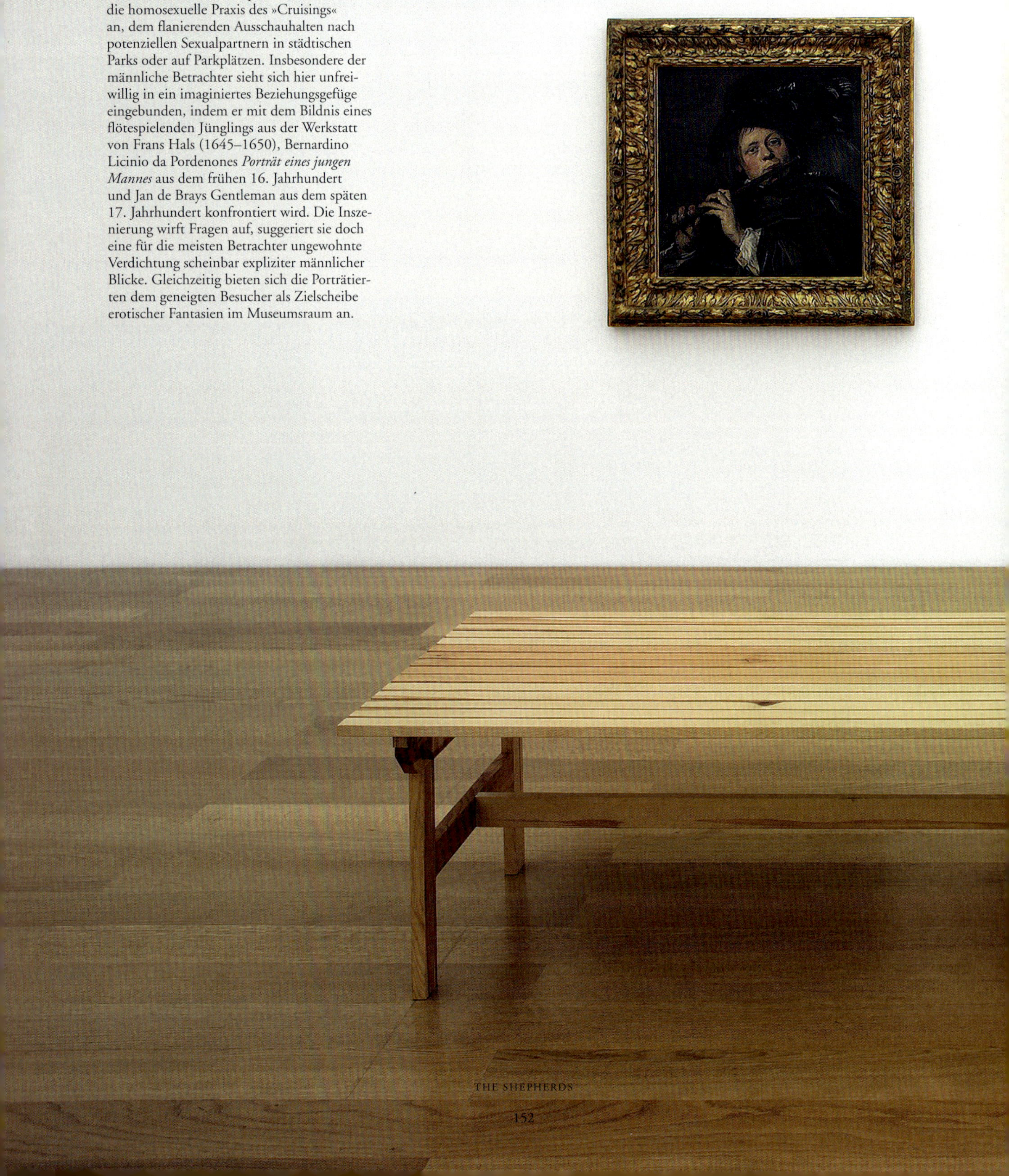

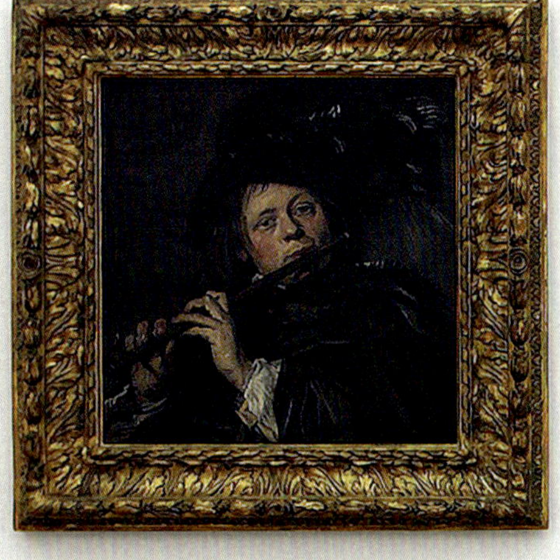

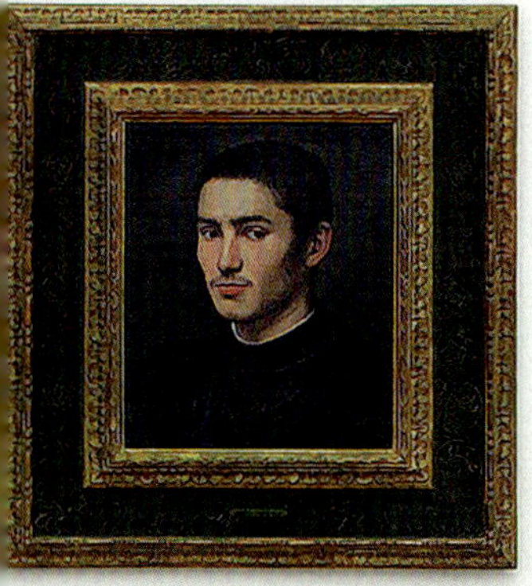

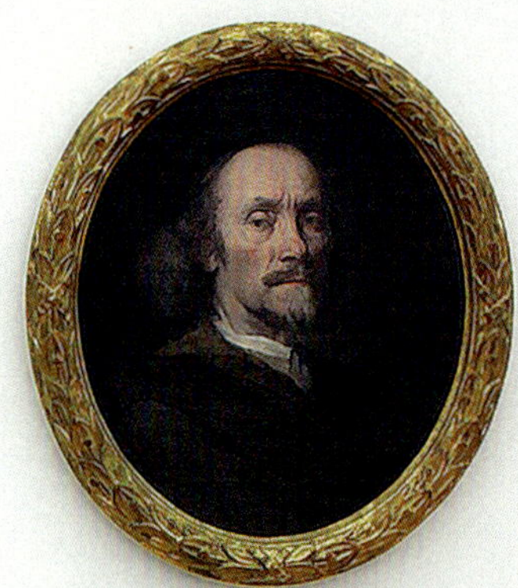

With the installation of three historical male portraits from the collection of the Liechtenstein Kunstmuseum, Leiderstam alludes to the homosexual practice of "cruising" of casually strolling around municipal parks or parking lots on the lookout for potential sexual partners. The male viewer, in particular, finds himself caught up in an imaginary web of relationships, in which he is engaged by the image of a flute-playing young man from the studio of Frans Hals (1645–1650), Bernardino Licinio da Pordenone's *Portrait of a Young Man* from the sixteenth century and Jan de Bray's late seventeenth-century portrait entitled *Gentleman*. The setting itself raises questions, suggesting for the majority of viewers an unusual concentration of apparently explicitly male ways of looking at people and things. At the same time, the subjects portrayed offer the suitably inclined museum visitor the opportunity to view the portraits as a target for erotic fantasies within the space of the museum.

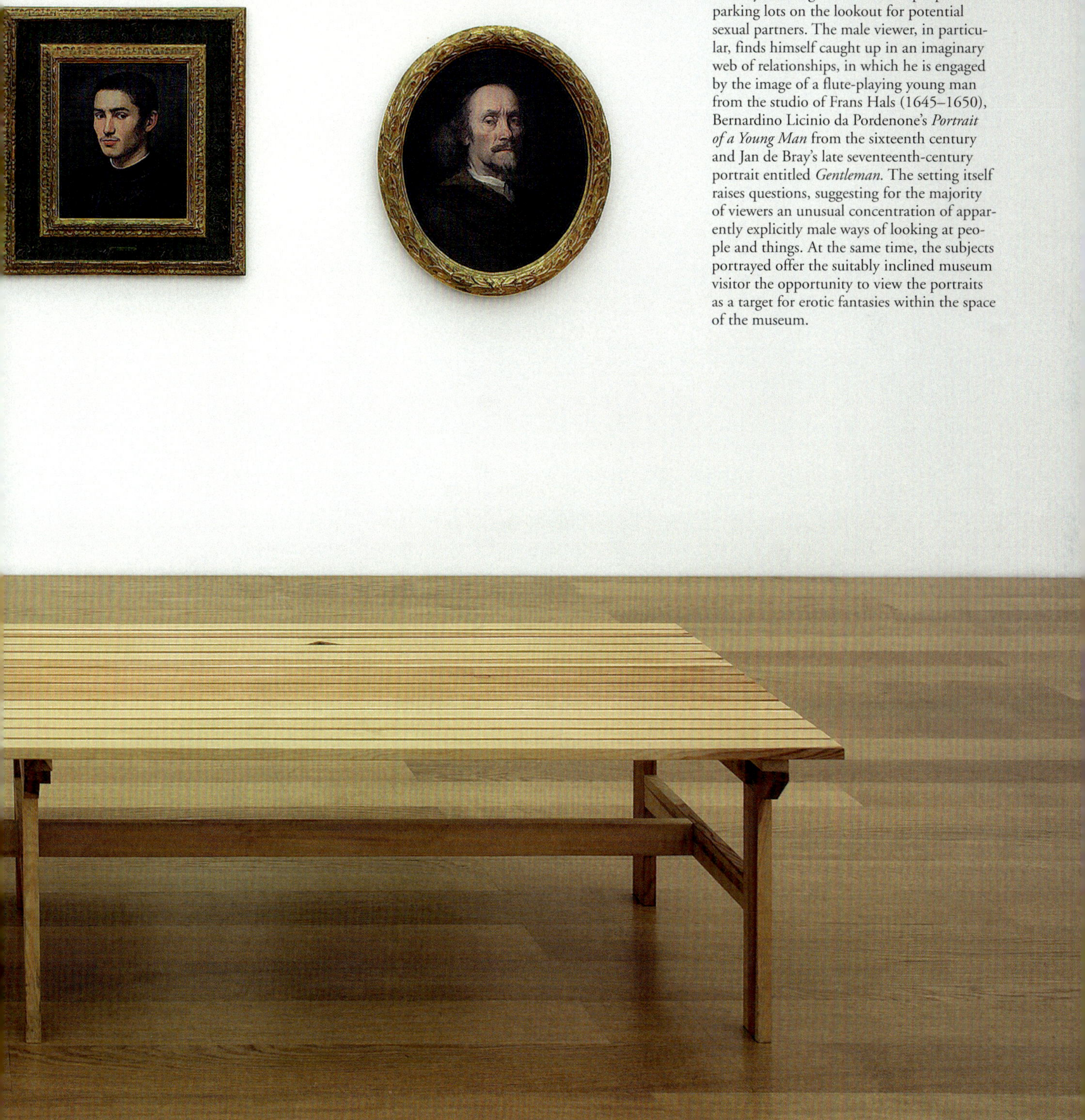

CRUISING WITH NICOLAS POUSSIN (MADE AFTER NICOLAS POUSSIN'S SPRING OR THE EARTHLY PARADISE, 1662–1664), 1996

Die ephemere Bodenarbeit *Cruising with Nicolas Poussin* realisierte
Leiderstam erstmalig im Rahmen der Ausstellung *See What It Feels
Like!* im Rooseum Center for Contemporary Art in Malmö. In der
Art eines Straßenmalers übertrug er Poussins Gemälde *Le Printemps
ou le Paradis terrestre* (1660–1664) mit Kohle und Kreide direkt auf
den Boden des Museums, wobei er lediglich die üppige Vegetation
übernahm, aber auf die Darstellung von Gott, Adam und Eva verzichtete. Er positionierte die Arbeit so, dass die Besucher es kaum
vermeiden konnten, über das Bild zu laufen und die Landschaft in
einem sehr wörtlichen Sinne zu betreten. Dabei nahmen sie mit
ihren Schuhsohlen Teile der Farbschichten auf und verteilten sie mit
jedem Schritt weiter durch die Ausstellung. Die idealisierte Natur in
der Malerei, für die Leiderstam hier exemplarisch Poussin zitiert,
diente den Landschaftsarchitekten des 18. Jahrhunderts als Vorlage
für die Entwicklung der sogenannten englischen Gärten und hat
auf diesem Weg unsere Wahrnehmung von der Natur als einer vom
Menschen geschaffenen Landschaft substanziell geprägt.

Leiderstam realized the ephemeral floor piece *Cruising with Nicolas Poussin* for the first time within the framework of the exhibition *See What It Feels Like!*, in the Rooseum Center for Contemporary Art in Malmö. In the manner of a street artist using chalk and charcoal, he transferred Poussin's painting *Le Printemps ou Le Paradis terrestre* (1662–1664) directly onto the floor of the museum by adapting only the lush vegetation here and forgoing the depiction of God and of Adam and Eve. He positioned the work in such a way that visitors could scarcely avoid walking across it and thereby literally entering the landscape. In so doing, they inadvertently picked up and removed parts of the layers of colored chalk on the soles of their shoes and subsequently spread them throughout the exhibition with every step. The aspect of idealized nature in painting, for which Leiderstam cites Poussin as a prime exemplar, served eighteenth-century landscape architects as a model for the development of the so-called English garden and has substantially shaped our perception of nature as a man-made landscape.

CRUISING WITH NICOLAS POUSSIN

RETURNED, 1997–1998

Für die Fotoserie *Returned* fertigte Leiderstam fünf Kopien von Nicolas Poussins Gemälde *Le Printemps ou le Paradis terreste* (1660–1664) an. Abweichend vom historischen Original verzichtete er jedoch auf die Darstellung Gottes sowie der Figuren Adams und Evas und rückte damit das Motiv der Landschaft in den Mittelpunkt. Anschließend stellte Leiderstam seine Adaptionen in solchen Parks und Grünanlagen verschiedener europäischer und US-amerikanischer Großstädte auf, die dafür bekannt sind, von homosexuellen Männern als Cruising-Sites frequentiert zu werden. Er fotografierte die Arbeiten dort und ließ sie anschließend zurück. Der Verbleib der Gemälde ist unbekannt.

For the photo series *Returned,* Leiderstam produced five copies of Nicolas Poussin's painting *Le Printemps ou le Paradis terreste* (1660–1664). Deviating from the original, however, he omitted the depiction of God, as well as the figures of Adam and Eve, thereby highlighting the landscape motif. Leiderstam subsequently displayed his adaptations in different European and American cities in those parks and green spaces known to insiders as cruising sites for homosexual men. He photographed the works there and afterwards left them behind. The whereabouts of the individual paintings are unknown.

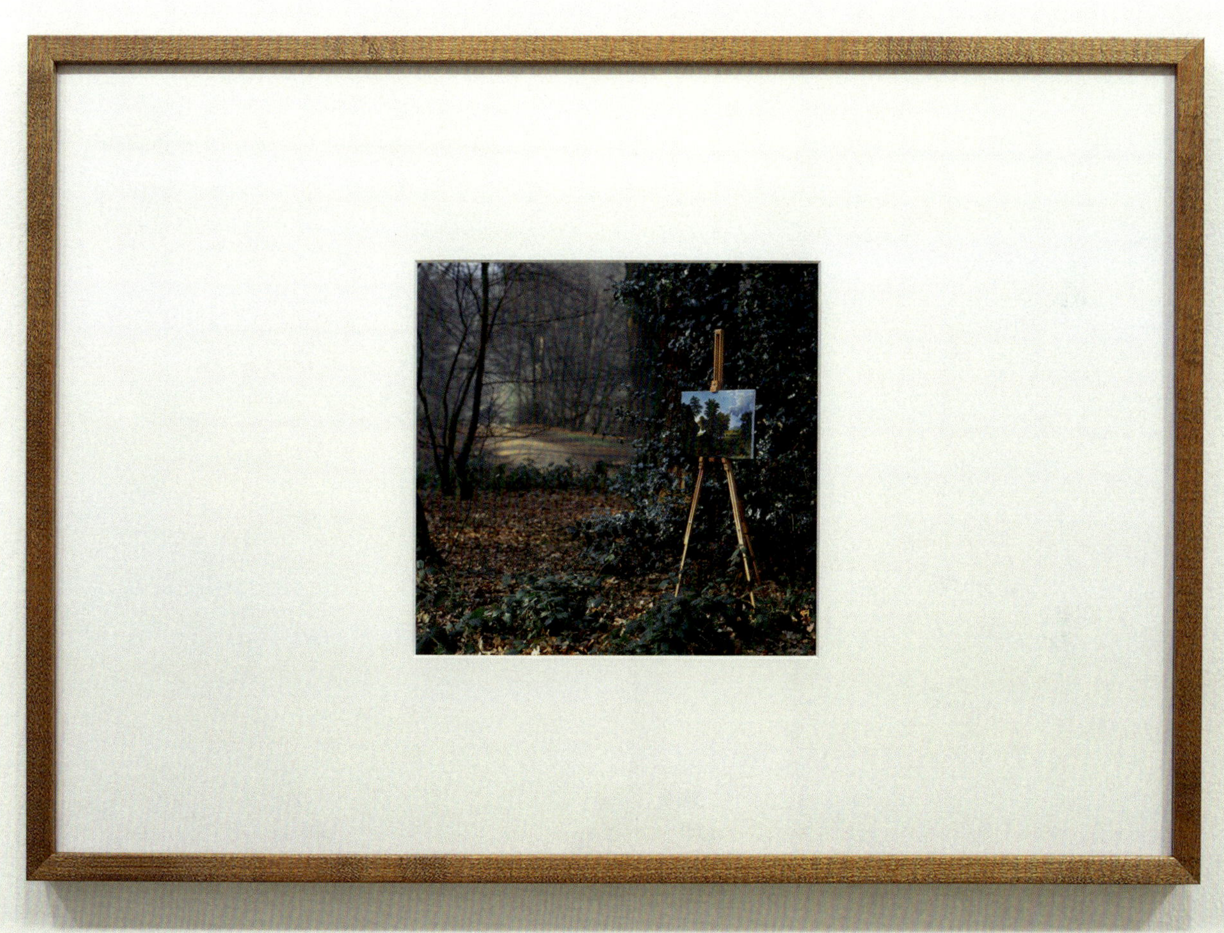

Returned Hampstead Heath, London, 1997

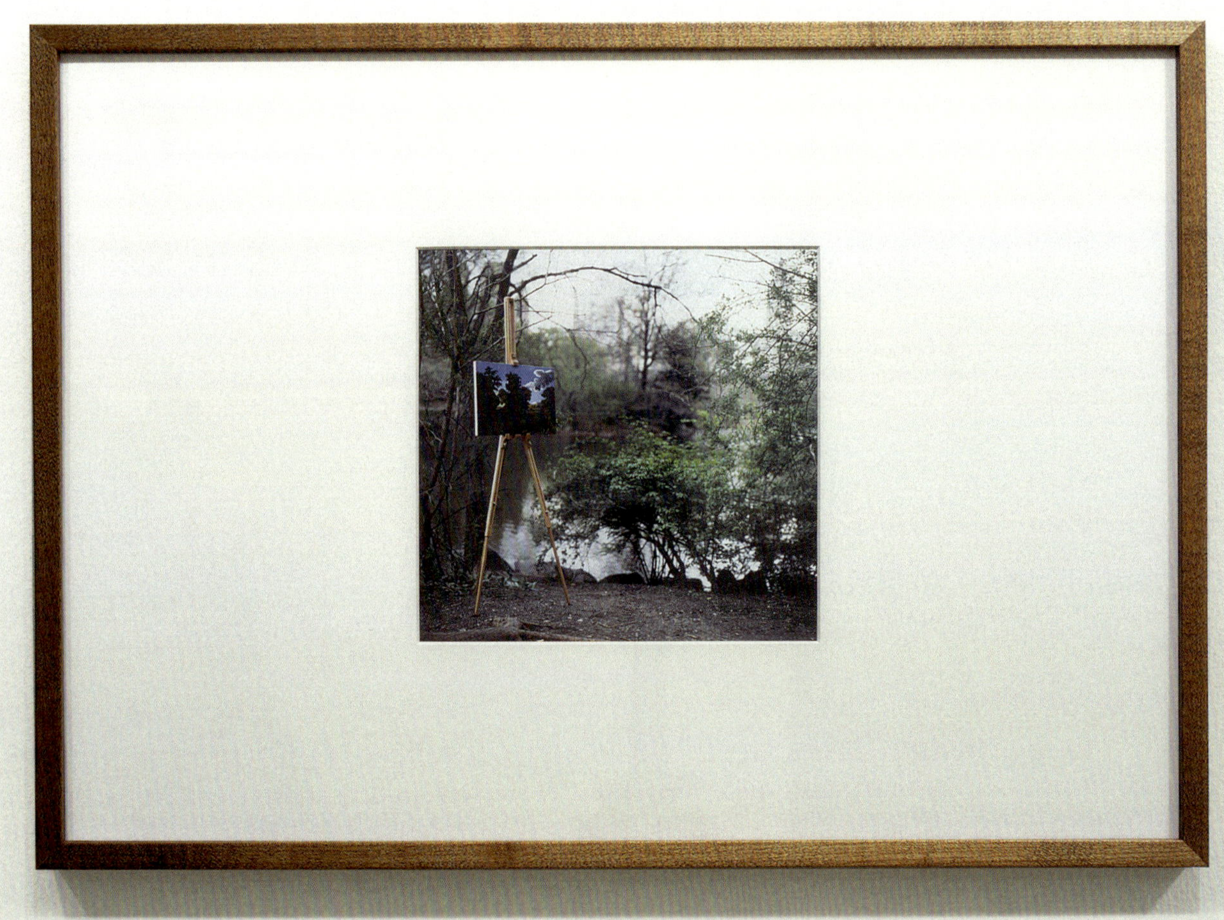

Returned, The Ramble, Central Park, New York, 1997

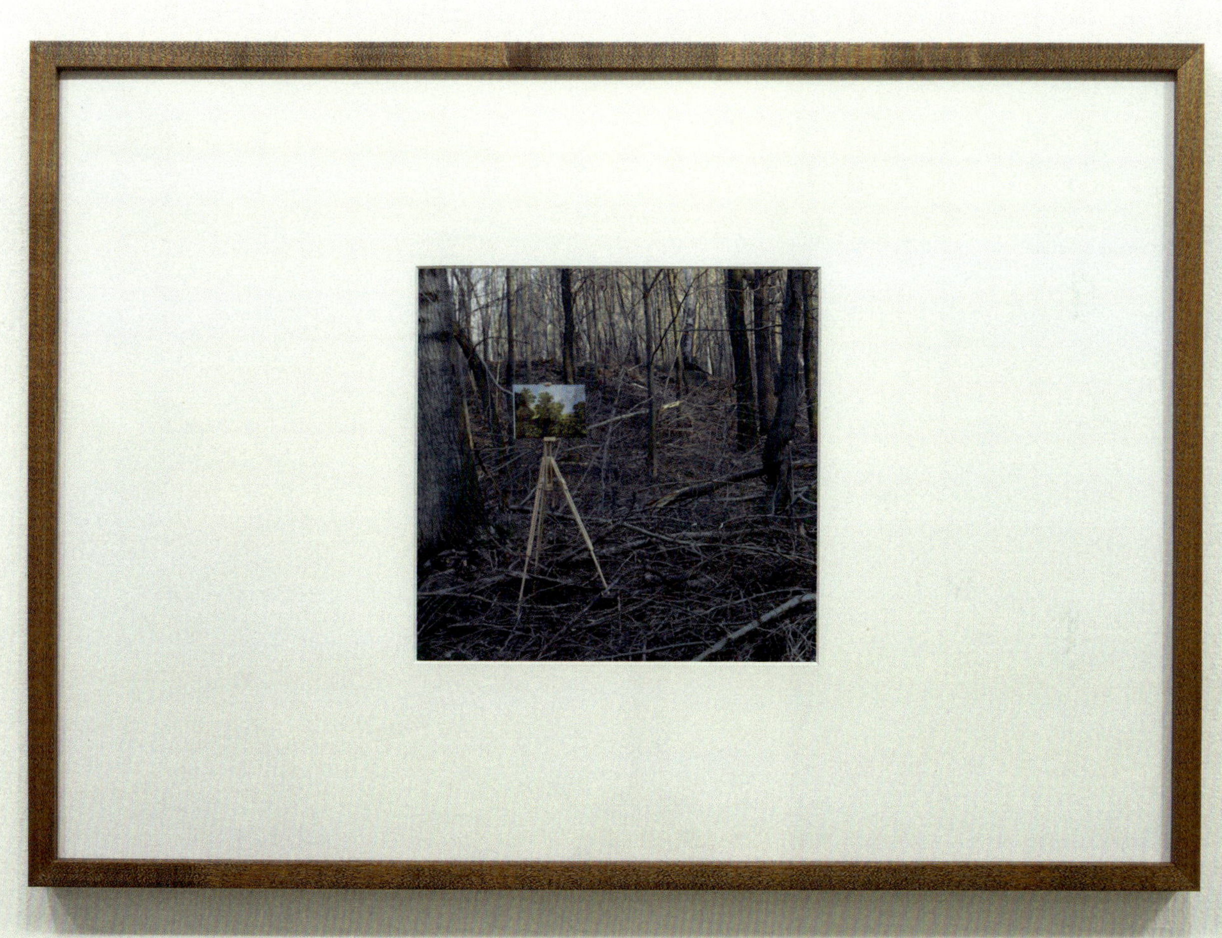

Returned, Parc Mont Royal, Montréal, 1998

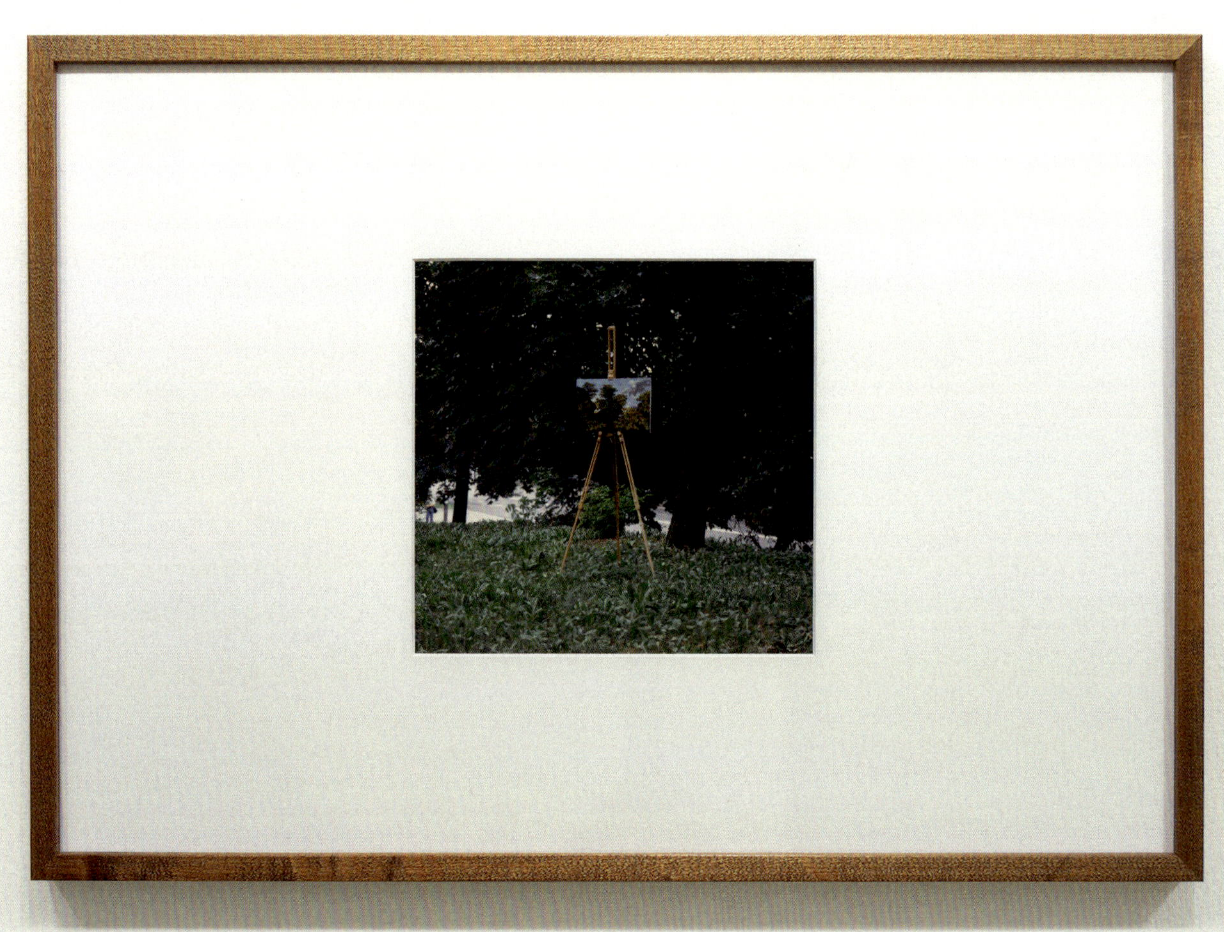

Returned, Park K. Marcinkowskiego, Poznań, 1998

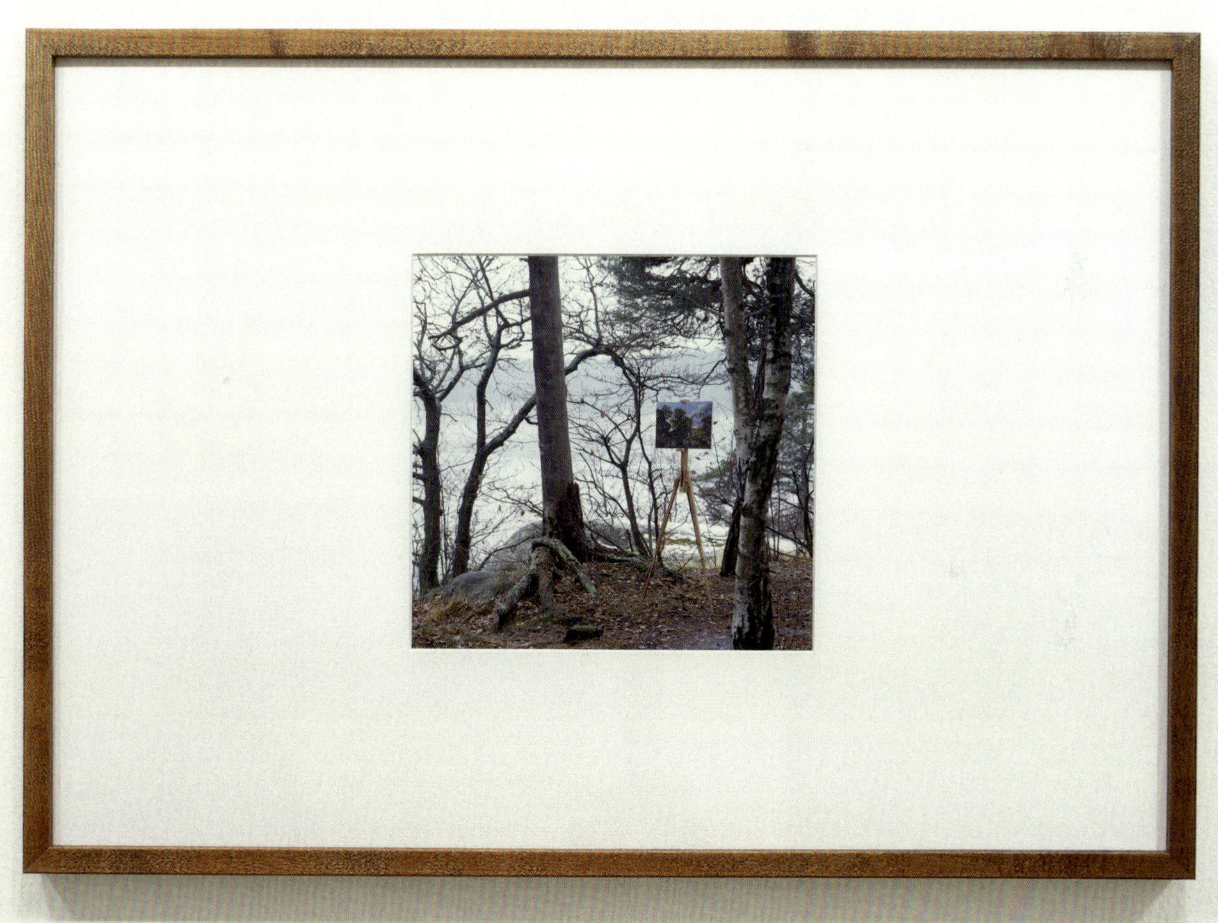

Returned, Frescati, Stockholm, 1998

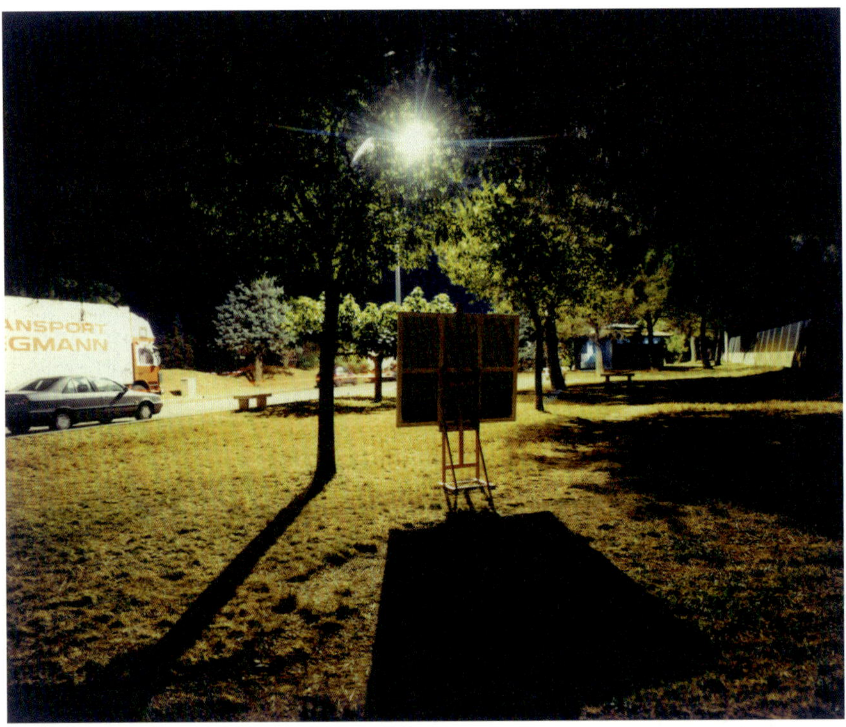

Gustave Courbets berühmtes Gemälde *Le rencontre, ou Bonjour Monsieur Courbet* (1854) zeigt ein fiktives Treffen des Malers mit dem Sammler Alfred Bruyas, der von seinem Diener begleitet wird. Ort der Begegnung ist ein Weg außerhalb Montpelliers. Leiderstam nahm diese Anekdote und die in der Kunstgeschichte ikonografisch codierte Darstellung der Begegnung von Künstler und Sammler zum Anlass, um eine ganz andere Form männlichen Zusammentreffens zu thematisieren: Heute befinden sich rund um Montpellier, wie beispielsweise auf den beiden Rastplätzen von Saint Aunès beidseitig der Autobahn A9, weithin bekannte Cruising-Sites, auf denen sich homosexuelle Männer zu spontanen intimen Treffen einfinden. Leiderstam fertigte zwei Gemälde mit Ansichten der besagten Autobahnraststätten an. Die Rückseiten der Gemälde fotografierte er auf der jeweils gegenüberliegenden Raststätte, deren Vorderseiten jedoch in seinem Atelier. Die Installation besteht aus vier großformatigen C-Prints, die im Ausstellungsraum auf je einer freistehenden Wand angebracht werden. Leuchten, die an Straßenlaternen erinnern, tauchen die museale Inszenierung in eine zwielichtige Atmosphäre.

Gustave Courbet's famous painting *Le rencontre, ou Bonjour Monsieur Courbet* (1854) depicts a fictitious encounter between the painter and the collector, Alfred Bruyas, who is accompanied by his valet. The meeting takes place on a road outside the town of Montpellier. Leiderstam took this anecdote and its representation, which has been iconically coded in art history, as catalyst for a completely different form of male encounter. Today, in the vicinity of Montpellier—for example, at the Saint Aunès service area on both sides of the A9 expressway—are a number of widely known cruising sites where homosexual men can casually meet for spontaneous intimate encounters. Leiderstam painted two pictures with views of these expressway service areas. He photographed the back sides of the paintings at the service area on the opposite side of the expressway, their front sides were photographed in the artist's studio. The installation is comprised of four large-format C-prints, each mounted respectively on a free standing wall in the exhibition space. Lights reminiscent of streetlamps immerse the museal setting in a louche atmosphere.

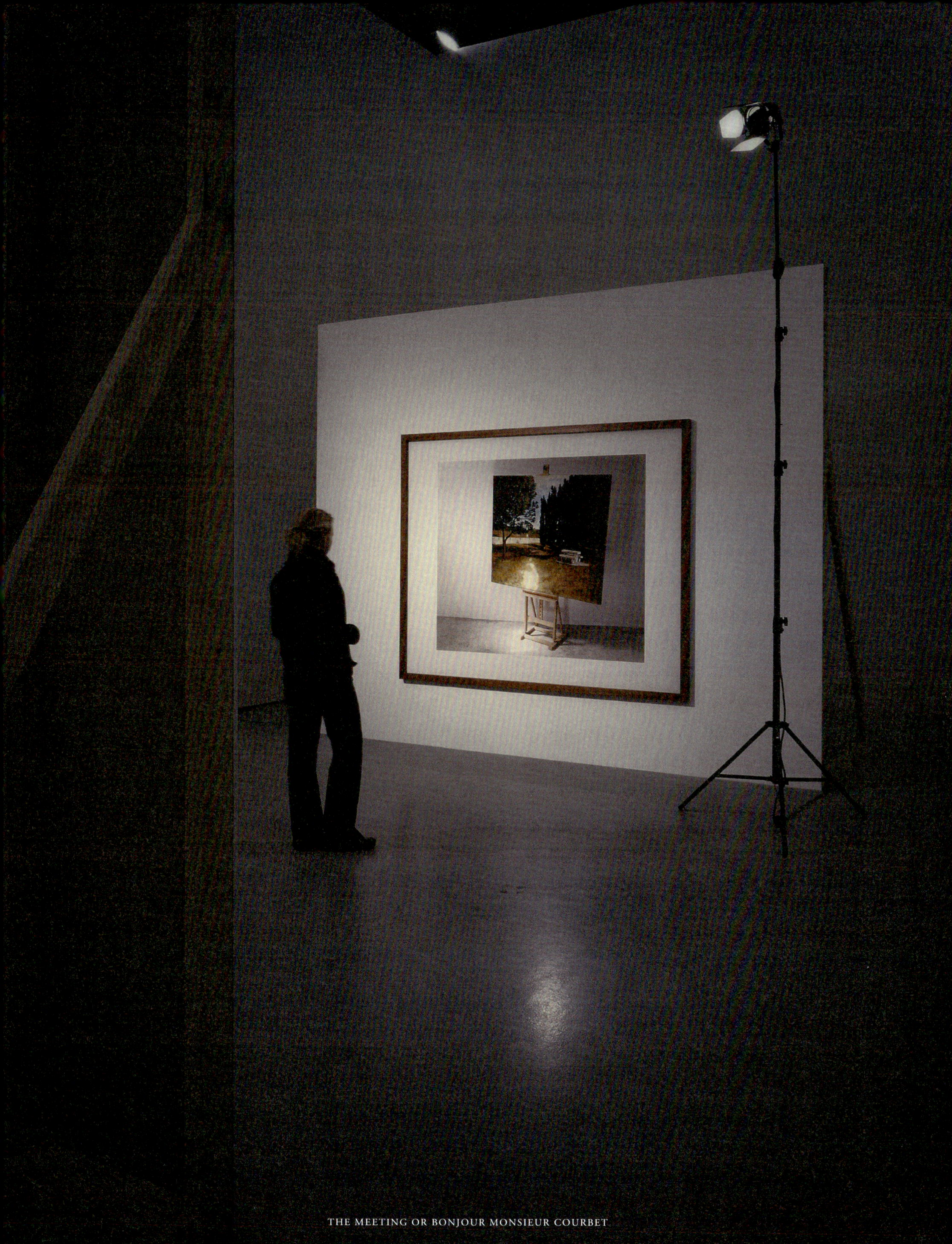

THE MEETING OR BONJOUR MONSIEUR COURBET.

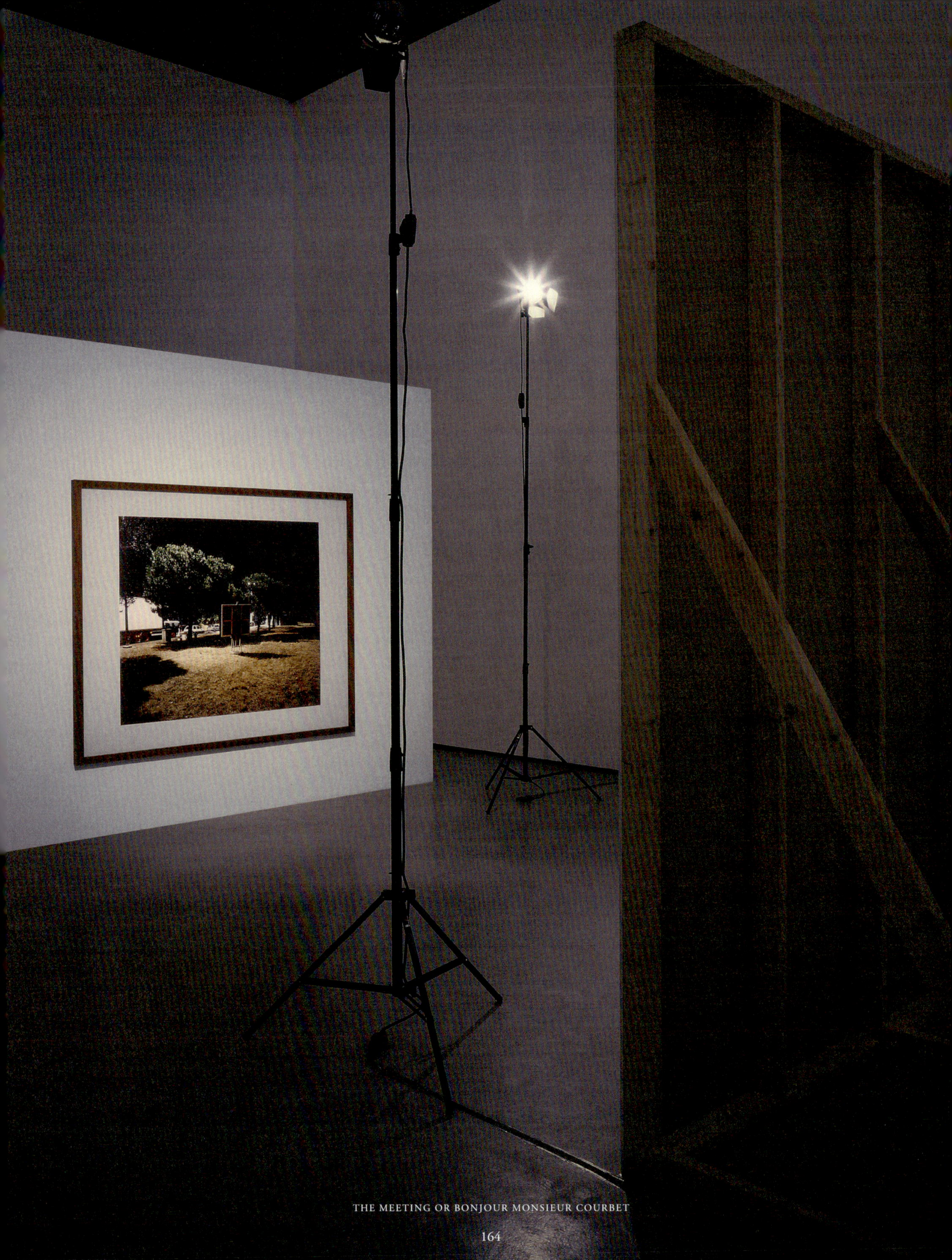

THE MEETING OR BONJOUR MONSIEUR COURBET

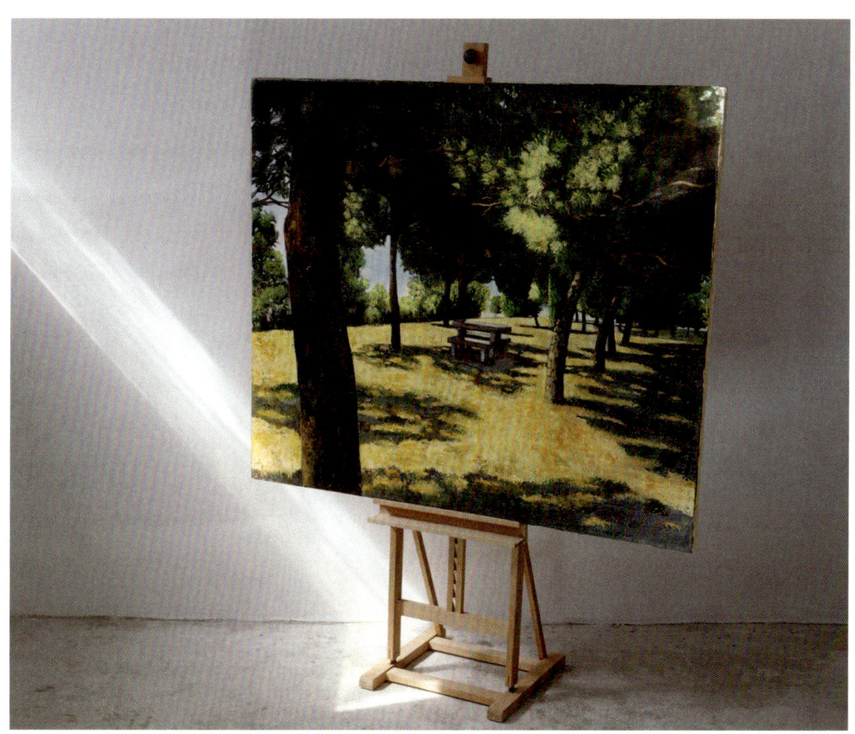

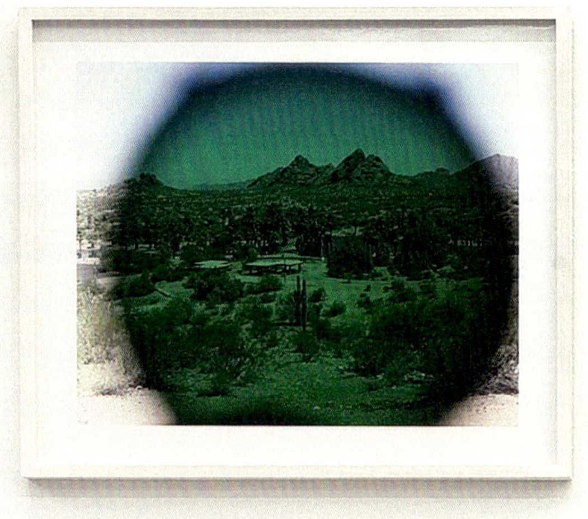

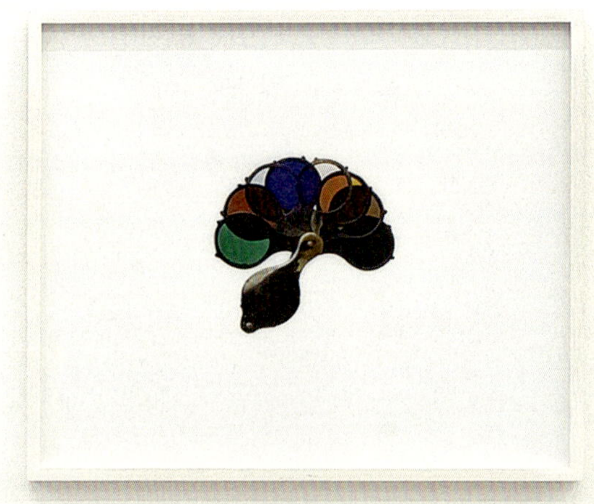
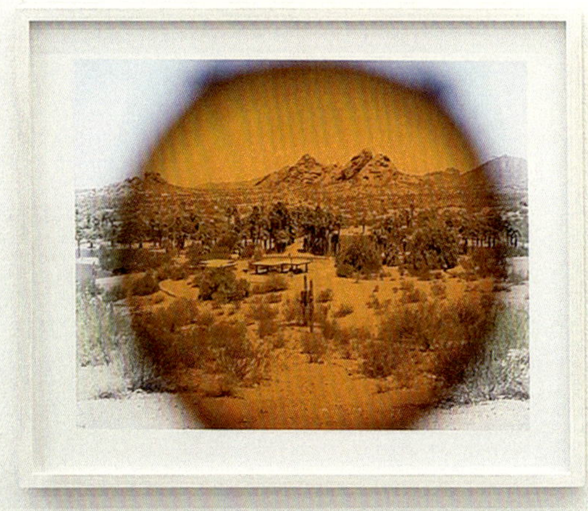
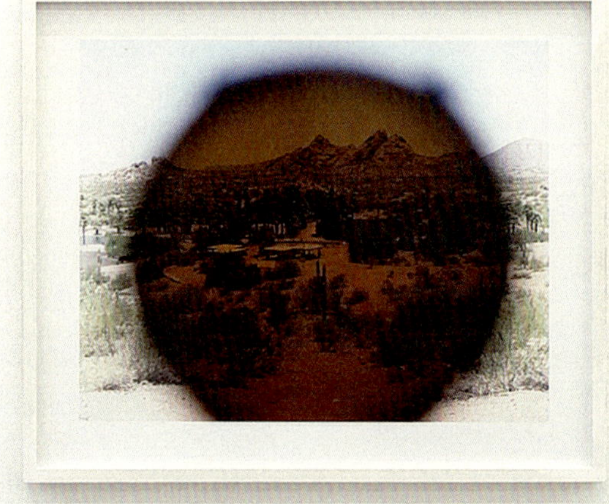

VIEW (PAPAGO PARK)

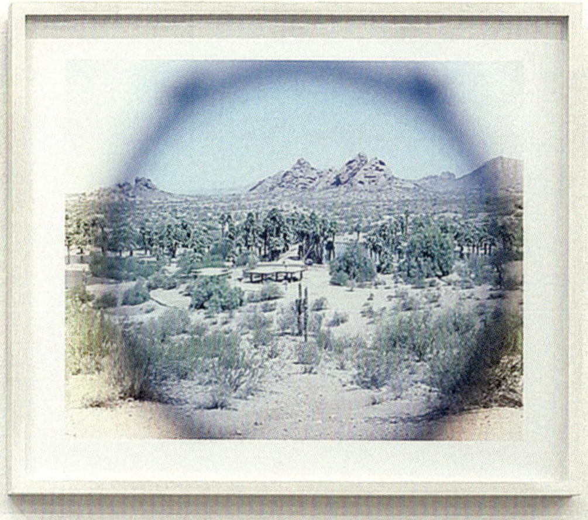

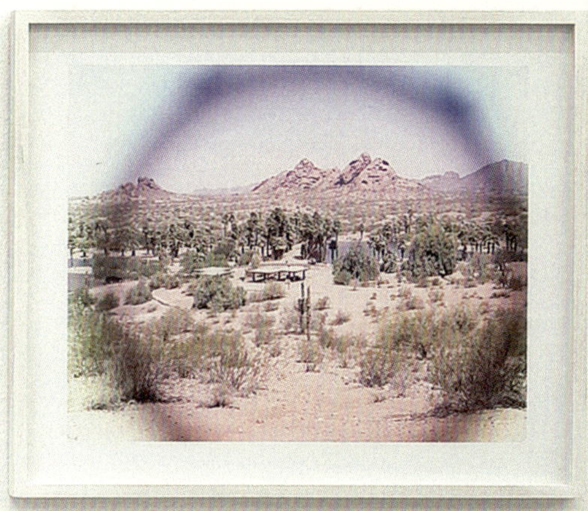

VIEW (PAPAGO PARK), 2007

In der neunteiligen Fotoserie *View (Papago Park)* arbeitet Leiderstam mit den sogenannten Claude-Gläsern, die Landschaftsmaler des 18. Jahrhunderts häufig als Malhilfe verwendeten, um farbliche Tonabstufungen besser erkennen und malerisch umsetzen zu können. Leiderstam benutzt dieses historische Instrument allerdings nicht, um empfindsame und raffinierte Lichtstimmungen zu erzeugen, sondern hält die einzelnen Filter mit wissenschaftlicher Systematik nacheinander vor das Objektiv seiner Kamera. Das Landschaftsmotiv, das nun in die Farben des jeweiligen Filters getaucht erscheint, ist dabei keineswegs ein unberührtes Arkadien, sondern ein Landstrich, der sich durch die heterogene Nutzung verschiedener Interessensgruppen auszeichnet. Während die Berglandschaft im Hintergrund der Arizona National Guard als Trainingsgelände dient, hat sich der Parkplatz im Vordergrund als Cruising-Site etabliert, die von Homosexuellen für zwanglose Begegnungen frequentiert wird.

In the nine-part photographic work entitled *View (Papago Park),* Leiderstam works with so-called Claude-glasses, which landscape painters frequently employed in the eighteenth century to help them determine tonal gradations more easily and realize them in paint. However, Leiderstam does not use this historic instrument to evoke sensitive, subtle moods by means of light, but instead systematically holds the individual filters one after another in front of the lens of his camera with scientific precision. The landscape motif, seemingly immersed in the colors of each respective filter, is by no means an unspoiled Arcadia, but rather a tract of land characterized by a heterogeneous uses by different interest groups. While the mountainous terrain in the background serves the Arizona National Guard as a site for training exercises, the car park in the foreground has become an established cruising site, frequented by homosexuals for casual encounters.

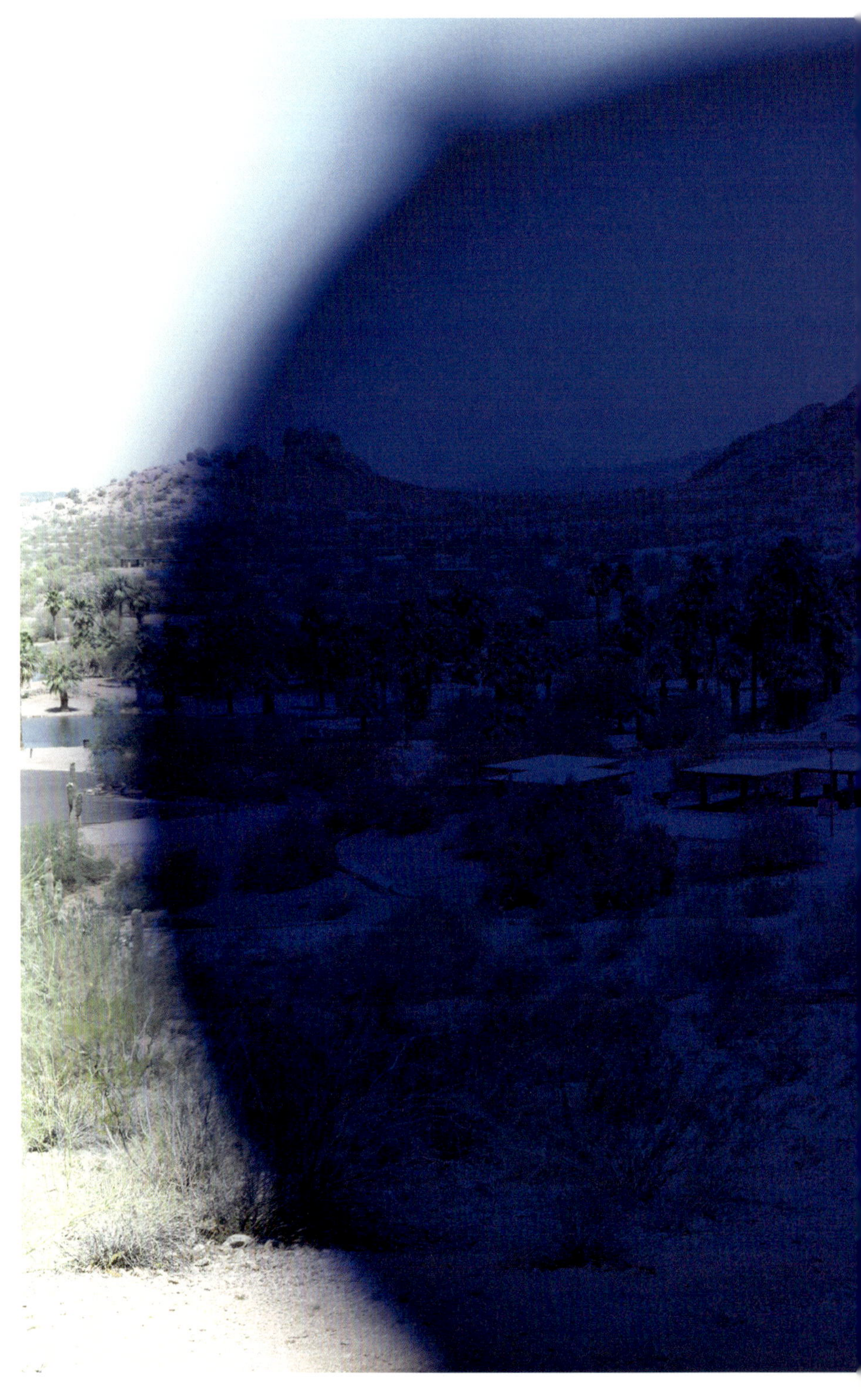

VIEW (PAPAGO PARK)

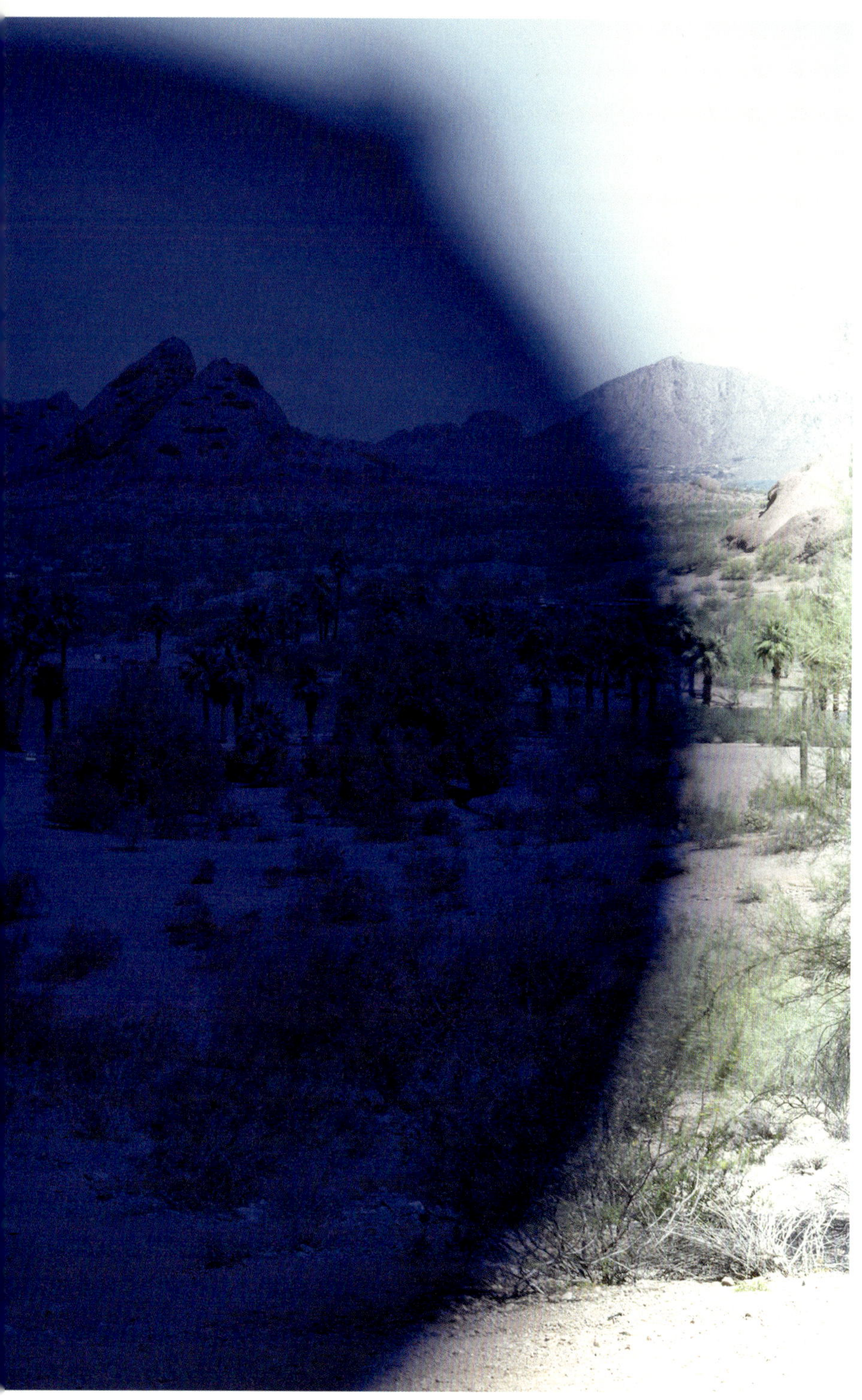

VIEW (PAPAGO PARK)

SEHEN: ANBLICKEN

Wie ihr bekannterer zeitgenössischer Namensvetter, der von den früheren Fotografie-Studenten von Bernd und Hilla Becher gebildet wird, widmete sich die ursprüngliche Düsseldorfer Schule der Landschaftsmalerei der Förderung neuer Arten des Sehens ebenso wie der Entwicklung neuer Arten der *Bildfindung (imaging).* Und wie es bei jeder Form von Landschaftsmalerei und/oder Landschaftsfotografie der Fall ist, entwarfen beide »Schulen« hierfür neue Instrumente der Rahmung – das heißt, sie wählten und gestalteten sowohl den Rahmen selbst als auch das, was sie mit ihm rahmten. Schließlich ist jede Landschaft, um mit dem amerikanischen Ikonologen W. J. T. Mitchell zu sprechen, »zugleich ein repräsentierter und ein präsentierter Raum, ein Signifikant und ein Signifikat, ein Rahmen und das, was ein Rahmen enthält, ein realer Ort und sein Simulakrum, eine Verpackung und die Ware in dieser Verpackung.«[1] Interessanterweise erweitert Mitchell seine bewusst durchlässig gehaltene Definition des Sujets – Sujet oder Umgebung? Sujet *und* Umgebung! – in den folgenden »ökonomischen« Begriffen: »Landschaft ist kein Genre der Kunst, sondern ein Medium. Landschaft ist ein Medium des Austauschs zwischen dem Menschlichen und dem Natürlichen, dem Selbst und dem Anderen. Als solches ist es wie Geld: An und für sich nutzlos, kann es potenziell eine grenzenlose Wertreserve ausdrücken.«

Mitchells Verweis auf die Idee des Geldes im scheinbar damit nicht zusammenhängenden historischen Kontext der Landschaftsmalerei des 19. Jahrhunderts erinnert an einen ähnlichen Vergleich, den Jonathan Crary in seinem wegweisenden Buch *Techniken des Betrachters* zog: »Fotografie und Geld werden im 19. Jahrhundert zu homologen Formen der gesellschaftlichen Macht. Sie sind ähnlich zusammenfassende und umspannende Netzwerke, die alle Subjekte in ein einziges weltweites Netzwerk der Wertung und des Begehrens einbinden. Was Marx über das Geld sagte, trifft auch auf die Fotografie zu: Sie ist eine große Gleichmacherin, eine Demokratisiererin, ein ›bloßes Zeichen‹, eine Fiktion, ›durch die sogenannte allgemeine Übereinstimmung der Menschen‹ sanktioniert. Beides sind magische Formen, die eine neue Menge abstrakter Beziehungen zwischen dem Individuum und den Dingen schaffen und diese Beziehungen als das Wirkliche darstellen. Durch die verschiedenen und sich gegenseitig durchdringenden Wirtschaftssysteme des Geldes und der Fotografie wird eine ganze gesellschaftliche Welt ausschließlich als Zeichen dargestellt und konstituiert.«[2]

Ich zitiere ausführlich Crarys Untersuchung aus mehreren Gründen, die mit historischer Koinzidenz zu tun haben: Zum einen wurden die ersten entscheidenden Schritte zur Etablierung der Fotografie als *dem* prägenden neuen Medium des 19. Jahrhunderts, zusammen mit Großbritannien und Frankreich, dank eines wenig bekannten Erfinders namens Carl August von Steinheil in Deutschland (oder genauer im Königreich Bayern) unternommen. Das Beharren der Fotografie auf der Genauigkeit ihres Blicks und die unterstellte Objektivität ihrer Aufzeichnung übten naturgemäß einen großen Einfluss auf die spätere Entwicklung der Landschaftsmalerei aus. Insbesondere die Düsseldorfer Malerschule war damals bereits weithin bekannt für ihre Hinwendung zum realistischen Detail und ihr Vertrauen auf die Wirklichkeitsnähe, die eine rigorose Pleinair-Praxis sicherstellte. (Frühe Kritiken des eigentlichen Realismus verurteilten die Bewegung wegen ihrer »wissenschaftlichen« Aspekte und ihres krassen Materialismus – das heißt gerade aufgrund ihrer Ähnlichkeit mit dem fotografischen Verfahren. Die Diskussion, in welchem Maße die Düsseldorfer postromantische Landschaftsmalerei Teil der realistischen Tendenz der Kunst war oder diese

1)   W. J. T. Mitchell, »Imperial Landscape«, in: Ders. (Hrsg.), *Landscape and Power.* Chicago 1994, S. 5.

2)   Jonathan Crary, *Techniken des Betrachters: Sehen und Moderne im 19. Jahrhundert,* übers. von Anne Vonderstein, Dresden / Basel 1996, S. 24.

The Labyrinthine View
Matts Leiderstam in Düsseldorf   DIETER ROELSTRAETE

LOOKING: GAZING

Like its better-known contemporary namesake, comprised of the former photography students of Bernd and Hilla Becher, the original Düsseldorf School of Painting was as much devoted to fostering new ways of *looking* as it was to producing new ways of *imaging*. And as is the case with all landscape painting and/or landscape photography, both "schools" did so by conceptualizing new framing devices—that is to say, by choosing as well as shaping both the frame itself and what to frame with it. All landscape, after all, in the words of American iconologist W. J. T. Mitchell, "is both a represented and presented space, both a signifier and a signified, both a frame and what a frame contains, both a real place and its simulacrum, both a package and the commodity inside the package."[1] Interestingly, Mitchell expands his deliberately porous definition of the subject—Subject or setting? Subject *and* setting!—in the following "economic" terms: "Landscape is not a genre of art but a medium. Landscape is a medium of exchange between the human and the natural, the self and the other. As such, it is like money: good for nothing in itself, but expressive of a potentially limitless reserve of value."

Mitchell's reference to the notion of money within the apparently incongruous historical context of nineteenth-century landscape painting is reminiscent of a similar comparison made by Jonathan Crary in his seminal *Techniques of the Observer:* "photography and money become homologous forms of social power in the nineteenth century. They are equally totalizing systems for binding and unifying all subjects within a single global network of valuation and desire. As Marx said of money, photography is also a great leveller, a democratizer, a "mere symbol," a fiction "sanctioned by the so-called universal consent of mankind." Both are magical forms that establish a new set of abstract relations between individuals and things and impose those relations as the real. It is through the distinct but interpenetrating economies of money and photography that a whole social world is represented and constituted exclusively as signs."[2]

I am quoting at length from Crary's study for a number of reasons that concern historical coincidence: firstly, along with Britain and France, it was in Germany (or rather, in the Kingdom of Bavaria), thanks to a little-known inventor named Carl August von Steinheil, that the first decisive steps were taken towards the establishment of photography as *the* defining new medium of the nineteenth century. Photography's insistence on the accuracy of its vision and the presumed objectivity of its record naturally exerted great influence upon the subsequent development of landscape painting. The Düsseldorf School, in particular, was then already widely known for its devotion to realist detail and its confidence in the verisimilitude assured by rigorous *plein air* practice. (Early criticisms of Realism proper condemned the movement for its "scientific" aspects and gross materialism—i. e. its likeness, precisely, to the photographic procedure. The discussion as to what extent Düsseldorf's post-Romantic landscape painting was either part of or presaged the Realist trend in art cannot be dealt with at length within the confines of this essay, though it is important to note the subtly *moralistic* undertones shared by both Realism in its more established manifestations—Caillebotte, Courbet, Millet etc.—and much of the proto-realist painting being practiced in Germany at around the same time.) Secondly, the reference to Marx in Crary's remark reminds us of yet another crossing of apparently haphazard trajectories: apart from photography, the electrical telegraph and the postage stamp—all inventions amounting to a true revolution in communications and the transport of imagery—the 1840s

1)   W. J. T. Mitchell, "Imperial Landscape," in W. J. T. Mitchell (ed.), *Landscape and Power* (Chicago: University of Chicago Press, 1994), p. 5.

2)   Jonathan Crary, *Techniques of the Observer: On Vision and Modernity in the Nineteenth Century* (Cambridge, Mass.: MIT Press, 1992), p. 13.

ankündigte, kann im Rahmen dieses Essays nicht ausführlich behandelt werden, doch ist es wichtig, die subtil *moralistischen* Untertöne zu bemerken, die dem Realismus in seinen bekannteren Manifestationen – Caillebotte, Courbet, Millet usw. – und einem Großteil der protorealistischen Malerei, die in Deutschland ungefähr zur gleichen Zeit praktiziert wurde, gemeinsam waren.) Zum anderen erinnert uns der Verweis auf Marx in Crarys Bemerkung an eine andere Überschneidung scheinbar zufälliger Laufbahnen: Abgesehen von der Fotografie, dem elektrischen Telegrafen und der Briefmarke – allesamt Erfindungen, die einer wahren Revolution der Kommunikation und des Transports von Bildsprachen gleichkamen – erlebten die 1840er Jahre auch die Geburt einer der führenden progressiven Zeitungen Preußens, der *Rheinischen Zeitung,* deren (Chef-)Redakteur von ihrer Gründung im Januar 1842 bis zu ihrer von der Regierung erzwungenen Einstellung im März 1843 niemand anderes als Karl Marx war (gelegentlich unterstützt durch Friedrich Engels, den Marx eigentlich erst durch ihre gemeinsamen Beiträge für diese Zeitung kennenlernte). Während der kurzen Zeit ihres Bestehens zeigte die *Rheinische Zeitung* auch ein ausgeprägtes Interesse an der (lokalen) Kunst ihrer Zeit und ging soweit, *Die Hussitenpredigt* (1836) von Karl Friedrich Lessing, zusammen mit Johann Wilhelm Schirmer einer wichtigsten Vertreter der Düsseldorfer Malerschule, für ihre Kampagne »gegen die Kirche und für spirituelle Freiheit« in Anspruch zu nehmen.[3] Auch hier war »Landschaft« – Lessing zeigt den böhmischen Häretiker und Vorläufer der Luther'schen Reformation Jan Hus bei einer geheimen Predigt im Wald, während im Hintergrund eine gotische Kirche brennt – nach und nach (vor allem) in eine *Bühne* transformiert worden, auf der sich ein breites Spektrum konfliktträchtiger zeitgenössischer kultureller Anliegen orchestrieren ließ, was einmal mehr beweist (und dies ist sehr wichtig im Hinblick auf Crarys eingangs erwähnte Diskussion verschiedener »Techniken des Betrachters«), dass das, was man sieht, nie einfach nur das ist, was man sieht – sondern vielmehr eine Reflexion über das sehende Auge/Ich und seine zahlreichen Bezugs-»Rahmen«.[4]

PHYSIOLOGISCHES SEHEN: INTERPRETIERENDES SEHEN

Ein Definitionsmerkmal eines großen Teils der Landschaftsmalerei der Mitte des 19. Jahrhunderts, wie sie vor allem in den deutschen Staaten praktiziert wurde, ist das häufige Auftauchen des *Fensterrahmens,* durch den viele der fraglichen Landschaften zu sehen sind. Schon in der deutschen Romantik, vor allem im Werk von Caspar David Friedrich (den Georg Friedrich Kersting 1812 in zwei berühmten Gemälden mit dem Titel *Caspar David Friedrich im Atelier*[5] porträtierte), erscheint das Fenster oft als zentrales Strukturelement – das, wodurch sich die ferne, potenziell bedrohliche Andersartigkeit der Natur ankündigt. Doch erst in der bildenden Kunst der retrospektiv als Biedermeier bezeichneten Epoche, genau zu der Zeit, als

3) Zit. nach Albert Boime, *Art in an Age of Civic Struggle 1848–1871: A Social History of Modern Art,* Bd. 4., Chicago 2008, S. 513. *Die Hussitenpredigt,* die als Dauerleihgabe in der Berliner Alten Nationalgalerie zu sehen ist, war ein besonders machtvolles Symbol des Konflikts zwischen Katholiken und Protestanten, der damals weite Teile des gesellschaftlichen und kulturellen Leben in Preußen – bis hinein in die Aktivitäten der Düsseldorfer Kunstakademie – prägte.

4) Zur »Theatralizität« eines großen Teils der Landschaftsmalerei, die aus der Düsseldorfer Malerschule hervorging, siehe die folgende Bemerkung von Boime: »Ein einzigartiges Merkmal der Düsseldorfer Kunstszene war ihre Beziehung zur Bühne. Karl Leberecht Immermann, der energische Dichter und Dramatiker, gründete ein Amateurtheater, das gelegentlich in Schadows eigenem Haus zusammenkam. Die Künstler selbst beteiligten sich an den Inszenierungen, entwarfen Bühnenbilder und Kostüme, schrieben Stücke oder traten in den Dramen auf. Immermann stellte oft Tableaux vivants auf, und die Maler liebten es, die wirkungsvollsten Tableaux einer gelungenen Aufführung auf der Leinwand festzuhalten. Der gesteigerte Realismus der Düsseldorfer Malerschule lässt sich teilweise durch die Beschäftigung der Künstler mit den Eigenschaften der zeitgenössischen Bühne erklären. Der flache Vordergrund und die Aufmerksamkeit für Gesichtsausdrücke, die so viele ihrer Werke kennzeichnen, entstammen ihrer Erfahrung mit dem Theater.« A. a. O., S. 511 f.

5) Eine Version dieses Gemäldes, die auf dem Umschlag [der englischen Ausgabe] von Hans Beltings vielversprechend betiteltem *Die Deutschen und ihre Kunst: Ein schwieriges Erbe* reproduziert ist, zeigt den Künstler nachdenklich posierend in einem Atelier, ausgestattet mit einem Fenster, dessen untere Hälfte merkwürdig abgeschottet ist und den Blick des Landschaftsmalers auf die Außenwelt versperrt – eine starke Metapher für das ambivalente Kultivieren von Innerlichkeit und Isolation, das für viele deutsche »Fensterbilder« charakteristisch ist, ein weiteres Beispiel dafür ist *Frau am Fenster* von 1822, das als eine Darstellung (des Rückens) der Ehefrau des Künstlers gilt. Beide Gemälde erschweren sicherlich eine trennscharfe kunsthistorische Kategorisierung, derzufolge Friedrich ausschließlich der Tradition der Romantik angehört, und zeigen stattdessen, dass sein Werk einen Übergangspunkt – und daher wiederum die Angemessenheit des Fenstermotivs – hin zu Fragestellungen des Biedermeiers markiert.

also saw the birth of one of Prussia's leading progressive newspapers, the *Rheinische Zeitung,* edited by none other than Karl Marx (sometimes helped by Friedrich Engels, whom Marx really only got to know through their shared contributions to the newspaper) from its foundation in January 1842 until its forced shut-down on government orders in March 1843. In its short lifetime, the *Rheinische Zeitung* also showed a keen interest in the (local) art of its time, going so far as to enlist *The Hussite Sermon* (1836) by Karl Friedrich Lessing, one of the leading lights, along with Johann Wilhelm Schirmer, of the Düsseldorf School, in its campaign "against the church for spiritual freedom."[3] Here too, "landscape"—Lessing depicts the Bohemian heretic and forerunner of the Lutheran reformation, Jan Huss, preaching clandestinely in a forest, with a gothic church burning in the background—had gradually been transformed into a *stage* (first and foremost) upon which a wide variety of conflicting contemporary cultural concerns could be orchestrated, proving once again (and this is all important with regards to Crary's aforementioned discussion of the varying "techniques of the observer") that what you see is never merely what you see—but instead, a reflection upon the seeing eye/I and its many "frames" of reference.[4]

LOOKING: SEEING

One of the defining features of much mid-nineteenth-century landscape painting, as practised in the German states in particular, is the remarkable recurrence of the *window frame* through which many of the landscapes in question are seen. Already in German Romanticism, most notably in the work of Caspar David Friedrich (famously portrayed by Georg Friedrich Kersting in a pair of paintings from 1812 titled *Caspar David Friedrich in his Studio*[5]), the window often appears as a crucial structuring element—that through which nature's distant, potentially threatening otherness announces itself. But it is really only in the pictorial arts of the retrospectively named Biedermeier period, at the precise time when painting is readying itself to ward off the first set of challenges from the emerging new art of photography, that the window becomes a true framing ("view-finding") device, effortlessly mobilized in the escalating conflict of rivalling scopic regimes and viewing techniques that is such a distinctive feature of mid-nineteenth-century culture. It is here that *landscape* painting in particular acquires its exemplary role as a testing ground for the development of new ways in which to relate to natural beauty (or nature in general) as both an easily allegorized aspect of everyday reality and a symbol of the fundamental instability of all political and societal processes. This project centrally revolves around the *domestication* of the Sublime, as the very act of "framing" nature—formerly represented almost exclusively by dramatically warped clouds, storms, dizzying mountainscapes and Biblical rainfall—comes to symbolize the political project of dampening the ungovernable force of the unruly mob as a natural phenomenon of sorts. In the Sublime's stead come more bucolic (i.e. "realistic," up-close) views of an amenable nature very far removed from the formerly apocalyptic vision of the wholly Other—quite close, in other words, to the landscapes preferred by the painters of the

3) Quoted in Albert Boime, *Art in an Age of Civic Struggle 1848–1871: A Social History of Modern Art,* vol. 4 (Chicago: University of Chicago Press, 2008), p. 513. The Hussite Sermon, on permanent display in Berlin's Alte Nationalgalerie, was a particularly powerful symbol of the Protestant/Catholic conflict shaping much of Prussia's social and cultural life at the time, up to and including the activities at the Düsseldorf Art Academy.

4) On the "theatricality" of much landscape painting coming out of the Düsseldorf School, see the following remark by Boime: "A unique feature of the Düsseldorf art scene was its relationship to the stage. Karl Leberecht Immermann, the energetic poet and dramatist, initiated an amateur theater that sometimes convened in Schadow's own house. The artists themselves participated in stage productions, designing sets and costumes, writing plays, or acting in the dramas. Immermann often posed tableaux vivants, and the painters enjoyed preserving on canvas the most effective tableaux of a successful performance. The heightened realism of the Düsseldorf School may be understood in part by the artists' preoccupation with contemporary stage properties. The shallow foreground and attention to facial expression that marks so much of their work grows out of their experience with the theater." Ibid., pp. 511–512.

5) One version of this painting, reproduced on the cover of Hans Belting's auspiciously titled *The Germans and their Art: A Troublesome Relationship,* depicts the artist pensively posing in a studio fitted with a window, the bottom half of which is curiously blocked off, disabling the landscape painter's view of the outside world—a powerful metaphor for the ambiguous cultivation of interiority and insulation typical of much German "window painting," *Woman at a Window* from 1822, thought to depict (the back of) the artist's wife. Both paintings certainly confuse the clear-cut art-historical categorization according to which Friedrich belongs to the Romantic tradition only, instead revealing his work to constitute a point of transition—hence, once again, the appropriateness of the window motif—towards Biedermeier concerns.

die Malerei sich bereit macht, die ersten Herausforderungen der neuen Kunst der Fotografie abzuwehren, wird das Fenster zu einem echten Mittel der Rahmung (zu einem »Sucher« [»view finder«]), mühelos mobilisiert in jenem eskalierenden Konflikt rivalisierender skopischer Regimes und Techniken des Sehens, der ein ganz entscheidendes Merkmal der Kultur des mittleren 19. Jahrhunderts darstellt. Hier nimmt insbesondere die *Landschaftsmalerei* ihre beispielhafte Rolle als Versuchsgelände für die Entwicklung neuer Möglichkeiten an, sich auf die Schönheit der Natur (oder die Natur im Allgemeinen) als einen leicht allegorisierbaren Aspekt der alltäglichen Realität und als Symbol der grundlegenden Instabilität aller politischen und gesellschaftlichen Prozesse zu beziehen. Dieses Projekt dreht sich im Kern um die *Domestizierung* des Erhabenen, da der eigentliche Akt der »Rahmung« von Natur – bis dahin fast ausschließlich durch aufgerissene Wolken, Stürme, atemberaubende Berglandschaften und biblische Regenfälle repräsentiert – sich darauf belief, das politische Projekt einer Schwächung der unbeherrschbaren Macht des widerspenstigen Mobs zu symbolisieren, als handele es sich bei diesem um eine Art Naturphänomen. An die Stelle des Erhabenen treten bukolischere (das heißt »realistischere«, aus der Nähe betrachtete) Ansichten einer zugänglicheren Natur, sehr weit entfernt vom apokalyptischen Anblick des vollkommen Anderen – ziemlich ähnlich, mit anderen Worten, den Landschaften, die die Maler der Düsseldorfer Schule bevorzugten, die wenig Wert auf Darstellungen endloser Weiten arktischen Eises oder unwirtlicher Bergregionen legten.

Das Fenstermotiv – von dem sich in der Düsseldorfer Malerschule, wo das Fenster in erster Linie ein allegorisches Instrument der Proxemik zu sein scheint, zugegebenermaßen nur wenige Beispiele finden – ließe sich als eigentliche Überbrückung der Kluft zwischen Romantik und Biedermeier bezeichnen. In einer Anspielung auf seine buchstäblichen Eigenschaften als Übergangsfigur und als etwas, das Übergang als solchen ermöglicht, bemerkt Malcolm Andrews, dass »das Motiv des Blicks aus dem Fenster, das manchmal eine hinausblickende Figur einschließt, mit spezifisch nordeuropäischen Überlegungen der Romantik assoziiert wurde, mit

der Sehnsucht, dem Eingesperrtsein zu entkommen, mit dem Ansporn, die Vorstellungskraft freizusetzen, um die weiten Regionen des Lichts zu erforschen. Das Motiv bringt, wie ein Kritiker formulierte, ›die Beschränkung eines Innenraums in den unmittelbarsten Kontrast zu der Unermesslichkeit des Außenraums […]. Das Fenster wirkt wie eine Schwelle und gleichzeitig wie eine Barriere.‹ Die Wirkung des Fensterrahmens um eine Landschaft besteht darin, das Gefühl der kulturellen und visuellen Distanz zu betonen, die diese Außenwelt gewinnt.«[6] Zu den berühmteren Beispielen, überwiegend aus der Dresdner Schule (die damals stark von Friedrichs Erbe beeinflusst war, obwohl die Datierungen in die frühen Jahre des Aufstiegs der Düsseldorfer Malerschule fallen), gehören Carl Gustav Carus' *Atelierfenster* (1823–1824) und *Gotische Fenster am Oybin. Fensterdurchblick am Chor* (um 1828); Johan Christian Dahls *Blick aus einem Fenster auf das Schloss Pillnitz* (1823–1824) und *Blick aus einem Fenster auf Quisisana* (1820) sowie Friedrich Wasmanns *Blick aus einem Fenster* (1832–1833).[7] Weiter westlich liefert Karl Begas' Porträt Die *Familie Begas* (1821) ein interessantes Hybrid: Obwohl es sich nicht um ein Landschaftsbild handelt, lässt sich durch das Fenster hinter diesem breit angelegten Gruppenbild ein aufschlussreiches Fragment der Außenwelt erblicken. Dieses erscheint lediglich wie ein Bühnenbild und besteht aus Ansichten des Kölner Doms und der Kirche St. Andreas als symbolischen, aber essenziellen Ergänzungen der Inszenierung häuslicher Seligkeit durch

6) Malcolm Andrews, *Landscape and Western Art*, Oxford 1999, S. 111. Das von Andrews zitierte Fragment stammt hingegen von Lorenz Eitner, »The Open Window and the Storm-tossed Boat: An Essay in the Iconography of Romanticism«, in: *Art Bulletin*, 37, 1955, S. 281–290. Andrews geht sogar soweit, die Ursprünge der Landschaftsmalerei im Allgemeinen in den »spezifisch nordeuropäischen« Überlegungen zu lokalisieren, das Problem von Innen und Außen verhandeln zu müssen: »Insbesondere Nordeuropäer sind fasziniert von der Schwächung scharfer Trennungen von Innen und Außen, Landschaft und häuslichem Interieur. Das Leben im Norden spielt sich so sehr im Inneren der Häuser ab, dass es sich stark von der Erfahrung der Menschen des Mittelmeerraums unterscheidet, wo sich Innen und Außen leichter durchdringen. Solche Überlegungen können zu einer Erklärung beitragen, weshalb die Landschaftskunst ursprünglich eine nordeuropäische Initiative gewesen zu sein scheint.« A. a. O., S. 110.

7) In seiner Diskussion von Dahls Blick auf Quisisana am Golf von Neapel bemerkt Andrews, dass das Gemälde bereits »mehr eine touristische Aufzeichnung einer berühmten Landschaft als ein flüchtiges Erblicken der Möglichkeiten der Romantik« ist. Die (teils buchstäbliche) »Domestizierung« der natürlichen Landschaft als geheiligter Stätte des Erhabenen war selbstverständlich ein wesentlicher Bestandteil der touristischen Erfahrung, die erst zu diesem Zeitpunkt ein gewisses Niveau von *Demokratisierung* erreichte.

Düsseldorf school, who didn't care much for depictions of endless expanses of Arctic ice or inhospitable mountain ranges.

The window motif—of which there are admittedly few examples from the Düsseldorf School, where the window seems to exist as an allegorical tool of proxemics first and foremost—could be said to properly bridge the gap between Romanticism and Biedermeier. Alluding to its literal quality as both a figure of transition and that which enables transition as such, Malcolm Andrews notes that "the motif of the window view, sometimes including a gazing figure, has been associated with specifically northern European Romantic preoccupations, the longing to escape confinement, the inducement to liberate the imagination to explore the vast regions of light. The motif, as one critic has put it, 'brings the confinement of an interior into the most immediate contrast with the immensity of space outside … The window is like a threshold, and at the same time a barrier'. The effect of a window frame around a landscape is to accentuate the sense of distance, cultural as well as visual, which that outside world acquires."[6] Some of the more famous examples, mostly taken from the Dresden School (then strongly influenced by Friedrich's legacy, though their dates coincide with the early years of the Düsseldorf School's ascendancy) include Carl Gustav Carus' *Studio Window* (1823–1824) and *Gothic Windows in the Ruins of the Monastery at Oybin* (ca. 1828); Johan Christian Dahl's *Blick aus einem Fenster auf das Schloss Pillnitz* (1823–1824) and *View from a Window at Quisisana* (1820), as well as Friedrich Wasmann's *View from a Window* (1832–1833).[7] Further west, Karl Begas's portrait of The Begas Family (1821) provides an interesting hybrid: although Begas's is not a landscape painting, a telling shard of outside scenery is glimpsed through the window in the back of this extended group portrait. Appearing as a theatrical backdrop only, it consists of a view of the Cologne Cathedral and St. Andreas Church as symbolic yet essential complements of the artist's staging of orderly domestic bliss. A much later painting by Austrian artist Moritz von Schwind, finally, is referred to by Albert Boime as a prime example of Biedermeier's aforementioned attempt to 'domesticate' the sublime landscape as inherited from the Romantic tradition: "In *Morning Hour* (1858), Schwind acts upon favorite motifs of Caspar David Friedrich and Philipp Otto Runge but neutralizes the allegorical tension of the latter's *Morgenrot* and the former's immensely silent reverential gaze. Instead, Schwind projects his scene from the receding perspective of a pleasant interior where the beholder must first traverse the boards of the rustic wooden floor and the compact Biedermeier furnishings on the way to the view out of the window. Substituting for the dwarfed and deserted "Rückenfigur" of Friedrich is the lighthearted girl who eagerly throws open the window to greet the dawn. It is from the safety of this Biedermeier staging platform that we follow her upward gaze to the summit of the glorious Zugspitze in the remote distance."[8] In quite a few of these paintings, the windows or window frames could easily be read as classic instances of the *parergon* as theorized most famously by Jacques Derrida in his 1978 collection of essays *The Truth in Painting:* the parergon is that which does not seem to belong to the work ("ergon") in the strict sense, but nonetheless appears attached ("par-") to it in a manner of some structural complexity, enabling it (or our experience of it).

Derrida quotes the examples of frames *around* paintings (rather than in paintings) and the (marble) drapes covering demi-nude Greek statues as primary representation of such "supplements," using them as art-historical arguments in his long-term philosophical interrogation of

6) Malcolm Andrews, *Landscape and Western Art* (Oxford: Oxford University Press, 1999), p. 111. The fragment quoted by Andrews is in turn taken from Lorenz Eitner, "The Open Window and the Storm-tossed Boat: An Essay in the Iconography of Romanticism," in *Art Bulletin* (1955), pp. 281–290. Andrews even goes so far as to locate the origins of landscape painting in general in the "specifically Northern European" preoccupation of having to negotiate interior and exterior: "For northern Europeans especially, there is a fascination with the relaxing of sharp distinctions between inside and outside, landscape and domestic interior. So much of the northerner's life is passed inside buildings that it differs a great deal from the experience of the Mediterranean where inside and outside interpenetrate more easily. Such considerations might help to explain why landscape art seems originally to have been a northern European initiative." Ibid., p. 110.

7) Discussing Dahl's view of Quisisana on the Gulf of Naples, Andrews notes that the painting is already "more a tourist's record of a celebrated landscape than a glimpse of Romantic possibilities." The (partly literal) "domestication" of natural landscape as the hallowed site of the Sublime was of course an essential ingredient of the tourist experience, which only at this point in time reached a certain level of *democratization.*

8) Boime 2008 (see note 2), p. 493.

den Künstler. Schließlich verweist Albert Boime auf ein wesentlich späteres Gemälde des österreichischen Künstlers Moritz von Schwind als ein vorzügliches Beispiel für den bereits erwähnten Versuch des Biedermeiers, die erhabene Landschaft, ein Erbe der romantischen Tradition, zu ›domestizieren‹: »In *Die Morgenstunde* (1858) folgt Schwind bevorzugten Motiven von Caspar David Friedrich und Philipp Otto Runge, neutralisiert jedoch die allegorische Spannung im *Morgenrot* des Letzteren und den ungeheuer stillen, ehrfürchtigen Blick des Ersteren. Stattdessen projiziert Schwind seine Szene aus der zurückgesetzten Perspektive eines angenehmen Interieurs, wo der Betrachter auf dem Weg zum Blick aus dem Fenster zuerst die Bohlen des rustikalen Holzbodens und die kompakten Biedermeier-Möbel hinter sich lassen muss. Friedrichs klein wirkende und verlassene Rückenfigur [i. Orig. dt.] wird ersetzt durch ein fröhliches Mädchen, das eifrig das Fenster aufstößt, um den Morgen zu begrüßen. Aus der Sicherheit dieser Biedermeier-Bühne folgen wir seinem nach oben gerichteten Blick auf den Gipfel der herrlichen Zugspitze in weiter Ferne.«[8] In einigen dieser Gemälde ließen sich die Fenster oder Fensterrahmen ohne Weiteres als klassische Beispiele des *Parergons* interpretieren, dessen berühmteste theoretische Untersuchung Jacques Derrida 1978 in seiner Essay-Sammlung *La vérité en peinture* (1978) lieferte: Das Parergon ist etwas, das dem Werk (»ergon«) nicht im engeren Sinne zugehörig, ihm aber durch eine strukturelle Komplexität beigefügt (»par-«) erscheint und es (oder unsere Erfahrung davon) ermöglicht.

Derrida zitiert die Beispiele von Rahmen *um* Gemälde (statt *in* Gemälden) und (Marmor-)Gewändern halbnackter griechischer Statuen als primäre Repräsentationen solcher »Supplemente« und verwendet sie als kunsthistorische Argumente in seiner langjährigen philosophischen Befragung traditioneller Hierarchien, die Innen (Oben) und Außen (Unten) voneinander trennen oder Zentrum und Peripherie einander gegenüberstellen. Was selbstverständlich die Frage aufwirft, warum die Landschaftsmalerei als solche nicht in Derridas summarischen Listen der Genres, Motive oder Tropen aufgenommen wurde, die in die Bewertung des Parergons einfließen. Entspricht nicht die gesamte Geschichte des Genres eben jenem Emanzipationsprozess, der die Landschaft von einem lediglich ornamentalen Zusatz oder »Hintergrund« in das Zentrum der malerischen Praxis verschiebt, das heißt sie zum eigentlichen Gegenstand der Landschaftsmalerei werden lässt? Und dass insbesondere das 19. Jahrhundert von den dramatischsten Fortschritten dieses Prozesses (in denen die Romantik eines, sagen wir, Friedrich, selbstverständlich eine entscheidende Rolle spielte) gekennzeichnet ist, hängt wiederum aufs Engste mit den zahlreichen Dezentralisierungen, vor allem jenen des Blicks, zusammen, die sich in seinem Verlauf ereigneten. Dazu gehörten beispielsweise signifikante neue Überlegungen zur eigentlichen Bedeutung von *Aufmerksamkeit* wie auch zu den Auswirkungen von Fokussierung und Zerstreuung auf die Sehfunktion bei der Organisation ihrer verschiedenen (In-)Formationen. Hier kann die Düsseldorfer Malerschule, bei all ihrer offenkundigen Bescheidenheit – oder besser noch *wegen* ihrer Bescheidenheit und durch ihre programmatische Hinwendung zu relativ unspektakulären Naturszenen –, wiederum eine zentrale symbolische Position einnehmen. Wenn die Zeit von 1810 bis 1840 (die ungefähr der Blütezeit des Biedermeiers entspricht) das »relativ plötzliche Aufkommen von Modellen des subjektiven Blicks in einem breiten Spektrum von Disziplinen« erlebt, wie Crary in seiner fesselnden Untersuchung zur Geschichte (und *Historizität)* der Aufmerksamkeit feststellt, dann scheint das Modell des subjektiven Blicks, das im Düsseldorf jener Jahre besonders verfeinert wird, in erster Linie auf der Entdramatisierung oder auf der Abkehr vom Narrativen der Landschaftsmalerei im postromantischen Zeitalter zu beruhen.[9] Und wenn dem heutigen Betrachter vieles von dem, was damals dort gemalt wurde, seltsam und bewusst ereignislos vorkommt, dann gerade deshalb, weil die Emanzipation des traditionellen »Parergons« der Landschaft in den neu errichteten skopischen Regimes der europäischen Moderne Mitte des 19. Jahrhunderts dies erforderte. Eine neue, aufmerksame Art der Betrachtung des Naheliegenden, des beinahe Übersehenen anstelle der wolkigen Andeutungen einer unerforschlichen Ferne – und so wandte sich die Kunst dem heimischen Herd zu.

8)   Boime 2008 (siehe Anm. 2), S. 493.

9)   Jonathan Crary, *Suspensions of Perception: Attention, Spectacle, and Modern Culture,* Cambridge / Mass. 1999, S. 12.

the traditional hierarchies that separate interior (superior) from exterior (inferior) or oppose center to periphery. Which of course leads one to wonder why landscape painting as such was not included in Derrida's summary lists of genres, motifs or tropes invested in the valuation of the parergon. Doesn't the whole history of the genre coincide, precisely, with a process of emancipation that shifts landscape from mere ornamental accessory or "background" to the center of painterly practice, i. e. to become the thing of landscape painting itself? And that the nineteenth-century in particular is marked by this process's most dramatic advances (in which the Romanticism of, say, Friedrich of course plays a crucial role) is again intimately tied up with the many decentralizations, of vision first and foremost, that took place throughout its course. These included the significant reconsideration of the true meaning of *attention* for instance, as well as of the effects of focus and dispersal upon the function of vision in the organization of its various (in)formations. Here again, the Düsseldorf School of landscape painting, in all its apparent modesty—or better still, *because* of its modesty, and through its programmatic dedication to relatively unspectacular natural scenery—may assume a position of symbolic centrality: if the period from 1810 to 1840 (that is to say, roughly coinciding with the flowering of the Biedermeier era) sees the "relatively sudden emergence of models of subjective vision in a wide range of disciplines," as Jonathan Crary asserts in his compelling study of the history (and *historicity)* of attention, then the model of subjective vision that is being honed in Düsseldorf during those years in particular appears to rely primarily upon the de-dramatization or de-narrativization of landscape painting in the post-Romantic era.[9] And if much of what was painted then and there may strike the contemporary viewer as oddly, deliberately uneventful,

it is precisely because that is what the emancipation of the traditional "parergo"' of landscape in the newly established scopic regimes of mid-century European modernity required. A new, attentive way of looking at the close-by, the almost-overlooked, rather than foggy intimations of the inscrutably far-off—and so art homed in on the hearth.

LOOKING: BEHOLDING

Any consideration of the Düsseldorf School of landscape painting, especially when viewed through the lens of contemporary art practice, must acknowledge the concurrence of its golden age with the wonder years of what was only retrospectively (and always disparagingly) called "Biedermeier." This was the exact period—1815 to 1848— during which Düsseldorf emerged as the pre-eminent center of Prussia's Rhineland province in both industrial and cultural terms. The immediate successor of heroic Romanticism as the dominant cultural "trend" in continental (and mostly central) Europe, Biedermeier has long been viewed as a retrograde movement characterized by petty bourgeois sentimentalism and an escapist cultivation of domesticity and interiority—the precise cultural equivalents, that is to say, of Prince Metternich's attempts at restoring the balance of power characteristic of the *ancien régimes* before they were either toppled by the onslaught of populist political passions unleashed by the French (*and* American[10]) Revolution or eroded by the Napoleonic wars that came in the latter's wake. For those in power at the time—whether they be Friedrich Wilhelm III or Hegel—the period of restoration following the Congress of Vienna necessitated the

9)   Jonathan Crary, *Suspensions of Perception: Attention, Spectacle, and Modern Culture* (Cambridge, Mass.: The MIT Press, 1999), p. 12.

10)   It is a little-known fact that the quintessentially American icon that is Emanuel Leutze's *Washington Crossing the Delaware* (1851) was actually started by the German émigré painter when he was still living in Düsseldorf in a close-knit community of political radicals (many of whom had had ties with the Academy) who had all been involved in the revolutions of 1848 that heralded the end of the Biedermeier era. One of Leutze's colleagues at the time, Johann Peter Hasenclever, painted one of the very few artworks concretely referred to by Marx in one of his many miscellaneous political writings, an 1853 letter to the editor of the *New York Tribune—Workers Confronting the Magistrature* (1850), one version of which is now on view at the Kunstmuseum in Düsseldorf. On a related note, and considering the fact that the Biedermeier period also witnessed a frenzied flurry of nation-building (of the type nostalgically celebrated, precisely, in Leutze's heroic portrait of Washington), it is interesting to note that the Düsseldorf Academy at this time attracted numerous aspiring landscape painters from many parts of the world, more specifically from America, Russia, and the Scandinavian countries. They came to Düsseldorf to master the art of landscape painting—starting with the generic basics, that is, to end up producing their own, "national" landscape. In Swedish art-historical accounts of the period in particular it is often observed that artists from Norway, Sweden and Finland had to travel to Düsseldorf to learn to both *see* and thereafter *produce* the properly Scandinavian landscape.

Alle Überlegungen zur Düsseldorfer Schule der Landschaftsmalerei, besonders wenn man sie durch die Linse der zeitgenössischen Kunstpraxis betrachtet, müssen die Gleichzeitigkeit ihres goldenen Zeitalters mit den wunderbaren Jahren jener Tendenz anerkennen, die erst retrospektiv (und stets geringschätzig) als »Biedermeier« bezeichnet wurde. Dies war genau der Zeitraum – 1815 bis 1848 –, in dem Düsseldorf in industrieller und kultureller Hinsicht als das herausragende Zentrum der preußischen Rheinprovinz hervortrat. Das Biedermeier, der direkte Nachfolger der heroischen Romantik als dem vorherrschenden kulturellen »Trend« in Kontinental- (und überwiegend Mittel-)Europa, ist lange als eine rückwärtsgewandte Bewegung betrachtet worden, die von kleinbürgerlicher Sentimentalität und einer eskapistischen Kultivierung der Häuslichkeit und Innerlichkeit geprägt war – mit anderen Worten, die exakten kulturellen Äquivalente zu den Versuchen Fürst Metternichs, das Gleichgewicht der Kräfte wiederherzustellen, welches die *Anciens Régimes* charakterisiert hatte, bevor diese entweder durch den Ansturm populistischer politischer Leidenschaften gestürzt wurden, die die Französische *(und* die Amerikanische[10]) Revolution ausgelöst hatten, oder von den Napoleonischen Kriegen untergraben wurden, die diese nach sich zogen. Für die Machthaber der damaligen Zeit – ob Friedrich Wilhelm III. oder Hegel – erforderte die Restaurationszeit, die auf den Wiener Kongress folgte, die Bändigung zahlreicher verdächtiger Kräfte, die mit der Blüte der Romantik in Zusammenhang standen; sie manifestierte sich in einem breit angelegten Programm politischer Unterdrückung (von unterschiedlicher Direktheit und Effizienz), das von einer neuen dominierenden Kultur mühelos und bereitwillig verinnerlicht wurde. Letztere schien sich damit zufriedenzugeben, am laufenden Band nichts als harmlose Historienromane und hohle Loblieder auf das Landleben zu produzieren, wobei das Bild der Natur mit seinem Reichtum an gedämpften religiösen und moralischen Zwischentönen, dem die Düsseldorfer Malerschule anhing, ein besonders wirkungsvolles eskapistisches Idyll bot. Doch die Biedermeierzeit, die vor allem im Rheinland durch eine schnelle Industrialisierung gekennzeichnet war, erlebte zugleich die Entstehung einer neuen urbanen Mittelschicht mit einer spezifischen Reihe gesellschaftspolitischer Bestrebungen, die sich nicht länger mit der reaktionären Politik Metternichs in Einklang bringen ließen, und in ihrem Windschatten folgte eine echte Demokratisierung der Kultur mit weitreichenden Konsequenzen. Während die deutsche Romantik ihre wichtigsten Befürworter noch fast ausschließlich aus der Aristokratie rekrutiert hatte, waren die Galionsfiguren der Düsseldorfer Malerschule und der Kultur des Biedermeiers im Allgemeinen (ebenso wie die Anführer der 1848er-Revolution) überwiegend Liberale aus der Mittelschicht, und der spätere kommerzielle Erfolg der Düsseldorfer Malerschule hing stark von der neu erworbenen Kaufkraft dieser Liberalen und von dem relativ neuartigen bürgerlichen Geschmack an einer unverfänglichen Genremalerei – je ereignisloser, desto besser – ab, die sich leicht in jedes häusliche Interieur integrieren ließ und trotzdem ihre subtile allegorische Macht behielt. (Die »Korrektur nach unten« in der Musik jener Zeit bietet einen weiteren aufschlussreichen Einblick in die private Ausrichtung vieler kultureller Aktivitäten: Auf die gewagte orchestrale Extravaganz Beethovens folgten die Lieder von Franz Schubert, das

10) Es ist eine wenig bekannte Tatsache, dass Emanuel Leutzes *Washington Crossing the Delaware* (1851), dieser Inbegriff einer amerikanischen Ikone, in Wirklichkeit von dem aus Deutschland immigrierten Künstler begonnen wurde, als dieser noch in Düsseldorf in einer engen Gemeinschaft politisch Radikaler lebte (von denen viele Beziehungen zur Kunstakademie gehabt hatten); alle waren in die 1848er-Revolutionen verwickelt gewesen, die das Ende der Biedermeierzeit einläuteten. Einer von Leutzes damaligen Kollegen, Johann Peter Hasenclever, malte eines der ganz wenigen Kunstwerke, auf die sich Marx in einer seiner zahlreichen kleineren politischen Schriften konkret bezog, und zwar 1853 in einem Brief an den Herausgeber der *New York Daily Tribune – Arbeit vor dem Magistrat* (1850), von dem heute eine Version im Kunstmuseum Düsseldorf ausgestellt ist. In diesem Zusammenhang und in Anbetracht der Tatsache, dass die Biedermeierzeit auch eine hektische Welle von Nationenbildungen (eben jener Art, die Leutzes heroisches Washington-Porträt nostalgisch feierte) erlebte, ist es interessant festzustellen, dass die Düsseldorfer Akademie damals zahlreiche aufstrebende Landschaftsmaler aus vielen Teilen der Welt, insbesondere aus Amerika, Russland und den skandinavischen Ländern, anzog. Sie kamen nach Düsseldorf, um die Kunst der Landschaftsmalerei zu beherrschen – das heißt, sie begannen mit den allgemeinen Grundlagen, um am Ende ihre eigene, »nationale« Landschaft zu produzieren. Insbesondere in schwedischen Abhandlungen über diese Epoche wird oft bemerkt, dass Künstler aus Norwegen, Schweden und Finnland erst nach Düsseldorf reisen mussten, um zu lernen, wie man die wahre skandinavische Landschaft *sieht* und dementsprechend *produziert.*

taming of many suspicious forces associated with the flowering of Romanticism, manifesting itself in an extensive program of political oppression (of varying directness and efficiency) which was effortlessly and readily interiorized by a new dominant culture that appeared content with merely churning out harmless historical novels and inane paeans to country life, with the picture of nature adhered to by the Düsseldorf School, so rich in subdued religious and moral overtones, providing one particularly potent escapist idyll. But the Biedermeier period, characterized by rapid industrialization in the Rheinland in particular, also witnessed the establishment of a new urban middle class with a particular set of socio-political aspirations that could no longer be reconciled with Metternich's reactionary politics, and in its slipstream followed a genuine democratization of culture with far-reaching consequences. Whereas German Romanticism had still recruited its main proponents almost exclusively from the aristocracy, the figureheads of both the Düsseldorf School and Biedermeier culture in general were (like the leaders of the 1848 Revolution itself) largely middle-class liberals, and the subsequent commercial success of the Düsseldorf School was hugely dependent on these liberals' newly-found purchasing power, as well as the relatively novel bourgeois taste for innocuous genre painting— again, the less eventful the better—that could easily fit into any domestic interior yet still retain its subtle allegorical power. (The "scaling down" of music during this period offers another revealing insight into the private thrust of much cultural activity: after the audacious orchestral extravagance of Beethoven came the lieder of Franz Schubert, the solo piano music of Robert Schumann and the chamber music of Felix Mendelssohn-Bartholdy.) Above all, however, we must appreciate Biedermeier's fundamentally *elegiac* quality.

Whether in literature, music or painting (as an anxious contemporary of photography), the central event of its every cultural expression was almost always remembrance of things past, and of things irretrievably lost—the presumed innocence of pre-industrial society and handicraft, for instance, or the virgin purity of Germany's woodlands; the noble simplicity of the early Reformation and the farming life; the sanctity of nature at its smallest, most familiar and least conspicuous. In its deeply rooted melancholy and sense of historical dislocation—the term was only coined *after* the cultural phenomenon it referred to had been relegated to a clearly closed-off past, its time thus by its very definition always "out of joint."[11] Biedermeier may well signal the first truly modern moment in art: the beginning of the long history of modern anxiety. This the painters of the original Düsseldorf School were doubtlessly aware of when they first set out to chronicle the unassuming beauty of their rural environs in its very twilight years, just before (or even during) the fateful advent of industrialization— the exact historical event so lovingly and nostalgically recorded by the "founders" of the *second* Düsseldorf School, Bernd and Hilla Becher, who came to see the Rurhgebiet's stranded armada of disused water and winding towers in much the same way as Achenbach, Lessing, Schadow, Schirmer et al. had seen the natural wonders of rock, tree and water that had once preceded these industrial artefacts: one-hundred and fifty years of beauty migrating to the eye of the beholder.

LOOKING: BACK

The once-picturesque valley of the Düssel is better known today as the cradle of modern paleo anthropology than as the preferred traipsing ground of the once-formidable Düsseldorf School of landscape painting. It is here, after all, in the summer of 1856, that the fossil remains of Homo Sapiens Neanderthalensis were discovered and identified— three years before the publication of Charles Darwin's *The Origin of Species* and fifteen years before the publication of *The Descent of Man.* (The discovery of the aforementioned remains by a couple of miners had itself been made

11) The term Biedermeier, a combination of the German adjective *bieder* (meaning both honest as well as conventional or conservative) and the familiar bourgeois surname *Meier,* was invented by two amateur poets, Adolph Kussmaul and Ludwig Eichrodt, who from 1853 onwards published parodic paeans to philistine contentment under the pseudonym of Wieland Gottlieb Biedermaier in an obscure satirical journal. Only from 1855 did these poems become popular, appearing with increasing regularity in Munich's *Fliegende Blätter*—and it took a couple more decades for the term to acquire the historiographic, denotative quality with which we now associate it.

Solo-Piano von Robert Schumann und die Kammermusik von Felix Mendelssohn-Bartholdy.)
Vor allem gilt es jedoch, sich der zutiefst elegischen Qualität des Biedermeiers bewusst zu
werden. Ob in der Literatur, in der Musik oder in der Malerei (als ängstlicher Zeitgenossin der
Fotografie), das zentrale Ereignis jedes kulturellen Ausdrucks war fast immer die Erinnerung
an Dinge der Vergangenheit und an Dinge, die unwiederbringlich verloren waren – wie etwa
die mutmaßliche Unschuld der vorindustriellen Gesellschaft und des Handwerks oder die jung-
fräuliche Unberührtheit der deutschen Wälder, die edle Schlichtheit der frühen Reformation
und des Landlebens, die Heiligkeit der Natur in ihren kleinsten, vertrautesten und unschein-
barsten Erscheinungsformen. Mit seiner tief verwurzelten Melancholie und seinem Gefühl
historischer Verschiebung – der Begriff wurde erst geprägt, *nachdem* das kulturelle Phänomen,
das er bezeichnete, in eine offenkundig abgeschlossene Vergangenheit verbannt worden war –
war seine Zeit daher per definitionem immer schon »aus den Fugen«.[11] Das Biedermeier
markiert wohl den ersten wirklich modernen Moment der Kunst: den Beginn der langen
Geschichte der modernen Angst. Dessen waren sich die Maler der ursprünglichen Düsseldorfer
Schule zweifellos bewusst, als sie sich daran machten, die bescheidene Schönheit ihrer länd-
lichen Umgebung in den Jahren ihrer Dämmerung, kurz vor (oder sogar während) des schicksalhaften Anbruchs der Industrialisierung, festzuhalten – eben jenem historischen Ereignis, das
von den ›Begründern‹ der *zweiten* Düsseldorfer Schule, Bernd und Hilla Becher, so liebevoll
und nostalgisch dokumentiert wurde. Letztere betrachteten die gestrandete Armada stillgeleg-
ter Wasser- und Fördertürme des Ruhrgebiets auf ganz ähnliche Weise, wie Achenbach,
Lessing, Schadow, Schirmer et al. die Naturwunder von Stein, Baum und Wasser gesehen
hatten, die einst diesen industriellen Artefakten vorangegangen waren: einhundertfünfzig Jahre
Schönheit, die an das Auge des Betrachters dringen.

ZURÜCK: BLICKEN

Das einstmals pittoreske Tal der Düssel ist heute eher als
die Wiege der modernen Paläoanthropologie denn als
bevorzugtes Terrain der einstmals Respekt einflößenden
Düsseldorfer Schule der Landschaftsmalerei bekannt.
Schließlich wurden hier im Sommer 1856 die fossilen
Überreste des Homo sapiens neanderthalensis entdeckt und
identifiziert – drei Jahre vor der Veröffentlichung von
Charles Darwins *Über die Entstehung der Arten* und fünfzehn Jahre vor der Publikation von *Die Abstammung des
Menschen.* (Die Entdeckung der erwähnten Überreste durch
einige Steinbrucharbeiter war ihrerseits möglich geworden
durch die rasche Entwicklung des Kalksteinabbaus in der
Region, weshalb die sagenhafte Naturschönheit des Tals
bereits der Vergangenheit angehörte, als der Begriff
»Biedermeier« geprägt wurde. Siehe Anm 11.) Diese drei
Ereignisse, zusammen mit dem überragenden Einfluss der
hegelianischen Geschichtsauffassung – Hegels Philosophie,
gleichgültig wie abstrus oder kunstvoll man sie interpre-
tierte, entsprach bereitwillig einer politischen Position der
Mitte und schien daher bestens geeignet, die politischen
und gesellschaftlichen Ansichten des Biedermeiers zu
legitimieren[12] –, helfen zu erklären, warum Fortschritt
(Geschichte, Entwicklung) die große Obsession der Kultur des 19. Jahrhunderts war. Und da dieses spezielle
19. Jahrhundert tatsächlich die Schmiede war, in der
»unsere« moderne Welt wirklich geformt wurde, erscheint

11) Der Begriff Biedermeier, eine Kombination aus dem
deutschen Adjektiv *bieder* (das sowohl »anständig« wie auch
»konventionell« oder »konservativ« bedeutet) und dem ver-
breiteten bürgerlichen Nachnamen *Meier,* wurde von zwei
Amateurdichtern, Adolph Kussmaul und Ludwig Eichrodt,
erfunden, die ab 1853 unter dem Pseudonym Wieland Gottlieb Biedermaier in einer obskuren satirischen Zeitschrift
parodistische Lobgesänge auf die spießbürgerliche Zufrie-
denheit veröffentlichten. Erst 1855 wurden diese Gedichte
populär und erschienen mit zunehmender Regelmäßigkeit
in den Münchner *Fliegenden Blättern* – und es dauerte noch
mehrere Dekaden, bis der Begriff jene historiografische, denotative Qualität annahm, die wir heute mit ihm assoziieren.
12) Hegels viel zitierte Maxime aus der Vorrede zu seinen
(1820 erschienenen) *Grundlinien der Philosophie des Rechts,*
»Was vernünftig ist, das ist wirklich; und was wirklich ist,
das ist vernünftig«, ist der vielleicht präziseste Ausdruck der
deutschen kulturellen Mentalität in den Jahren zwischen dem
Wiener Kongress und den 1848er-Revolutionen. Im Kontext seiner Schriften wurde sie oft als letzter und definitiver
Beweis der unerschütterlich konservativen politischen
Ansichten des großen Philosophen interpretiert; im Kontext
der ästhetischen und/oder künstlerischen Revolution des
Realismus hingegen wäre es als ein einzigartig mutiges Statement verstanden worden – etwas, das direkt aus Gustave
Courbets *Realistischem Manifest* hätte stammen können.

possible by the quickly-paced development of limestone quarrying in the region, the reason why the valley's fabled natural beauty was already a thing of the past by the time the term "Biedermeier" was coined. See note 11.) These three events, together with the overarching impact of the Hegelian view of history—Hegel's philosophy, no matter how abstruse or elaborately interpreted, readily corresponded to a middle-of-the-road political position, thus appearing eminently suited to legitimate the Biedermeier view of politics and society[12]—help to explain

why progress (history, development) was the great obsession of nineteenth-century culture. And inasmuch as this particular nineteenth century was really the smithy in which "our" modern world was truly forged, it seems only apt that contemporary art regularly looks back at it with great expectations—in the hope of solving the mystery of our present-day gaze perhaps, or (at least) of locating the fateful moment when man and nature finally parted ways. When nature was suddenly given its accolades and locked inside the realm of *cultural* production—a process of the imagination that required inventing new ways of looking (back) at the old: the subject of Matts Leiderstam's work.

12   Hegel's oft-quoted maxim from the preface to his *Philosophy of Right* (published in 1820) that "what is rational is real; and what is real is rational" is perhaps the most accurate expression of the German cultural mindset in the years between the Congress of Vienna and the 1848 Revolutions. In the context of his writing, it has often been interpreted as final and definitive proof of the great philosopher's staunchly conservative political views; in the context of the aesthetic and/or artistic revolution of Realism, however, it would have been read as a singularly audacious statement—something straight out of Gustave Courbet's *Realist Manifesto*.

es nur angemessen, dass die zeitgenössische Kunst immer wieder mit großen Erwartungen darauf zurückblickt – in der Hoffnung, womöglich das Rätsel unseres heutigen Blicks zu lösen oder (wenigstens) jenen schicksalhaften Moment auszumachen, als sich die Wege von Mensch und Natur endgültig trennten. Als die Natur plötzlich den Ritterschlag erhielt und in dem Bereich der *kulturellen* Produktion eingeschlossen wurde – ein Prozess der Imagination, der es erforderte, neue Arten des (Rück-)Blicks auf das Alte zu erfinden: der Gegenstand von Matts Leiderstams Arbeit.

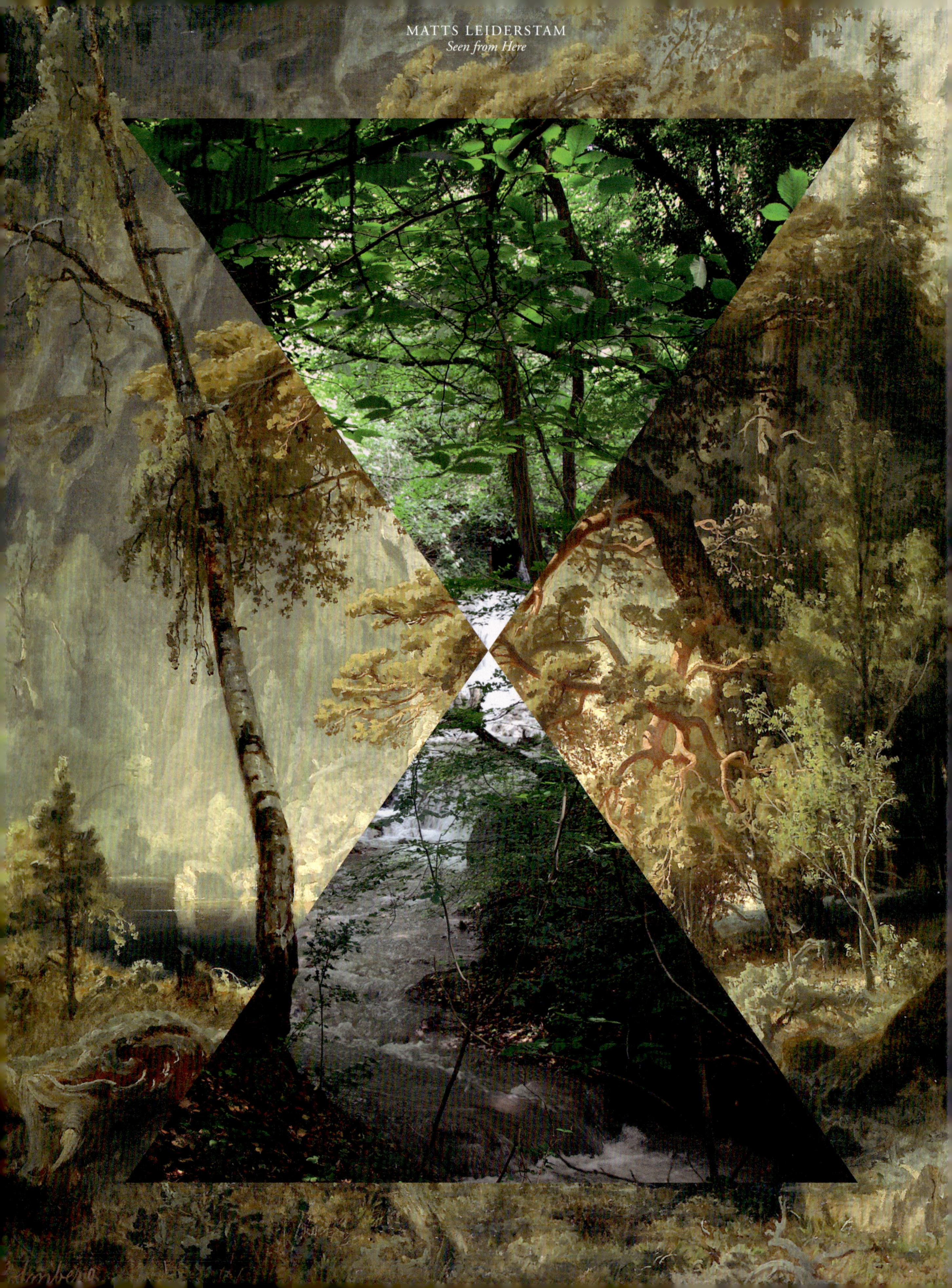

MATTS LEIDERSTAM
Seen from Here